The Patapsco

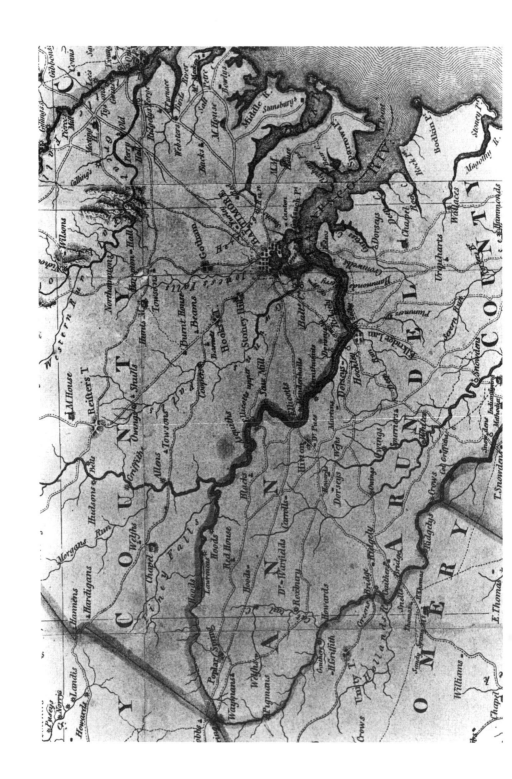

The Patapsco

BALTIMORE'S RIVER OF HISTORY

2nd Edition

PAUL J. TRAVERS

Published in association with
The Maryland Historical Society

4880 Lower Valley Road • Atglen, PA 19310

Travers, Paul J. (Paul Joseph)
The Patapsco : Baltimore's river of history / by Paul J. Travers.
—1st ed.
p. cm.
Includes bibliographical references and index.
ISBN 0-87033-400-X
1. Patapsco River Valley (MD)—History. 2. Patapsco River (MD)— History. 3. Baltimore (MD)—
History. I. Title.
F187.B2T73 1990
975.2′6—dc20   89-40785

Library of Congress Control Number: 2016935335

Designed by Danielle D. Farmer
Cover design by Molly Sheilds
Type set in Book Antiqua

ISBN: 978-0-87033-644-7
Printed in China

Published by Schiffer Publishing, Ltd.
4880 Lower Valley Road
Atglen, PA 19310
Phone: (610) 593-1777; Fax: (610) 593-2002
E-mail: Info@schifferbooks.com
Web: www.schifferbooks.com

For our complete selection of fine books on this and related subjects, please visit our website at www.schifferbooks.com. You may also write for a free catalog.

Schiffer Publishing's titles are available at special discounts for bulk purchases for sales promotions or premiums. Special editions, including personalized covers, corporate imprints, and excerpts, can be created in large quantities for special needs. For more information, contact the publisher.

We are always looking for people to write books on new and related subjects. If you have an idea for a book, please contact us at proposals@schifferbooks.com.

Frontis. **In the Griffith map of 1795, the Patapsco extends from the Chesapeake Bay. Note the size of the Main Branch. On today's maps, it appears as a barely distinguishable line.** *Courtesy Maryland Historical Society.*

To Catherine, Cynthia, and Deborah,
the belles of the Patapsco

Contents

Foreword

The Patapsco River. What stories lie buried in its memories: bloody Indian wars, devastating floods, raging fires, the ravages of erosion, heart-stopping explosions, tales of courage, accounts of hard work, tragedies of fighting, narratives of joy, dramas of sadness, sagas of men and women who performed great deeds and of those knowing the heartbreak of failure.

Those who live in the heartland of the Baltimore metropolitan area have had a centuries-old love affair with that river, so primeval, which has housed untold tales for thousands of years.

The river banks, once frequented by tribes of Piscataway, Susquehannock, and Seneca Indians, were rich in minerals — marble, granite, limestone, and iron ore. Its waters abounded with catfish, perch, sunfish, carp, and rock. Groves of cedar, oak, maple, hickory, gum, sassafras, and dogwood blossomed in the river valley.

Its marble lives in history in the Capitol and Library of Congress buildings. Granite from the Patapsco valley is the foundation of the Smithsonian Institution and the old Treasury Building (now the Executive Office Building) in Washington and the Courthouse in Baltimore.

Memories. That river generated power for mills that were world famous for their products: flour, cotton, silk, sails, and cotton duck. The Patapsco was a source of commerce, manufacturing, recreation, pleasure; yet its wrath resulted in great tragedies, destroying in minutes and hours what the brightest and strongest men had created over decades and scores of years.

Its harbor in Baltimore made the most mortal of men into princes of commerce. Eyewitness to constant change, the port over time has been food canning center of the world and the globe's leader in fertilizer production, and once housed the largest and most modern sugar plant and the largest spice house in the world. It is also the port that has seen a steel industry whose strength led to the development of a community — Dundalk — second only in size in the state to Baltimore City.

A burgeoning soap industry flourished. The city became a refuge for emigrants from Europe seeking freedom in the new world. In fact, Baltimore was second only to New York in numbers of immigrants landed.

The port has seen the era of famed night boats in the age of excursion boats steaming to places such as Tolchester and Betterton. Amusement parks — Riverview and Bay Shore — once graced the shoreline.

This port has seen the might of our shipbuilding industry during World War II when over 5 million tons of shipping — more than 500 ships — were built. That production accounted for ten percent of the American fleet. More tonnage and more ships were constructed here than in any other of the wartime mass production yards in the nation.

Once the harbor was ringed by great forts, including one whose heroic defense led to the masterful poetry of our national anthem and another whose looming ghostlike silhouette still lies moldering in the harbor entrance, relics from a bygone era.

Baltimore's attractions as a port led to the creation of America's railroad system. At the time of its construction it was necessary to provide inexpensive access to the treasure trove of the Ohio Valley. The most obvious route for its construction paralleled the Patapsco riverbed. Several of the bridges crossing the Patapsco were the first of their kind in the world and structurally so sturdy that they are still in constant use to this very day.

Great men of those times, the mid-1820s, were involved in the Baltimore and Ohio Railroad construction: George Brown, head of the investment house founded by his father and the oldest investment house in America, Alex. Brown & Sons; Charles Carroll of Carrollton, signer of the Declaration of Independence and wealthiest man in America; philanthropist Johns Hopkins; Ross Winans, whose pioneering inventions and innovations are still in use today; Thomas Ellicott of the Ellicott Mills; William Patterson, one of the wealthiest men in the state and father of Betsy, who married Napoleon Bonaparte's brother; John Eager Howard, one of the military heroes of the Revolutionary War and large landowner; and Philip Thomas, president of one of the leading banks in Baltimore, who would become the railroad's first president.

Memories. Once it was the export center for early tobacco planters. Its forges once produced the arsenal for Washington to fight our War of Independence.

Where once rotted wharves and warehouses stood — beside an inner harbor awash with sodden tires, fruit rinds, and railroad ties — a mystical phoenix has arisen. That part of the Patapsco River that kisses the main section of downtown Baltimore has become a mecca for visitors from around the world. The tourism and convention industry of Baltimore's Inner Harbor is now a billion-dollar-a-year industry. An apt demonstration of the adaptability of that river and its inhabitants.

The Patapsco River, some fifty-two miles in length, has seen great transition. Thriving industrial towns along its length are mere shadows of themselves. Where commerce once flourished, there are now mostly bedroom communities of Baltimore and, to some extent, Washington.

One element remains consistent down through the annals of time. The river, the valley, and its inhabitants have been able to cope with great change. Transition has been handled in stride. The future of the river and its people is bright, no matter what course of fate looms on the horizon.

This painstaking effort, lovingly written by Paul Joseph Travers, is important. For as a wise man once said, "People who don't learn from history are subject to relive it."

As a public servant who has labored for the people of the Patapsco valley for more than a third of a century, I am vitally interested in its rich history and tradition and dedicated to achieving the very best in the future for our people.

In my mind's eye, I can see some of the river's memories. A Baltimore clipper ship preparing to berth at the piers in Canton, laden with riches from the Orient. The struggle in Baltimore along Pratt Street as Southern sympathizers engage in pitched battle with Union soldiers, resulting in the first bloodshed of the Civil War. A picaresque vignette of giant hogsheads of tobacco being manhandled at picturesque Elkridge Landing, bound for the markets of Europe. The maiden trip of the *Tom Thumb* as it marked the beginnings of the "Iron Horse."

Now — if I could only get that river to speak!

William Donald Schaefer
Former Governor of Maryland

Preface

Listen to the song of the Patapsco! It is a symphony that echoes the history of America, a collection of passionate verses that tell of work and wars, railroads, ships, shipyards, mills, and milltowns. In a mood which ranges in tone and temperament from the hushed overtones of a string quartet to a raucous, sometimes bawdy, seafarer's chanty, it is a song titled "The River That Built America."

A rather grand and imposing title for such a small river, some people may think, but don't be fooled by statistics. The Patapsco's size belies the enormous historical value of the river as a living link with some of the most glamorous events in America's past. While the waterway will always be tied to the city and port of Baltimore, it is more than the "Baltimore connection." The events that have occurred on and along the Patapsco have had local, regional, national, and international impact. From the late 1700s to the late 1800s, the river witnessed the development of America into an industrial and military power. Its history is the American saga, a series of classic confrontations pitting man against man, man against nature, and man against machine. The title "River of History" bestowed upon the Patapsco is not the promotional phrase of an overzealous historian; it is a hard-earned, well-deserved distinction.

I first heard the song of the river during my early days at St. Stanislaus parish school, about a block away from Fell's Point. The melody was hypnotic and entrancing and its effect was magnetic. Lunchtime recess provided the opportunity to scale the schoolyard walls and explore the piers, warehouses, canneries, and back alleys. For me, classroom history lessons came alive with the sights, sounds, and smells of the waterfront. While the history books had the *Mayflower*, the *Constitution*, the *Monitor*, and the *Merrimac*, I had a fleet of rusting freighters, aging tugboats, and an occasional schooner. My fascination with ships made the port come alive and fueled my imagination—ships, all shapes and all sizes, coming from exotic ports of call, carrying with them a cargo of a thousand stories about tropical islands and life on the high seas. Vignettes of the desolate frigate *Constellation*, anchored in Colgate Creek like an abandoned pirate ship, and the sullen steamer *City of Richmond*, tied to the docks at Pratt Street waiting for her last run down the Chesapeake, are forever etched in the memory of my childhood.

College days brought me a new perspective on the river, as I spent many a weekend night imbibing local spirits in the salty neighborhood pubs that fronted on the water. However, the seeds for the book were not planted until my days as a park ranger at Patapsco Valley State Park in the early 1980s. It was there along the river valley that I began to piece together the fragmented history of the river as it ran from Parr's Spring to the Chesapeake Bay. After years of research and countless hours at the typewriter, I finally had in my hands this story of the Patapsco.

Today, more than ever, the river is a collage of sharply contrasting images. In many ways, it mirrors the character of the people it serves. Like the city of Baltimore, the Patapsco can be appropriately labeled "blue collar" — although its role in the colonizing and industrializing of the nation ended decades ago, the river still toils in the shadow of office buildings and condominiums, moving people and products in a nonstop effort. The river has suffered the price of its hard work, and in many places its banks have been weathered by age and soiled by occupation. In comparison, the glitter of the new inner harbor, a mecca for tourists and real estate developers, is only a small reflection in the harbor basin. Still much in evidence is the rough and tumble atmosphere reminiscent of Marlon Brando's *On the Waterfront*.

Along the Main Branch, however, the river still combines the elements of woods and water in a visual display of nature's magical power to delight. Its waters flow through pastoral settings, past small towns, under railroad bridges, over abandoned dams, and by the ruins of the river's halcyon mill days. The scenic panorama of the river valley, so often captured in the postcards and calendars of a bygone era, displays sensual qualities to inspire modern poets and writers.

This book was designed to be an entertaining and educational history of one of Maryland's best-kept secrets. Use it as a key to unlock the door to the past. Go down to the river. Stroll the harbor promenade, hike the river valley, and leaf through these pages. Stop to listen, and you'll hear the song of the Patapsco.

The story of the Patapsco River involved working thousands of hours and traveling thousands of miles. The task of compiling the river's history would have been impossible without the assistance of libraries, museums, historical societies, various state agencies, and people of the river. Over the years of searching and researching, writing and rewriting, the river and the author made new friends and renewed old acquaintances. With great sincerity, I would like to express my gratitude to the following individuals: Tim Baker, Dr. George H. Callcott, William Sager, Governor William Donald Schaefer, Janet Schwartzberg, and Jane Warth; and to the following organizations: Baltimore County Historical Society, Baltimore County Libraries, Maryland Room at the Enoch Pratt Free Library, Fire Museum of Maryland, Fort McHenry National Monument, Howard County Historical Society, Howard County Libraries, Maryland Historical Society, Maryland Port Administration, Patapsco Valley State Park, and the US Army Corps of Engineers Baltimore District.

The "greening of the Patapsco" (chapters 14 through 19) would not have been possible without the time, talent, and enthusiastic support from the following individuals and organizations: Judd Anderson and the Baltimore Rowing Club, Baltimore Rowing Center, Laura Bankey and the National Aquarium, Jonathan Flesher and Beatty Development, David Flores and Blue Water Baltimore, Joanne Heckman and the Sierra Club, illustrator extraordinaire turned map maker Jedediah Kahl, Adam Lindquist and the Waterfront Partnership, Cary Lynch and General Ship Repair Corporation, Serena McClain and American Rivers, Betsy McMillion and the Patapsco Heritage Greenway, "Captain" Vince Metallo and his good crew who sail out of Old Road Bay, Dottie Mitchell and the US Coast Guard Yard, Lee Oxenham, Matthew Scales and the Maryland Port Administration, Justine Shaeffer and the Benjamin Banneker Historical Park and Museum, Joe Stewart, Steve Stover, Victoria Ann Streitfeld and Honeywell International, Olympic gold medal visionary Patrick Terranova, Patrick Taylor of the *East County Times*, Lorraine Warnick and the Masonville Cove Environmental Education Center, and Deborah Stiffler.

The Patapsco

CHAPTER ONE

A Diverse Natural Resource

PATAPSCO: THE NAME AND ITS ORIGINS

> The westerne shore by which we sayled we found all along well watered, but very
> mountainous and barren, the valleys very fertile, but extreame thicke of small wood
> as well as trees, and much frequented with wolves, beares, deere, and other wild
> beasts. Wee passed many shallow creekes, but the first we found navigable for a
> ship, we called BOLUS, for that the clay in many places under the clifts by the high
> water marke, did grow up in red and white knots as gum out of trees; and in some
> places so participated together as though they were all of one nature, excepting the
> colour, the rest of the earth on both sides hard sandy grauell, which made us think
> it bole-armoniack and terra sigillata.
>
> — From the journals of John Smith (Smith 1910)

The Patapsco, first explored by Captain John Smith in the spring of 1608 on
his maiden voyage to the upper waters of the Chesapeake Bay, was originally
named Bolus Flu. The descriptive name was derived from the large masses
of red clay, or "bole-armoniack" sighted at the jagged red cliffs which later
became the steep, manicured slopes of Federal Hill, at the southern edge of the
Baltimore harbor. The clay hills, renamed in honor of Maryland's ratification
of the Constitution in 1788, later served as a lookout point for incoming ships,
and as a Union fortification during the Civil War.

By the late 1600s, the name Bolus Flu had been replaced by several
variations on the present Indian derivative, Patapsco. Early maps show that
the river was called Patapscoe (1666) and Patapsico (1673), and records refer to
it as Potapscoo (1699), Potapscoe (1701), and Pattapscoo (1706). The different
spellings are best explained as attempts by the first settlers and explorers to
reproduce the original Indian sound in English. The Fry and Jefferson map of
1751 is the first recorded document in which the river's name is spelled in its
present form. The spelling became popular and appeared thus on the majority
of recorded and legal documents during the late eighteenth century. But the
evolution of that spelling still remains a mystery. In colonial times, it was easier

to use a previously recorded version that economized on letters, rather than one of the many variations, which risked possible confusion.

The word Patapsco was derived from the Indian tongue of the Algonquian tribal group, who inhabited the Eastern Seaboard at the time of the first English settlements. Although the exact meaning of the word is unknown, two theories offer the most plausible explanation. Both combine the elements of known Algonquian dialects. One theory claims the word Patapsco means "backwater" or "tide covered with froth." The other theory reconstructs the word to arrive at another descriptive meaning. By using word fragments, modified stem words produce a translation meaning "rocky point." This linguistic deduction may hark back to the White Rocks, a group of limestone rocks jutting fifteen feet out of the Patapsco near Rock Creek and the Chesapeake Bay. Although all of the theories have shortcomings, they are useful tools to help explain the origins of the river's name.

THE RIVER SYSTEM

When Captain John Smith sailed up the Patapsco, he failed to realize he was entering a complex river system, encompassing miles of shoreline and numerous creeks and tributaries. In a shallow draft vessel designed for exploring inland bodies of water, Smith sailed to within sight of the present Baltimore harbor basin. Finding no inhabitants or unusual developments, Smith left the area and later recorded his sightings in his journal.

On a map, the Patapsco looks simply like an extension of the Chesapeake Bay. Unlike rivers whose boundaries can be readily established by a quick glance at a map, the Patapsco requires a detailed examination to determine its perimeters. The river system, approximately fifty-two miles in length and covering an estimated watershed drainage of 540 square miles, is divided into two major components: the tidewater or river basin (known as the harbor) and the Main Branch. To understand the river's scope, it is best to take the unorthodox route and examine the river by starting at its end.

The river basin, Baltimore's harbor, is a two-pronged estuary of the Chesapeake. The basin is located on the Bay's western shore, 170 miles upstream from the Atlantic Ocean. Divided into the Northwest Harbor and the Middle Branch, the basin composes the larger body of water most people recognize as the Patapsco. Although water movement there is directed by the tidal changes in the Chesapeake Bay, the basin remains a part of the river system, extending the flow of its inland branches. The harbor's perimeters include the edge of Baltimore's downtown business and industrial districts and extend fourteen miles in a southeasterly direction to the Chesapeake Bay. At the point where the Patapsco meets the waters of the Bay, the river reaches its greatest width of approximately four miles, measuring from Fort Howard on the north bank to Fort Smallwood on the south bank.

Heading upriver from the Bay, the harbor basin gradually decreases in width, creating a funnel-like effect. The broken shoreline is interrupted by a number of shallow and deep creeks. Bodkin Creek, Rock Creek, and Stony Creek (so-called pleasure creeks because they have remained free from heavy industrial development), as well as the industrialized Curtis Creek and Curtis

Bay, are the major inlets extending from the river basin into the south bank. On the heavily industrialized north bank—which includes Bethlehem Steel's Sparrows Point plant and the Dundalk Marine Terminal—Bear Creek, which empties near the Francis Scott Key Bridge, is the major break in the shoreline.

Eight miles from the mouth of the river basin, at the site of the Baltimore Harbor Tunnel, the basin reaches its narrowest width, one mile. From this point northwestward, the river divides into two sections, resembling a distorted U or horseshoe. With the Harbor Tunnel as the bottom portion of the horseshoe and Fort McHenry/Locust Point in the central space, the basin branches to the right in a northwest direction as the Northwest Harbor, and to the left in a southwest direction as the Middle Branch. The Harbor Tunnel can be used as an arbitrary reference for dividing the lower Patapsco into two sections: the bay basin being the lower section extending to the Chesapeake Bay, and the harbor basin extending west to the edge of Baltimore.

Headwaters of the Patapsco River at Parr's Spring.
Photo by the author.

Included in the harbor basin are prong-like streams that flow through Baltimore City and empty into the river. Jones Falls, which was piped and paved over in the early 1900s, empties into the river just north of Baltimore's revitalized inner harbor, whereas Gwynns Falls empties into the Middle Branch. Both tributaries generally go unnoticed until a prolonged rain swells the streams, which carry the junk, trash, and filth of a large city and deposit it in the river.

A larger and more important prong that empties into the Middle Branch is the Main Branch of the Patapsco. This second component of the river system, often designated as a line on most maps, is tucked away along the southern bank of the Middle Branch. The Main Branch flows unheralded into the harbor basin near the site of Harbor Hospital Center, its entrance marked and disfigured by a marshland turned into a city landfill. From this point, the Main Branch extends southwestward six and a half miles to the town of Elkridge. At Elkridge, the river turns in a westerly direction and continues uninterrupted for twenty-six miles, passing the communities of Ellicott City, Oella, Daniels, and Woodstock. At a point just below Marriottsville, the river forks into the North Branch and the South Branch. The North Branch heads north for two and a half miles and dead-ends at the concrete monolith known as Liberty Dam. The reservoir above the dam is fed by streams that run through the rolling farmlands of Carroll County. The South Branch heads west for eighteen miles, past Marriottsville, Sykesville, Hood's Mill, and Woodbine.

The mouth of the Patapsco as it empties into the Bay. In the left background is Bethlehem Steel at Sparrows Point. *Photo by the author.*

At a small farm pond south of the intersection of Interstate 70 and Route 27, the Patapsco begins its journey to the Chesapeake Bay. Parr's Spring, a pond covering less than an acre on the Four Corners Farm, is recognized as the headwaters of the Patapsco. The clear, cold, spring-fed pond, surrounded by a row of pine trees, reflects the character of the entire river: a small natural preserve of scenic beauty and historical significance, it is surrounded by residential developments and superhighways. The pond, also the point where the counties of Carroll, Howard, Frederick, and Montgomery meet, is marked by a small gray engraved stone that lists statistical data about the pond and the river. In many ways, the small monument serves not only as a landmark but also as a tombstone bearing the epitaph of the Patapsco.

From its humble beginning in the hills of central Maryland, the river runs through a variety of landforms. Starting in a series of gentle sloping valleys, the river passes through narrow rock-lined canyons before emptying into the harbor basin at the marshland near Baltimore. Along its route, the Patapsco serves as a natural border for Carroll, Howard, Baltimore, and Anne Arundel counties before entering the Middle Branch through the southern tip of Baltimore City.

The physical statistics of the Main Branch are unimpressive. Unlike the harbor basin, which has channel depths of up to fifty feet (needed for large vessels in a deep-water port), the Main Branch is consistently shallow in depth and narrow in width for much of its journey southward. From Parr's Spring to Elkridge, the river averages two to four feet in depth and ranges from ten to fifty feet in width. As the river continues its natural progression and the terrain changes, the volume of water widens and deepens the river. Below Elkridge to the Middle Branch, the Main Branch reaches its deepest and widest points. Along this section, the river ranges from three to six feet in depth and from fifty to seventy-five feet in width. At the junction of the Main Branch and the Middle Branch (the point where the Main Branch enters the harbor), the river spreads into a lazy-flowing backwash 300 feet wide. The only radical changes in depth and width along the Main Branch occur at the sites of former and present dams. Here the river slows into silt-filled pools of various widths, with sharp fluctuations in depths that can be deceiving and dangerous.

The Main Branch at the harbor has changed drastically from its days before the immigration of white settlers. However, from Parr's Spring to Marriottsville, the river has suffered the least from natural phenomena and man-made developments, and it flows fast and clear through rural countrysides as it did hundreds of years ago.

The remaining sections of the river have undergone considerable alteration through floods, erosion, and the intrusions of man. The large number of dams has contributed to decreasing the volume of water flow and to lowering the water table of the river. Erosion and runoff from farms and construction sites have clogged the river and changed not only the dimensions of its banks but also its width and depth. One of the more evident changes in the river's makeup is seen at Elkridge, once the site of Elkridge Landing, a major colonial seaport. During the colonial period when the seaport prospered, the river at a point just below present-day Route 1 (Washington Boulevard) was similar in size to the Main Branch where it empties into the harbor basin. Today the same section of river resembles an oversize stream or creek.

With the changes in the physical geography of the river came the disappearance of one of the river's trademarks. Approximately three-quarters of a mile above Elkridge Landing, just below Avalon, stood the Great Falls of the Patapsco. The waterfalls, a rock ledge or outcropping approximately ten feet in height, were often mentioned in books and journals and frequently pictured in lithographs in the mid-1800s. At this point near the fall line, water passing over and around the rocks provided a natural song for the river and prevented navigation farther into the river valley. Today the falls are nothing more than a ripple of water over a gradually descending stone riverbed. As a result of the loss in water volume and depth, the river is characterized by numerous rock outcroppings which were once an underwater part of the riverbed. Even with a thorough examination of the river's topographical features, it is extremely

Fort McHenry and Locust Point. To the right is the Northwest Branch; in the center background is the harbor basin; the Middle Branch begins at bottom left. *Courtesy Maryland Historical Society.*

The Middle Branch as seen from Locust Point. In the background is the Hanover Street Bridge. *Courtesy Maryland Historical Society.*

difficult to picture the river as it was when the rocks were covered by the river's natural depth.

The tidewater limit (the uppermost point where the river rose and fell in unison with the harbor tides) during the 1700s was located about a half-mile above Elkridge. Near the present-day Thomas Viaduct, it was a popular fording place known as the Falls of the Patapsco. Before the Flood of 1868, small barges transported raw materials upriver to the Avalon Iron Works, about a mile above Elkridge. Today the tidewater limit extends only a few miles upstream from the Middle Branch at the harbor basin.

RIVER GEOLOGY

The geology of the Patapsco, as diverse as its boundaries, incorporates a number of major features. The key to understanding the river and its valley is the fall line and its effects. The physiographic term *fall line* refers to the fall or drop of streams as they pass through certain defined regions. Maryland's fall line, where the streams drop from the central piedmont region to the lower coastal plain, crosses the state along a diagonal line running from the state's northeast boundary with Delaware, around the head of the Chesapeake Bay, through Baltimore, and southwesterly to Washington, DC. Over its length of forty miles, the Main Branch drops from its highest point of 800 to 1,000 feet at Parr's Spring to sea level at the harbor basin. The fall line is clearly evident at Elkridge where the river rushes forth from the steep-walled rocky canyon after making a 300-foot drop in elevation between Woodstock and Elkridge. At this point, the fall line divides the river valley into two major geological regions, the piedmont and the coastal plain.

The piedmont (meaning foot of the mountain) extends from the fall line at Elkridge northward to the Catoctin Mountains in Frederick County. This area, which includes the upper part of the Main Branch from Parr's Spring to Elkridge, is noted for its gradually descending rolling hillside situated on a complex series of crystalline rocks lying just below the surface cover of soil and vegetation. The steep, rocky river canyon, visible from Ellicott City to Elkridge, is not a feature of the piedmont region, but a unique feature formed by the flow of water. The gorge is a result of the water current of the river cutting through the crystalline base while meeting resistance from the harder rock formations of gneiss, granite, and gabbro. These formations originally surfaced in what scientists call a "recent" geological uplift, "recent" being millions of years ago.

The coastal plain, extending from the fall line to the Atlantic Ocean, includes the river from Elkridge southward to the harbor basin and the Chesapeake Bay. It is distinguished by a rolling to flat land surface and is underlaid with sedimentary deposits of sand, clay, and gravel. The many ponds that dot the lower portion of the Main Branch are not natural terrain features but abandoned gravel pits and excavation sites. The effects of the fall line on the coastal plain are seen in the sluggish backwater of the harbor basin extending into the Main Branch.

The diverse rock formations have provided in the past and also in the present an industry for supplying raw material utilized in construction and manufacturing. Marble, granite, sand, and gravel are quarried at various places along the river. Many of the older houses lining the river were built with stone taken from nearby quarries. The river's banks and hillsides provided limestone, charcoal, and the iron ore needed for production of iron, the industry that fostered industrial and commercial development in the valley. Marble quarried at Granite in Baltimore County, and at Marriottsville and Ellicott City in Howard County, was used in the construction of the US Capitol, the Washington Monument, the Library of Congress, and buildings at the Naval Academy in Annapolis. Granite quarried at these locations was also used in the construction of bridges for the Baltimore and Ohio Railroad.

WATER QUALITY AND POLLUTION

Any river's value is reflected in its ability to sustain life within its waters and support life within its reach. The Patapsco River, serving as a vital link between man and his natural environment, exemplifies the delicate and fragile relationship among mutually supportive ecological systems. The lifeline for both man and nature along the river is the water and the quality of that water. The Patapsco is a collection of various water types with overlapping pollution problems.

On the South Branch, the uppermost portion of the river, the water quality is rated very good to excellent. From the headwaters at Parr's Spring to the junction with the North Branch below Marriottsville, the river runs cold and fast like a mountain trout stream. The effects from fertilizers, farm chemicals, manure, and failing septic tanks (always a constant source of pollution) have been minimal. In the last decade, the boom in residential development in the region has posed a new threat.

On the North Branch, the water quality is rated good. However, the impoundment of water at Liberty Dam presents a unique problem. Water quality in some seasonal periods is marked by sharp fluctuations. During periods of prolonged drought, water flow above and below the dam is minimal, allowing water to pool and stagnate. The result, especially during summer months, is algal blooms, an abundant growth of algae. These excessive algal populations occur when high levels of nitrogen and phosphates from natural and man-made sources enter the water system. Bacteria that decompose the dying algae utilize the oxygen dissolved in the surrounding water and thus compete with other aquatic organisms for the available dissolved oxygen. Algal blooms destroy the aesthetics of the reservoir and river by turning the water into a slimish pea soup and emitting the rotten-egg odor of hydrogen sulfide.

On the Main Branch, water quality varies from good to poor. From Marriottsville to Elkridge, where the river runs swiftly through the rocky valley gorge and is fed by a number of small, steep, well-shaped streams, the water is rated fair to good. Small amounts of industrial pollutants and sewage, though, continue to degrade the health of the river. From Elkridge to the Middle Branch, where the river flattens and slows into a backwater, the water is rated fair to poor. This lower portion suffers not only from the pollutants being washed downriver but also from the inflow of harbor pollutants during ebb tides. However, while the report card on the Main Branch may seem mediocre, it is an encouraging sign of continued improvement—only two decades ago, the river was an ecological disaster area.

The Main Branch of the Patapsco, at one time a national disgrace and blatant example of wanton and indiscriminate dumping, has made a comeback. Back in the mid-1960s, the river was a bubbling, foamy cesspool, capable of supporting only the lowest of life forms. Natural colors had been replaced by new industrial shades. The water was brown and the banks were edged in a green slime. Detergents dumped in the river and activated by swift currents produced a foamy white outer covering that contrasted sharply with the brown water and gave the river a permanently winter-like appearance. By any environmental standards or textbook definitions, the Patapsco was dead. It resembled an open sewer more than it did a natural resource. Government officials labeled it "grossly polluted," while reporters described it as an "aquatic junkpile." In the shallows, junk, scrap metal, lumber, tires, auto parts, and appliances could be seen protruding from the water. Any species of wildlife or marine life living in or along the river were identified as endangered, regardless of their number.

The pollution problem involved the dumping of industrial wastes and the discharge of raw sewage. The industrial waste that found its way into the river was as diverse as the industries that were dumping it. A liquor distillery was discharging grain, a box factory was discharging pulp and fibrous material, and a textile mill was discharging dye and detergent. Other wastes included oil, chemicals, solvents, and food scraps. Every day, thousands of gallons of raw sewage were being discharged into the river by nearby communities. All of this man-made garbage produced bacteria which decomposed the organic matter and depleted the dissolved oxygen in the water. The bacterial action was identical to that of the algal blooms. A heavy sulphuric odor permeated the air along the river valley and a thick green slime coated the banks. In prior years, the river had been able to gradually break down the majority of wastes before they could accumulate to a dangerous level. When the river flow was impeded by the construction of Liberty Dam and the consequent loss of its tributaries, the river's self-cleaning mechanisms were overloaded and eventually broke down under the strain. To be succinct, there was more waste than water in the river.

The raw sewage threatened more than the wildlife. Sewage dumped into the river skyrocketed the normal bacteria count and contaminated the water with infectious bacteria, fungi, and viruses which could cause cholera, dysentery, typhoid fever, polio, and hepatitis in humans. Predominant were *Pseudomonas*, bacterium *E. coli*, *Proteus*, and enteric bacilli, which infect the eyes, ears, throat, intestines, respiratory system, and urinary tract. The solution was simple: the construction of a sewer interceptor pipeline to carry raw sewage to wastewater treatment plants. For decades, this issue was a political hot potato that was discussed then quickly discarded as too costly. It was not until 1982 that Oella, the last community without public sewage hookup, was funded money for the construction of a sewage system to eliminate the discharge of untreated waste into the Patapsco.

On the Middle Branch and Northwest Harbor, which are commonly referred to as the harbor and harbor basin, the water quality is poor. Decades' worth of dumping of toxic wastes by riverfront industries have destroyed the river's ability to produce and maintain aquatic life. Bottom grasses essential for finfish, shellfish, and waterfowl were long ago buried under a layer of industrial sediment. This harbor muck has the consistency of mayonnaise and contains toxic layers made up of cadmium, mercury, copper, chromium, arsenic, and synthetic chemical compounds, including PCBs and DDT. Surface samples reveal low to mid-level concentrations of pollutants and chemical wastes.

Despite the harbor's being an ecological dead zone, its surface area has shown cosmetic improvement in recent years. While credit for the cleanup can be given to stricter dumping regulations and watchdog environmental groups, the clearer and cleaner water is the result of the harbor's natural flushing mechanism. Researchers in the early 1960s discovered that the top and bottom layers of water flow into the harbor while a middle layer of mixed fresh and salt water flows out of the harbor. This unique three-level flow system combines with the tidal flows to replace ten to twelve percent of the harbor's water volume on a daily basis. As a result, the harbor has survived three centuries of being a dump for raw sewage, animal wastes and carcasses, spoiled foodstuffs, and storm runoff, which in the past ignited epidemics of cholera, typhoid, and scarlet fever. Although the harbor remains a sterile habitat for marine life, there are signs of improvement. In recent years, worms, tiny clams, and microscopic organisms have been found in the uppermost level of bottom sediment. Another optimistic indicator is the efforts by city and state officials to restore the wetlands that once proliferated around the harbor. These tidal marshes, which once constituted three square miles, had shrunk to nineteen acres by the mid-1970s, but an agreement between environmental officials and developers requires the developers to create new wetlands in the harbor for portions of the harbor that were filled in during construction.

Conservation Activities

The ecological future of the Patapsco is a continuing battle that depends on the success and survival of grass roots conservation groups formed in the early and mid-1960s. In the 1980s, the lower Patapsco has emerged as a new battleground for environmentalists and industrialists. With the deterioration of the Chesapeake Bay — a growing problem that has attracted federal funding and national media attention — the spotlight has been recently focused on the Patapsco as a pollution site. The numerous heavy industries along the Northwest Branch and Middle Branch have been identified as major sources of toxic wastes and chemicals that eventually flow into the Bay. For decades, the institutionalized thinking prevailed that the dumping of industrial wastes into the river was part of the trade-off that had to be made between nature and man. Because these industries were licensed by the state and the federal government to dump a certain portion of their byproducts into the water, the question was asked: How bad could the problem of pollution be? The answer was: Monumental. Industries were using the river as a convenient dumping ground for every waste that required bureaucratic red tape, restrictive handling practices, or additional expense for proper disposal. Many dumpers were operating in excess of their permits, with expired permits, or without any permits. Minuscule fines levied by state and federal regulatory agencies were barely a slap on the wrist, and only served to condone more dumping and more pollution. The only recourse was through the court system. However, even this approach failed as high-powered corporate attorneys tied up the system with lengthy appeals that often lasted for years. In the meantime, the dumping continued.

The cries to stop these practices, uttered by a small number of activist conservation groups, fell on deaf ears. Industry had been the economic backbone of the region for years, and industry meant jobs. The idea of compatibility between industry and ecology sounded nice, but to most people it was a pipe dream. For them, the choice was simple: you either had a clean river and no jobs, or a filthy, foul body of water and jobs. The gains made in the 1960s and 1970s were being threatened by apathy, which was creeping its way back into the minds of the public. For years, the question went begging of who could take on these powerful industrial giants and expect to win. It remained unanswered until 1982. With the arrival of Greenpeace, a modern environmental David and Goliath story came to life in the port of Baltimore.

The nonprofit, highly idealistic, international ecological group was known more for its campaigns to save the whales and seals and at first did not appear to be a worthy opponent. In the summer of 1982, the group's forty-foot ketch *Aleyka* sailed up the Patapsco to battle the major polluters. The war to save the Chesapeake Bay depended on a victory at the "Battle of the Patapsco." Not since the British had sailed up the Patapsco in September 1814 had the city seen this kind of battle preparation. The group's tactics of active confrontation and passive resistance were ideally suited for this type of campaign. Battle dress consisted of rubber boots, rubber gloves, decontamination suits, and gas masks. Beach landings were to be made from a fleet of canoes and inflatable rafts. Newspaper and television reporters stood nearby, ready to focus on every detail of the upcoming skirmish. With the attention of the media quickly captured, Greenpeace had secured the first objective of its battle plan.

In the 1982 campaign, the group targeted the SCM Corporation and centered its attack on a beach landing near a drainage pipe that was discharging large quantities of wastes from a leaking chemical holding pond. Their efforts to stop the flow by inflating a portable raft inside the pipe failed but the publicity made the campaign a success. In 1983 and 1984, Greenpeace returned to do battle along the Patapsco with the American Recovery Corporation, a major waste recycler and polluter. In 1983, the group claimed squatters' rights and took up temporary residence in a drainage ditch at the plant. In 1984, they scaled the plant's 185-foot water tower and painted "Recover the Bay . . . Save the Bay" in letters large enough to be seen around the harbor. Also in 1984, attention was turned to the Bethlehem Steel Company. The attack group made its way to the Sparrows Point plant and strung a sixty-foot banner with the words "We Can Save the Bay" across the mouth of polluted Humphrey's Creek.

For their theatrics, amounting to only a few futile gestures with symbolic overtones, group members were arrested and later fined on charges ranging from trespassing to defacing public and private property. It was a small price to pay for victory. Accounts of the battles made front-page news. For the first time in years, industry was being held accountable for its actions. Its rationale and reasoning for dumping wastes into the Patapsco were scrutinized by the media and the public. Each accusation made by Greenpeace produced a flimsy alibi from the polluters to justify their position. The business concepts of cost-cutting and increased profit margins at the expense of the Patapsco and the

Chesapeake were found to be totally unacceptable. The issue of pollution now involved a question of morality, not only legality.

As a result of the efforts of Greenpeace, polluters were investigated and reinvestigated. Fines were levied, lawsuits were initiated, and tighter controls were placed on user industries. More important, the Greenpeace initiative was continued by local activist and community groups, who now realized they could make these industrialists accountable and liable for their actions.

The Fishery

For hundreds of years, the Patapsco River provided a means of survival for all living creatures in the region. The predator-prey cycle, which included the dominant species of man, centered on the healthy habitats and abundant food sources supplied by the river. From the waters of the Patapsco, a variety of fish, shellfish, and river wildlife provided a vital link in the food chain. Even in hard times, when game animals were scarce, hunting parties could always depend on the river for an ample harvest.

With the influx of white settlers, the river's production began a slow but steady decline. The first ominous sign was seen in the 1780s, when the Ellicott brothers noticed a decrease in the migrating schools of herring and shad due to dam construction. By the mid-twentieth century, the harbor basin and sections of the Main Branch were dying. Sport-fishermen were among the first to notice the symptoms as sport species began gradually to be replaced by rough fish. The days when large schools of fish could be spotted just offshore became memories, and a few hours on the river could no longer produce enough fish to feed a large family. One explanation of the seemingly sudden decline occurred in the late 1940s when Baltimore City began dumping ashes from its nearby incinerator plant onto the adjacent mud flats. A newspaper article of that time lamented the passing of a time when "a 100 pound bag of hard crabs could be caught by a single crabber in several hours. Yellow and white perch, sunfish, catfish, carp and rock abounded. In summer, the mud flats yielded jumbo soft crabs. In the winter, trappers caught thousands of muskrats. Reedbirds fed on the wild oats that flourished on the mud flats. Now residential and commercial structures are going up on the reclaimed lands." (*Baltimore Evening Sun*, November 17, 1946)

Another popular outdoor pastime that had disappeared by the 1940s was gudgeon fishing along the banks of the Main Branch just south of Relay. When word went out that the gudgeon were running in the river, fishermen and their families, including mothers and daughters, flocked to secure a good position along the crowded bank. Gudgeon fishing was strictly a family affair and many a Baltimore sportsman began his fishing career in quest of the lowly gudgeon. Equipment and supplies were minimal: one only needed a tiny fly hook baited with a worm, a spool of cotton for a line, and a branch from the nearest sapling for a rod. The gudgeon, a member of the carp family, averaged five inches in length and was easily recognized by its iridescent blue back and glittering silver belly and fins. In the spring, the spawning fish moved from the saltier Bay to the fresh waters of the river, appearing in such great numbers that they literally clogged the small spawning streams leading to the river. A good day could produce a catch of eighty to one hundred fish. Frequently, they were cleaned, rolled in cornmeal, and fried in bacon fat over fires right on the banks where they were caught. Enthusiasts claimed the fish was a feast for the gods.

Since the 1960s, the fishing in the Patapsco has gradually returned. It is not spectacular, and the number and size of the fish are not exceptional. The amazing fact is that there are any fish in the Patapsco, given its marginal water quality.

Many anadromous species (which come from the sea to spawn in freshwater streams) have been eliminated by the numerous dams that not only impeded the movement and migration of fish but reduced and altered habitats by decreasing water flow and volume. The large loss of water from the upper reaches of the river triggered warmer water temperatures and a heavy buildup of sediment which made spawning impossible. The biggest change in the river's makeup came with the construction of its biggest dam. Liberty Dam, completed in the early 1950s, stopped the flow of millions of gallons of water daily. As a result, water flow from the North Branch was reduced to a trickle. But, while fishing below the dam declined, the new lake behind it became a fisherman's paradise.

While the dams along the Patapsco provided good fishing holes, they were directly responsible for the decline in the number and variety of fish in the river. These impassable structures limited the access of migrating species and caused buildups of silt, which covered the sand and gravel beds used for spawning and feeding. The negative effects of the dams were counteracted, strangely enough, however, by the destructive forces of nature.

The severe floods, which wiped out every living thing in their paths, had the long-term effect of improving the river as a suitable habitat for marine life. Deposits of silt and pollutants were washed away, leaving the river's banks and bottom capable of sustaining life.

Although twenty species of fish have been documented in the river, the fishing is only rated as fair. Along the river's upper reaches, where the water quality is considered good, bass and seasonal trout fishing are available to the more intense fishermen. The lower portions hold the most common species: carp, catfish, sunfish, suckers, and a number of rough fish. At the mouth of the Patapsco, where the river meets the Bay, white perch, bluefish, and rockfish are caught despite the heavy industrialization of the river. An encouraging sign is the fishing and crabbing along the harbor basin at the edge of the city's boundaries. In the summer months, it is not uncommon to see fishermen and crabbers lining the piers and bulkheads at the lower end of the harbor basin and the south bank of the Main Branch. The number and species of fish that make their way to the edge of downtown Baltimore raise the issue of whether this is a result of improved water conditions or the ability of the fish to survive in a tainted environment. Health department surveys and samplings reveal "safe" concentrations of toxic substances in fish and crabs. It is doubtful that the fishing in the Patapsco will ever return to its former excellence, when schools of herring, shad, rockfish, and bluefish could be seen churning the surface; however, with continued care the fishing should slowly improve in future years, just as it slowly died in the past.

CHAPTER TWO

Children of the Sun: The Piscataway and Susquehannock Indians

When Captain John Smith sailed up the mouth of the Patapsco in 1608, he noted with amazement the absence of any type of Indian activity. What he did not know was that the region had already been abandoned due to the sporadic but constant warfare among the area's Indian tribes. Although never a permanent home for any one tribe, the region was frequently utilized by various tribes from areas soon to be designated as the colonies of Maryland, Virginia, and Pennsylvania. Valued for its prized hunting and fishing grounds, it was a source of conflict for those who desired exclusive land and water rights. The Patapsco River Valley abounded with large and small game, including black bear, elk, beaver, turkey, and deer. The river teemed with fish and shellfish, including herring, shad, rockfish, clams, oysters, shrimp, and crabs. The river region and adjacent wilderness areas provided a rather easy and steady means of existence for those who controlled the entire area. It would be the warlike Susquehannocks and the peaceful Piscataway Indians whose mutual claims to the Patapsco region would spill over into bloodshed. Their individual histories would combine to form the history of the American Indian along the Patapsco, and the river, which provided for the survival of both tribes, would be the common denominator in the eventual downfall and extinction of these once proud and mighty nations. Conflicts among these and other rival Indian tribes, spilling over and involving the early settlers, would be a terrible experience repeated continually as the colonies expanded west. Hostilities ceased only when the supply of land and the supply of Indians were completely depleted.

The Piscataways, or Conoys, the first Indian group to be documented along the Patapsco near the site of Elkridge, were a major tribe in a confederation of Algonquian tribes, which included the smaller tribes of the Mattawomans, Patuxents, Chopticans, Potopacs, Mattapanys, and Yaocomicoes. These tribes lived in an area south of the Patuxent River that is bordered on the east by the Chesapeake Bay and on the west by the Potomac River. The tall, dark-skinned Piscataways lived along Piscataway Creek, on a point of land on the Maryland side of the Potomac River below Washington, DC, across from present-day

Mount Vernon. After their long-time village of Moyaone was destroyed by fire in 1622, the tribe moved a short distance east, near the present-day town of Piscataway. The new village of Kittamaqundi became the new home of the Piscataway tyac (emperor) and the capital of the Piscataway empire.

An accurate and vivid description of the Piscataways can be found in the narratives of Father Andrew White, a Jesuit missionary who landed with the first Maryland settlers at St. Clement's Island in Southern Maryland in February 1634. Father White wrote in his journals:

The natives of person be very proper and tall men, by nature swarthy, but much more by art, painting themselves with colours in oile a darke read, especially about the head, which they doe to keep away the gnats, wherein I confesse there is more ease then honesty. As for their faces they use sometimes other colours, as blew from the nose downeward, and read upward, and sometimes contrary wise with great variety, and in gastly manner. They have noe bearde till they be very old, but insteed thereof sometimes draw long lines with colours from the sides of their mouth to their eares. They weare their [hair] diversly some haveing it cut all short, one halfe of the head, and long on the other; others have it all long, but generally they weare all a locke at the left eare, and sometimes at both eares which they fold up with a string of wam- pampeake or roanoake about it. Some of their Caucorouses as they terme them, or great men, weare the forme of a fish of Copper in their foreheads. They all weare beade about their neckes, men and women, with otherwhiles a haukes bill or the talents of an eagles or the teeth of beasts, or sometimes a pare of great eagles wings linked together and much more of the like. Their apparell is deere skins and other furrs, which they weare loose like mantles, under which all their women, and those which are come to mans stature, weare perizomata of skins, which keep them decently covered from all offence of sharpe eies. All the rest are naked, and sometimes the men of the younger sort weare nothing at all.

Their weapons are a bow and a bundle of arrowes, an ell long, feathered with turkies feathers, and headed with points of deeres homes, peeces of glasse, or flints, which they make fast with an excellent glew which they have for that purpose. The shaft is a small cane or sticke, wherewith I have seene them kill at 20 yards distance, little birds of the bignesse of sparrows, and they use to practise themselves by casting up small stickes in the aire, and meeting it with an arrow before it come to ground. Their bow is but weake and shoots level but a little way. They daily catch partridge, deere, turkies, squirrels and the like of which there is wonderfull [plenty?], but as yet we dare not venture ourselves in the woods to seeke them, nor have we leasure.

Their houses are built in an halfe ovall forme 20 foot long, and 9 or 10 foot high with a place open in the top, halfe a yard square, whereby they admit the light, and let forth the smoake, for they build their fire, after the manner of ancient halls of England, in the middle of the house, about which they lie to sleep upon mats, spread on a low scaffold hafe a yard from ground. In one of these houses we now doe celebrate, haveing it dressed a little better then by the Indians, till we get a better, which shall be shortly as may be.

The naturall wit of these men is good, conceiveing a thing quick to. They excell in smell and taste, and have farre sharper sight than we have. Their diett is poane, made of wheat, and hominie, of the same with pease and beanes together, to which sometimes they add fish, foule, and venison, especially at solemne feasts. They are very temperate from wines and hote waters, and will hardly taste them, save those whome our English have corrupted. For chastity I never see any action in man or woman tendinge to soe much as levity, and yet the poore soules are daily with us and bring us turkie, partridge, oisters, squirells as good as any rabbit, bread and the like, running to us with smileing countenance and will help us in fishing, fouling, hunting, or what we please.

They hold it lawful to have many wives, but all keep the rigour of conjugall faith to their husbands. The very aspect of the women is modest and grave; they are generally so noble, as you can doe them noe favour, but they will returne it. There is small passion amongst them. They use in discourse of great affaires to be silent, after a question asked, and then after a little studdie to answere in few words, and stand constant to their resolution. If these were once Christian, they would doubtlesse be a vertuous and renowned nation. They exceedingly desire civill life and Christian apparell and long since had they beene cloathed, had the covetous English merchants (who would exchange cloath for nought but beaver, which every one could not get) held them from it. (God forbid we should do the like)

As for religion we neither have language as yet to finde it out, nor can wee trust therein the protestant interpretours. (White 1874)

The peaceful Piscataways, initially shy and retiring, quickly befriended the settlers and gradually became accustomed to the peculiar ways of the white man. Fishing, hunting, and farming techniques were shared, and trading later developed whereby settlers could obtain food and furs in exchange for ornamental bells, beads, clay pipes, knives, axes, fish hooks, and cooking implements. Firearms, at first banned as items of trade, were later made available by black-market traders. The settlers' sincere effort to coexist with the Piscataways was reflected in the actions of Leonard Calvert. Prior to deciding on the location of the Maryland colony, Calvert visited the Piscataways at their village on Piscataway Creek for the purpose of establishing a peaceful and productive connection. The resulting relationship, which at first was beneficial to both parties, later proved disastrous to the Piscataways—the tribe, which numbered almost 2,000 in 1634, could only count 150 members by 1675: diseases, such as smallpox and tuberculosis that were previously nonexistent among the Indians, ravaged the tribe, killing hundreds at a time.

The loss in numbers, combined with the death toll from the war with the Susquehannocks, drastically reduced the impact that the Piscataways later had in dealing with the settlers. The tribe that had befriended the settlers and shared their secrets and skills for survival in an untamed frontier found themselves dependent on the settlers for the necessities of life—clothing, weapons, tools, and utensils. Less than fifty years after the arrival of the colonists, the Piscataways had almost forgotten how to make bows and arrows. The surrender of large tracts of land to the settlers also limited the Piscataways in hunting and farming and altered their accustomed lifestyles. The fatal blow to the Piscataways was a result not of what the settlers did for the tribe, but of what they failed to do. The much-desired and desperately needed alliance with the settlers to fight the Susquehannocks failed to materialize. The Piscataways quickly learned that the settlers' guns and firearms were reserved almost exclusively for the best interests of the settlers. Their fight became a no-win situation: the Piscataways found themselves fighting for land that was being grabbed by the settlers. The tribe whose empire once extended as far north as

Elkridge found itself running out of land and people. The area between the Patapsco and Severn rivers, which had been depopulated by the Indian fighting, was taken and divided among the colonists. Even the constant attacks by the Susquehannocks did not stop the establishment of several large plantations in the 1670s. The colonists' eagerness and desire for land, which translated into power and wealth, knew few restraints.

The final displacement of the tribe came in the late 1600s. For their cooperation and friendship with the settlers, the Piscataways found themselves rewarded by confinement to a reservation. Reservations were established at Zekiah Swamp, near present-day La Plata in Charles County, along Nanjemoy Creek near Nanjemoy, and on the south side of Piscataway Creek. Although the reservations solved the settlers' problem of what to do with the remaining Piscataways, they did not solve the Piscataways' problems with rival Indian tribes. In 1697, after suffering repeated attacks from the Susquehannocks while on their reservations, the Piscataways moved to Heater's Island in the Potomac River near present-day Point of Rocks. Again on the move after other Indians attacked settlers in Virginia, the Piscataways fled to Pennsylvania. From there the now-nomadic tribe—which had occupied its village at Moyaone for an estimated 1,000 years—headed northwest to join the Iroquois in upstate New York, though a sizable group of Piscataways did remain near the Zekiah Swamp Reservation. The exodus finally ended with the absorption of the remaining Piscataways into the western tribes of the Mohicans and the Delawares.

THE SUSQUEHANNOCKS

It was an ironic twist of fate that the fierce, warlike Susquehannocks eventually sought refuge and made a final stand against armed settlers in the old fortification of their former enemy, the Piscataways. The Susquehannocks encountered the same problems faced by the Piscataways in dealing with the colonists. However different their approach, activities, and attitudes, the results would prove the same.

With the downfall of the Piscataway empire in the 1590s, signaled by the retreat of the Piscataways to Southern Maryland and the Potomac River, the Susquehannocks had emerged as the dominant tribe in the Patapsco River Valley region.

The Susquehannocks, a family tribe of the Iroquois, lived in a series of villages on the Susquehanna River, approximately twenty-two miles from its junction with the Chesapeake Bay. From their main village, located two miles below Conowingo near the mouth of the Octoraro River, the Susquehannocks gathered in hunting parties before departing for their fall and winter hunting grounds to the south.

The Susquehannocks were a tall, well-built people, who in physical stature overshadowed neighboring Indians and settlers. Their warlike image and fierceness were reflected in both their physical appearance and dress. The head of the brave was usually shaved on one side, leaving a long mane on the other side and a brushlike strip of hair in the center. The face was decorated with four vertical stripes of red, green, white, and black. A necklace of shells and animal claws, usually bear or eagle, was frequently highlighted with a small animal head hanging from the center. The brave's chest was adorned with a tattoo of the symbol of his clan—a bird, mammal, or reptile. On the legs and arms were numerous tattoos depicting deeds of valor and courage. From a leather belt tied or wrapped around the waist hung a leather apron decorated with small shells or leather fringes. The brave was barefoot in the summer and wore one-piece soft-soled moccasins during the winter months. His winter wardrobe also included a three-quarter- to full-length robe of animal skins, worn over the shoulders. Captain John Smith's journal provides an excellent firsthand description of the Susquehannocks:

> They were noble warriors. One was like a giant, the calf of whose leg was three quarters of a yard about, and all the rest of his limb so answered that proportion that he semmed the goodliest man we ever beheld. His hayre, the one side long, the other shaved close, with a ridge on his crown like a cock's comb. His arrows were five quarters long, headed with the splinters of a white crystall like stone in form of a heart, an inch broad and an inch and a half long. These he wore in wolf's skin at his back for his quiver, his bow in the one hand, and his club in the other. All were dressed in bear and wolf skins, wearing the skins as the Mexican his poncho, passing his head through a slit in the center, and letting the garment drape naturally around the body from the shoulders. (Smith 1910)

With the close of summer and the final harvest of crops, braves readied themselves for the fall and winter hunting parties that would carry them south to the Patapsco River Valley. Armed with bow and arrow and spear, the Susquehannocks hunted large game such as black bear, elk, deer, wolf, cougar, and bobcat, in addition to abundant small game such as turkey, squirrel, raccoon, beaver, rabbit, and opossum. Small game birds were also hunted, and fish and shellfish were harvested on a limited basis to provide an additional food source. However, it was the larger game, namely deer and bear, that provided the meat and hides necessary for the survival of the village.

Deer antlers were used in the making of tools and glue. Tendons and sinews were made into bow strings and sewing thread, and intestines were cleaned and used as vessels for carrying water. Farming implements were made from shoulder blades, while various other bones were made into fishhooks, needles, and weapons. Warm winter robes were made from bear skins, and bear fat was melted down and used as a seasoning with wild berries and fruit. Bear oil was used as hair ointment, insect repellent, and as a paint base for plant dyes for body decoration. The hide of the wolf made fine arrow quivers. Several hides sewn together made a useful and comfortable robe. Rabbit skins were cut into strips and woven into warm blankets. The hides of the small game animals, such as skunk and raccoon, were used for winter caps. Caps were also fashioned from bird feathers by the warriors, while the chiefs used the feathers to create and accent their regal robes.

The seasonal hunting lodges that dotted the Patapsco region consisted of a small group of huts called wigwams by the Algonquian Indians. The slanted structure was basic and simple, and the huts could be quickly put up or taken down depending on the circumstances. Saplings were staked out in a circle and drawn together at the top, then lashed to form a sphere. The frame, which was covered with animal skins or bark, supplied space for a few

European view of Susquehannock village in the mid-1600s.
Courtesy Maryland Historical Society.

warriors or a single family. Rock formations and natural caves also provided the hunting parties with shelter.

The arrival of the first white settlers in Maryland signaled the rapid decline of the Susquehanna nation. The desires of the Susquehannocks to expand their territory and remain independent would lead to the eventual extinction of the tribe. The settlers, who were rapidly expanding in the upper regions of the Chesapeake Bay, took quick advantage of the warring Indian tribes. They befriended the Piscataways and other Southern Maryland tribes, converted them to Christianity, supplied them with arms and ammunition, and rallied behind them in their war with the Susquehannocks. The Susquehannocks, resenting this intrusion and collaboration with their enemy, now included the settlers in their raids. In 1638, the colonists passed a militia law, and a military force was formed for protection. Attacks grew so frequent and intense that on September 13, 1642, acting Governor A. Giles Brent proclaimed the Susquehannocks enemies of the state. This legislation unified the settlers, who were splintered politically and scattered geographically. Earlier legislation, passed in June 1642, prohibiting the trading of munitions to the Susquehannocks, had proved ineffective. The Susquehannocks merely turned to the Swedish traders in Delaware, who eagerly traded arms and munitions for furs and hides.

Retaliation by the settlers took the form of raiding parties that copied Indian fighting tactics. Captain Thomas Cornwallis was commissioned to lead an expedition of 53 Marylanders; they encountered a group of about 250

Susquehannocks north of the Patapsco and killed 29 warriors in the ensuing battle. After this incident, defensive measures centered around the formation of local militia groups. Known throughout the state as the Maryland Rangers and locally as the Patapsco Rangers, these were men of certified good character who were selected for their ability to track, and to handle firearms. These colonial guerrillas, Maryland versions of Davy Crockett, proved to be a formidable foe for the raiding Indian parties. Frontier outposts, simple stone and log fortifications, were first established from the Patapsco to the Susquehanna and later as far south as Georgetown on the Potomac. Captain John Oldton, who built Fort Garrison in 1692, commanded the regiments from the Patapsco to the Susquehanna, and Captain Thomas Brown's command included the regiments from the Patapsco to the Potomac. Along the Main Branch of the Patapsco, Colonel Ninian Beall commanded a garrison of rangers stationed in a log cabin between the Falls of the Patapsco and Gwynns Falls. Beall's rangers were able to monitor and limit Indian activity on the Seneca Trail, the major north-south transportation route that crossed the Patapsco at the main falls above Elkridge and connected the Susquehanna and the Potomac.

The desired peace between the settlers and the Susquehannocks came as a result of the tribal war between the Susquehannocks and the Iroquois Confederacy. The confederacy, composed of the Onondaga, Cayuga, Mohawk, Seneca, and Oneida, needed the Susquehannocks to strengthen its political and military sovereignty over the mid-Atlantic tribes. Numerous invitations extended to the Susquehannocks led to a declaration of war when the confederacy passed a rule to destroy any tribe which refused to join.

During the time that the settlers began to retaliate against the Susquehannocks, the Cayugas and Senecas came down from New York State with firearms obtained from the French and began their offensive against the defiant tribe. Faced with the prospect of a two-front war that would spell quick defeat, the Susquehannocks made a hasty peace with the settlers. Survival with the settlers seemed a more viable choice than subordination and possible elimination at the hands of the Iroquois Confederacy.

In 1652, five chiefs of the Susquehannocks, in the presence of a Swedish Council, met with Maryland colonial government representatives (then called the Maryland Council) at the present site of St. John's College in Annapolis. At the meeting, a treaty was signed whereby the Susquehannocks ceded to the colonists all their claimed territory from the Patuxent River to Palmer's Island on the western shore and land from the Choptank River to the northeast branch of the Elk River on the Eastern Shore. In return for relinquishing most of their land in the Maryland province, the Susquehannocks now believed they had the strong ally needed to repel the invasion of the Iroquis Confederacy. This "paper" ally produced only firearms and munitions through the renewed trading agreement of the treaty. The treaty did not provide colonial troops, and none were offered by the settlements. The alliance not only offered little help but was short-lived. Continued outbursts of violence by the Susquehannocks aroused the colonists' hidden anger and dissolved this uneasy friendship of convenience.

In May 1661, a summons sent out to the borders of the Patapsco River Valley by the governor and his council gathered settlers who had suffered from the recent Indian violence. At this meeting on Spesutia Island (offshore from the present site of the Aberdeen Proving Grounds), complaints were heard and investigated. The meeting resulted in the reaffirmation of one of the terms of the Treaty of 1652—to live peaceably with the Susquehannocks. By 1662, the violence between the Susquehannocks and the settlers had subsided. However, the peace once again proved to be short-lived. The settlers soon found themselves caught in tribal warfare. Seneca Indians coming into Maryland to obliterate the Susquehannocks killed not only their native enemy but also the settlers who happened to be in their path. A settler was reported to have been killed by the Senecas near the Patapsco River.

With the Senecas rapidly driving south of the Patapsco, the Susquehannocks and the settlers once again turned to each other for help. In August 1663, Chief Wastahanow met with the Maryland Council at George Goldsmith's home on the Bush River to sign a peace treaty of mutual self-interest. It was hoped that a mutual defense treaty could stop the invading Senecas. The new allies, combining for a concentrated military effort, received an unexpected ally from the north. Fleeing Hurons, survivors of the Iroquois Confederacy offensive, took refuge with the Susquehannocks and declared an all-out war against the confederacy. But this new ally added too few warriors to the ranks of the Susquehannocks, whose number was already greatly diminished due to years of constant warfare.

By 1674, the Susquehannocks could muster only 300 warriors from a force that only a few years before had numbered 700. The long years of warfare with the Senecas following the Treaty of 1663 depleted the tribe to the point where their extinction became only a matter of time. Another somewhat surprising factor that contributed to the destruction of the tribe was the unauthorized attacks by the settlers. In one incident, five Susquehannock chiefs were killed while under a flag of truce. Colonial militia Major Thomas Trueman lost control of his troops, who murdered the Indians. Seneca attacks were also being unjustly attributed to the Susquehannocks. A Seneca raid on the settlers near the Patapsco, in which one person was killed and two boys carried off, was blamed on the Susquehannocks. Cases of mistaken identity were quickly utilized by the settlers to widen the gap between the two tribal groups and to renew the animosity. It was another ironic twist of fate that the Susquehannocks' legendary fame as warriors, as reported by the settlers before 1663, worked against them in the following years when they tried to maintain a peaceful existence. A final factor influencing the destruction of the Susquehannocks was the smallpox epidemic that ravaged the tribe; it could not be stopped by either white or red medicine.

The final defeat of the Susquehannocks occurred in 1675. After mounting an unsuccessful counterattack against the Senecas, the Susquehannocks left their Susquehanna River home and journeyed southwest across the Patapsco to Piscataway Creek, a few miles below Washington, DC. Here they took up residence in a wood-and-earth fort previously occupied by their former enemies, the Piscataways. The arrival of the Susquehannocks on the western shores of the Potomac raised the heated protests of nearby farmers and plantation owners, who feared the warlike nature of the tribe. With the retreat of the Susquehannocks to the Potomac River, the Senecas had clear passage through the Patapsco River Valley. Fearing the effects of a tribal war and eager to drive out the Susquehannocks, Marylanders and Virginians joined together to form a military expedition to remove the approximately 100 Susquehannock men, women, and children from the fort.

Virginians, led by Colonel John Washington, the grandfather of George Washington, and Marylanders, under the command of Major Thomas Trueman, formed an army of approximately 1,000 men in an effort to negotiate a peaceful removal of the Susquehannocks. On Sunday, September 26, 1675, the combined armies gathered at the earthen fort for the first meeting. Trueman initiated the action by sending two messengers to the fort with an invitation to the Susquehannock chiefs for a conference. The chiefs quickly accepted and sent six leaders outside the walls of the fort. The peaceful meeting quickly turned into a heated argument, with accusations of murder and violence placed against the Susquehannocks. The explanation that the recent attacks had been committed by the Senecas, who were now camped at the head of the Patapsco, failed to satisfy the military leaders. After denying murder charges made by Colonel Washington and Colonel Mason of the Virginia forces, the Indian leaders returned to the fort with a promise to meet the following morning. Early the next day, while the second meeting was taking place in front of the fort, Captain John Allen, a well-known leader of the Maryland Rangers, was dispatched to the home of Randolph Hanson for supplies. Arriving at the house and finding the Hanson family murdered, Allen promptly returned to the camp with the mangled bodies. The conference was immediately stopped as Washington and Trueman decided upon the appropriate reaction to these murders. As word spread throughout the camp, the emotions of the militia reached a fever pitch. Trueman was faced with the difficult task of subduing the Virginia officers, who called for immediate execution of the Indian leaders. The overwhelming sentiment of the mob prevailed, and five of the six chiefs, who had been detained with the news of the Hanson family, were brought forth and clubbed to death.

For his part in the murders, Trueman was indicted by the Maryland Assembly. He pled guilty under mitigating circumstances, and, after the lower and upper houses of the Assembly failed to decide on a sentence, he was fined 10,000 pounds of tobacco and was ordered to post a bond of 150,000 pounds to ensure his future good conduct. Washington was cleared of any wrongdoing by Virginia authorities.

This act of colonial "justice" served only to strengthen the resolve of the Susquehannocks holed up in the fort. During the next six weeks the fort came under frequent but unsuccessful attack by the militia. After six weeks of heroic defense, the Susquehannocks, who numbered about seventy-five, ransacked the inside of the fort and escaped through the lines of soldiers, killing ten guards who were asleep. The Susquehannock survivors combined with several small Virginia tribes and headed into Virginia. Still angered and outraged at the slaughter of their leaders, the Susquehannocks avenged the unjust deaths by taking the lives of sixty Virginia settlers. This rampage and the savagery of their actions aroused the strong outcries of Virginia settlers.

When their protests appeared to fall on the deaf ears of their government representatives, the settlers took matters into their own hands. Nathaniel Bacon, later to become immortalized for Bacon's Rebellion, felt the sting of the Susquehannocks with the death of his plantation overseer. Bacon formed an army of armed servants and settlers and swept the countryside in search of the Susquehannocks. One by one, the renegade Indians were hunted down and killed.

The few remaining Susquehannocks retreated northward to Pennsylvania, where in 1701 they became a subject tribe of the Onondagas in the Iroquois Confederacy. Converted to Christianity and trained in the ways of the white man, the Susquehannocks were permitted to live along the Susquehanna River near the town of Conestoga. The survivors of this once-powerful, independent tribe remained along the Susquehanna until 1763, when the Pontiac War broke out along the Pennsylvania frontier. Rioting settlers, inflamed by this new Indian war, massacred the last group of twenty Susquehannocks in the jail yard of Lancaster, Pennsylvania. Fearing for their safety, the Susquehannocks had sought refuge and shelter at the hands of the white man.

CHAPTER THREE

A Port and Its Forts

THE PORT OF BALTIMORE

The port of Baltimore is at the head of the navigable portion of the Patapsco, approximately twelve miles northwest of the 4,400-square-mile Chesapeake Bay, the largest estuary in the United States.

The port is 150 nautical miles north of the Virginia capes, the entrance to the Bay from the Atlantic Ocean. Vessels also have access to the port from the ocean by way of the sea-level Chesapeake and Delaware Canal and Delaware Bay, a distance of 113 nautical miles. The canal, extending from Reedy Point, Delaware, to the Chesapeake Bay, provides unencumbered ship passage between Baltimore and other North Atlantic ports or the open Atlantic Ocean. The Patapsco enters the Chesapeake Bay about nine and a half miles below Fort McHenry at Baltimore. The river is about four miles wide at its mouth, between North and Bodkin points.

The port area of Baltimore includes the navigable part of the Patapsco below Hanover Street; the Northwest and Middle Branches; Curtis Bay and its tributary, Curtis Creek; and parts of Colgate, Bear, and Jones Creeks. The Northwest Branch, known locally as the inner basin, extends about three miles in a northwesterly direction from Fort McHenry to its head at Calvert Street, and varies in width from 1,200 to 3,000 feet. Middle Branch, also known locally as Spring Garden, extends about one and a half miles in a northwesterly direction from Ferry Bar past Hanover Street to the foot of Eutaw Street, and varies in width from 1,000 to 4,000 feet. Curtis Bay is an estuary, about two miles long and seven-tenths of a mile wide, on the southwest side of the Patapsco, six miles above the river mouth. Curtis Creek empties into the head of Curtis Bay from the south between Sledds and Ferry points, on the southwest side of Curtis Bay. The harbor comprises approximately forty-five miles of waterfront, encompassing nearly 1,600 acres of sheltered waters. The mean range of the tide is about one foot at Baltimore, although prolonged winds of constant direction may cause substantial variations. Currents in the harbor are too weak and variable to be predicted, but they still require the attention of anyone using the harbor waters.

The climate of the Patapsco system is controlled by the Chesapeake Bay and the Atlantic Ocean to the east, and the Appalachian Mountains to the west. These topographical features produce more equable and moderate weather patterns when compared with other locations farther inland at the same latitude. Rainfall distribution throughout the year is rather uniform. The average amount of yearly precipitation is forty-four inches. The greatest intensities of rain are confined to the summer and early fall months, the seasons for severe thunderstorms and hurricanes. Hurricane-force winds in excess of seventy-four miles per hour may occur on rare occasions when a cold front or a thunderstorm moves into the area.

January is the coldest month and July is the warmest. Temperatures during fall and winter (October–March) average 41.6°F; during spring and summer (April–September) 67.6°F. Winter and spring months have the highest average wind speeds. Changes in wind direction are frequent and contribute to the changeable character of the weather. Snowfall occurs on about twenty-five days per year, with an average of only nine days producing snowfalls greater than an inch. The heaviest amounts of snow generally fall in February, with occasional heavy falls as late as March.

The seaport takes its name from George Calvert's title as the first Lord Baltimore. George Calvert, the son of Leonard Calvert, a country gentleman from Yorkshire, England, served as secretary of state to King James I and as a member of the Privy Council. His political career, during which he was knighted by the king and bestowed with the title Sir George Calvert, ended when Catholicism became unpopular in England in the seventeenth century. In 1625, James I, who wished to maintain as much political support as possible, compensated Calvert for his work in English politics by bestowing upon him the title of Baron Baltimore, of Baltimore, Ireland. Baltimore, its name taken from the original Irish *Beal-t-more*, meaning *great place* or *circle of Baal*, the sun god, was a tiny fishing village on the south coast. In addition to the title received from James I, George Calvert also received a grant of land north of the Virginia colony. The distinction of founding the colony and being the first lord proprietary of the Maryland province fell to Calvert's son Cecil, the second Lord Baltimore. In 1633, Cecil sent his brother Leonard to head the expedition to the new colony. Sailing in the *Ark and the Dove* with 200 colonists, Leonard Calvert arrived at St. Clement's Island on March 25, 1634, and took possession of the land grant that later became Maryland.

Baltimore was officially chartered as Baltimore Town in 1729. A large portion of the land around the harbor basin belonged to Thomas Cole, who in 1668 obtained a warrant for 550 acres of land where Jones Falls enters the Patapsco. Growth of the village as a seaport was slow. Elkridge Landing, Joppa, Fell's Point, and Whetstone Point offered a more convenient access to ships and tobacco planters. By 1752, the town consisted of about twenty-five houses and two hundred inhabitants. One small finger pier serviced the limited tobacco trade, which used the town for export purposes.

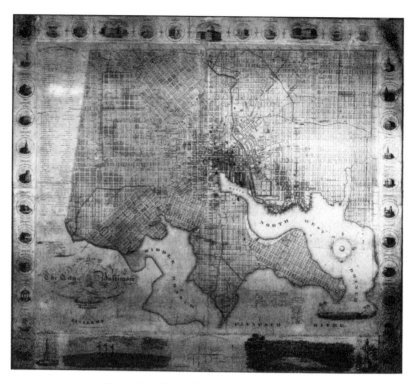

Plan of the City of Baltimore dated 1792.
Courtesy Maryland Historical Society.

As the town gradually developed, the shipping business expanded and diversified. In 1752, Nicholas Rogers sailed his brig, the *Phillip and James*, to Barbados with a load of tobacco, flour, iron, and various food staples. The success of the new trade route between Baltimore and the West Indies prompted Dr. John Stevenson, a physician turned shipping entrepreneur, to experiment with grain shipments to Ireland and to markets on the mid-Atlantic seaboard. The capability to handle the grain exports provided the impetus for the development of flour mills near the port. The opening of farmlands in central Maryland and the flour production of the Ellicott brothers at their Patapsco Flour Mill supplied the port with an abundant export commodity and a financial base for continued growth.

During the American Revolution, Baltimore blossomed into a major seaport and surpassed Annapolis as the colony's center of trade. Fell's Point, annexed by Baltimore in 1773, became the much-needed deep-water port. Fell's Point had been founded in 1730 by English shipwright William Fell and laid out as a separate town by his son Edward in 1763. The deepwater location east of the harbor basin made it an ideal shipping and shipbuilding center. The first frigate of the Continental Navy, the *Virginia*, was one of the many noted vessels turned out by the shipyards to battle the British for control of the high seas. Military contractors and suppliers were not the only ones to benefit from the war. Baltimore merchants and shippers took advantage of the British blockade to expand markets in the West Indies and Latin America. The British fleet sailed up the Chesapeake Bay, blockading Annapolis and leaving Baltimore undisturbed. [Other than the attack on Baltimore in 1814, only once did the British fleet anchor at the mouth of the Patapsco.] The show of force did not stop Baltimore's entrepreneurs.

In August 1785, Captain John O'Donnell made a celebrated arrival into the Baltimore harbor from China. His ship, *Pallas*, carried a cargo of tea, china, silks, and satins. This first of many cargoes opened up new trade routes to the Orient. O'Donnell became so enchanted with the town that he purchased 1,809 acres of waterfront property east of Fell's Point. He built an Oriental style house and named the estate Canton in honor of the Chinese city that had brought him fortune and fame. [The property was purchased in 1827 by an investment group headed by Peter Cooper.] An ironworks founded by Cooper was later sold to Horace Abbott, who during the Civil War contracted with the federal government to provide iron plates for the Union Navy's first ironclad vessel, the *Monitor*.

In 1797, at Harris Creek in Canton, the frigate *Constellation* was launched. The first ship in the new Continental Navy was named by George Washington. During her illustrious career, the *Constellation* defeated the French ships *L'Insurgente* and *La Vengeance* on the high seas, fought the British fleet in the War of 1812, opened trade with China in the 1840s, helped break up the slave trade off the coast of Africa in the 1860s, transported food to Ireland during the famine of 1880, and served continuously until the end of World War II, during which time she was commissioned the flagship of the Atlantic fleet under Admiral Ernest J. King and moored at Newport, Rhode Island.

Harbor basin in the 1870s during the heyday of the steamboat.
Courtesy Maryland Historical Society.

By 1790, seven regularly scheduled packet services were sailing from Baltimore to other East Coast ports. Maritime services were expanded and enhanced due to the development of the Baltimore Clipper. Characterized by a sharp bow and a V-shaped, streamlined hull, and topped with two masts set back at an angle, the clipper ship could outdistance and outmaneuver anything afloat. Designed primarily for speed rather than durability, the clipper ship proved vulnerable to the stormy waters of the North Atlantic. However, the clipper was ideally suited for sailing to the tropics and established an impressive performance record for carrying trade in those waters. The ultimate clipper ship was the *Anne McKim*, which was built for Baltimore merchant Isaac McKim and launched on June 4, 1833. Rated at the time as the fastest sailing ship in the world and the largest clipper ship (at 143 feet in length), the *Anne McKim* carried shipments of flour around Cape Horn to Peru in exchange for copper ore. Along with other clippers, the *Anne McKim* would be replaced by a sailing vessel with larger and more profitable cargo holds. During the American Revolution and the War of 1812, the fleet of clippers served as privateers. Colonial pirates, or privateers, were privately owned and armed vessels commissioned to capture or destroy enemy ships while continuing their merchant duties. After the War of 1812, clippers found new work in the slave trade. The Baltimore clipper was ideally suited to engage in carrying cargoes of human misery. The swift clipper easily outran the British vessels guarding the African coast. Attempts to enforce the legislation of the Congress of Vienna, which outlawed international slave trade in 1816, proved futile. The final chapter in the history of the glamorous clipper ship is both unforgettable and regrettable.

By the early 1800s, Baltimore had gained an international reputation as a financial and commercial center. The expansion of the import firms of Robert Oliver and the investment and banking concerns of Alexander Brown led the way in creating a favorable financial environment to lure more trade into the port. In 1812, the *Niles Weekly Register* reported that Baltimore had risen "from absolute insignificance to a degree of commercial importance which has brought down upon it the envy and jealousy of all the great cities of the Union."

In 1813, sail power gave way to steam power on the Chesapeake Bay and signaled a new era in transportation. Only six years after Robert Fulton sailed the *Clermont* up the Hudson River, Baltimore built and operated its first steamer, the *Chesapeake*. Within a few years, Baltimore became the home port for a large fleet of steamers designed for Bay trade. Through the 1820s and 1830s, a number of steamship lines made regular runs from Baltimore to Norfolk and points south. In 1839, the most famous of all lines was incorporated as the Baltimore Steam Packet Company, more commonly known as the Old Bay Line.

On the afternoon of April 14, 1842, the company unveiled its newest steamer, the *Medora*, a 180-foot vessel with a lever-beam engine by John Watchman and boilers of the best Pennsylvania iron. On board for the trial run down the Chesapeake were seventy-nine people, many of whom were company officials, invited guests, and shipyard workers. At approximately 2:30 p.m., the departure bell sounded and the steamer backed away from Cully's Wharf on the south side of the harbor basin. As the paddle wheels made their second revolution, the boiler exploded, splintering a large portion of the upper deck and blowing the smokestack 100 feet into the air. The boiler, described as an "immense one of iron" (Brown 1940), was launched upwards and came back down, landing on and shattering the remaining portion of the deck. The muffled explosion threw up scalding clouds of steam and fragments of wood and iron from the ship. Bodies with arms and legs extended were hurled through the air with a whirling motion. Within seconds of the explosion, the *Medora* sank to her guards (paddle wheel covers). Many who survived the blast were carried down with the ship. Twenty-six people were killed and thirty-eight others injured. Among the dead were Andrew F. Henderson, the company's president, and John C. Moale, the general agent. An investigation into the accident failed to determine the cause of the explosion. The disaster was only a temporary setback to the profitable and popular line. The hulk of the *Medora* was salvaged and within a year rebuilt and christened the *Herald*.

For nearly a century, steam packets were the port's economic lifeline, carrying passengers and freight to cities along the Atlantic coast. The Patapsco was ideally suited as a home port for these shallow-draft vessels, which resembled a cross between a small ocean liner and a barge. Many of the steamboats built in the late 1800s and early 1900s were as elaborately furnished and decorated as luxury liners, complete with wood-paneled hallways, gilt-and-ivory dining saloons, and staterooms with brass beds. The steamers proved so rugged and reliable that a few were pressed into service for convoy duty in the North Atlantic during World War II. Following the war, the steamers were victimized by the ever-increasing truck and automobile traffic on the nation's expanding highway system. A prime example was the construction of the Chesapeake Bay Bridge in 1952, which closed the gap between the eastern and western shores, making automobile ferries obsolete. The steam packets, which had begun to decline in the 1930s, managed to survive until the early 1960s when the Old Bay Line discontinued its run to Norfolk.

The founding of the Baltimore and Ohio Railroad in 1827 ushered in a new era of prosperity for the port. With the development of a practical steam-driven locomotive, the industrial and agricultural products of mid-America were hauled to the head of the Patapsco for domestic distribution and overseas export. The boom created by the railroads helped the port develop into a major railway center. Coal and grain, two of the major exports, could be brought directly to dockside in larger quantities in less time and at less expense than ever before.

By 1844, Baltimore shipowners were importing vast deposits of bird guano from the islands off the Peruvian coast. One customer, who gained unwanted notoriety, was Junius Brutus Booth, the father of presidential assassin John Wilkes Booth. Booth mixed the guano with bone dust to fertilize the fields of his Harford county farm. In the late 1850s, the port began importing phosphate lime and became the nation's leader in the fertilizer and chemical industries.

With the outbreak of the Civil War, the city found itself caught in the center of the North-South controversy and in the uneasy position of being half-heartedly committed to the cause of the Union. The city's allegiance was ensured in May 1861 when General Benjamin Butler seized and occupied the city with his contingent of Union forces. Federal Hill became a Union fort, with artillery batteries pointing over the harbor and the center of the city. Baltimore's strategic location as a seaport and railway center between

Washington and the major northern cities made it imperative that it remain in the Union at all costs. The occupation saw Baltimore's maritime and commercial traffic slow to a trickle. Area industries became major producers of military supplies for the federal government. Exports dropped 60 percent as regional trade disappeared. Baltimore was turned into a military installation operating at the discretion of President Lincoln. The weak link in the chain of northern cities outfitting the war remained the vital connection in preserving the Union.

With the surrender of the Confederate Army in April 1865, Baltimore businessmen immediately turned their attention to the task of rebuilding the shipping industry. Steamship services to Charleston, South Carolina, and Havana, Cuba, were launched to reopen trade routes. The B&O, the port's lifeline to the Midwest and the South, was reconstructed under the guidance of its president, John Garrett. Throughout the war, the railroad suffered frequent damage to its tracks, bridges, stations, and rolling stock at the hands of Confederate raiding parties. It was essential that the railroad be rebuilt and renovated in order to ensure the survival of Baltimore as a major seaport. Garrett also bought and rebuilt three former blockade runners to initiate the port's first postwar transatlantic service. For three years, these ships were the only US flag ships involved in European trade. Not an overwhelming success, the service did result in a business venture with the North German Lloyd Company, providing direct service to Bremen, Germany. Regular passenger service from Bremen to Baltimore resulted in an influx of thousands of German immigrants. The line continued to land passengers at the B&O terminal at Locust Point until the outbreak of World War I in 1914. Baltimore at one time ranked second only to Ellis Island, New York, in processing immigrants from European countries.

Between 1840 and 1860, Irish and German immigrants comprised the majority of new arrivals in Baltimore. From the 1880s to the end of the 1920s, the new immigrants were Italians and Greeks from Southern Europe, and Poles, Lithuanians, Ukrainians, Hungarians, Czechs, and Jews from Eastern Europe. Leaving behind poverty, political oppression, and religious persecution, they disembarked at registration points in Locust Point, Canton, and Fell's Point for a chance at a new life. Many stayed in the neighborhoods where they arrived and found work in the nearby shipyards, factories, canneries, and packinghouses. Today these diverse nationalities are reflected in Baltimore's well-preserved ethnic neighborhoods. Since 1820, more than two million immigrants have sailed up the Patapsco, the first sight of their new country being the Stars and Stripes waving over the ramparts at Fort McHenry.

By 1872, newly built, rail-financed grain elevators brought the Midwestern wheat market to Baltimore for shipment to European markets. In 1874, *Scribner's* magazine, commenting on Baltimore's rapid development, declared that the city had become "the Liverpool of America." Two years later, the port ranked as the sixth largest in the world, bolstered by the large movement of heavy commodities from the Midwest. Favorable postwar economic conditions combined with a new immigrant work force to make industrial expansion a necessity rather than a risk. By the mid-1880s, Baltimore was firmly established as a great industrial and shipping center. One of the largest cities on the Eastern Seaboard, it ranked only behind New York and Philadelphia in population and maritime production. During the late 1800s, an era of unprecedented economic growth was instituted with the development of a heavy industry base.

In 1887, the Pennsylvania Steel Company acquired land at Sparrows Point for the production of pig iron. A new plant was built and it revived an industry that had slumped to near extinction after the Civil War in the face of competition from larger, more modern operations in the Midwest. The peninsula on the north side of the Patapsco where it empties into the Chesapeake Bay had been first patented by Thomas Sparrow in 1652. In 1891, the plant added Bessemer converters for the production of steel and a rolling mill for the manufacture of rails. The plant also established a shipyard for the construction of steel-hulled vessels. In 1916, the steel plant and shipyard were acquired by the Bethlehem Steel Company. The plant continued to expand its operations and its product line of steel products. During its heyday, the plant was one of the largest steel mills in the United States, as well as the largest private employer in the State of Maryland.

Sunday, February 7, 1904, dawned as another cold, gray, overcast winter's day. Few late morning churchgoers paid attention to the horses pulling Engine No. 15 as they raced along Liberty Street. No one on the streets realized that the clanging fire bells were prelude to a disaster that would literally re-create the city of Baltimore.

National Automatic Alarm No. 854, located outside the Hurst Building at Hopkins Place and German (now Redwood) Street, sounded at 10:40 a.m. By the time Engine No. 15 arrived, smoke was already billowing from the top floors of the six-story building. The heat-sensitive alarm indicated that the fire was in the basement. Captain John Kahl and his men smashed through the glass doors, carrying a three-quarter-inch chemical line and a two-and-one-half-inch water line, and headed for the stairwell. Before they could get to the bottom of the stairs, the building was rocked by two explosions. The first threw Kahl and his men out of the building; the second blew out the windows and blasted the roof off, scattering flaming debris onto nearby buildings.

Southwest winds quickly spread the fire across German Street. Within minutes, two city alarms were sounded, the first at Box 414. At 11:45 a.m., Fire Chief George W. Horton dispatched a distress message to Washington asking for immediate help. In the early afternoon, with twelve blocks engulfed in flames, Mayor Robert McLane gave permission to dynamite buildings to create a firebreak. By late afternoon, the dynamite finally arrived and the demolition began, but it was too little too late. Many of the sturdy stone buildings failed to collapse, and the explosions merely aided in spreading the fire. Winds reaching twenty and thirty miles per hour spread the flames horizontally from building to building. The inferno raged into the night with temperatures spiraling to an estimated 2,500°F. The six-story, "fireproof" Continental Building was gutted, its ornamental copper and brass fixtures melted into globs of metal. By dawn of the next day, firemen and equipment from Pennsylvania, Delaware, and New York had joined the fight, many having arrived during the night on special trains. A gallant all-day stand at Jones Falls by lines of exhausted firemen weakened the fire and finally turned the tide of battle. By 5:00 p.m., the conflagration was declared under control.

An area of 140 acres, bordered by Liberty Street to the west, Jones Falls to the east, Fayette Street to the north, and the harbor basin to the south, smoldered in ruins. The downtown business district, an estimated 1,500 buildings, was

The harbor district after the Great Fire. View looking west up Baltimore Street. Right of center is the cupola of City Hall.
Courtesy Maryland Historical Society.

destroyed. Damage was estimated at between $125 and $150 million, of which $32 million was insured. Two thousand firms were out of business and 35,000 people were out of work. A total of 1,671 firemen had been utilized including the 460 men of Baltimore's fire department. The fire ranked as the third worst city fire in American history, behind the Chicago fire of 1871 and the San Francisco earthquake fire of 1906. The most amazing statistic is that not one life was lost in the blaze.

What started the fire? It is believed that a cigar or cigarette, discarded on Saturday night, fell into an unplugged two-inch eyelet in the sidewalk and landed among bolts of cotton cloth being stored in the basement of the Hurst Building. There it smoldered until the following morning when it ignited and activated the alarm.

Within a few days, a new city began to rise from the ashes. New streets, utilities, and buildings were constructed using the latest technology. The tired, aging, cramped city with its many obsolete buildings and dilapidated warehouses was gone. To many optimistic Baltimoreans, the fire was a blessing in disguise.

The opening of the Panama Canal in 1914 enabled the port to move westbound cargo more quickly and cheaply than its northern competitors. The worst shipping disaster in the port's history had a connection with the canal. On March 7, 1913, at 10:30 a.m., the British freighter *Alum Chine* exploded while anchored off Hawkins Point. The ship had been loading 350 tons of dynamite for use in the construction of the canal. Thirty-three men were killed and sixty injured as the 1,800-ton vessel and two railroad barges tied alongside (carrying six boxcars of dynamite) were ripped to pieces and sent to the bottom of the harbor. When huge fragments of steel and iron were hurled aboard the coal transport *Jason*, several crewmen were killed. The tugboat *Atlantic* sank while trying to escape. The shock wave following the explosion resembled an earthquake, shattering windows throughout East Baltimore. Earth tremors were felt as far north as Philadelphia and Atlantic City. According to the investigation conducted by the city coroner, the explosion was caused by a stevedore sticking a bale hook into a box of dynamite that had been placed crookedly. The dynamite caught fire and gave off a thick column of smoke before exploding into a fireball a few minutes later.

The worst maritime accident on the waters of the Patapsco was not related to the shipping industry but occurred during a social excursion along the river's bank. On the night of July 23, 1883, a few minutes after nine o'clock, sixty-three Baltimoreans lost their lives when a finger pier collapsed. The victims, who were trapped by pilings, debris, and the mass of other struggling victims, drowned in less than six feet of water. The social outing, which was sponsored by the newly formed parish of the Corpus Christi Catholic Church, turned into a nightmare that left the city stunned at its loss. The tragic day had started on a happy note as friends and family of the predominantly Irish parish gathered at the downtown edge of the harbor basin to await their ride. A steam-powered tugboat pulling a large, flat barge had been hired for a fifteen-mile trip downriver to Tivoli, a popular summer spot later engulfed by Bethlehem Steel's Sparrows Point plant. The day was filled with food, friends, and leisure activities, and ended all too soon; as twilight fell on the waters of the Patapsco, weary excursionists lined up near the pier for the return trip. The anxious crowd surged past a restraining gate and funneled themselves onto the length of the pier. The aging timbers squeaked and groaned under the weight of the crowd until the main supports snapped with a thunderous clap. Within seconds, more than 100 people found themselves immersed in water and darkness. Although a number of victims were pulled to safety, rescue efforts were thwarted by hysteria, panic, and the darkness of the moonless night. Many of those in the water were crushed by others struggling for safety. The official death list recorded thirty-four women, twenty-four children, and six men killed in the accident.

When the United States was drawn into World War I in 1917, the shipyards of Baltimore were ready to assist in the hurried shipbuilding program. The increased flow of supplies and equipment bound for the war theater stimulated the construction of numerous piers and warehouses by the three railroads that served the port. The increased cargo and sea traffic revealed some of the inadequacies in the port facilities. After the war, in 1920, the State of Maryland passed legislation providing loans of up to $50 million for major harbor improvements. The investment paid off handsomely. Over the next decade, thirty-nine overseas steamship lines sailed regularly from the port, and thirteen coastal and nine inter-coastal cargo and passenger services operated on a regular schedule. Channel improvements in the Patapsco, made possible through federal funding, lowered the channel depth to thirty-eight feet to accommodate a new line of larger ships, as well as providing a new cutoff channel that shortened the distance between Baltimore and the Chesapeake and Delaware Canal.

During World War II, the port operated at peak efficiency and established new production and performance records. In 1941, Bethlehem Steel Company leased the shipyard of the Union Shipbuilding Company at Fairfield, west of Curtis Bay, and began to turn out the first Liberty ships. The first Liberty ship, the *Patrick Henry*, was launched on September 27, 1941, some five months after the keel-laying ceremony. By early 1942, the shipyard operated around the clock, employing an estimated 47,000 workers. Completion time from keel-laying to launching was reduced to an average of thirty days. In 1944, the shipyard switched to building Victory ships, a larger, more practical version of the Liberty ship. Before the war ended, Bethlehem-Fairfield built 384 Liberty ships, 94 Victory ships, and 30 LSTs (landing craft). During the war, the shipyard built more ships and outproduced all other shipyards. Baltimore shipyards built a total of 608 ships, in addition to repairing thousands of others.

At the end of the war, the shipping facilities were in desperate need of repair. Attempts by different owners and agencies to update the port revealed a total lack of communication and direction on the part of all those involved in the industry. By the early 1950s, it was clear that some authority needed to be established to coordinate all port activity. The Port of Baltimore Commission was organized to seek more liberalized loans for port improvements. In 1956, the commission was succeeded by the Maryland Port Authority. Created by the Maryland General Assembly, it was the single agency charged with coordinating the maritime efforts of city, state, and private concerns. In 1971, the Maryland Port Authority was redesignated the Maryland Port Administration. The task of maintaining the port as a productive and innovative world leader in maritime commerce remained the same.

Taking advantage of its location as the nation's farthest inland deep-water port, Baltimore has maintained its place of world prominence in the maritime industry. Supported by excellent rail, highway, and air systems, the port has access to America's most productive agricultural and industrial areas. In 1981, Baltimore ranked fifth nationally in overall tonnage and second in containerized cargo. In the 1960s, Baltimore was one of the first US ports to become involved in the revolutionary concept of containerization. Specialized handling facilities, such as those at the Dundalk Marine Terminal, helped the port maintain a competitive edge over other Atlantic seaports. Today major cargo-handling facilities at Locust Point, Canton, and Port Covington handle millions of tons of cargo a year in containerized and break-bulk form, as well as dry and liquid products. Export and import products include automobiles, chemicals, construction materials, heavy equipment, machinery, textiles, and sugar. Since the eighteenth century, coal and grain have remained the major export commodities.

The essential factor in the formula that produced prosperity for the port has been the maintenance of the Patapsco's bottom. The entire harbor basin is a shallow bay which historically averaged between sixteen and twenty feet in depth. This was more than adequate for the clipper ships that called on the port and dominated the shipping business until the Civil War. However, as sail gave way to steam and cargo capacities were increased with larger ships, deeper water was required to service the port. Deeper water on the Patapsco meant dredging.

Since all but the earliest days of the port, survival of the maritime industry has required continuous dredging of the harbor's man-made channels. Dredging projects have been a cooperative effort between the city of Baltimore and the federal government. Assistance from the federal government came not only via congressional funding but also in the form of machinery and manpower from the US Army Corps of Engineers. The role of the Baltimore district of the corps has been instrumental in making Baltimore a major seaport. Their achievements in channel construction and maintenance have allowed the port to keep pace with the latest maritime trends and technology.

Dredging first began in 1798 when the city provided money to build and operate a primitive dredge, similar to the "mud machine" already being operated by the Ellicotts at their waterfront terminal. For the next fifty years, dredging and federal funding for dredging were sporadic. Involvement of the Corps of Engineers was limited to harbor surveying projects. In 1852, dredging became a priority with the appointment of Captain Henry Brewerton as Baltimore district engineer. Aided by generous federal funding, Brewerton planned for the excavation of the harbor from Fort McHenry to four miles beyond North Point into the Chesapeake Bay. In the fall of 1853, dredging began with the use of two modern steam dredges. At the time, the main channel averaged only seventeen feet at mean low tide. Brewerton hoped to carve out a channel twenty-two feet deep and 150 feet wide. By 1857, five dredges were working in the harbor. On August 7, 1858, the city celebrated the arrival of the *Empress of the Seas*. Drawing nineteen-and-a-half feet of water, she was the largest ship ever to have entered the port. Dredging operations continued until the outbreak of the Civil War. When digging stopped, six miles of channel had been dredged to a depth of twenty-three-and-a-half feet. To honor the tireless efforts of the project leader, the city named the lower channel (extending from below Fort Carroll to North Point) Brewerton Channel. The upper portion of the channel, extending from Fort McHenry to Fort Carroll, was named the Fort McHenry Channel.

In November 1865, Major William P. Craighill, who served for two years as an assistant to Brewerton, was appointed district engineer. Craighill's first task was to finish dredging the Brewerton Channel. This easy project, which remained unfinished after eight years, took on a new urgency when it was discovered that the channel had shoaled extensively beyond North Point. Cross currents from the Patapsco, the Susquehanna, and the Chesapeake Bay were moving bottom sediment into the channel at an alarming rate. To neutralize the effects of the currents, Craighill proposed a new channel in alignment with the currents, running approximately three miles in a southerly then southeasterly direction. The new channel, which measured twenty-two feet deep and 200 feet wide and opened for traffic in the summer of 1869, was not wide enough for the larger ships, which feared running aground on the nearby oyster beds. In 1874, the deficiency was corrected when dredging widened the channel to 400 feet with a depth of twenty-four feet.

Craighill lobbied continuously among political circles in Washington and frequently allied himself with local businessmen, most notably John W. Garrett, B&O president. While critics questioned his methods, they could not question his motives. Craighill firmly believed in maintaining the status of the port by maintaining the harbor. During his tenure, dredging and federal funding continued on a regular basis. When Craighill left in 1895 for the post of chief of engineers in Washington, the main channel was twenty-seven feet deep and up to 600 feet wide. Craighill's efforts not only placed the port in a position of prominence on the Atlantic Coast, but highlighted the contributions of the Corps of Engineers. Most importantly, he established the working relationship between the city and the corps that would continue until today.

Craighill's legacy lived on as one dredging project after another was completed throughout the 1900s. At the outbreak of the Spanish-American War in 1898, the channel was thirty-five feet deep and 600 feet wide. By 1916, the approach channels to the city and the inner harbor were dredged to thirty-five feet. As larger ships serviced the port, businessmen continuously clamored for a deeper main channel and a width of 1,000 feet. Their cries were challenged by local watermen, who questioned the dumping of harbor mud in the Bay. The waterman claimed that thousands of acres of oyster beds had already been destroyed and feared that the oyster industry in the upper Chesapeake would disappear. In 1917, Congress settled the issue by requiring that all dredged material be deposited behind bulkheads supplied by the local community. For the next fifty years, the controversy remained dormant, and the dredging continued. In the 1930s, the channel averaged thirty-five feet. In 1954, the channel was dredged to a depth of thirty-nine feet with a recommendation by the Corps of Engineers that the channel be dredged to forty-two feet in depth and 800 feet in width. Two Congressional vetoes delayed the project until the 1960s.

No sooner had this latest project been completed than another dredging proposal was on the drawing board. Congress authorized plans to dredge the main channel from forty-two to fifty feet at a width of from 800 to 1,000 feet. The dredging project became a political hot potato that was juggled for fifteen years. Environmentalists immediately questioned the effect dredging toxic layers of bottom sediment would have on the environment. A central issue was the man-made dike at Hart and Miller islands and its ability to safely contain contaminated sludge that had the consistency of mayonnaise. The Hart-Miller program involved depositing dredge material into a man-made dike between the two islands near the mouths of the Back and Middle Rivers. The dike, approximately 29,000 feet long with a capacity of at least 53 million cubic yards of dredge material, was to be later reclaimed and turned into a 1,140-acre wildlife and recreational facility for public use. Citizen groups, fearing that the local taxpayer would be financially squeezed to pay for the project, added to the controversy by asking who was going to foot the bill, estimated at $400 million.

The dike was finally completed in 1983 and used to hold materials from maintenance dredging of the harbor. In July 1985, the political stalemate was resolved when the US Senate approved House-passed legislation that included start-up money to dredge the harbor. The bill called for the federal government to pay about half of the $220 million total cost for dredging the main channel to fifty feet.

THE RIVER FORTS

In the 1800s, permanent coastal fortifications became the military trend in protecting Baltimore. The burning of Washington in August 1814 and the bombardment of Fort McHenry in September 1814 during the War of 1812 showed the vulnerability of coastal cities to attacks from the sea. In 1818, the

War Department proposed the construction of forts at Sollers Point Flats and Hawkins Point to provide a line of defense farther downriver from Baltimore. The proposal was scaled down and resulted in immediate funds for the repair of Fort McHenry and long-term funding and plans for a fort at Sollers Point Flats. Prior to construction at Sollers Point Flats in 1847, Fort McHenry had been the city's only coastal defense. In 1894, the secretary of war approved recommendations by the US Army Corps of Engineers to protect the entrance to the Patapsco River with batteries at Fort Carroll, Hawkins Point, North Point, and Rock Point.

Construction on the batteries began in 1896 and was completed in 1902. In the spring of 1903, all batteries were armed and operational. The batteries were reinforced concrete gun emplacements with parapets and sunken gun platforms over top underground magazines. At Hawkins Point, seven miles below the city on the south bank of the Patapsco, stood Fort Armistead, named in honor of Brevet Lieutenant Colonel George Armistead, who commanded Fort McHenry during the British attack on September 13 and 14, 1814. The fort had four batteries with cannons of various size. At North Point, seventeen miles below the city, where on September 12, 1814, 3,500 British soldiers landed uncontested to march on Baltimore, stood Fort Howard. Named after Colonel John Eager Howard, Revolutionary War leader and former governor of Maryland, the fort had six batteries of guns and mortars. At Rock Point, on the south bank of the Patapsco across from Fort Howard, stood Fort Smallwood. Named after General William Smallwood, Revolutionary War hero, the fort had three batteries.

During World War I, only Fort Howard and Fort Smallwood remained active. At Fort Howard, called the "Bulldog at Baltimore's Gate," the garrison was doubled and put on wartime alert. Guns from Fort Carroll and Fort Armistead were transferred to other units or placed on mobile mounts. In 1921, the forts were officially abandoned by the Army. Fort Armistead and Fort Smallwood were deeded to the city and developed into public parks. During World War II, Fort Armistead was temporarily reclaimed by the Navy and used as an ammunition dump until 1947. In 1952, the Army briefly used the site for an antiaircraft battery. In 1940, the property at Fort Howard was transferred to the Veterans Administration to be the site of a hospital. Late in the 1960s at the height of US involvement in the Vietnam War, the fortifications at Fort Howard were utilized by the US Army Intelligence School headquartered at Fort Holabird. A training site was constructed that included a mock-up of a Vietnamese village complete with underground tunnels, booby traps, and a prisoner-of-war camp. The sunken bunkers and amphitheater style gun emplacements, which resembled the French colonial architecture prevalent in many parts of Vietnam, added an eerie sense of realism to the training camp. When Fort Holabird closed in 1972, the Department of the Army deeded the sixty-two-acre parcel to Baltimore County, which later developed the land as a public park.

One of the most unusual structures built for coastal defense was Fort Carroll. Named after Charles Carroll, signer of the Declaration of Independence, the fort was constructed in the middle of the Patapsco River near the main shipping channel at the end of Sollers Point Flats. In 1848, after a year of surveying work, construction on the fort began. Major Cornelius A. Ogden served as chief engineer until November 15, 1848, when he was replaced by Brevet Colonel Robert E. Lee. From the start, the project encountered engineering problems, which proved costly and time-consuming. But by 1852, the 3.4-acre man-made island on which the fort would be built was finally completed.

In May 1852, Colonel Lee was assigned to the position of superintendent of the US Military Academy at West Point and was replaced by Captain Henry Brewerton. Under Brewerton's command, construction continued intermittently. In 1853, Brewerton was able to have a wooden-frame lighthouse built atop the fort. A year later, the lighthouse received a lantern and its keeper became the island's only permanent resident. By the late 1850s, Congress, aware that current naval weaponry made the fort obsolete from a military viewpoint, cut off funds for any further construction. Due to the loss of funds, the original building plans, which called for a regular hexagon with three tiers of gun casements and one barbette, were compromised. The result was one level of masonry and stone fourteen feet high. When the first shots of the Civil War resounded from the island fortress at Fort Sumter in Charleston Harbor, Fort Carroll was incapable of defending Baltimore from any sea or land attack.

For three decades after the Civil War, the fort remained an unfinished, decaying landmark. Conversion plans by the Army Board of Engineers in the 1880s to enable the fort to house the heaviest of rifled guns with thick armor protection were never realized. During the Spanish-American War, twelve-inch guns were installed and used for training by units from Fort McHenry. In 1918, the army dropped plans for an elaborate searchlight defense that would utilize the fort, and a short time later abandoned the structure. In 1920, an automated light replaced the lighthouse. In 1941, the Coast Guard used the fort for small-arms training, and during World War II, foreign sailors were detained there while their ships were fumigated before entering the port.

In 1958, the fort was purchased for $10,000 by Baltimore attorney Benjamin Eisenberg. After extensive renovation, which included mounting replicas of the fort's original guns, Fort Carroll was opened to the public in 1960. However, plans for a restaurant were dropped and the fort closed after Eisenberg became entangled in legal battles concerning tax assessments on the property. Subsequent efforts to rezone the property and turn the fort into an island casino failed to gain any political support.

The most practical and historic of the defensive fortifications along the banks of the Patapsco was constructed at Whetstone Point, a couple of miles southeast of downtown Baltimore. The end of the narrow peninsula, dividing the Northwest Harbor and the Middle Branch of the Patapsco, was the key strategic position to anchor any defense for Baltimore. From this slightly elevated vantage point next to the water's edge, river and land traffic could be monitored. Whoever controlled Point Whetstone also controlled Baltimore and the port.

During the Revolutionary War, the Council of Safety was directed to provide for the defense of Baltimore. Local patriots responded to the call and, on March 16, 1776, reported to the council, "Our fort at Whetstone is ready to mount 8 guns and we shall use every exertion to expedite it." (Roberts 1987) The fortification never came under enemy fire during the war, but served as a visible deterrent to British warships operating in the Chesapeake Bay. By

1795 the fortification, now known as Fort Whetstone, consisted of a battery, magazine, barracks, and hospital.

In 1793, the Maryland House of Delegates, concerned by the volatile state of affairs in Europe, passed a resolution authorizing the governor to erect a more substantial fortification at Point Whetstone. In 1795 Congress enacted legislation for the construction of a fort in the Baltimore harbor. John Jacob Rivardi, an experienced artilleryman and military engineer, was directed by the secretary of war to visit Baltimore and draw up plans for a permanent harbor defense. Samuel Dodge was appointed supervisor, and in 1798 money was finally appropriated to begin construction of the fort. Due to limited funds, much of the construction work was accomplished by local volunteers who donated not only time but also money. Shortly before the turn of the century, James McHenry, a resident of Baltimore who had been an aide to General Washington and secretary of war in both Washington's and John Adams's cabinets, was honored with the bestowal of his name on the fort.

An 1806 report by the secretary of war described Fort McHenry as a "regular fortification of mason work, with batteries, magazines, and barracks, erected principally in year 1798, 1799, 1800." (Roberts 1987) At this time, the fort comprised a pentagon with a bastion at each angle forming the five-pointed "star fort," a dry moat, and a number of interior buildings. Defense included an upper and lower battery of cannon and powder magazines. Along the entire seawall was a parapet where additional guns could be mounted. For over a decade the fort served as a regular army garrison and artillery unit base.

THE BATTLE OF BALTIMORE

Preparations that made Fort McHenry an impregnable fortress proved invaluable during the latter half of the War of 1812. Following the burning of Washington on August 24, 1814, British troops retraced their steps two days later to rejoin the troop convoy in the Patuxent River as stragglers and deserters from the ranks pillaged nearby farms. Taking matters into his own hands, Dr. William Beanes, who had graciously welcomed the British and hosted dinner for Major General Robert Ross and Rear Admiral George Cockburn on their way to Washington, helped capture six or seven of the highwaymen. When one of the prisoners escaped and reported the incident to his command, an enraged Ross had Beanes arrested and thrown into the brig aboard the British flagship *Tonnant*.

To secure Beanes' release, his friends secured the services of Georgetown lawyer and amateur poet Francis Scott Key. On September 5, Key and John S. Skinner, the American prisoner of war exchange agent, boarded a truce-of-war sloop and sailed down the Patapsco River. They found the British fleet in the Chesapeake Bay near the mouth of the Potomac River preparing to sail north. Armed with a packet of letters from British prisoners, who attested to their favorable medical treatment at the hands of the Americans, Skinner and Key eventually persuaded Ross to free Beanes. But before the trio would be released, they would have to witness the attack on Baltimore.

After regrouping at Tangier Island in the lower bay, campaign commander Vice Admiral Alexander Cochrane decided to attack Baltimore instead of

Sketch of the bombardment of Fort McHenry.
Courtesy Maryland Historical Society.

Rhode Island. Baltimore, the third largest city in the country with a population of 45,000 and one of the wealthiest due to its prosperous maritime business, had incurred the wrath of the British since the beginning of the war. The port, commonly called a nest of pirates by the British, was home to over 120 privateers. This private fleet, which operated under government licenses known as "Letters of Marque," seized over 500 British merchant vessels since the beginning of the war. Most of the privateers were sleek, fast-sailing, two-masted schooners or brigantines known as Baltimore Clippers. Cochrane opined in one of his letters that "this town ought to be laid in ashes" in retribution for alleged American atrocities in Canada. The combined land and sea operation would land troops at North Point who would march thirteen miles to Baltimore and flank the city, while Cochrane's fleet would sail up the Patapsco and attack Fort McHenry to support the ground offensive.

On Sunday, September 11, at 1:00 p.m., the early afternoon stillness was shattered by three cannon shots from the courthouse green to muster the troops. The British had been sighted in the lower Patapsco. Remembering the fate of Washington, panicked citizens, to include pessimistic city officials, grabbed whatever possessions they could carry and headed to the safety of the surrounding countryside. Meanwhile, the city's defenders, under the leadership of Major General Sam Smith, who had been recently appointed the commander of Baltimore's defenses, exuded a quiet, almost cocky, confidence. Predicting the British battle plan, the sixty-two-year-old politician, local merchant, and Revolutionary War hero strengthened the river's gun batteries and defensive line. On the morning of August 28, citizens of all ages and color started digging trenches and building earthworks on a line that extended northeast from the harbor to the high ground at Hampstead Hill and beyond. At the same time, thousands of volunteers and militia from surrounding states, many without weapons or provisions, streamed into the city with scattered units from the Battle of Bladensburg. Smith was adamant that his forces would not suffer another frenzied retreat from three weeks earlier that was jokingly referred to as the "Bladensburg Races."

Back at the fort, Major George Armistead had fifty-seven guns and a thousand men to defend the city. Upon assuming command in the spring of 1813, he reported to Smith that "We, sir, are ready at Fort McHenry to defend Baltimore against invading by the enemy. That is to say, we are ready except that we have no suitable ensign to display over the Star Fort and it is my desire to have a flag so large that the British will have no difficulty seeing it from a distance." To remedy the situation, local flag maker Mary Pickersgill was commissioned to produce a garrison flag measuring thirty by forty-two feet, and a storm flag measuring seventeen by twenty-five feet. Working late into the night with help from her daughter, two nieces, and an indentured African-American girl, Pickersgill stitched the flags from a combination of dyed English wool bunting (red and white stripes and blue union) and white cotton (stars). Each star was approximately two feet in diameter and each stripe twenty-four inches wide. In August, the flags were delivered to the fort at a cost of $405.90 for the large one and $168.54 for the small one.

A few hours after the alarm had been sounded on September 11, Smith sent out a strike force of 3,200 men under the command of Brigadier General John Stricker to delay the British so the finishing touches on his defenses could be completed. Early that evening, Stricker stopped at the Methodist Meeting House, about halfway between North Point and Baltimore, and placed his defensive line in a farm clearing at the junction of the two roads leading to Baltimore. With water on both sides and only a half-mile wide, this narrowest point of the peninsula was the ideal spot to engage the enemy. After camping under the stars, Stricker and his troops arose early the next morning and waited anxiously for the British to arrive.

In the early morning hours of August 12, British transports started ferrying some 4,500 troops ashore at North Point. By 7:00 a.m., the advance column began marching to Baltimore under the watchful eye of General Ross and naval coordinator Admiral Cockburn. In the early afternoon, following a leisurely breakfast at the Gorsuch farm, Ross rode north to where shots had been heard. He was unaware that Striker, peeved that British troops had failed to appear, had sent out a detachment of about 250 riflemen to locate the enemy. After arriving at a skirmish line where both sides were still exchanging fire, Ross rode back alone to hurry along the light companies. A shot rang out and tore through the general's right arm, piercing his chest and knocking him from his mount. Found crumpled upon the ground, the mortally wounded Ross was carted back to a shade tree near the Gorsuch farm where he died. Colonel Arthur Brooke, who had been second-in-command, quickly reorganized the troops to press the attack. At around 2:30 p.m., guns from both sides opened fire. The Battle of North Point had begun. A half an hour later, a British bugler sounded the charge and the Redcoats advanced. After twenty-minutes of dueling at close quarters, British troops were able to turn Sticker's left flank. As American troops streamed back into the woods, Stricker coordinated an orderly retreat that ended at Hampstead Hill.

British casualties included 40 to 45 killed in action and 280 wounded. On the other side, the Americans officially listed 24 dead, 139 wounded, and 50 taken prisoner. Despite retreating, Stricker's troops were not discouraged. They had stood toe-to-toe with battle-hardened veterans fresh from the defeat of Napoleon and delayed the British advance. General Ross, who earlier in the day had responded that he would "sup in Baltimore or hell" when questioned about his evening meal, arrived early for his dinner date with the devil. Aboard ship, his body was placed in a hogshead of rum for eventual interment in Halifax, Nova Scotia.

Later that day, Brooke's army bivouacked just north of the battlefield. The hot and humid weather with intermittent rain showers that would eventually give way to a heavy downpour over the next two days was not conducive to long marches in wool uniforms after an exhausting battle. As the British rested and tended to their wounded, Cochrane and his fleet laboriously sailed up the shallow Patapsco. Later that afternoon, with his flagship and other vessels anchored about five miles below Fort McHenry, five bomb vessels and a rocket ship maneuvered to within two-and-a-half miles of the fort. Surveying the harbor's fortifications that included gun barges at the mouth of the Northwest Branch, Cochrane discovered that a number of vessels had been sunk in front of the barges, making the channel impassable. His only hope to seize the city was to somehow capture Fort McHenry.

By 4:00 p.m., the attack flotilla numbered sixteen warships and a small fleet of support vessels. The following morning, on September 13 between 6:30 and 7:00 a.m., the bomb vessels and the rocket ship inched closer to the fort and opened fire. With the British ships now within their mile-and-a-half range, the well-trained batteries at the fort returned deadly and damaging fire. Cochrane immediately pulled his ships out of range. From a safe distance of about two miles, his attack vessels could now safely, but not as accurately, lob shells and launch rockets at the fort. With five bomb vessels firing forty to fifty shells an hour, Cochrane assumed it was only a matter of time before the fort surrendered. With the British out of range, Armistead reluctantly ordered his guns to cease fire. Artillerists in the bastions hunched close to the ground and soldiers huddled in the dry moat behind the fort to weather the withering cannonade. At 3:00 p.m., Cochrane, sensing the quiet fort may be mortally wounded, ordered the bomb vessels and rocket ship to move closer for the fatal blow. Once again, the fort's guns roared to life with devastating fire. Sustaining serious damage to several ships, Cochrane once again pulled back.

Back on the peninsula, Brooke came within sight of Hampstead Hill (present-day Patterson Park), the high ground that served as Smith's command post. Estimating the enemy troop strength at 22,000, more than twice the actual number, he reconnoitered the line for any weak spots. Finding the flanks heavily reinforced and his movements being shadowed by Stricker's brigade, Brooke concluded the only hope for victory was a night-time bayonet attack at the center. To divert the defenders, he requested that Cochrane feign an assault along the Ferry Branch.

At midnight, twenty boats, carrying a landing party of 300 men led by frigate commander Captain Charles Napier, set out in the driving rain. Lost in the night, eleven boats mistakenly rowed towards Baltimore before returning to their ship. The remaining nine vessels with 128 men continued silently past

Fort McHenry in the right direction. Upon hearing muffled oars sweeping the water, gun batteries at Fort Babcock and Fort Covington opened fire into the black void. Seconds after Napier's men returned fire, the fleet and the fort began the fiercest artillery duel of the battle that shook buildings in Baltimore. The night was ablaze with muzzle flashes from both sides as 200-pound British bombshells burst over the fort and Congreve rockets trailed fiery, red streaks. At 3:00 a.m., Napier, thinking that the diversion had succeeded, began rowing back. He was unaware that Brooke had called off the attack and was marching his army to North Point. Hoping to slip silently by the fort, his boats again drew gunfire after a signal rocket was launched to alert the fleet of their return. At least two boats were sunk and three seamen killed.

By 4:00 a.m., the battle was over. Sporadic gunfire continued throughout the morning darkness as both sides anxiously waited for dawn. At 7:00 a.m., Cochrane signaled his ships to cease fire and withdraw. Two hours later, as the British fleet weighed anchor and sailed down the Patapsco, the fort's storm flag was lowered, and the garrison flag was raised on the ninety-foot flagpole to a rousing version of "Yankee Doodle Dandy" with fife and drum. The British had launched between 1,500 and 1,800 bombshells and 700 and 800 rockets at the fort, killing 4 and wounding 24. One shell scored a direct hit on the gun battery at the southwest bastion, killing Lieutenant Levi Claggett and Sergeant John Clemm. Another shell, one that could have obliterated the fort, crashed through the roof of the powder magazine. The fuse sputtered menacingly before being doused with water.

Anchored downriver with the fleet near the present-day namesake bridge, an anxious Francis Scott Key waited for the day's first light to pierce the heavy mist. Peering through a spyglass, Key strained to focus on a point above the fort where a flag hung limply in the morning stillness. Shades of red and blue were visible, but with the tattered flag clinging to the mast, it was impossible to determine if the colors belonged to the Union Jack or the Stars and Stripes. When a slight breeze finally stirred the air, Key had his answer. Fort McHenry had held. Key, who had become caught in the emotions of the night's battle and his own personal battle questioning his religious beliefs and patriotic duties, felt compelled to put his feelings down on paper. Using the back of a crumpled letter that had been stuffed in his pocket, he deliberately began to pen immortality for himself and the fort with the words that would eventually become "The Star-Spangled Banner."

On September 16, Key and his companions returned to Baltimore where Key took a room at the Indian Queen Hotel to finish the four verses of his poem. The next day, at the urging of Judge Joseph Nicholson, his wife's brother-in-law who had commanded a volunteer company at Fort McHenry, copies were printed and distributed to the fort's defenders. Originally titled "The Defence of Fort McHenry," the handbill included instructions to sing the song to the popular British melody "Anacreon in Heaven."

After the gallant stand in 1814, the military importance of the fort lessened. The development of more powerful weapons rendered the structure obsolete, and the rapid expansion of the harbor below the fort minimized the strategic location of Whetstone Point. Despite recommendations by the War Department in 1818 and 1820 that the fort be abandoned, it continued to be utilized by the army. Beginning in 1829 and continuing until the late 1830s, construction was undertaken to repair and remodel the fort. The batteries that had defended the city in 1814 were removed and newer ones closer to the fort were emplaced. Repairs and additions, such as the building of guardhouses and the increasing of barracks space, were designed to expand the facilities and increase the fort's diversity. The garrison life of drills, inspections, and parades continued until the Mexican War in 1846. From 1846 to 1848, Maryland troops were trained at the fort before being sent to the Southwest.

During the Civil War, Fort McHenry became a prison for Confederate prisoners, court-martialed Union troops, and treasonous civilians, and served as a temporary detention center for prisoners awaiting transfer to the larger prisoner-of-war camps. The facility normally processed between 250 and 300 prisoners monthly. Although never reaching the size of Andersonville, Georgia, or Point Lookout, it became a typical Civil War prison camp, supplying only the basic necessities of life for the inmates, under conditions often termed unfit for animals. During the times of frequent overcrowding, food, clothing, shelter, and medical services became luxuries.

Within the first months of the war, the detention facility temporarily housed a number of well-noted citizens of Baltimore, including politicians, city officials, newspaper editors, and judges. Mayor George Brown, Congressman Ross Winans, Police Commissioner Charles Howard, editor Francis Key Howard (grandson of Francis Scott Key), and George Armistead Appleton (grandson of Lieutenant Colonel George Armistead) were jailed under suspicion of disloyalty to the Union. As the occupation of Baltimore continued and the war expanded, the prison population swelled. In February 1863, the fort processed 400 Union soldiers found guilty of misconduct, 250 captured Confederate troops, and 30 civilians accused of conspiracy with the enemy. After the battle of Gettysburg in July 1863, the number of prisoners soared to almost 7,000. Between 1863 and 1865, there were 38 escapes and 15 recorded deaths. Three men were known to have been executed: in March 1862, a Union soldier was hanged for the murder of an officer. In May 1864, Confederate sympathizer Andrew Laypole, also known as Isadore Leopold, was hanged after being found guilty of murdering two civilians while engaged in guerrilla warfare. And in September 1864, another Union soldier was shot after being convicted of desertion and the attempted murder of several citizens. By 1865, only a small detachment of troops and a handful of prisoners remained at the fort. The surrender of the Confederate Army in April 1865 closed the grimmest chapter in the fort's history.

Following the war, garrison life continued until the Spanish-American War in 1898 when Maryland National Guardsmen were drilled there. On March 31, 1907, the army announced that the fort would be abandoned. Five years later, in the twilight on July 20, 1912, the last of the garrison troops marched out the gates. On May 21, 1914, Congress officially leased the fort to the city of Baltimore for use as a park. The next summer saw the city open a beach and swimming pool, featuring mixed bathing for both sexes.

With the entry of the United States into World War I, the fort was reclaimed by the army. In 1917, Fort McHenry officially became US Army General Hospital No. 2. Under the command of Lieutenant Colonel Harry Selby Purnell, the fort was transformed into a hospital complex with 109 buildings of wood and concrete. There were nearly 13,000 beds for the wounded and a staff population of nearly 4,000 Army doctors and nurses, Red Cross nurses, corpsmen, and reconstructive aides. The role of the hospital gradually shifted from a receiving station to a surgical center as great strides were made in developing new techniques and procedures in neurosurgery and plastic surgery. In 1921, the nation's first rehabilitation school for disabled veterans was established at the hospital. In 1923, the last patients were transferred to other local hospitals and the fort was vacated again.

In March 1925, President Calvin Coolidge signed a bill designating the fort as Fort McHenry National Park and placing it under the jurisdiction of the army. By the fall of 1926, all the hospital buildings had been razed, leaving the fort as it had been prior to the massive construction effort in 1917 (special consideration had been given then to ensure that the hospital was built around the fort and other historical landmarks to protect its historical integrity). In 1933, the fort was transferred to the National Park Service. Since then the park service has operated and maintained Fort McHenry National Monument and Historic Shrine as a living monument to the birthplace of the national anthem.

CHAPTER FOUR

Crossroads of the American Revolution: Elkridge

This village does not deserve noticing on account of its size, as it countains only about 15 houses, 2 stores, and a few shops for mechanics; but for being a place of business, long before Baltimore was inhabited. Here all the business was conducted on a large scale, it being the deposit of all the tobacco raised for a considerable distance, where it was inspected and sent to Europe. It is on the turnpike Road to Washington, 7 miles from Baltimore, on the south side of the River Patapsco.

— From the writings of an anonymous British traveler
(Andrews 1965)

Claimed to be the oldest settlement in Howard County, Elkridge was the answer to regional tobacco planters in the early and mid-1700s who needed an export center for their crop. Elkridge, originally known as the Ridge of Elk and later as Elk Ridge, included the large region of hills and ridges that paralleled the Patapsco and extended west to Charles Carroll's Doughoregan Manor above Ellicott City, and south to Oakland Mills. The region was first settled by wealthy tobacco planters, such as the Dorseys, the Hammonds, and the Ridgelys, many of whom built summer homes along the ridgeline to escape the oppressive heat and humidity of the low-lying farmlands. Adam Shipley was recorded as the first settler to obtain land in the area that became the settlement of Elkridge. In 1687 he obtained 500 acres that he named Adam the First, and in 1692 he acquired an additional 282 acres, called Adam's Trust. In 1688 land grants included Major's Choice to Major Edward Dorsey, and Dorsey's Adventure to John Dorsey. Thomas Browne, John Hammond, Henry Ridgely, and Richard Warfield soon followed with large land grants in the area. The largest land grant in Elkridge belonged to Dr. Mordecai Moore. In 1695, he obtained a tract of 1,368 acres, which included the great ridge overlooking Elkridge Landing. This land, along with the adjacent Rockburn tract, was later acquired by ironmaster Caleb Dorsey.

Elkridge Landing in the early 1770s. From a painting by Joan Hull.
Courtesy Patapsco Valley State Park.

Development in the region was rapid. Elkridge, believed to be first settled by Job Larking in the late 1690s, was originally an undistinguished stopover for settlers, tradesmen, and frontiersmen heading west. By the early 1700s, most of the accessible land had been opened up to settlers who were putting it to agricultural use. Although Elkridge would develop into a viable community that would survive through decades of economic prosperity and depression, it was the river port known as Elkridge Landing that would secure a place of prominence in Maryland colonial history as the "gateway" to the Patapsco River Valley.

The success of Elkridge Landing was directly related to its geographical location on the Patapsco. Located below the tidewater limit known as the Falls of the Patapsco, the landing was the upper limit of navigation for shallow-draft sailing ships and barges. At this point, the river formed into a large expanse of tidal backwater and flowed slowly six-and-a-half miles to the harbor basin. The river ranged in width from 300 to 500 feet with a depth between 10 and 20 feet, averaging 14 feet in the main channel. A lagoon, approximately 200 to 300 feet in width, existed across from the landing. The lagoon was wide and deep enough to allow ships and barges to turn around for the return trip to the deep waters of Moore's Place, where larger ships were anchored.

To cross the Patapsco at places other than natural fords, ferry service was initiated. During the late 1770s at Elkridge Landing, Robert Long began a ferry service, which consisted of a small barge connected to a rope anchored on both banks and propelled with the aid of long poles. The ferry business at Elkridge Landing was later assumed by Edward and Samuel Norwood, who named it the Patapsco Upper Ferry. William Hammond later supplied a similar ferry service below the landing. When bridge construction put the Patapsco Upper Ferry out of business, Hammond built a pontoon-type bridge to replace his ferry. The bridge featured a movable section that could be opened to allow passage for watercraft to and from Elkridge Landing. The access provided by the river to a centralized embarkation point was matched by the overland routes. The network of "rolling roads" — crude dirt paths that twisted and curved along the ridgelines — connected with the major roads in the area and facilitated the transportation of the tobacco crop. Hogsheads, large wooden barrels capable of holding up to a thousand pounds of tobacco, served as giant wheels when fitted with temporary axles and makeshift frames. The awkward barrels were then pulled down to the river by horses, oxen, and sometimes slaves.

Elkridge Landing quickly grew into a major seaport and soon ranked second to Annapolis in the colony. A customhouse, inspection office, and tobacco warehouses were some of the first buildings to be constructed. Private residences, taverns, craft shops, and a church soon followed. The landing's sudden popularity was due to its accessibility by land and water routes. In 1700, the General Assembly of Maryland took advantage of the landing's centralized location between Baltimore and Annapolis and sat in session there. This official visit by Maryland's political elite recognized the landing as more than a way station for pioneers heading west. Many frontiersmen and settlers decided to stay behind and became full-fledged colonists, taking on the trappings of colonial living previously associated with wealthy planters and landowners. In the transition, enterprising planters and farmers became merchants and shopkeepers. The commodities market expanded so rapidly that by the 1730s Elkridge had developed into a major commercial center. Increased import-export trade provided maritime, agricultural, and financial business associated with the tobacco and shipping industries.

By 1734, the ever-increasing numbers of people, wharves, finger piers, and wood buildings were unofficially recognized as a town. Influenced by the Act for Advancement of Trade, which had been passed by the Legislature in 1683 to encourage the creation of towns, the Maryland Assembly directed that Jansen Town be established at the landing. The initial legislation called for a tract of thirty acres to be subdivided into forty lots. The name Jansen Town was never formalized, and the ramshackle settlement became known as Elkridge Landing.

In the mid-1700s, Elkridge Landing was enjoying its best years as a colonial seaport. In 1763, 1,695 hogsheads (a figure which represented nearly half of the crop from Anne Arundel County) were shipped overseas. Also in 1763, the first public tobacco warehouse, as prescribed by law, was erected on the land of John Hammond. This centralized warehouse alleviated many of the transportation problems for local planters who shipped their tobacco from individually owned wharves located along the river. Now for the first time, the crop could be inspected, taxed, and loaded for export without lengthy delays.

As the town flourished with the tobacco trade, so did the fortunes of its citizens. The elaborate and ornate town houses of planters and merchants rivaled those of Annapolis. Ladies and gentlemen sported the latest in fashion and fads from England. Ships often anchored at the landing with tons of furniture, silverware, china, linens, silk, and other household items, which would be exchanged for cargoes of tobacco, cotton, grain, and iron. The era of prosperity seemingly had no end. Schools and churches were built, and private libraries were acquired by the new class of wealthy intellectuals. Social sports of the day, such as cockfights, fox hunts, and horse races, enjoyed immense popularity. Colonel Joshua Griffith operated a racetrack on the outskirts of town where the wealthier bettors waged tobacco, livestock, and land on the outcome of the races. In 1764, John Howard, impressed by the business boom occurring at Elkridge Landing, built a small wharf across from the landing. Howard's Landing, later named Norfolk, experienced only limited growth. By 1770, another wharf area, Rag Landing, was built on the far side of the river to handle the overflow of port business.

In 1755, the economy of Elkridge was bolstered by the addition of the iron ore industry. In that year Elkridge Furnace, also known as the Ellicott Elkridge Furnace, originated with a land patent of 100 acres to Caleb Dorsey, Alexander Lawson, and Edward Dorsey of Annapolis. Caleb Dorsey took controlling interest in the operation and became the catalyst for the expansion of the iron ore industry along the Patapsco.

Dorsey's furnace, taking advantage of access to the river and the nearby surface deposits of limestone and iron ore, was built on the south riverbank approximately one-half mile east, or downriver, from Elkridge Landing. By 1756, the cold-blast, charcoal-burning furnace produced over 1,000 tons of pig iron, most of which was shipped to England and Scotland. In 1759, a forge was added to the site. Dorsey operated the furnace and forge until his death in 1771. From this point until after the Revolution, the operation was run by Samuel and Edward Dorsey. During the war, it is believed, the site produced cannons and arms for Washington's army. In the early 1800s, the furnace was leased to John Ellicott and Andrew Ellicott Jr. The brothers rebuilt the furnace to a height of thirty-two feet and a width of eight-and-a-half feet. The blast was driven by water power from the Patapsco. A millrace from nearby Deep Run was added, and a water-powered forge was rebuilt next to the furnace. In 1826, the operation employed around 100 men and had an annual output of 1,400 tons of pig iron, which was produced in castings for water and gas pipes. In 1836, the Ellicotts purchased the furnace and until 1854 ran the business under the name of Jonathan Ellicott and Sons. The property was sold to Robert Howard who, in 1858, sold it to the Great Falls Iron Company for $71,000. By this time, the furnace had been converted to a steam-and-water, hot-blast charcoal operation, capable of producing 500 tons of forge iron per year for major iron manufacturers, such as the Avalon Ironworks, located upriver. In the next decade, the furnace changed hands several times as the fading iron industry proved to be a financial risk. The Flood of 1868 washed away portions of the furnace and forge, and the site was abandoned in 1872.

In the mid-1760s, Elkridge became a crossroads for the American Revolution; and for the next decade and a half, the town witnessed the passing of men, material, and politicians on the way to military and political battlefronts.

Although outside the sphere of radicalism emanating from New England, Elkridge, like other Maryland communities, was quick to adopt the obstinate politics of the Northern colonies. In 1765, the Lower House of the Maryland Assembly passed a resolution to protest the imposition of the Stamp Act.

Zachariah Hood, a merchant with stores in Annapolis and Elkridge, was Maryland's appointed stamp officer. Hood, a descendant of John Hood, one of the first settlers on the Patapsco at Hood's Mill (later to become Ellicott's Upper Mills), encountered widespread resistance to his collection of the tax. Animosity toward Hood quickly reached the boiling point. In late 1765, effigies of Hood were burned in the streets of Baltimore, Annapolis, and Elkridge. When his Annapolis warehouse was destroyed by an armed mob, Hood, fearing for his life, fled to New York, and later to Bermuda. In 1766, though, he was reimbursed for his losses at the Annapolis warehouse by the Maryland Assembly.

The Boston Tea Party of December 16, 1773 — when patriots masquerading as Indians dumped chests of tea into the harbor — had a counterpart in Maryland ten months later. In October 1774, the citizens of Annapolis witnessed the burning of the brig *Peggy Stewart*. The brig, owned by James Dick and his son-in-law Anthony Stewart, an Annapolis merchant, dropped anchor at Annapolis to unload her cargo. The owners hoped to sell their contraband load of imported tea at a considerable profit, and quickly depart. Upon hearing of their intentions, Dr. Charles Alexander Warfield (who later became an officer in the Elkridge militia), along with Dr. Ephraim Howard, Captain Thomas Hobbs, and others from the radical Whig Club of the Elkridge area, marched to Annapolis. Their purpose was not only to take part in the protest against Dick and Stewart but also to burn the vessel and its cargo.

Political groups throughout the colony appeared in Annapolis to air their opinions in this great tea debate. The dock where the *Peggy Stewart* was anchored witnessed a meeting that grew from a heated debate into a chaotic series of shouting matches. Emotionally charged soapbox speeches, voiced to decide the fate of the vessel, filled the air. In response to the radicals' demands that the vessel be burned, Charles Carroll the Barrister (the father of the signer of the Declaration of Independence) led the moderates in calling for the destruction of only the cargo of imported tea. During the proceedings, Stewart addressed the gathering and seemingly convinced both moderates and radicals to let the brig sail from the port undamaged. After Stewart's speech, however, Warfield and his fellow Whigs erected a makeshift gallows and ordered Stewart at gunpoint to either burn the ship or hang. Considering the passionate plea from his wife to save his own life, Stewart acceded to the demands of the radicals and reluctantly set fire to the *Peggy Stewart*. While Stewart watched the flames burn the brig to her waterline, the fire of the Revolution was already rapidly spreading throughout the colonies, fueled by the arrogance of the British military hierarchy and fanned by the winds of political rhetoric.

The shots fired in the skirmishes on April 19, 1775, at the Battles of Lexington and Concord marked not only the beginning of the Revolutionary War but also signaled the colonies to prepare for war. Elkridge moved immediately to establish itself as a regional manufacturing and distribution hub for Maryland. Eager to advance the cause of independence as well as to better their own financial situations, merchants, manufacturers, shippers, and entrepreneurs were quick to offer their goods and services. In addition to cannons and other weapons from Dorsey's furnaces and forges, Elkridge became a military supplier for foodstuffs, medical supplies, and military field equipment, ranging from tents and sails to belt buckles.

Military activity began as early as January 1776, when Elisha Riggs was recommended to be captain of the Elkridge Battalion. By the next month, the unit was formed. Reporting on the ranks, the battalion field officers wrote that "many of the men are without weapons while others have arms that could be repaired at small expense." *(Calendar of Maryland State Papers* 1953) Five months later, the battalion was sufficiently trained and armed to be placed on duty at Annapolis. The Elkridge Battalion, part of the Maryland Line that served so nobly and bravely, included among its officers names familiar throughout Maryland history: Colonel Thomas Dorsey, Lieutenant Colonel John Dorsey, Major Dr. Charles Alexander Warfield, Major Ed Gaither, and Quartermaster Benjamin Howard.

Correspondence directed to the Council of Safety reveals the extent of the activity in Elkridge. The council had been formed to "superintend the execution of the orders and resolutions of the convention and occasionally from time to time promote the prudent and necessary preparations for defense." *(Calendar of Maryland State Papers* 1953) As the war intensified, the council's responsibility in coordinating all related activities broadened.

Before the end of August 1776, Samuel Dorsey Jr., of Elk Ridge Furnace, sent a tent of his own design as well as a pattern tent to the council for its selection. At the same time, William Jacobs placed orders at Elkridge for more cloth to make military tents. On December 7,1776, Dorsey Jr. again wrote to the council stating he needed "someone to prove guns; a few have been made which Swarinham or Hamilton of Elk Ridge Landing near by can test." *(Calendar of Maryland State Papers* 1953) In April 1777, John Dorsey, the son of Edward Dorsey of Anne Arundel, was appointed as a collector of blankets in the Elkridge Hundred. He was ordered to collect the blankets and to deposit them with Charles Wallace Howard of Annapolis. In 1777, a letter from the council contracted Samuel Dorsey Jr. and John Onion to produce twenty-four-pound cannon and swivels.

At the beginning of 1777, the Elkridge Battalion was on an alert "to be ready to march in 7 or 8 days." *(Calendar of Maryland State Papers* 1953) The battalion was composed of Elkridge citizens who could be called to duty when needed. It was not until August 20, when the pace of activity increased, that the unit was activated. Ephraim Howard of Henry wrote to Governor Thomas Johnson that he expected "to leave with the four Elk Ridge Companies on Thursday and be in Baltimore on Friday." *(Calendar of Maryland State Papers* 1953) The next several days at Elkridge were frantic. Twelve ships and one galley of the British fleet were reported in the mouth of the Patapsco, and the public stores from Baltimore were rushed to safety at Elkridge. A note dated August 24 indicated that room for all public stores could be arranged at Elkridge, but accommodations for only sixty of the sick could be had, "several houses prepared for them having been rented." *(Calendar of Maryland State Papers* 1953)

The month of September proved no less exciting for Elkridge residents. Medical supplies and wagons loaded with muskets and cartridges funneled into and through the village. Dr. Richard Tottell of Annapolis wrote Governor

Johnson that "John Bullen had been requested to remove the sick by vessell to Indian Landing and from there to Elk Ridge by wagon." *(Calendar of Maryland State Papers* 1953) On September 10, Robert Long of Elkridge Landing wrote that the road to haul cannon (originally Gun Road) had been opened and that the "iron workers" would assist in bringing timber sheels (shells) from Back River. Five days later, the transporting of cannon had begun, and a request for scows on which to load them was made by Long. By September 20, Long stated that "a fleet had been sent" and told of the distribution of the cannon.

With the coming of fall and winter, the war effort slowed. Jesse Hollingsworth, a government employee, requested of Governor Johnson, on October 7, some funds from the treasury "if the treasury is still at Elk Ridge." *(Calendar of Maryland State Papers* 1953) Thomas Dorsey, appointed by Governor Johnson to act as a county purchasing agent, indicated that he had received 121 head of cattle from John Holsher. Walter Warfield, the surgeon's mate in Dorsey's battalion, requested a supply of clothing from the provincial stores. A government source recorded that salt was a scarce item in the Elkridge area and that residents had disposed of all their extra meats.

The year 1778 was composed of minor troop movements, alerts, and the issuance of commissions to area residents. In that year, the War Board authorized the establishment of a "communication line" *(Papers of the Continental Congress* 1778) between Elk Ridge Landing and Albemarle Sound in North Carolina. The line was to carry 500 barrels of meat weekly by boat and wagon. The order authorized the governor of Maryland to request Continental Treasury funds to construct the necessary roads and buildings. It was not until 1781 that the excitement of the war effort returned when the Continental Army and allied forces rushed southward to force a British surrender in southern Virginia. On April 19, 1781, the Marquis de Lafayette crossed the Patapsco at Elkridge. At the time, the river was so wide and deep that scows were used to ferry the men and supplies across. During the crossing, one scow sank and nine men were drowned. Once on the southern shore, the troops encamped within sight of the Patapsco Canyon's mouth near the village. From here Lafayette arranged for the use of carts and wagons to carry his men, many of whom were barefoot and dressed in ragged clothes, to the Potomac River.

Lafayette's plight while passing through Elkridge, and the support of the Baltimore area merchants, are best pictured from a letter written in Baltimore on April 16, 1781, from James McHenry to General Greene:

> While I admire your policy, I have more than once pitied the Marquis' situation. His troops passed here yesterday, discontented almost to general desertion, destitute of shirts, and proper equipments, and in most respects, unprovided for a march. You know the Marquis. He has been with us two days, but, in this time, he adopted an expedient to conciliate them to a degree which no one but himself would have thought of. To-day he signs a contract, binding himself to certain merchants of this place, for above two thousand guineas, to be disposed of in shirts, overalls and hats, for the detachment. Without these the army could not proceed, and with these, he has managed to reconcile them to the service. He is also bent upon trying the power of Novelty on their minds by giving to the march the air of a frolic. His troops will ride in wagons and carts from Elkridge Landing to the limits of this state, and how much farther he will continue this mode of movements depends on

Virginia. The assistance rendered to Lafayette by the citizens of Baltimore restored tranquillity and discipline to this command. Every cart and wagon that could be procured being put in requisition, the troops who had been encamped near Elkridge Landing, on the 19th of April, took up their line of march for Virginia. They crossed the Patapsco at Elkridge (by crowding too many men into the ferry boat in one of its trips across the ferry, the boat sank, and drowned nine soldiers) and by leaving the baggage and artillery to follow on, they arrived with the help of wagons and horses, at Alexandria, on the 21st. (Scharf 1967)

On September 12, 1781, the village of Elkridge again witnessed the passing of troops. On this occasion, the famous General Comte de Rochambeau was leading his French regulars toward Yorktown, Virginia, to assist Lafayette and Washington in forcing the surrender of Lieutenant General Charles Earl Cornwallis and the British regiments. Upon reaching the Patapsco, Rochambeau's troops made a detour upstream from the Elkridge area and forded the river just below the dam used by the Dorsey forge (near the present site of the Interstate 95 bridge). The map of Rochambeau's 34th camp on that day notes the danger and difficulty in crossing the Patapsco:

It is not necessary to make much of a detour in order to ford the river and I calculate the distance to be from about three-fourths to one mile. The ford path is bad and filled with rocks and cut trees. On arriving at the ford, it is dangerous to follow the steep bank because the river is very deep in places where the water is held back to run the ironworks. It is good to follow the path here indicated, staying close to the big stones; for if one strays away one finds big boulders and stones. (*Herald Argus* 1967)

From Elkridge, Rochambeau made his way to Annapolis and later sailed to Virginia. Through the combined efforts of General Washington, Marquis de Lafayette, and Comte de Rochambeau, the British forces were defeated at Yorktown on October 19, 1781. After the signing of the Treaty of Paris on January 20, 1783, Governor William Paca declared April 25, 1783, to be "Victory Day," celebrated in Annapolis, Baltimore, and Elkridge with banquets featuring thirteen toasts. Regiments of the Maryland Line, numbering 500 men, arrived at Annapolis and were disbanded under General Mordecai Gist.

As the American economy continued to expand, it seemed only a matter of time before Elkridge Landing would supplant Annapolis as the major seaport in the colony. Ironically, the industries that brought prosperity to the landing would spell its eventual downfall. Deforestation from tobacco cultivation, charcoal production, and surface mining for iron ore created major erosion problems. By the late 1770s, so much silt clogged the Patapsco that only small sailing vessels were able to reach Elkridge Landing. The problem was first noticed in 1753 by the Maryland Assembly, which passed an act prohibiting the throwing or dumping of earth, sand, or dirt, which would cause the channel to fill up and thus impair the river's navigability. The law was enacted to curb a practice of large sailing ships that were required to carry ballast when sailing with an empty cargo hold: they dumped the ballast, usually sand, in the channel prior to loading hogsheads of tobacco. As the erosion continued, and ships couldn't reach the seaport, its economy slowly died. The fate of Elkridge Landing was sealed by the spectacular growth of Baltimore Town, which was chartered in 1729 by the Maryland Assembly. This sleepy little river community, numbering only 200 residents in 1750, provided the convenient, deep harbor for exporting the products of nearby ironworks, flour mills, textile plants, and farms.

On May 7, 1825, a fire in Elkridge Landing destroyed nine of ten houses as well as two small stores. On July 24, 1868, a raging flood engulfed the landing and washed away the remaining traces of the seaport. Despite the loss of its maritime business and these disasters, the landing's final demise was still years away. In 1871, the *State Gazette* still listed thirty-seven merchants and craftsmen living in or around the landing.

Although Elkridge Landing faded into history, the community of Elkridge survived the losses of the landing and the furnace. Resiliency became the trademark for the town, which suffered continued economic setbacks. In the early 1900s, land around the abandoned furnace blossomed into willow groves, which provided a new light industry. Baskets and reed by-products were manufactured until the early 1960s. Following the completion of the Thomas Viaduct in 1835, the town enjoyed the business brought by the B&O Railroad on its north-south rail link. From 1850 to 1880, before the popularity of Pullman and dining cars, station hotels sprang up to serve the needs of long-distance travelers. With advancements in railroad technology, Elkridge was bypassed as trains traveled longer distances without stopping. The advent of the automobile in the early 1900s saw the town revitalized with the building of the Washington Turnpike, the first highway to link Baltimore and Washington. Businesses were located along Main Street to provide the services needed by drivers and passengers on their long, weary, and often hazardous journeys. As the automobile became more dependable and sophisticated, the turnpike was moved a block west to become US Route 1, bypassing the main business district. The construction of superhighways in the 1960s and 1970s saw the town "overpassed" and sealed off from the interstate traveler. Today Elkridge, only ten miles south of Baltimore, remains a quiet, relaxed community with a rural atmosphere, dotted with roadside businesses and light industries.

CHAPTER FIVE

The River Valley Comes of Age: Ellicott's Mills

The Industrial Revolution arrived along the Patapsco with the appearance of three young Quakers from Pennsylvania. Joseph, John, and Andrew Ellicott, the sons of Andrew Ellicott and the descendants of an old Devonshire, England, family first introduced large-scale manufacturing and production techniques to the wooded and rocky region that was still considered wilderness in the late 1700s. With the development of the flour industry under the Ellicotts, the reign of tobacco as the "king" crop and cornerstone of Maryland's colonial economy was coming to an end. A new wealth was waiting to be harvested in golden fields of wheat. Through the foresight and perseverance of the Ellicott brothers, the potential of the Patapsco as an industrial center was fully realized. Their efforts led the way for other entrepreneurs willing to gamble on making the region a prosperous and productive business community.

Sometime around 1770, the Ellicott brothers pooled their financial resources and embarked on a journey to establish a commercial flour mill for the grinding of wheat and other grains. Prior to deciding on a mill site, the brothers spent weeks on horseback traveling through the remote regions of Pennsylvania and Maryland. After inspecting the wilds of Maryland from the Patapsco to the Blue Ridge Mountains, the Ellicotts decided on a stretch of land along the Patapsco some ten miles west of Baltimore Town and six miles upriver from Elkridge Landing. In 1772, the brothers purchased two miles of riverfront property on both sides of the river, with all water and power rights for two miles above and below the proposed mill site. The unlimited capability for adapting water power proved to be the deciding factor in selecting a site. Most of the land was purchased from William Williams for a reported price of three dollars an acre for 700 acres. A wealthy Englishman, Williams sold cheaply, fearing that the outbreak of war between the colonies and England would result in the seizure of his land holdings. The Ellicotts provided a most opportune chance to dispose of some undesirable property at a reasonable profit. Other acreage was obtained under a Maryland law of 1669 that allowed any man who built a mill to take up to twenty acres of land on either side of the stream or river and to hold the land for a period of fifty years. For the Ellicotts, the heavy financial risk would come with the building of the first gristmill and the large outlay of capital for buildings and machinery.

Back in Pennsylvania with the land acquisitions finalized, the Ellicotts, filled with anxieties and second thoughts, prepared for the long, hard journey southward. Relocating their flour industry was an extremely difficult, almost impossible task. Their selected mill site, known as The Hollow, was an untamed wilderness covered with forests of centuries-old trees and rimmed by rock outcroppings that composed a formidable barrier of steep cliffs. Wagons, carts, wheelbarrows, mechanical devices, agricultural implements, draft horses, and household goods for workers and their families were loaded aboard vessels at the port of Philadelphia and transported down the Delaware River to New Castle. From New Castle the equipment was loaded into wagons and carts and driven across the peninsula to Head of Elk. There, everything was once again loaded aboard ship and sailed down the Chesapeake Bay to Elkridge Landing on the Patapsco. At Elkridge Landing, all materials were unloaded and readied for the wagon train to The Hollow. This last part of the trip proved to be a very long six miles. Because only Indian trails led the way, a road had to be constructed by clearing trees, brush, and rock along the route as the wagons slowly inched forward. At a point about one mile from its destination, the caravan was forced to stop because of rocks and precipices. With the way impassable for wagons, the traveling party had to carry the supplies and equipment on top of wooden poles to their final destination. Making a return trip, the men dismantled the carts and wagons and hand-carried the pieces over the rugged terrain.

Proving to be concerned environmentalists as well as industrialists, the Ellicotts carefully cleared the land and controlled the amount designated for commercial use. With ample portions of ground cleared and a rough road constructed south to Elkridge Landing, the brothers were ready to build their first mill. In the fall of 1774, after nearly two years of work, the mill, with dam and millrace, was completed. Described as a "house, one hundred feet long and of proportionate breadth and height" (Tyson 1871), it was used to store grain and to house the necessary equipment. A small village of houses for the mill workers was constructed along with the mill. Forced by their geographical location to be self-sufficient, the Ellicotts also opened a sawmill and granite quarry to serve the needs of the mill and the town.

After the harvest in 1774, the Ellicotts were ready to grind wheat. In one month, 300 barrels of flour were sold to William Lux Bowley, a leading merchant captain, and delivered to Bowley's Wharf at Elkridge Landing. The mill's capacity at this time was 200 barrels of flour a day from about 400 barrels of grain from neighboring farmers.

The concept of using water power to turn millstones had been successfully employed since Roman times. The operation of the Ellicotts was only slightly more sophisticated. A natural or man-made dam was used to divert water into a narrow, shallow channel called a millrace.

The water was then funneled into a flume to direct the flow of water to the waterwheel and returned to the river by a tailrace, a continuation of the millrace. The wheel powered an elementary system of wood and iron gears that turned

Panoramic view of the Patapsco above and below Ellicott's Mills.
At bottom center is the Patterson Viaduct and the Ilchester Flour Mill.
Upriver in the next bend is Ellicott's Patapsco Flouring Mills.
Farther upriver on the east bank is the Granite factory and then the
Alberton factory. At top left is the Union Manufacturing Company.
Courtesy Maryland Historical Society.

the millstones. Inside the mill, two large millstones were used as grinding
elements. The circular stones with holes in the center, marked by grooves and
indentations extending outward from the center hole, were stacked horizontally,
close to the waterwheel and machinery. The bottom stone, or bedder, was
fastened to the floor, while the top stone, or runner, was delicately balanced
on a wood axle passing from underneath the floor through both stones. As the
top stone began to slowly turn, the miller poured grain into the center hole of
the top stone. The grain forced its way between the two stones, and centrifugal
force carried it across the stones to the edge, during which time it was slowly
ground to a fine texture. As time passed, more complicated devices were
added to increase productivity. However, the operation of grinding remained
basically the same until the late 1800s and the introduction of roller mills. The
Ellicotts' mill was a vertical mill, where the waterwheel was attached upright
to an outside wall of the mill. This was a common design in the Baltimore area.

The brothers first transacted business under the name Ellicott and
Company. Within a short time, the mill became the largest merchant mill for
grinding flour in colonial America and an example of industrial success copied
by other businessmen around the nation. Although the mill was operating at a
profit, the Ellicotts faced the difficult task of convincing local growers to change

their farming habits and concentrate their efforts on wheat as the major cash crop. For several years, the majority of wheat ground by the Ellicotts came from their own fields. Tobacco was still the primary cash crop. Planters were unwilling to discard their livelihood until they were assured that wheat and corn could yield a reasonable and steady profit. Until the arrival of the Ellicotts, wheat had only been grown on large plantations to provide enough white flour for the planter and his family. Most of the grinding was done at a small gristmill at Elkridge Mill or hand-ground by slave labor at the plantation.

The Ellicotts did not attempt to force their ideas and techniques on local planters. Considered dreamers and half-hearted fools by many people, the brothers slowly and quietly established a solid reputation as knowledgeable businessmen. Despite the initial negative reaction from local growers, the Ellicotts were able to keep their attention firmly fixed on developing the resources of central Maryland and advancing Baltimore as a major seaport on the Eastern Seaboard. Even after the American Revolution, the Ellicotts continued to offer a fair price for local wheat, but still found few planters willing to contract wheat for the mill. The Ellicotts believed that by creating a demand they could create a sufficient supply of wheat. To assist local planters the Ellicotts imported large amounts of gypsum from Nova Scotia. A special mill was built to reduce the raw material into a fine powder. The gypsum, used as fertilizer and a soil nutrient, brought life back to the soil, which had been severely depleted by continued tobacco crops. The rejuvenation of the land encouraged more wheat growing and convinced many planters to continue farming along the Patapsco River Valley. At one point, many of Maryland's leading families located in the region, such as the Dorseys, Worthingtons, Ridgelys, and Meriweathers, had been considering a move to the fertile lands available in Kentucky and Tennessee. The efforts of the Ellicotts helped change a prevailing opinion among farmers that growing wheat was robbing the soil, when in fact tobacco was the culprit.

The cause of the Ellicotts in convincing farmers to switch to wheat had unknowingly received a tremendous boost years earlier in the early 1700s, when a large number of German immigrants from the Palatinate of the Rhine settled in the rolling hills of central Maryland. Fleeing the constant devastation of their land by war, these hardy people, many of them farmers in their homeland, were encouraged by the prospect of coming to the colonies for a new start in life. Despite the problems of cultivating undeveloped land and an occasional Indian raid, these German farmers were able to firmly establish themselves in the region. When the Ellicott brothers founded their mill in 1774 and advertised for grain, the frontier farmers were able to provide the mill with enough grain to keep the operation running.

In 1774, Joseph Ellicott, the oldest of the brothers, left the firm of Ellicott and Company to establish his own milling operation at Hollofield. The site, three miles upriver from the original mill, was inadvertently named Hollofield when a clerical error resulted in the misspelling of the name of the Hollifield family, the last owners of the Upper Mill before its financial and physical collapse. Joseph Ellicott purchased the land from James Hood who, in 1768, had built a dam and a gristmill. The old mill was torn down. A new one, using the latest mechanical devices, was constructed and named

Ellicott's Upper Mills. A dry-goods store, which offered the finest in cloth goods and household items, was built for the mill community. Accommodations for mill workers were also constructed at the mill site. The family home built by Joseph Ellicott became a wonder talked about throughout the state. The two-story building, equipped with running water from nearby springs, included an ornamental rare flower garden, a fish pond, and a fountain that rose ten feet. When the Upper Mills was resurveyed in 1797, the tract was appropriately renamed Fountainville.

The decision of Joseph Ellicott to leave the partnership with his brothers was made in part to allow him the time to pursue his other interests. Already a wealthy man from previous business associations and the liquidation of his great-grandfather's estate in England to which he was heir, Joseph gradually eased himself out of the flour business to tinker in mathematics, clockmaking, and inventions. A published author in scientific journals, Joseph became preoccupied to the point of obsession with his new endeavors. His most famous invention was a musical clock. The four-faced grandfather clock, which played twenty-four tunes and marked seconds and minutes, was built by Joseph and his son Andrew while they still resided in Bucks County, Pennsylvania. The clock, which stood in the middle of a specially built room, was best described by Joseph's grandson, Charles W. Evans:

> The case of the clock is of mahogany, in the shape of a four sided pillar or column, neatly though plainly finished, and on the capital is the clock, with four faces, it being designed to stand in the middle of an apartment, or sufficient distance from the wall, to enable the observer to walk around it. On one face is represented the sun, moon, and all the planets moving in their different orbits, as they do in the heavens. On another face are the hands which designate the hours, minutes, days, weeks, months and years, the years representing one century. On the third face are marked twenty-four musical tunes of the times previous to the American Revolution; in the centre of this face is a pointer, which being placed against any named tune, this tune is repeated every fifteen minutes until the pointer is moved to another. On the fourth face is a plate of glass, through which you see the curious mechanism of the clock. (Tyson 1871)

The turning point in the fortunes of the Ellicotts came with the friendship of Charles Carroll of Carrollton. To sway the opinion of Carroll to their viewpoint, the Ellicotts had built a road to Carroll's county residence, Doughoregan Manor, five miles west of Ellicott's Mills. Carroll, believing in the future of the flour industry and seizing a rare opportunity to increase his own fortune, became a staunch supporter of the Ellicotts. Not only did he become a financial backer, thus allowing the business to be expanded, but he also converted much of his farmland from tobacco to wheat. At the time, Carroll was one of the wealthiest men in colonial America and was considered the "great banker" of Maryland. His support of the wheat industry influenced others to convert their fields to wheat and other grains.

Doughoregan Manor, the final resting place of Charles Carroll of Carrollton, was the largest and most impressive of the Carroll family homes. The long, narrow, two-story house was constructed of brick and painted yellow. Consisting of a main building with two wings, one of which was the chapel marked by a bell tower and the other the kitchen with living quarters for servants, the entire structure measured 300 feet in length. Doric columns framed the front and back entrances, and double-paneled doors graced the two L-shaped wings. A cupola adorned the top of the main building, and a widow's walk extended outward from it, covering the full length of the house. The country estate, complete with slave cabins and an estate manager's home among its many outbuildings, was part of an original land grant of 15,000 acres given to Charles Carroll Jr. During its early history, the manor played host to some of the most noted and influential men in America. George Washington, Thomas Jefferson, John Adams, Benjamin Franklin, and Bishop John Carroll — the cousin of Charles Carroll and the first Roman Catholic bishop in North America — were a few of the many guests entertained at the estate.

The road to Doughoregan Manor was built at the expense of the Ellicotts, with help from local planters. A horse-drawn house on wheels was constructed for the workers and equipped with a kitchen for cooking everything but bread products. Other roads, constructed west to Frederick and east to Baltimore, were part of the great highway system known as the National Road. Frederick Turnpike, which passed through the Lower Mills and replaced the old Frederick Road at the Upper Mills, became the major thoroughfare linking Baltimore with the central and western sections of the state. The roads were repaired and maintained by "wheel-barrow men," convicts sentenced for lesser crimes and assigned to work projects.

Joseph Ellicott died in 1780, and the household at Ellicott's Upper Mills was maintained by his wife, Judith, until her death in 1809. Their son Andrew, following in the footsteps of his father as a man of science, went on to a most remarkable career as a nationally known surveyor. In 1789, Andrew was appointed to survey land located between Pennsylvania and Lake Erie. With his brothers Joseph and Benjamin, he later made the first accurate measurements of the Niagara River and its famous falls. In 1791, with the assistance of Benjamin Banneker, Andrew was called upon to finish the surveying work for the nation's capital after George Washington was forced to dismiss the temperamental Major Charles L'Enfant. Although most of the city had been planned and surveyed under the direction of L'Enfant, Andrew Ellicott had the distinction and honor of completing this monumental and historic project. The recognition of his . work resulted in his appointment as surveyor-general of the United States. His outstanding surveying accomplishments included the extension of the Mason-Dixon Line westward, the Georgia-North Carolina boundary line, and the border shared by Spanish-owned Florida and the United States. His final survey was the 45th parallel between New York and Canada, as dictated by the Treaty of Ghent, which ended the War of 1812. In 1813, President Madison appointed him professor of mathematics at the United States Military Academy at West Point. Andrew Ellicott died at his West Point home and was buried with military honors on the grounds of the academy. His brother Benjamin entered politics and served as a member of Congress from New York.

By the late 1770s, the supply of wheat from local planters had increased dramatically. The Ellicotts, anticipating the end of the Revolutionary War, made preparations to ship their flour to foreign markets. For this purpose, they bought a waterfront lot in Baltimore and built their first wharf at the corner of Pratt and

Water Streets. A log warehouse constructed at the wharf was managed by Elias Ellicott, the son of Andrew Ellicott. Daily communication between Ellicott's Mills and the Baltimore shipping operation was effected by the drivers of flour-laden wagons. At the waterfront property, the Ellicotts made the first attempt to deepen the Baltimore harbor. Their "mud machine," a drag with iron scoops drawn by horses and raised by a windlass, was a primitive but effective device for removing sediment from the bottom of the harbor.

Following the end of the American Revolution, Ellicott and Company entered its most prosperous and controversial era. The 1798 federal tax list showed the Lower Mills to have a frame coal house, a sawmill (60' × 14'), a stone millhouse (100' × 36'), and a stone storage house with cellar (53' × 37'). Productivity at the mill increased sharply with the addition of mechanical devices. Due to increased competition in the market, mill owners were forced to become inventors in order to survive. The Ellicott brothers, millers by trade during their earlier days in Pennsylvania, became innovators in the field and developed a number of improvements, loosely classified as inventions, on mill machinery. In the early 1760s, "hopper boys" and "elevators" of some type were used by the Ellicott brothers at Petitt's Mill in Buckingham, Pennsylvania. Believing manufacturers should have the use of their "inventions," the Ellicotts did not apply for patent rights on the devices. Until the establishment of a federal patent office in Washington, patent rights were granted separately by state legislatures. Keeping track of inventions on items, such as milling machinery, was a difficult task for colonial bureaucrats. The situation was compounded by the fact that numerous minor inventions could be added to improve machinery still considered simple by engineering standards. Prior to the creation of the US Patent Office, the Maryland Legislature had granted only three patents. One of these was a patent granted to Oliver Evans in 1787 for an "elevator," a "hopper boy," and a "steam carriage" with the exclusive right for fourteen years of making and selling them within the state. The "elevator" was a continuous belt or strap fitted with small buckets, scoops, or rakes to move the grain in various mill operations. Grain could be funneled, channeled, loaded, and unloaded with a minimum number of workers. The "hopper boy" was a twelve-foot rake that pushed ground meal from the loft floor and funneled it down the chute to the bolting box. The device eliminated the worker who performed the same job with an oversized rake. Evans later developed a set of concentric revolving screens used with a fan to sift grain and blow off any debris or impurities lighter than the wheat. He served as a mail-order consultant for the construction of new mills, while continuing to develop new methods for bolting, sifting, and regrinding grain products by improving on the design and function of the waterwheel. After Evans's death in 1819, technological advances in the milling industry remained dormant. This changed in the 1870s when steam power and steel grinding rollers were introduced.

Oliver Evans, a self-taught technological genius from Delaware, became the major force in revolutionizing the milling industry. His inventions automated the mills and drastically cut production costs. Baltimore's prominence as the center of the flour industry was due in large part to Evans's milling advances, which ultimately reduced the need for unskilled laborers in the mill. On May 4, 1789, Evans visited Ellicott's Upper and Lower Mills to interest the family in steam power. At the mills, he observed the Ellicott inventions and suggested a number of improvements. It appears that Evans, while traveling around the state to advertise his inventions, often stopped at Ellicott's Mills to update himself on progress there. According to historian Martha Tyson, when the Ellicotts learned of Evans's patents, they demanded an interview with Evans and ended any further association with him. Whether the Ellicotts and Evans clashed over the issue of patents was irrelevant at the time. In 1790, Thomas Ellicott wrote a testimonial for Evans's handbook on mill building. The statement signed by the Ellicott family proclaimed:

> We do certify that we have erected Oliver Evans' new-invented mode of elevating, conveying, and cooling meal, etc. As far as we have experienced, we have found them to answer a valuable purpose, well worthy the attention of any person concerned in merchant, or even extensive country mills, who wished to lessen labor and expense of manufacturing wheat into flour.

John Ellicott
Jonathan Ellicott
George Ellicott
Nathaniel Ellicott

— Ellicott's Mills, Baltimore County, State of Maryland
Aug. 4, 1790 (Evans 1795)

Employing Evans's inventions, the Ellicotts reportedly raised the daily production of processed flour and saved $4,875 in annual labor and production costs. The largest mill in the country was now the most automated. All the machinery in the mill was now powered by the waterwheel. Technology at Ellicott's Mills attracted the interest of foreign businessmen, engineers, and travelers. The mill became a necessary stop for anyone passing near the area. In 1791, a French traveler, Ferdinand M. Bayard, described the loneliness at "Hellicotts Lower Mill" and remarked that "the profits that one can obtain from a mill in this place makes the owners indifferent to the horrors which are thick about him . . . he lives contently in his frightful retreat; the noise of the waters which wear away the rocks does not disturb his sleep at all." (Tyson 1871) Benjamin Banneker, Oella's famous son, became a frequent visitor to the mill.

The issue of patent rights surfaced again in 1812 when the statement made by the Ellicott family in Evans's handbook was used by Evans in a patent infringement suit involving Evans versus Samuel Robinson and Charles C. Jones. The Ellicotts entered the case to testify on behalf of Robinson and Jones and to deny the unique character of the inventions as claimed by Evans.

In 1813, the case of patent rights inevitably spilled over to include the Ellicotts. Evans brought suit against the Ellicott family for patent infringement. By the time the lawsuit came to court, the firm of Ellicott and Company had changed leadership and ownership. Joseph had already left the partnership to build his own mill at Hollofields; John died suddenly in 1795; and Andrew gave his share of the business to his sons, Jonathan, Elias, and George, and retired from active participation in business affairs. The younger Ellicotts built other mills on Gwynns Falls but failed to take out a license with Evans to use his patented inventions. After a five-day trial in Baltimore, the federal court decided in favor of Evans and awarded him $1,000 in damages and ordered the Ellicotts to secure a license from him.

Richard Ridgley and Luther Martin, expert legal counsel for the Ellicotts, defended their clients by demonstrating to the court that Evans's inventions were the sole inventions of Ellicott and Company. William Pinckney and Robert Goodloe Harper, Evans's lawyers, stated that the Ellicotts could not clearly claim full ownership of the inventions. They contended that if the patent claims made by the Ellicotts were valid then their exclusive right to maintain ownership of the inventions had expired. The Ellicotts' failure to have their inventions patented when first designed in the 1760s was undoubtedly a major factor in influencing the decision of the jury. The verdict of the jury in some aspects agreed with the opinion of those historians who believed the Ellicotts were the actual inventors and the victims of Evans's "duplicity." Although the Ellicotts were disappointed by the verdict, they were not discouraged from pursuing technological developments. A wagon brake used to check or slow the downhill speed of wheeled, horse-drawn vehicles was first made in the shops of Ellicott's Mills and tested on mill wagons. John Ellicott, using a detailed description supplied by a family member, James Brooke Ellicott, was responsible for introducing the brake to the United States. The brake, widely used in some European countries, replaced the old-style brake that checked wagon speed by locking one of the wheels with a heavy chain.

In spite of legal problems, Ellicott's Mills continued to grow and Patapsco Flour became a familiar trademark recognized around the world. The labeling of the company trademark on flour barrels with a stencil instead of a branding iron was another first from the Ellicotts. However, despite a bright future, the years of prosperity did not pass without adversity. The first setback occurred in 1809, when a disastrous fire gutted the mill and destroyed log homes and buildings in its vicinity. Salvaging machine parts, the Ellicotts quickly rebuilt the mill and resumed normal operation. For the next two decades, the flour business remained static. The construction of the B&O to Ellicott's Mills in 1809 gave the mill town the new economic dimension it desperately needed. With the means now available to transport large quantities of flour in less time from their mills, the Ellicotts gained a decisive advantage over the competition.

Worsening economic conditions, which culminated in the Panic of 1837; saw the beginning of the end for the Ellicott empire. The Ellicott family, "trading under the name of Jonathan Ellicott & Sons, being embarrassed in their circumstances and largely indebted to many individuals" (McGrain 1980), was forced to convey its business holdings to a court-appointed trustee, Robert Mickle. The deed of trust, containing a recitation of the facts pertinent to the case, listed twelve pages of accumulated assets. The family name continued to suffer from the effects of the economy when the Union Bank of Maryland, closely connected with the Ellicott family, collapsed. Thomas Ellicott was singled out for abuse in an anonymous poem that appeared in 1836. The poem voiced displeasure with the bank's conduct:

HEROIC POEM DEDICATED TO STOCKHOLDERS
OF THE UNION BANK OF MARYLAND

When the Devil Had Started at Ellicotts Mills And Stopped at Ellicotts Store
He thought he was doomed to ride and run Betwixt Ellicotts—ever more.

Old Nick went on to the Capital to get rid of the Ellicott Name;
And were you half as wise as the Devil You'd endeavor to do the same. (McGrain 1980)

The Ellicotts sold their mills to Charles Carroll, a nephew of Charles Carroll of Carrollton, and Charles A. Gambrill. The partnership continued from 1844 until Carroll's death in 1863. After the Flood of 1868, the mills were purchased and rebuilt by Gambrill and his two nephews, Richard G. and Patrick H. Magill. The mill became Patapsco Mill A of the Gambrill chain and boasted the oldest brand name in the country. Steam power and roller machinery were added to allow the mill to compete with Midwestern wheat. In 1906, the rebuilt mill had a production capacity of 2,000 barrels of flour and corn products daily. Destroyed by a fire in 1916, the mill was again rebuilt in 1917 with a daily capacity of 2,400 barrels.

During World War I, the Magill Company manufactured pancake flour at the mills. Immediately following the war, the company went bankrupt when sugar they had contracted to buy at twenty-one cents a pound plummeted to four cents a pound. Unable to break the wartime contract, and at the same time losers in a lawsuit, the owners put the company up for auction. The plant was bought by Morris Schapiro and operated as the Continental Milling Company, continuing to manufacture a line of cake mixes and flours. The plant suffered flood damage in 1923 but continued operation. In 1930, it was leased to the Doughnut Corporation of America, whose name was later changed to simply DCA. For the next twenty-five years, the plant manufactured doughnut-cooking equipment capable of making 20 to 600 dozen doughnuts per hour, and made mixes of flour enriched with milk and eggs. At its peak, the doughnut company annually processed the harvest from 40,000 acres of grain, used the equivalent of 2.5 million gallons of powdered milk, and consumed 8 million eggs. The six-story plant building contained eight sifters and twenty-four grinders. After a major fire in 1941, DCA rebuilt and diversified their product line to include radar components and gun parts. During World War II, the company assisted the war effort by supplying a canteen type truck that traveled to war bond rallies, offering free doughnuts to bond subscribers. In 1955, DCA acquired title to the property. In 1967, it sold the mill to the Wilkins-Rogers Company of Washington, DC, which manufactured flour under the Washington Flour brand name. In spite of the Flood of 1972, which caused an estimated $1 million in damages, the company relocated its entire operation to Ellicott City. The site of the original Ellicott's Lower Mills is now marked by the massive concrete building and silos of the Wilkins-Rogers Company.

ELLICOTT'S MILLS: A VILLAGE, TOWN, AND CITY

Before the completion of the Ellicott brothers' first mill, the town of Ellicott's Mills was being cut and hammered into place. The first building constructed by the Ellicotts was a large log boardinghouse. Built on the river's northern bank, it contained a number of apartments for the workers and their families. With the completion of a sawmill, a number of wood houses, described as a small village of "comfortable houses," sprang up on the river's south bank. The Ellicotts, following the completion of residences for their families and stables for their draft horses, directed the building of a school for area children. Staffed by the finest teachers available, the school provided all children, regardless of the social stature or income of their parents, with an education in the essential academic skills. The costs and expenses of running the school were paid for by local property owners. The last building erected, in 1790, was a stone warehouse and storehouse. The storehouse grew to become a general merchandise store and company shop. Amply stocked with articles needed by mill workers and farmers, the store became a regional shopping center that attracted shoppers from Frederick, Washington, and Baltimore. Fine fabrics, such as silk and satin, glassware, pottery, imported china, mathematical instruments, iron household and farm implements, groceries, wines, and liquors were some of the items for sale proudly displayed on shelves behind curtained glass cabinets and protective drawers.

Through the end of the 1700s, the town of Ellicott's Mills experienced limited growth. The village consisted of residences for the small number of clerks, millers, coopers, blacksmiths, wheelwrights, and millwrights living and working in the area.

With the death of John Ellicott in 1795, a family cemetery was established on the ridge running along the river's south bank. In 1800, the Ellicotts built a Quaker meetinghouse on the cemetery grounds and opened the cemetery to the public. The four-acre site became known as Quaker Ridge. The first service performed at the new meetinghouse was the wedding of Cassandra Ellicott, the widow of John Ellicott, and Joseph Thornburg from Baltimore. In 1816, a lack of membership forced the meetinghouse to close its doors. The building was pressed into service during the Civil War as a hospital, following the Battle of Monocacy in 1864. The building served as a school and later it was remodeled as a private residence.

As the financial success of the Ellicotts' flour mill increased, new industry was attracted to the river location. In 1794, Ellicott and Company disposed of a mill site downriver to Thomas Mendenhall for a paper mill. In 1804, Joseph Atkinson, leasing property from the Ellicotts, built an oil mill and a carding mill for wool. Ellicott and Company also sold eight acres to a fellow Quaker, Samuel Smith, who built a tanyard for tanning and currying leather. In 1808, the company sold 900 acres upriver to the Union Manufacturing Company of Maryland.

The Ellicotts expanded their own operation in 1806 by establishing next to Smith's tanyard an ironworks for rolling and slitting bars of iron. Nails were manufactured at the works and exported to southern markets. On November 12, 1814, *Niles Weekly Register* reported that there was "a machine at Ellicott's Mills that cuts (please observe, I do not say will cut, but cuts) twelve hundred nails in one minute, more perfect than any heretofore finished." Later added were machinery for making wrought iron utensils and a furnace for rolling and sheathing copper.

In 1809, the fire that destroyed the mill also burned down most of the log cabin village. Following the fire, new structures were built of brick and stone. The cost, which earlier proved prohibitive to the average mill worker, was now considered financially feasible. The opening of nearby granite quarries, credited with supplying the stone for the Baltimore cathedral, changed the fabric and design of the mill village. Rebuilt and concentrated on the river's south side, the village centered on a main street wedged between a twenty-foot cliff and the Tiber River, a feeder stream to the Patapsco. As the village grew, it encompassed two southern ridges: Quaker Hill to the east and Courthouse Hill to the west. A series of squat stone structures, running diagonally along Quaker Hill, served as homes for a number of mill workers. Tongue Row, built in the early 1800s by a gentleman named Tongue, stands today as one of the town's best-known landmarks and most photographed attractions.

By 1825, the population of Ellicott's Mills had swelled to over 3,000. Businesses began to settle in stone buildings along Main Street and large country homes began to dot the hillsides. One of the more popular buildings was the Colonial Inn and Opera House, which reportedly witnessed the theatrical debut of an aspiring actor named John Wilkes Booth. In 1830, the Patapsco Hotel was dismantled stone by stone and then rebuilt to accommodate the increasing number of railroad passengers. The hotel frequently hosted vacationing merchants and, on occasion, a visiting celebrity. It was reported that the famous statesman Henry Clay once addressed a gathering from its porch. When the railroad traveled through the mill town, it passed by the hotel alongside a steep embankment where a stop had been created that allowed departing riders to step from the train to the hotel's second floor. In 1831, the B&O built its first terminus at the foot of Main Street across the street from the Patapsco Hotel. The stone station, located next to the river, included a turntable that allowed trains to be turned around for the return trip to Baltimore. Today, the station is a National Historic Landmark and operates as a railroad museum, offering a unique look at Ellicott's Mills and the B&O in the 1800s.

One of the most unusual homes built in the town was Castle Angelo. Constructed in 1831 by Frenchman Samuel Waughn, the structure was said to be an exact miniature copy of a French castle bearing the same name. Located on the eastern side of Courthouse Hill, the castle became a popular tourist attraction. In 1833, it was auctioned in a lottery by its owner, Andrew McLaughlin. The structure later served as the rectory for the first Catholic priests in the area until St. Paul's Church was completed. The first Catholic mass in Ellicott's Mills was said at the castle. Directly below Angelo Cottage, as the castle later became known, stood Tarpeian Rock. Located next to the B&O tracks, the top-heavy column of balanced rock, later removed by the B&O, was a familiar landmark and an unusual attraction.

St. Paul Catholic Church, built on land acquired from George Ellicott and constructed with gray granite from a nearby quarry, was dedicated on December 13, 1838. From its lofty perch on a steep hillside overlooking the town and the river, the oldest active parish between Baltimore and Pittsburgh has dutifully witnessed the triumphant and turbulent history of Ellicott City. On at least two occasions, it was also a participant. In addition to serving as a hospital for Southern and Northern troops during the Civil War, the church claims a footnote to one of baseball's greatest players. Standing in front of the first pew on October 17, 1914, Baltimore's George Herman Ruth, the "Babe" as he was nicknamed, married Helen Woodford, a waitress he had met earlier that year at a coffee shop in Boston. On July 9, 1914, the unheralded nineteen-year-old rookie had been sold by the minor-league Baltimore Orioles to the Boston Red Sox. Two days later, Ruth made his major league debut as the winning pitcher against the Cleveland Indians.

As the population of the mill town grew, the number of churches and schools increased. No structure was more prestigious than the Patapsco Female Institute. Built on one of the town's highest hills, it was a select finishing school for Southern belles to be tutored in the liberal arts and the social graces. The 33,000-square-foot porticoed mansion was constructed of yellow granite on land donated by the Ellicotts. Designed by noted Maryland architect Robert Carey Long Jr. in the Greek Revival style, the school opened its doors on January 1, 1837. It quickly gained a reputation as one of the finest women's liberal schools in the country. Its noted alumnae included Winnie Davis, the daughter of Jefferson Davis. Headmistresses of note were Almira Lincoln Phelps, a noted educator and author, and Sarah Nicholas Randolph, the great-granddaughter of Thomas Jefferson. Following the Civil War, this symbol of Southern aristocracy suffered from financial troubles and was eventually forced to close in 1891. In that year, the institute was purchased by James E. Tyson and turned into a summer retreat. In 1905, his daughter Lily took possession of the building and renamed it Berg Alnwick after Alnwick Castle, the ancestral home of the Tyson family in England.

In 1917, the structure was turned into a fifty-bed hospital for returning World War I veterans. Known as the Maryland Women's War Relief Hospital, it solicited a contribution of one dollar from every woman in Maryland. In 1930, the hospital became the Hill Top Theatre, the first professional summer stock theater in Maryland. The building eventually passed into the hands of Dr. James Whisman, whose will in 1965 deeded it to his alma mater, the University of Cincinnati. In 1966, the property was purchased by the Board of County Commissioners. In cooperation with the Friends of Patapsco Institute, a historic preservation group, the board made an effort to raise funds to restore the old institute as a cultural and recreational center. The ravages of time and vandals, however, proved to be insurmountable and restoration efforts were abandoned.

In 1843, a massive stone structure atop the western ridge overlooking the town was completed. The building became an administrative and judicial center—the Howard County Courthouse—when the Anne Arundel district was designated a separate county in 1851. The new county took its name from John Eager Howard, Maryland's Revolutionary War hero. In 1867, a city charter was obtained and Ellicott's Mills became Ellicott City. In 1935, the city's charter was revoked by the Maryland Legislature, and the town began a gradual decline that would last more than three decades.

In 1940, the old millrace to the original mills, measuring fifteen feet wide and six to eight feet deep, was filled by the States Roads Commission. The millrace, partially uncovered by floodwaters in 1972, was the scene of steam experiments conducted by John Ellicott in the late 1780s and early 1790s. While he was testing his steam-powered boat, a boiler exploded, costing him the loss of an arm. According to an old monograph, *The Rise and Progress of Ellicott Mills*, written by John S. Tyson, "one-armed John Ellicott, son of the first John, sped along the canal in front of his residence in 1789." The monograph added that "had not John Ellicott shortly after lost one of his arms by the explosion of its steam boiler, he would, in all likelihood have perfected the invention and anticipated Robert Fulton by at least ten years. However, he demonstrated the principle that vessels could be propelled through the water by steam. It was

then along Ellicott's Canal that the first steamboat in America was propelled."
(Baltimore Sun, July 28, 1940)

After World War II, Ellicott City began to have the appearance of a decaying industrial community. Businesses that had thrived on defense contracts closed forever under bankruptcy petitions or opted for better working conditions and a cheaper labor force in the new industrial South. The economic collapse slowly strangled the town's main business district. Vacant storefronts began to proliferate along the narrow streets. The stone buildings, which had survived nearly two centuries, never looked more tired or worn. Nearby slum-like communities still lacking running water and indoor plumbing contributed to giving the area the appearance of an Appalachian shanty town. The biggest postwar event, according to local people, occurred in 1957, when the town was invaded by movie makers from Hollywood. The movie to be produced, *The Goddess*, was about the rise of a Hollywood starlet from humble origins in a small, dilapidated, Southern town. Two hundred residents were employed as extras in a movie that ironically reflected the plight of Ellicott City.

In the early 1960s, after more than a decade of restless sleep, the town awakened to find that it had been bypassed by residential and commercial development. Five miles to the south, Columbia was being hailed as the model residential community of the future. Thirteen miles to the east, Baltimore was preparing plans for major renovations of its downtown business district and waterfront areas. Ellicott City was still being plagued by problems that had been addressed by other cities and towns years earlier. In the late 1960s, members of the community, including businessmen, civic leaders, and politicians, took stock of their precarious economic position and began to look for ways to revive the town. After studying all possibilities for development, it was decided that the future of Ellicott City depended on capitalizing on the town's past. A rediscovery of the town's historic roots served as the catalyst for a well-planned, concentrated effort aimed at revitalizing the business district and creating a new commercial identity. In 1973, the town's boundaries were re-established, and the town was designated a Historic Preserve. While the rebirth has been a slow process, it has been successful. Today Ellicott City is a charming blend of historical and commercial interests. Stylish stone buildings, resembling those in a European mountain village, retain their old-world flavor in spite of contemporary changes. Antique, craft, and specialty shops along Main Street reflect the new energy that moves the town, while historical attractions instill a new awareness of its past.

CHAPTER SIX

Mills along the Patapsco: Avalon, Orange Grove, Ilchester, Gray's Mill, Oella, Granite, and Daniels

AVALON

Seeking to expand his industrial empire, ironmaster Caleb Dorsey looked to riverfront property north of Elkridge. In 1761, he acquired a large tract of land called Taylor's Forest, stretching from Rolling Road (near present-day Catonsville Community College) to near the edge of the Patapsco. Later in the same year, Dorsey acquired the desired river frontage, a 375-acre tract called Long Acre, in a purchase from John Owings. The property was first harvested for timber to supply raw materials for his other industrial operations. Taking advantage of the potential of the property, Dorsey shortly after built a forge and a small furnace on the southeastern corner of his property, which was later to be known as Avalon. According to historians, Dorsey's forge operated at a limited capacity, primarily producing crowbars. The seemingly insignificant iron tool was an innovation for colonial manufacturers, because up until this time all hand tools had been imported from England. When Dorsey died in 1771, the forge and related holdings passed to his sons, Edward and Samuel.

In 1775, the Dorsey brothers entered into an agreement to lease the forge and two acres of land to William Whetcroft. Whetcroft, who had contracted to supply arms to the Continental Army, had invested in the ironworks to manufacture cast-iron parts for muskets. In Annapolis, Whetcroft maintained assembly facilities where the muskets were completed. In addition to the use of the ironworks, the agreement stipulated that a slitting mill, a dwelling, and other convenient buildings were to be operational within five months of the agreement. Whetcroft's business at Avalon remained operational until 1778, when it became the center of a heated and contested

Avalon Nail and Iron Works in 1857.
In the background is the Thomas Viaduct.
Courtesy Maryland Historical Society.

legal controversy concerning the lease agreement. In 1777, with the death of his brother Samuel, Edward Dorsey (nicknamed "Ironhead Ned") refused to execute a written agreement with Whetcroft. Dorsey claimed that at the time of the verbal agreement he had been a minor and thus not legally liable for the contract. Whetcroft petitioned the Maryland General Assembly to adjudicate the matter.

The assembly decided the issue in favor of Whetcroft, and in 1779 they passed an act forcing Dorsey to continue the original lease. An influencing factor in the decision was Whetcroft's claim of having spent his own money in making the facilities operational. In 1780, Dorsey executed the lease and also agreed to raise the height of the dam. The dam, located about 600 feet below the ironworks, was raised a foot higher with "sound logs and gravel and a millrace thirty feet wide and five feet deep was dug to Whetcroft's slitting mill. To compensate Dorsey after the bitter legal confrontation, Whetcroft agreed to buy all his bar iron from Dorsey at the Baltimore Company Ironworks and promised not to operate his forge to the detriment of Dorsey's forge or gristmill. Annual rent for the property was 28 pounds sterling or one ton of bar iron.

In 1780, Whetcroft formed a new partnership with Alexander McFadon and reopened his mill at Avalon. The slitting mill offered rods, sheet iron, and slit iron. In 1783, that operation was seized for unpaid taxes by the sheriff of Baltimore County, William McLaughlin. In 1785, the property was auctioned to Samuel Godman, a merchant from Anne Arundel County, who sold the property to Edward Dorsey. Lawsuits and counter suits were initiated by Whetcroft and Dorsey. The struggle continued in the courts for years and was carried on by their sons. The circumstances surrounding the question of property rights and ownership were partially revealed in a bill of complaint filed by Robert Dorsey in one of the court proceedings. The complaint stated:

> That the said slitting mill lay entirely useless for several years after Edward Dorsey purchased her; That after the Federal Government was established and the duties laid on foreign goods made the manufacture of iron an object, the said Edward Dorsey rebuilt the mill at a Considerable expense: That the said Whetcroft suffered the said Dorsey to rebuild the mill and never gave him any notice that he meant to contest the validity of the sale made by (Sheriff) McLaughlin until the mill was put in completed order by Edward Dorsey: That Whetcroft in the year 1792, or 1793 brought an ejectment against the said Edward Dorsey to recover said property. (McGrain 1977)

The Dorsey forge affair was settled in 1815 when the property was ordered to be sold by the High Court of Chancery. The ironworks was sold to the highest bidders—Benjamin and James Ellicott, of the well-known and wealthy Ellicott family. In 1819, a five-sevenths interest was given to Jonathan, Elias, George, Andrew, and Thomas Ellicott. Individual shares in the forge were incorporated, and in December 1822, the Avalon Company was chartered. This reference to Avalon was the first appearance of the name in that area. Avalon would later lend its name to the community of Avalon and the Avalon Nail and Iron Company, both of which were established at the site of the original forge.

The ironworks continued to operate during the years of legal arbitration over the claims to ownership. The federal tax list of 1798 listed a number of buildings on the property, including a stone forge, stonesmith shop, frame millhouse, stone coal house, sawmill, frame granary, and open shed. As the product line of the ironworks expanded, the plant facilities increased. The 1806 tax list showed the addition of a coal house, 70' × 30', and described the main works as "1 forge with three fires, three fine wheels, two hammer wheels and two hammers, sixty feet by forty-five."

Production statistics assembled in 1820 by Evan T. Ellicott for his ironworks revealed the amount of manufacturing taking place along the Patapsco. In compiling his figures, Ellicott combined the output of both his mills at Ellicott's Mills and Avalon. The two plants were equipped with four rolling mills, six pairs of rollers with necessary furnaces, and twenty-four patent nail machines, as well as other equipment for making nails. At the time, the Avalon works used the automated nail machine (capable of cutting 1,200 nails a minute) introduced at the Ellicott ironworks. The works employed fifty men and thirteen boys and consumed 500 tons of iron bar and 300 tons of scrap annually to produce $120,000 worth of bar iron, sheet iron, boiler plates, nail plates, nails, and brads. Gross sales for these iron products was reported at $220,000. Ellicott stated that "the business for some years back has been regular and moderately profitable, but now will not pay an interest of six percent on the capital employed ... The importation of sheet iron and boiler plates interferes in a considerable degree with the manufacturer here—and we believe many mills are out of employ." (Singewald 1911)

The financial picture was not as bleak as painted by Evan Ellicott, but the increase in local competition and imports had a negative effect on the industry. A report of 1840 on iron manufacturing in the State of Maryland

Orange Grove flour mill, a typical milling operation along the river in the 1890s. The footbridge at right center connected the town with the mill. Today, a swinging bridge is an attraction in Patapsco Valley State Park. *Courtesy Enoch Pratt Free Library.*

listed thirty employees and 150 horses, mules, and oxen on the site. The plant continued to manufacture bar iron at a rate of 4,500 tons annually and was later expanded to manufacture merchant iron, such as sheet iron and hoops. In 1848, another rolling mill was added, and rails were rolled for the B&O. The old nail factory burned down in 1845 and was not rebuilt until 1850, when the plant was purchased by John McCrone and Company. The 1850 census listed this company at the Avalon Iron and Nail Works with $105,000 in capital, 140 hands, and water-powered production of 40,000 kegs of nails worth $140,000 made from 2,000 tons of iron. In 1854, the works was pulled down and rebuilt. The new plant consisted of seven puddling furnaces, three heating furnaces, three trains of rolls, and forty-four steam-driven nail machines. Nail output in 1856 reached 44,000 kegs.

In 1857, the plant was listed as the property of Joseph C. Manning and Company of Baltimore. Joseph C. Manning's half-interest in the ironworks, which was listed in a trustee's sale notice, included a rolling mill twenty-two feet tall, a former nail factory, a mill, a stone pattern house, a cooper shop, a stone store, and a large number of tenements.

The ironworks operated until 1868, when floodwaters swept down the river valley and destroyed the factory and the company town. The Avalon Iron and Nail Company, owned at the time by H. L. Brooke and Company (who also owned the ill-fated Elkridge Furnace), never resumed production because of the cost of rebuilding, as well as competition from modernized plants. The *American and Commercial Advertiser* reported on July 25, 1868, that "the Patapsco washed entirely through the lower portion of the large nail factory at Avalon . . . and the machinery at the works was damaged to a very great extent, and the stock on hand carried away. The houses of the workmen, surrounding the factory, and like it, situated on low ground, were inundated, the water reaching the second story of some of them. It is not known that any lives were lost at this place, but many families lost all their household property." A number of residents returned to their homes, but the community faded when the industry abandoned the area. By 1898, only a few houses and a small Catholic church were occupied. The town of Avalon officially passed into history in the early 1930s when St. Paul's Episcopal Church, the last remaining building, was demolished.

Until the flood, a small steamer named the *Great Western* made regular runs up the Patapsco to a small wharf below the Avalon ironworks, pulling barges with scrap iron upriver to the ironworks and returning downriver to Baltimore with manufactured iron. Ross Winans and the owners of the ironworks funded construction projects to straighten and deepen the river channel. One wharf was built near the Thomas Viaduct and several more on Winans's riverfront farm property. Floodwaters splintered the wharves and filled in the river channel. This marked the last time that ships were to travel up the Main Branch of the Patapsco to Elkridge and Avalon.

In 1901, the Baltimore County Water and Electric Company obtained land and built a water filtration plant on the site of the former ironworks. A large brick building was constructed to house the machinery, and concrete holding ponds were built behind the structure. A new dam, pumping stations, and a canal were built upriver from the plant. Water was diverted from the river, channeled into the filtration plant for purifying, and then pumped into nearby Baltimore City and County communities. The waterworks operated until 1928.

ORANGE GROVE

The success of the Ellicott brothers in the flour-milling business gave rise to similar milling operations along the Patapsco. One of the most successful was the flour mill at Orange Grove. The mill became known worldwide as a producer of quality flour products. Two of the more well-known and best-selling brand names were Orange Grove and the high-grade Patapsco Superlative, which was ground from the whitest part of the kernel. Flour products from the Orange Grove mill became a common sight in kitchens around Maryland and the mid-Atlantic region. Under the ownership and skillful management of Charles A. Gambrill, the trade was expanded to more distant northern and southern states. Flour products were eventually marketed in Europe, South America, and the West Indies. Throughout the mill's existence, claims were made that it was the largest mill in the South and the largest east of Minneapolis.

In 1856, George Bayly and George Worthington acquired valuable riverfront property on both sides of the Main Branch between Elkridge and Ellicott's Mills. Located a mile and a half above the Avalon ironworks and downstream from Ilchester, it was ideally situated for a commercial milling operation. The mill, which was set into the hillside on the river's north bank, was a four-story brick structure with two levels of attic space. It was powered by the river's main stream, which was spanned by a half-curved wooden overshot dam. The ten-foot dam was anchored on the north bank by a heavy timbered cage filled with large boulders, and on the south bank by an abutment of stone masonry. The water impounded by the dam created a placid lake reaching back to Ilchester. The large stretch of backwater provided seasonal recreational opportunities: boating in the summer and skating in the winter. Standing next to the stone abutment was a fish ladder.

Water was drawn from the river above the dam into a massive wooden tank called the forebay. The forebay extended across the full width of the mill. It was about fifteen feet deep, and its top was level with the mill's first floor. The top of the tank was open except for a narrow catwalk along the side of the mill extending from the front end of the tank to the rack house at the rear. The rack, made of closely spaced metal bars set in the floor of the tank at a sharp upward angle, collected any debris that might cause damage to the waterwheels. Water in the forebay was maintained at a constant temperature, and the flow of water to the waterwheels was controlled by headgates.

The mill complex was wedged on a narrow shelf of land between the steep embankment supporting the B&O and the high retaining wall next to the river. The mill was unique in design in that Gun Road, built as an access road during the Revolution, passed through the center of the ground floor by way of an arched passageway. The portals, which added to the charm of the structure, were boarded up after the Flood of 1868 washed away major sections of the roadway. For the first-time visitor to Orange Grove, it was an unusual sight to see horse-drawn wagons being swallowed by the massive groaning and grinding four-story brick structure only to reappear on the other side.

The second floor of the mill, called the grinding floor, was where grain was ground into flour. The third floor was the bolting floor. Here, the partially processed flour was sifted through fine silk cloth, known as bolting cloth. Several times a day samples were taken to see that any foreign particles were removed and to ensure that high-grade texture and quality were being maintained. The fourth floor was the packing floor, where the finished product was loaded into freight cars. This level was even with the floor of a boxcar on the siding and allowed for convenient and simplified loading. Directly across the tracks from the mill was a passenger station, which was divided into two waiting rooms with built-in seats around the walls.

An eight-story grain elevator (100' × 150') adjoined the mill on the upstream side, and an engine and dynamo room, furnace, and coal room were located on the downstream side. A tall, square smokestack of stone and brick towered above the complex and became an identifying landmark. Also downstream from the mill stood the superintendent's house. The three-and-one-half-story brick structure had electric lights, hot and cold running water, and a zinc-lined wooden bathtub, all luxury items at the time.

Across the river from the mill, on the south bank, stood a small mostly company-owned village consisting of seven houses for workers and a combination one-room school and church. The Bathgate House, occupied by night engineer John Bathgate, was the only house in the village not company-owned. (The house later served as park headquarters for the Patapsco Valley State Park, until it was washed away during Tropical Storm Agnes in 1972.) A swinging bridge was later constructed that linked both riverbanks and allowed mill workers easier access to their place of work. Drinking water was supplied by a community well, and foodstuffs were obtained from traveling grocers and butchers or during trips to Ellicott City, Elkridge, or Baltimore. Every third Sunday, church services were conducted by a traveling minister. It is believed the mill and village were named Orange Grove after the Osage orange trees that were common to the area.

In 1860, Bayly and Worthington sold Orange Grove to the C. A. Gambrill Manufacturing Company for a reported $45,000. At the time, the mill produced 300 to 500 barrels of flour daily. For Charles A. Gambrill, who already owned the Patapsco Flouring Mills in Ellicott City (originally built by John and Andrew Ellicott in 1773), the purchase was a needed expansion of his prosperous flour business. In the early 1880s, Gambrill again enlarged the business by building the first roller mill in Maryland, at Smith's Wharf in Baltimore. A company advertising card from 1884 displayed the company's three mills: Patapsco Mill A, Ellicott City, Maryland; Patapsco Mill B, Baltimore, Maryland; and Patapsco Mill C, Orange Grove, Maryland. Patapsco Mill C at Orange Grove was described as a large, well-built brick building, situated at a very picturesque point on the Patapsco River. Fourteen standard brands of flour, sold in barrels, half-barrels, and in quarter, eighth and sixteenth sacks, were listed in the advertisement.

After the death of Charles A. Gambrill, believed to have been hastened by his witnessing the destruction of his mills and their associated communities in the Flood of 1868, the mill at Orange Grove was operated by his son and his nephew. In 1873, steam power was introduced to the mill when a Corliss steam engine and boilers were added to supplement the waterpower. Ten years later, the stone gristmills were replaced with steel rollers. In spite of the economic recession felt by the flour industry in Maryland, Orange Grove continued to expand its productivity. An 1880 census showed that the Gambrill mills had a combined yearly output of 171,381 barrels of flour. The flour mills at Orange Grove and Ellicott City exceeded the output of the fifty nearby water-powered gristmills, which produced a total of 68,803 barrels of flour.

By 1900, two stories of frame and metal siding were added to the four-story mill. The mill (150' × 175') was powered by a coal-fired steam-driven Corliss engine and three horizontal waterwheels. An electric generator was installed to light the mill complex. William A. Clayton, the day engineer at the time, named one of his sons Corliss, in tribute to the highly dependable steam engine.

In the early 1900s the decline in the flour trade caught up with the C. A. Gambrill Manufacturing Company. In 1901, after experiencing a number of shutdowns and spells of half-time, management announced the closing of Orange Grove due to the scarcity of wheat. The mill was soon reopened under the management of George W. Carr, but the events of 1904 appeared as a premonition of the eventual fate of the Orange Grove mill.

In January 1904, a sudden thaw slowly turned loose giant cakes of ice. On January 22, ice cakes and chips began tumbling over the Orange Grove dam. Instead of floating downriver, the jagged ice forms began to pile up just below the dam. As new ice crashed into the jam, the mountain of ice rose higher and higher until it rose above the wooden walkway of the swinging bridge. Before the ice jam broke free, it banked to a height of thirty feet, demolishing the swinging bridge and four wooden utility buildings. The bridge was unable to withstand the tremendous pressure of the ice, broke away from its mooring on the south side, and swung around downriver while still firmly anchored at its north end. A young boarder at the Bathgate House was the last person to cross the bridge at the instant it broke loose. Ignoring the frantic warnings shouted by frightened spectators, the young man crossed the bridge and jumped to safety as it gave way from the south riverbank.

In February 1904, the Great Baltimore Fire, which burned and destroyed 1,545 buildings over a 140-acre area of the business and harbor districts, destroyed Gambrill's Patapsco Mill B on Smith's Wharf.

Orange Grove mill came to a sudden and violent end on May 1,1905. On that Monday evening, the mill burned to the ground, with all its machinery and a large quantity of wheat stored for grinding. The fire was discovered at about 7:00 p.m. in the basement of the engine room. George W. Carr,the superintendent in charge, was notified by phone at his Ellicott City home. The fire quickly spread, shooting flames hundreds of feet into the air. The glow in the early evening darkness was seen for miles.

At the time of the fire, the mill was the largest in the state, producing 1,200 to 1,500 barrels of flour daily. The loss was put at $200,000. Insurance coverage was carried for $175,000. The previous fall, new machinery had been installed at a cost of $50,000. The mill was about to shut down for the day when the fire was discovered. All company books and papers were saved by one of the millers.

The intense heat and flying embers carried the fire to several dwellings near the mill. Quick action by residents and neighbors salvaged personal articles and some furniture. Several explosions from stored oil and kerosene tanks erupted from the inferno. Above the mill, the Orange Grove station of the B&O and several outbuildings were burned. Firefighting teams, inadequately equipped and poorly trained, were limited in their ability to contain such a fire in a remote area. The Catonsville chemical engine, responding to the fire, worked effectively in saving a number of dwellings in the area.

By the following morning, the mill complex was in smoldering ruins. The thirty-five people employed at the time of the fire would never again return to work in the mill. The gutted shell was boarded up, and portions of unsupported standing walls were torn down. Vandals, floods, and the passing of time took their toll on the surviving structures in the abandoned village and mill complex. In 1972, floodwaters washed away most of the remaining ruins. Today the dam abutment on the south bank and the hillside foundation of the mill on the north bank are visible. The archway near the railroad tracks, where coal was unloaded by gravity from hopper cars, also remains standing in the rubble.

With the demise of Orange Grove, another era along the Patapsco passed into history books and memories. The subdued rumble of the mill heard from early Monday morning to late Saturday evening, the muffled, unbroken roar of water pouring over the high wooden dam, and the shrill whistles from the long freight trains passing day and night, described by Orange Grove historian Thomas L. Phillips in his memoirs of childhood, would never again be heard by the workers and families of Orange Grove.

ILCHESTER

This site of unparalleled natural beauty was first viewed by John and Andrew Ellicott in 1772 as they cleared their way through the dense woodland in making a roadway from Elkridge to their tract of land five miles upriver. After two-and-a-half miles of slow and unsteady progress in the covered forest, the working party broke through to a clearing, where the sun warmed their faces and dried their sweat-soaked clothes. Before them was one of the most scenic views encountered along the Patapsco. The narrow river valley was funneled into a narrower river canyon. On each side of the river, rocky cliffs were embedded in the steep hillsides, topped by a dense tree line that ran the length of the river. The rugged terrain, which closely resembled a mountain gap, was cut on the south bank by a turbulent falling stream. The roaring of the Patapsco and the rushing of the Bonnie Branch echoed and reverberated off the canyon walls. The sights and sounds of nature's symphony overwhelmed the senses of the early travelers, leaving them awed and humbled by the grand display of nature. The location was later to be the site of Ilchester, a mill and village named after Joseph Holland, Earl of Ilchester.

The first mill recorded at the site was the Dismal Mill, also known as the Vortex or Cornwait's Mill. In 1812, a gristmill (80' × 42') owned by John Cornwait was listed in the Ellicott family's deed of partition. In the early 1830s, George Ellicott replaced the old Dismal Mill with a new four-and-one-half-story stone and brick building on the south bank. When the railroad passed through the area, the mill was wedged between the river and the railroad embankment. The mill became a familiar landmark to travelers, signaling the final approach to Ellicott's Mills. The land and water rights were sold to George and Jonathan Ellicott by Elias Ellicott with the stipulation that the mill would grind only grain from Baltimore County. The mill, known as the Ellicott Ilchester Flour Mills, was severely damaged by the Flood of 1868. It was partially rebuilt and used by the Thistle Mill Company to grind grain in a smaller-scale operation.

In 1837, George and William Morris, two Scottish brothers from Philadelphia, built a cotton print mill, known as the Thistle Cotton Mill, on a 106-acre tract along the river's north bank, opposite the site of Ellicott's Mill. The tall, elongated factory and the mill village were constructed of granite from nearby hills. The first products from the mill were silk and cotton, followed by silk yarn and cotton thread. The 1850 census listed William and George Morris at the factory with an $80,000 investment, and 71 male and 106 female workers. Also listed was a water-powered output of 1.3 million yards of sheetings and drill. To power the mill, a dam was constructed upriver. As with other mills, a millrace diverted water from the river to power the essential machinery.

By 1900, the mill had been converted to spinning only silk. In 1919, the works was taken over by Edward and A. A. Blakeney and Company for use as a cotton-duck works. The plant was later sold to a New York corporation interested in making tire fabric. In 1922, the plant was sold to the Bartgis brothers for use as a paper plant. The works were acquired in 1957 by the New Haven Board and Carton Company, which continued to manufacture cardboard. At the time the plant was purchased, it had two pasteboard machines, 500 employees, and an annual output of 40,000 tons of light cardboard products. Recyclable wastepaper was used as the raw material to be processed. In 1963, Leon Simkins became president of the company, and, when the company announced its closing in December 1963, he took over control of the operation. In 1972, Simkins Industries was temporarily disabled by the flood, suffering damages estimated at $1 million. The plant was further damaged by a four-alarm fire that burned out of control for more than two hours on November 29, 1972. The plant was rebuilt in the gutted stone shells and expanded along both riverbanks. Despite its hazardous location next to the river, the company remained in the area.

In the 1830s, a company town, resembling a typical village in northern Wales, was built on the steep hillside above the river's north bank. In 1830, when the railroad blasted through the gorge and ran track alongside the mill, a railroad station and post office were built to accommodate the villagers. The post office situated at the foot of the cliff on the south bank measured 8' × 10' and was believed to be the smallest post office in the state. On the hillside above the post office, one of the Ellicotts built a stone hotel and tavern. That station complex was abandoned after the facility failed to receive the needed railroad business.

In 1867, on the river's south side, high above the mill and the old Ellicott Hotel, the Redemptorist Fathers established St. Mary's College. A massive five-story brick building was built as a novitiate for young seminarians in this Roman Catholic order. (The novitiate was a one-year training period for young men aspiring to become members of the order.) Granite for the foundation was quarried from nearby hills. Until the completion of the main building, which housed dining rooms, classrooms, offices, sleeping quarters, a chapel, and a gymnasium, the Redemptorists used the old hotel and other structures built by the Ellicotts. In the late 1960s, the college was sold after the order moved the novitiate to Wisconsin; at the same time, the order was also forced to relocate the cemetery located behind the college. Subsequent plans to convert the college to an apartment complex or nursing home never materialized. At the foot of the college once stood Ilchester's only church, Our Lady of Perpetual Help, which was built by the Redemptorists.

In 1903, the B&O was rerouted through Ilchester Mountain on the river's north bank. A long brick tunnel took the place of a steel-girder suspension bridge, which had replaced the Patterson Viaduct, washed out in the Flood of 1868.

GRAY'S MILL

In 1794, Ellicott and Company sold a tract of land below Ellicott's Mills to Peter Mendenhall of Philadelphia. Mendenhall built a large paper mill on the north side of the Patapsco to take advantage of the soft curve in the river. Before the construction of a local church, Methodists used the mill building for religious services and prayer meetings. Within a few years of operation, Mendenhall found that a paper mill was only a marginally profitable business. On December 18, 1797, the mill was advertised in the *Federal Gazette* as a three-story stone mill (100' × 38') with three engines, two vats, excellent iron screws, seizing houses, vat houses, and enough water for six engines. The mill was again offered for sale in 1805 and 1807 when it was advertised as 120' × 40', with "four sets of hands and the most productive paper mill in the United States." In 1807, the mill was purchased for $20,000 by Joseph Conrad, a bookseller from Philadelphia.

Following a chancery suit, the mill was advertised for sale by Samuel Moale in local newspapers.

In 1813, the complainants in the suit, Edward Gray, Samuel F. Bradford, Robert Taylor, and John Inskeep, bought the mill for $16,000. Later that year, Gray and Taylor bought out the other two partners. A short time after this transaction, Gray purchased Taylor's controlling interest and became the sole owner of the mill.

Edward Gray, who turned the former paper mill into one of the largest producers of cotton duck in the country, was born in the parish of Bowera, near Londonderry, Ireland, on July 16, 1776. A fervent admirer of the heroes of the American Revolution, particularly George Washington, Gray emigrated from Ireland to the United States around 1794. He never tired of telling the story of how he arrived at the Philadelphia wharf on a Sunday morning and passed the great general as he walked up Chestnut Street. Gray's first residence was in the same building where Alexander Hamilton was temporarily living. Gray's first job, that of a messenger for a commercial house, frequently brought him into the presence of these men and other Americans made famous as a result of the American Revolution. After a series of uneventful business ventures, Gray formed a business partnership and eventually gained control of the cotton spinning factory to be known as the Patapsco Cotton Factory and still later as Edward Gray's Cotton Manufactory.

On January 21, 1820, the factory and all its machinery were destroyed by fire. At the time, some 16 boys, 104 girls, and 10 men were employed to operate the 4,000 spindles and 32 looms. The mill processed cotton into cotton yarn, shirtings, sheetings, plaids, stripes, and denim. Incorporated as the Patapsco Manufacturing Company, the millworks advertised white and blue yarn from Sea Island cotton.

After the disastrous fire, Gray built a larger, more productive, and more efficient mill. The tariff of 1824 on foreign textile imports resulted in an unprecedented increase in business. The demand kept the mill busy around the clock. In 1847, the value of the mill was reported at $300,000. During the productive years in the 1840s and early 1850s, Gray enjoyed a personal income from the mill of an estimated $70,000 a year.

After Gray's death in 1856, the mill continued operating as a manufacturing plant for cotton goods. The flood of 1868 ruined the machinery and stock, but the bend in the river at the mill site spared the mill from serious structural damage. The mill was operated by Gray's daughter Martha and Hugh Bone until 1888, when it was permanently shut down as a textile mill. The mill was purchased by John Bone, who sold it to the Patapsco Electric and Manufacturing Company, which was headed by Victor G. Bloede. It was later sold to the Consolidated Gas Electric Light and Power Company, which utilized the site as a power substation for local communities until the 1930s.

Edward Gray built a residence for his wife and two daughters adjacent to the mill on the east side (downriver). The original manor house was built in the old post-frame style. Later, wings of granite were added in a rather hard rectangular castle-like style of architecture rising two-and-a-half stories. Gray lived the life of a lord of the manor. Pride in his business and home was reflected in the care and upkeep given to the structures. As his wealth and prestige grew with his business, Gray enlarged his home and spent a considerable amount of money beautifying the grounds with shrubs, trees, and terraced gardens. He became known as a lavish entertainer and a gracious host who was seldom without a guest. During his lifetime, he was a man known in many social circles. His acquaintances included well-known artists, writers, statesmen, lawyers, physicians, and businessmen. However, the social circle of his noted son-in-law, John Pendleton Kennedy, was of greater diameter and encompassed many of the most brilliant characters of the golden age of American literature, art, and statesmanship.

In 1829, John Pendleton Kennedy, a young Baltimore lawyer, married Elizabeth Gray. The twenty-year-old daughter of Edward Gray was described as a strikingly beautiful girl with dark eyes set in a flawless heart-shaped face. Writing to Edward Gray, Kennedy said that Elizabeth "will always receive from me the homage of an ardent affection and most sincere devotion to her welfare." (Bohner 1961) After their marriage, Kennedy and his bride moved into the Gray mansion along the Patapsco. They enlarged the home and continued to live there until the Flood of 1868.

Extracts of a letter from Kennedy to E. L. Stanley give an insider's view of the leisurely life along the river:

> You will find us pleasantly entrenched in our cottage close on the banks of the Patapsco, in one of the most romantic and beautiful nooks in the world. You shall have all manner of rural felicities, among which I enumerate the war of waters and spindles, rich cream, ham, chicken, much talk, plenty of books, backgammon, etc. The railroad is only distant by the span of our bridge; our country store is within a hundred and fifty yards, where you will find a most choice assortment of fashionable tinware, nests of buckets, and all kinds of calicoes, straw bonnets, coffee and cheese. The turnpike road gives a delightful publicity to this magazine of fashion, and affords an opportunity twice a day to observe that striking wonder of civilization, the omnibus, surcharged, inside and out, with the elite of our village. My library, which I shall put entirely at your disposal, is full of miracles of art in a choice collection of photographs, stereoscopes, portraits and inkstands. It has two windows, each opening on a balcony, one of which looks toward the mill dam through pendant willows, glorious to behold, the other at the bridge, which is the most romantic and picturesque of pontificals. (Davidson 1967)

Later in the letter, Kennedy noted the present state of affairs along the river: "Here where I live on the Patapsco, ten miles from Baltimore and near the Baltimore and Ohio Railway, troops are passing in trains almost every hour, and as they see my flag, which hangs from the library, I get the cheers of a regiment at a time. 100,000 have gone by, hurrahing, shouting, sometimes dancing on the tops of cars."

In 1854, noted author Washington Irving was an honored guest at the Gray home. After his stay, Irving wrote to Mrs. Kennedy:

> I envy K. [Mr. Kennedy] that job of building that tower, if he has half the relish for castle building that I have — air castles or any other. I should like nothing better than to have plenty of money to squander on stone and mortars and to build chateaus along the Patapsco with the stone that abounds there; but I would first blow up

the cotton mills — your father's among the number — and make picturesque ruins of them; and I would utterly destroy that railroad and all the cotton lords should live in baronial castles on the cliff; and the cotton spinners should be virtuous peasantry of both sexes, in silk shirts and small clothes and straw hats with long ribbons and should do nothing but sing songs and choruses and dance on the margin of the river. (Duffy 1928)

Irving's words were prophetic. The Flood of 1868 swept away portions of the mansion, as well as the trees, fences, and outbuildings. The manicured grounds were covered with between three and four feet of white sand, and Kennedy's prized library was strewn over the banks of the river. All household articles, including furniture, paintings, and sculptures, were lost to the floodwaters. Of the flood, Kennedy wrote that "the devastation has so completely altered the aspect of the place that I should not know it." *(Jeffersonian* 1933) With the destruction of their home, the Kennedys were forced to move from the river valley they had come to love.

John Pendleton Kennedy, a writer and littérateur who was one of his era's best-selling novelists, was born in Baltimore on October 25, 1795. His father was an Irish immigrant and his mother a descendant of an old Virginia family. After graduating from Baltimore College in 1812, he enlisted for service in the War of 1812 and took part in the battles of North Point and Bladensburg as a member of Captain Warfield's company of Maryland Militia.

After the war, Kennedy studied law and was admitted to the Baltimore bar in 1816. His literary career began in 1818, when he and Peter Hoffman Cruse became joint editors of the *Red Book*. Throughout his lifetime, Kennedy corresponded with many of the day's leading writers and statesmen. The impressive list included, among others, Edgar Allan Poe, Oliver Wendell Holmes, James Fenimore Cooper, Washington Irving, Charles Dickens, William Makepeace Thackeray, Zachary Taylor, Millard Fillmore, Andrew Jackson, James Madison, Jefferson Davis, Commodore Perry, and General Lew Wallace. Kennedy saved most of the letters and accumulated seventeen volumes, which proved to be priceless treasures for historians and literary scholars. In 1820, he was elected to the Maryland House of Delegates and three years later was appointed secretary of the legation to Chile by President Monroe.

In 1832, Kennedy produced his first novel, *Swallow Barn, or a Sojourn in the Old Dominion*. Three years later, he published his second and most famous novel, *Horse-Shoe Robinson, A Tale of the Tory Ascendency*. This was followed in 1838 by *Rob of the Bowl, a Legend of St. Inigoes* and in 1840 by *The Annals of Quodlibet*.

In 1838, he was elected to represent Maryland in the lower house of Congress. Although reelected in 1840 and 1843, he failed to win the seat in 1846. In 1852, Kennedy returned to official life as secretary of the navy under President Fillmore. In 1856, he became chief advisor and first assistant to George Peabody in the development and execution of his plans for the establishment of the Peabody Institute. In 1865, while resting in Europe after the publication of his last book, the *Paul Ambrose Letters*, he was appointed by Secretary of State Seward as one of the US commissioners to the Paris Exposition.

As a member of the Delphian Club, Kennedy was closely associated with Francis Scott Key, John Neal, William Gwynn, Paul Allen, Jared Sparks, Robert

Goodloe Harper, Samuel Woodworth (author of *The Old Oaken Bucket*), William Wirt, John Howard Payne (author of "Home, Sweet Home"), Rembrandt Peale, Peter Hoffman Cruse, and other celebrities. As a corresponding member of the Massachusetts Historical Society, he came into close touch with James Russell Lowell and other New England poets, essayists, and novelists. Lowell once said of Kennedy: "One could not be in his company for never so short a time without being touched by that gentle consideration for others which is the root of all good breeding." *(Jeffersonian* 1933)

Kennedy was also a close and helpful friend to Edgar Allan Poe. At Kennedy's suggestion, T. W. White, the publisher of the *Southern Literary Messenger* in Richmond, appointed Poe his assistant editor in 1835. In response to an appeal from Poe a year later, Kennedy exerted his influence with Philadelphia publishers Carey and Hart to persuade them to use some of Poe's stories in their *Annuals* or *Gift Books*. The first Poe story appearing in *The Gift* was published by them in 1836.

In August 1869, while visiting Newport, Rhode Island, Kennedy suffered a serious illness, later diagnosed as an abdominal tumor. Seeking relief from his discomfort, he again traveled to Newport in July 1870. On August 18, 1870, Kennedy died in Newport. His body was returned to Baltimore and buried in the family plot at Greenmount Cemetery.

OELLA

The community of Oella still remains a collection of picturesque stone houses nestled on the steep hillside along the north bank of the Patapsco. Located off Frederick Road, the main thoroughfare passing through the heart of Ellicott City, the village is bypassed by sightseers. The colorful history of this former mill town goes equally unnoticed; the town is greatly overshadowed by its historic neighbor across the river. Attention was recently focused on the community when the construction of long- awaited water and sewer lines became a reality. The controversial issue, often a political hot potato, received a tremendous amount of regional attention when revived and reviewed by the critical eyes of the media. For years, Oella had dumped its raw sewage into the Patapsco despite outcries from environmental groups. The publicity highlighted the name Oella but failed to mention its history. When the mill industry peaked along the Patapsco in the early and mid-1800s, Oella became a bustling mill town, serving two of the major mills in the area.

The Union Manufacturing Company, at one time the largest textile mill in the state and one of the largest in the country, was begun in 1808 when a group of prominent Baltimoreans, headed by John McKim, the company's first president, formed a corporation for the manufacture of cotton and cotton products. President Thomas Jefferson's embargo, prohibiting the importation of foreign cloth, opened the door for American businessmen to reinvest in an industry with an unlimited demand. Production at the Union Manufacturing Company began in an old gristmill on a 458-acre site purchased from the Ellicotts. The first report to stockholders, issued in January 1809, updated the mill's development and progress.

First Stockholders Report:

Near the Northern boundary of the land, and on the West side of the stream, stands an old millhouse which has been put in complete repair and fitted up as a machinist's shop, with lathes, etc., to be turned by water; adjoining thereto a saw mill has been erected, which is now in operation. On the same side of the stream are three small buildings which have been repaired, and are now tenanted by useful mechanics. A convenient Smith's shop has also been erected with two fires, and is occupied by a tradesman in the Company's employ. A few perches below this spot a bridge has been thrown over the river. Not far above the bridge a dam has been constructed across the falls, of the most substantial materials, and completed in a manner which promises great duration.

From this dam a race, or canal is leveled of twenty feet in breadth, extending down the east of the stream upwards of a mile and a quarter, to the commencement of the first range of mill seats. This canal is estimated to convey all the waters of the Patapsco, and besides affording a good boat navigation for that distance, has an elevation of 50 feet, 25 feet of which is intended to be used in the first range of buildings, proposed to [be] eight in number, and the remaining 25 feet in the second or lower range. Here then when the funds of the company will admit, and the situation of the country requires, the amazing number of 10,000 spindles may be kept in motion all by the same stream of water, with the expense of only one dam which is already erected, and the cutting of one canal, more than 300 perches (4,950 feet) of which are completed.

The building of one mill house was commenced late in the season. It is now nearly two stories high, 106 feet in length by 44 in breadth, and calculated to contain 500 spindles.

Contiguous to the mill seats, there have been erected five small buildings of wood, and two of stone, for the accommodation of the workmen, and one commodious stone house is now under roof for the use of the superintendent, also one small smith shop, and two stables. A good road has been opened from the works, which unites with the turnpike two miles east of Ellicott's Mills, and eight miles from Baltimore. (*American,* January 4, 1809)

The first textile mill, completed on October 6, 1809, was five stories high and housed 800 spindles. In 1811, the company had its landholdings of 865 acres resurveyed and patented under the name Oella. The Hall of Records listed the patent as "865 acres, resurveyed the twenty-fourth day of January one thousand eight hundred and ten, and called 'Oella' in commemoration of the first woman who applied herself to the spinning of Cotton on the Continent of America." The full identity of the woman whose name was given to the mill town was never discovered and remains a mysterious footnote to the mill's history. A behind-the- scenes look at the cotton mill was provided in 1811 when the British minister to the United States, Sir Augustus John Foster, visited the mill. Foster reported a cotton factory at Ellicott's Mills under the guidance of an Englishman, Matthew Waddell, who in spite of being paid two dollars a day was eager to quit the works and seek employment elsewhere. Some 220 pounds of raw cotton from New Orleans were spun daily into yarn, jean, and royal rib for vest material. Over 300 employees labored from sunrise to sunset, with a half-hour off for breakfast and an hour off for dinner. Foster noted that the workday was too long and that the workers were driven too hard.

A second mill with the same dimensions as the first was constructed in the spring of 1813. The new mill housed 5,500 spindles. The combined total of 6,300 spindles made the Union Manufacturing Company the largest manufacturer of cotton goods in the United States. The *Niles Weekly Register* of November 12, 1813, announced that the company would begin construction on a third mill as soon as the second was completed, "and begin to count upon a fourth . . . they have seats for sixteen mills in the space of a few hundred yards, to be turned by the Patapsco."

In 1815, disaster struck the mill complex. The *Baltimore American* reported the fire on Friday, December 15: "FIRE—With regret we state the destruction of the first cotton Works belonging to the Union Company of Maryland, near Ellicotts Mills—It burnt on Wednesday, but no suspicion is entertained of its being the deed of an incendiary—the loss sustained by this unfortunate incident is estimated at $60,000." Despite the uninsured loss, the company was able to regroup and resume operations after only one month of downtime.

In 1817, disaster struck again. A severe flood in August destroyed the western abutments of the dam, the head gates, and about 700 feet of the millrace bank. The untimely flood not only decimated the mill complex but severely strained the company's reserve capital. The decision was made not to rebuild the mill but to operate 5,500 spindles in the 1813 building.

In 1820, power looms (looms run by water-driven shafting) were introduced, and 150 of the new looms and 7,000 spindles were installed in a new building. The 1820 census listed the employment of 10 men, 16 boys, and 104 girls. Annual consumption was 150,000 pounds of cotton, with a production of 120,000 pounds of yarn and 240,000 yards of and 4/4 cloth. Products were advertised in Richmond and Fredericksburg, and in 1825 the company's bleached shirtings were among "Goods Exhibited in the Capitol." Even with the expansion, the mill's output was declining in the wake of competition. By the early 1820s, the Union Manufacturing Company lost its lofty ranking on the American textile scene and could be advertised as merely the largest textile mill outside New England. Once the textile industry peaked, mills such as the Union Mill faced the problem of overproduction and huge inventories. On April 26, 1834, the *Niles Weekly Register* reported that both "great cotton mills" had stopped production and several hundred workers had been furloughed. In 1838, the mill switched to the production of cotton duck. The 1850 census showed the mill making $150,000 worth of muslin and drill. In 1854, a bridge was built across the Patapsco to link the mill complex and the B&O.

It was reported in the *Maryland Journal* on October 14, 1882, that a new building (234' × 55') was being constructed at the Union factory at a cost of $20,000. The mill was built with wood floors and beams and had 400 horsepower of water. The 1867 tax ledger had listed "3 stone Factory buildings" and numerous utility buildings. In January 1887, the mill and 1,525 acres of property were advertised for sale. At the auction on February 12, the bid of $125,000 by William J. Dickey was accepted as the purchase price. After debts and liabilities were processed, only $15,000 remained to be divided among the former owners.

The life of William J. Dickey was another rags-to-riches American success story. Born in Ballymena, Northern Ireland (the same town that produced Baltimore's merchant-banker Alexander Brown), Dickey came to the United States as a small boy with his family. Disappointed in his desire to become a Presbyterian minister, Dickey went to work for his father in the wool-manufacturing business. In 1836, at the age of twenty-four with only $75 in capital, he was able to start his own weaving business. The business grew, and in 1871 Dickey was able to purchase the entire mill operation of Wetheredsville, later to become Dickeyville, just northwest of Baltimore.

Upon acquiring the Union Manufacturing Company in 1887, Dickey renamed it Oella Mills for the name previously given to the property. At the time, Oella was believed to be the old Indian name for the land. Textile production in 1895 consisted of wool jerseys, plaid linseys, cotton duck, brown sheetings, and cassimeres (a twilled fabric). The plant was called "one of the finest manufacturing concerns anywhere in the South."

After Dickey's death in 1896, the company was reorganized as W. J. Dickey and Sons, Inc. During World War I, while at work on government contracts for the production of military uniforms for the US and Italian armies, the mill complex was destroyed by fire. On January 26, 1918, a large electric globe had exploded, starting a blaze that consumed three main mill buildings and a warehouse. The company suffered damages estimated at $500,000. Again, the company rebuilt and, on July 1, 1919, opened a new glass and brick plant as its main base of operations. The last remaining building of the original Union Manufacturing Company was demolished when the plant was expanded.

During World War II, the company utilized sixty percent of the mills' output for the production of thirty-two-ounce olive-drab overcoat material. The company had survived the Great Depression and in 1934 began a record of continuous employment considered remarkable, when taking into account the fluctuating state of the economy. The employment record would stand until the 1960s, when foreign fabrics and synthetics flooded the American market and slowed production. The increased demand for double-knit products proved to be another serious setback. Double-knit fabrics could not be manufactured on the weaving machinery at the plant. As the subsequent demand for wool fabrics decreased, operating losses increased. In March 1972, following the closings of the Dickey plants in South Carolina and North Carolina, the Oella plant was shut down. The quality trademark "Dickey-Sheep Brand-Since 1838" and the marketing slogan "Fabrics with a Heritage" became mementos of a passing era. Disposal of the property left the mill intact. The building was later leased for storage space to local businesses.

Sitting high on the hillside above the Patapsco, the mill village of Oella was spared by the floods and served only as a witness to their immense destructive powers. The village today retains much of its character as a company town. The homes of log, stone, and brick embrace the span of mill village architecture from the prewar era of 1812 to the postwar era of World War I. The company houses range from eight-room frame cottages to six-room rowhouses. Many of the frame duplexes were built along the lines of those found in Baltimore, complete with ornamental cornices and decorative ironwork. In 1973, the number of former mill dwellings was 108. Federal tax lists from the 1800s, when the cotton industry peaked, record as many as 130 houses in the community. Colorful names, such as Brick Row, Herring Hill, Log Town, Granite Hill, Pleasant Hill, and Dutch Hotel, accurately described the town's streets and houses.

Life in Oella during the late 1800s and early 1900s was peaceful and pleasant. Townspeople were summoned to Sunday church service by the tolling of church bells in the center of the town. On Friday nights, the old community hall served as the local entertainment center. Tranquility was ensured by a town ordinance prohibiting any tavern or business from dispensing intoxicating beverages within the town's jurisdiction. The streets were patrolled by one police officer, who also serviced the street lamps. Community recreation consisted of a baseball team and a noted town brass band. Two doctors, paid by the company, operated a regularly scheduled clinic at the hall. The company and the town enjoyed a unique relationship built on trust and care. The consideration shown by the company toward its workers and their living conditions was reflected in the employees' attitudes and actions toward the company. During the 1930s and the Great Depression, the company provided free living quarters to its unemployed. Such thoughtfulness and kindness were never forgotten. The company was repaid on several occasions when the workers voted not to unionize, despite tremendous pressure from organized labor groups.

While the fame and fortune of the mills provided Oella with a place in the annals of Maryland history, it would be the contributions from one of its native sons that would place the name of the mill town in the pages of American history. Oella's most famous citizen was Benjamin Banneker, a black self-educated farmer, who later in life received recognition as one of the nation's outstanding mathematicians and astronomers. Banneker was born on November 9, 1731, of free parents on a small farm located along the north side of the Patapsco. His grandmother was Molly Welsh, a white English servant who was sentenced to involuntary emigration to America for stealing a bucket of milk which she vehemently swore had been kicked over by a cow. During her seven years of indentured servitude, Molly saved enough money to buy a piece of land near her former master and two slaves, one of whom was named Banaky, the son of an African king. She later set Banaky free and married him. The marriage produced four children, the oldest a daughter named Mary. Mary married a native African man, who took the name of Robert when he was given his freedom upon accepting Christianity and being baptized into the Church of England. For 7,000 pounds of tobacco, Mary and Robert purchased a farm of a hundred acres where Benjamin grew up with his three sisters and spent most of his life.

First taught to read and write by his grandmother, who took pleasure in teaching him from her imported English Bible, Benjamin intermittently attended a Quaker school near Ellicott's Mills until he was old enough to help with the heavy farm work. From an early age, he displayed a strong interest in mathematics and a keen insight into mechanics. Sometime in his twenties, he constructed a clock, using only a borrowed watch as a model. For the first forty years of his life, Banneker lived in obscurity along the Patapsco, which was still isolated from any large settlements. Although admired as a free black landowner and a master of mechanical devices, he remained unknown outside the community. The situation changed in 1774 with the arrival of the Ellicott brothers and the building of the first large-scale mill in the area. Banneker, who hovered for hours about the mill studying its machinery in motion, was befriended by George Ellicott, one of the sons of the original founders. Despite their age difference (Benjamin was forty-seven and George was eighteen), the pair met often to discuss their mutual passions of mathematics and astronomy.

Banneker's knowledge in calculating the movement of the stars and planets was recognized in his farm almanacs, which were published from 1792 until 1797. The almanacs, the most popular books in the farm region, contained astronomical calculations and information to aid farmers in planting and harvesting crops. The friendship with the Ellicott family resulted in Banneker's most noted accomplishment. In 1789, Banneker served as an assistant to Andrew Ellicott when Andrew was called upon to finish surveying the city's boundaries that would become the nation's capital, along the banks of the Potomac River. Banneker, who was then sixty years old, worked in the base camp, where he maintained the astronomical clock that was used to determine longitude of the boundary line. The survey work lasted only a few months, but Banneker's reputation as a mathematician and astronomer spread throughout the United States. On October 9, 1806, he died peacefully at his small cabin.

Banneker's obituary in the *Federal Gazette*, October 28, 1806, read:

> He was well known in the neighborhood for his quiet and peaceful demeanor, and among scientific men as an astronomer and mathematician. In early life he was instructed in the most common rules of arithmetic, and thereafter with the assistance of different authors, he was able to acquire a perfect knowledge of all the higher branches of learning . . . Mr. Banneker is a prominent instance to prove that a descendant of Africa is susceptible of as great a mental improvement and deep knowledge into the mysteries of nature as that of any other nation.

On the day of Banneker's funeral, a fire swept through his cabin, destroying his possessions, including the hand-made clock.

GRANITE

The Granite cotton mill, also known as the Granite factory, was built on the site of the former Ellicott ironworks, just below its rival, the Union Manufacturing Company. Whereas the Union mill was built on the hillside away from the river, the Granite factory was situated on the river's north bank. In 1846, the Granite Manufacturing Company was chartered and shortly thereafter construction on the mill began. The four-story granite mill (168' × 48') was equipped with steam heating and gaslight and contained two overshot wheels capable of using the whole volume of the river. Inside the plant, 101 muslin and drill looms were operated. A one-story foundry with an iron roof (85' × 75') and a three-story machine shop with an iron roof (84' × 45'), previously used as a shovel factory, completed the mill complex. In 1863 the works was sold to W. W. Spence for $36,000.

Mills along the Patapsco: Avalon, Orange Grove,
Ilchester, Gray's Mill, Oella, Granite, and Daniels

On July 24, 1868, the mill, advertised as "newly erected at a cost of $190,000," with a dam valued at $25,000 and dwellings worth $250,000, was reduced to rubble by the flood. Located on a sharp bend along the river canyon, the mill had acted as a breakwater, temporarily holding back the rising floodwaters. As the water rose higher and higher, the stone building, with walls twenty feet thick, began to crumble. Moments later, the mill and tower collapsed with a thunderous roar, unleashing a forty-foot tidal wave on the lower valley. After the flood, the Union Manufacturing Company leased the grounds and the remains of the granite dwellings. In 1875, the same company took title to the property but made no effort to replace the ill-fated mill, which only briefly lived up to its name as the "rock of the Patapsco."

DANIELS

The first mill at the site later known as Daniels was erected in 1840 when the Elysville Manufacturing Company was formed to manufacture cotton and woolen goods. In 1845, the partnership, consisting of the Ely brothers—Thomas, Asher, Beale, and William—and Hugh Balderson, ran into financial difficulties in operating the three-story stone mill. The group decided to form a new corporation and to solicit needed funds from new stockholders. Carrying out the corporate strategy, the Elysville Company sold the mill to the newly formed and incorporated Okisko Company in exchange for $25,000 of Okisko stock. The Okisko Company was founded by Lemuel W. Gosnell, William P. Bangs, Francis T. King, Thomas Meredith, Richard Sewell, and Thomas Hambleton.

Even with new money pumped into the company and physical improvements made to the mill, the business floundered. In July 1849, trustees were appointed by the court to sell the property of Okisko to pay off creditors. At this time, the Elysville Company, which maintained a separate existence under the corporate reorganization, brought suit against the Okisko Company. The Elysville Company claimed that the sale to the Okisko Company should have been voided, because Thomas Ely as president of the Elysville Company did not have the authority to sell the company. It also claimed that the Elysville Company did not have the authority to hold stock in another company, and that the initial agreement required payment in cash rather than in stock. The Elys requested that the mill be returned or sold for their benefit.

The suit was dismissed, and on September 29, 1849, the mill was auctioned for $21,000 to Hugh Ely, who had left the family firm. After receiving the property, Hugh sued the trustees, claiming that the property had been falsely advertised. Ely claimed that the property had been advertised with a fifteen-foot fall but had at most a fourteen-foot fall. He further stated that his brothers, Thomas in particular, had objected to his emptying the Okisko tailrace opposite the works. The court ruled that it was Ely's own folly to buy the company without finding out about the outflow rights. The court also held that the property was not misrepresented, and, as an original member of the Okisko firm, Ely had knowledge far superior to the trustees. Appeals reached the state's highest court three times before finally being rejected.

Throughout the 1850s, the mill was bought and sold by a number of corporations, many of which were reorganizations of previous owners. At one time, the mill was owned by the Alberton Manufacturing Company. Jacob Albert, the owner and a former Okisko creditor, gave the 106-member community—which consisted of the mill, an oakum factory, a store, a church, and a school—the name Alberton. After the 1857 panic, the mill was reorganized as the Sagouan Manufacturing Company. In 1861, James Sullivan Gary and his son Albert formed a partnership and took control of the mill. It was the elder Gary's wealth and influence that resulted in another son, James A., being appointed postmaster general under the McKinley administration. James A. Gary also served as the principal leader of the Maryland Republican party until his death in 1920.

Under the ownership of Gary, the mill prospered and became a financial success. In 1860, the mill employed 50 men and 120 women and operated 120 looms and 3,000 spindles. During the Civil War, the company received several large government contracts for canvas tents. By 1915, the mill complex had grown to include the main mill (with 400 employees and 14,000 spindles), a carding room, cloth room, dryer building, wheel house, belt house, heating plant, carpenters' shop, general stores, two schools, three churches, and a fire brigade of twenty men.

Following World War I, business at the mill slowed. The failure to update and modernize equipment hindered production efforts for decades. The Great Depression nearly succeeded in closing the mill permanently. Many employees were forced to accept cutbacks in work schedules; they could work only one or two days a week. After defaulting on a loan from the Reconstruction Finance Corporation, the owners were forced to sell the business at auction.

On November 23, 1940, C. R. Daniels Company of New Jersey purchased the mill, the village, and over 500 acres for $65,000. At the time of the purchase, the complex consisted of 550 acres fronting the Patapsco, a three-story stone mill (48' × 230'), a machine shop (30' × 60'), a brick seizing house (28' × 46'), 118 dwellings averaging 5 rooms each, spindles, and a concrete dam furnishing 400 horsepower and generating surplus electricity that was sold to the Baltimore Gas and Electric Company.

The demand for canvas and denim generated during World War II revived the industry and continued to sustain the mill during the postwar years. In 1968, the Daniels Company razed all the company houses, claiming it could not afford the expense of bringing the buildings into compliance with housing code standards. Many of the dwellings still lacked interior plumbing when they were finally demolished. The mill continued to operate until 1972 when Tropical Storm Agnes swept through the mill complex, literally washing away the industry. The property then passed through a number of owners, at one time selling for a paltry $25,000. In 1973, the mill complex was placed on the National Register of Historic Places. In September 1978, a fire gutted the main mill building, destroying the few remaining traces of its checkered past.

CHAPTER SEVEN

River Communities: Relay, Woodstock, Granite, Sykesville, and Mount Airy

RELAY

In 1829, as America's first gandy dancers finished laying the track between Baltimore and Ellicott's Mills, carpenters were constructing a relay station just east of the Patapsco River Valley where the tracks headed north to follow the river. Unlike other communities that grew up secondary to the railroad, Relay was created out of necessity and convenience. Until the B&O officially opened the line to Ellicott's Mills, the station and stables at Relay served as the first terminal. Located approximately seven-and-a-half miles from Baltimore and five-and-a-half miles from Ellicott's Mills, the site was the most suitable for the first horse-drawn trains. Not only was it close to midpoint between the two terminals, it was also the last piece of suitable terrain before the rails turned up the steep river valley. Here teams of fresh horses from the nearby B&O farms (later the site of the Calvert distillery) were stabled. When trains pulled into the station, teams were changed and passengers were given the opportunity for a light meal. As commercial and residential business increased in the area, Relay was the name given to the railroad station and the nearby community.

Following the opening of the Washington branch in 1835, a "mealing station" was built to provide hot meals to long-distance travelers. During the Civil War, Relay House played host to Union regiments whose mission was to protect and defend the vital railroad link. In the late 1860s, the station also included a continuous row of frame buildings: a baggage room, an agent's express office, and a post office, which stood on the south side of the Washington branch. By 1870, railroad technology made Relay nothing more than a whistle-stop. Faster steam engines eliminated the need for comfort, maintenance, and meal stops. With each passing train, the future of Relay grew dimmer.

In July 1872, however, Relay received a new lease on life when construction began on a combination hotel-station. In an unusual move, B&O President

The Viaduct Hotel in the early 1900s. The obelisk at left center was erected to commemorate the completion of the Thomas Viaduct. *Courtesy Enoch Pratt Free Library.*

John W. Garrett selected Relay as the site for one of the B&O's showcase hotel-stations, which were being built along the line from Baltimore to Chicago. The hotel was to serve as a transfer point and meal stop for passengers traveling from Midwestern cities to Philadelphia and New York. Passengers were scheduled to arrive thirty minutes ahead of trains from Washington and dine at the hotel while awaiting their next departure. At the time, the B&O's service terminated in Baltimore.

The site for the hotel-station was the center of the Y formed by the junction of the main branch and the Washington branch, which was adjacent to the Thomas Viaduct. Built in a Gothic style with blue Patapsco granite and red Seneca stone trimmings, the building was an architectural cross between a Victorian mansion and a medieval castle. The hotel section consisted of a three-story main building (55' × 70'), which featured a huge dining room (25' × 50'). The two-story station, which fronted the hotel, was 43' × 52' with a waiting room 23' × 40'. A handsome two-story rear porch with ornamental iron railing overlooked the river and offered a spectacular panoramic view of the valley. Decorative dormers, turrets, and towers accented the top floors. Steep angled slate roofs of various patterns and colors topped with iron cresting covered the entire structure. The building was heated by steam and lighted by gas produced on the site. The kitchen and laundry, which were situated in an outbuilding, were connected to the serving and dining rooms by an enclosed porch. Three sides of the building were surrounded by a large oak platform. The rear or river side featured a garden of graveled walkways, flowers, hedges, and evergreens, highlighted by a white marble monument in honor of the Thomas Viaduct. The Viaduct Hotel, with a total cost of $50,078.41, opened in August 1873.

Prior to the opening of the hotel-station, accommodations for ill or weary travelers had been limited, and food service dismal. It was to remedy this situation that the B&O had decided to establish its own facilities. The Viaduct Hotel not only supplied comfortable overnight accommodations but also provided stopover patrons with good food in a pleasant dining atmosphere. To prevent passengers from fearing that the train would leave without them, the conductor was served at a table in full view of the dining room. He did not rise from his table until the twenty or twenty-five minutes for the stop were expended.

For the convenience of those who desired only light refreshments and meals, a lunchroom was established in one of the larger waiting rooms. The service and hospitality of the hotel became renowned in railroad circles. Railroad travelers were often heard to say they would not think of passing Relay without entering the hotel for at least a cup of coffee. Mr. Thomas R. Sharpe, master of transportation, would often say that he was not at all dissatisfied if the hotel did not make a profit; the good will and advertisement secured by the personalized service was a sufficient return on the investment. Railroad officials believed that if everything possible was done for the comfort and convenience of the passengers, they would continue to use the line and induce their friends to do the same. At the time the hotel was constructed, it was said to be the first such structure erected by a railroad for exclusive use by railroad passengers.

Although the heyday of the Viaduct Hotel for railroad passengers was to last only to the late 1880s, when parlor, dining, and sleeping cars were introduced, the hotel and village were to gain an immense popularity that would last until the early 1900s. By the turn of the century, Relay had become a popular summer tourist attraction for many Baltimoreans. Before the opening of Druid Hill Park and other recreational and amusement parks in Baltimore, Relay provided a convenient spot to which city people could escape and enjoy open grounds and fresh air.

Near the railroad station were a dancing pavilion and bandstand surrounded by a grove of trees. Near the pavilion, carnival booths offered prizes to those who tested their abilities at games of chance and skill. For patrons more inclined to experience the peace and quiet of the country, paths leading down to the river offered the chance to take a leisurely stroll or have an uninterrupted picnic under a canopy of leaves and sky. During the summer, scarcely a week passed without one or more train excursions arriving. Special trains brought vacationers from Baltimore early in the morning, and returned them home late in the evening. The most disheartening sound amid the merriment was a loud whistle blast from the steam engine, signaling it was time to head for home.

Another nearby excursion destination offered more amusements, such as bowling and the ever-popular rides. Swings and flying horses allowed the more daring day tripper with a cast-iron stomach to briefly defy the laws of gravity. The flying horses were quite different from today's versions. A large center pole was set up and guyed with four booms, each suspending a two-seat frame. When all the seats were filled, two men stationed near the center would push the boom around.

The highlight of every summer season was the Fourth of July. Additional trains accommodated the thousands who eagerly awaited the annual outing. Round-trip tickets were an affordable twenty-five cents. The park near the Viaduct Hotel, filled with flowers and shrubs, was a popular gathering spot for the older celebrators and offered a refuge form the noise and excitement of the holiday festivities. The flying horses spun around almost nonstop, seemingly ready to lift off the ground. Orchestra music filled the air and echoed down the river valley as couples swirled and twirled in the dancing pavilion. Smoke filled the air near the booth where cigars could be won by tossing baseballs at a man's head sticking through a canvas backdrop. Adults bought large mugs of beer from a long table set up each year by the portly German manager of the hotel. Meals were served under the shade of the trees outside the hotel. Yankee Bell of Elkridge operated an ice-cream and soft-drink stand. Crowds lined the riverbanks as far as one could see, and lovesick couples embraced and kissed out in the open. Ball games with beer kegs at the bases always drew a large number of participants and spectators more interested in the bases than the score. In the evening, the railroad put on a fireworks display while the Elkridge Band played "The Star- Spangled Banner," "Yankee Doodle," and "My Country 'Tis of Thee." So much litter and debris were left after these outings that the B&O discontinued holiday rail service in the early 1900s.

With the end of summer outings, Relay became a railroad ghost town. The long row of freight offices was abandoned and later torn down. The Viaduct Hotel witnessed only the passing of military freight and troop trains during the Spanish-American War and World War I. Troops often stopped at the hotel while awaiting rail transportation to their duty stations. With the repeal of the Prohibition amendment in 1933, local businessmen hoped that the station-hotel would survive as a freight station for shipping distilled liquors. The business failed to materialize, and in 1938 the hotel was abandoned and boarded up to keep out vandals and railroad hobos. The building was razed in 1950 and later a commemorative plaque was placed at the site.

Although Relay faded from railroad maps as the automobile became the preferred method of transportation, the railroad community survived. The surrounding hillsides on the north side of the tracks were first settled by B&O officials who rode to work with free railroad passes. As Baltimore's residential development expanded into the surrounding counties, more property owners settled in the area. Across the tracks, the town of St. Denis was created by this new breed of suburban commuter. St. Denis was the name originally given to the community's post office. In the early days of the railroad, Denis A. Smith, who claimed to be a former state treasurer, bought property at the junction of Sutton and Washington Avenues and built a luxurious stone house for his residence. A high roller who entertained lavishly and extensively, Smith was jokingly nicknamed "St. Denis" by his associates. When the post office was finally built, it was named after the man who was instrumental in the structure's funding and construction.

Smith's 400 acres in Relay were later sold to Samuel Sutton. The low swampy land, called Chile Valley before being renamed St. Denis, was drained and turned into fine pastures for Sutton's herds of imported livestock. After the Civil War, the property was sold to real estate developers, who divided it into building lots. Chartered trains brought excursionists from Baltimore to attend auctions of these lots. Rebates of $100 to the first taker, $75 to the second, and $50 to the third were used as inducements to lure prospective buyers. The small-scale real estate boom saw the area change seemingly overnight from a rural community to a suburban village.

When the Thomas Viaduct opened up the western side of the Patapsco in 1835, affluent Baltimoreans took advantage of the opportunity and built country estates and summer retreats on the wooded hillsides overlooking the river valley. This land was once part of the 1,600-acre Belmont estate belonging to Caleb Dorsey. By 1917, when the estate passed into the hands of Mary Bowdoin Bruce, only 720 acres of the original Dorsey estate belonged to Belmont. The property had been sold and subsequently divided into a number of smaller parcels.

In 1840, Judge George W. Dobbin selected a piece of land on the southern bank above the river to build his estate, The Lawn. The site — offering seclusion and a retreat from city life but still convenient to the cities of Baltimore and Washington by either rail or horse-drawn carriage — soon attracted another legal professional. John H. B. Latrobe followed Dobbin's example and built the architectural wonder named Fairy Knowe. The country home, a charming mix of gingerbread house and medieval castle with ornamental woodwork and ribbed towers topped by cone-shaped roofs, was built on property described by Latrobe as "the very lovely spot which has grown to its present beauty from the end of the spur of a chestnut ridge overlooking the Patapsco, where this stream breaks through the primitive rock to wind its way through alluvial land to the Chesapeake Bay . . . as pretty a place as there is in Maryland." (Young 1937) In 1850, Fairy Knowe caught fire and burned to the ground. By the time Latrobe was able to rush there from his Baltimore office, the house was a mound of smoldering ruins. Fairy Knowe was rebuilt, using the design of the original building. Tradition says that Latrobe had the site cleared of debris by midnight, and the next day had contractors working. Within two months, a second Fairy Knowe was completed. The house stood for a number of years, until it again fell to the ravages of fire. No plans were ever made for a third Fairy Knowe.

Thomas N. Donaldson, a distinguished Baltimore attorney and leader in the Howard County Bar until his death in 1877, built Edgewood in 1843, a large country home described as luxurious but not frivolous. The building boom, which attracted legal professionals and the social elite, did not go unnoticed by local residents, who quickly dubbed the area Lawyer's Hill.

Throughout its existence, Relay witnessed history in the making. The tracks at the main junction moved the men and machinery that moved the nation. In the 1800s, a number of presidents rode their way into history books along rails through Relay. On June 6, 1833, Andrew Jackson boarded the train at Ellicott's Mills for a pleasure trip to Baltimore and became the first president to ride on a railroad train. A few months earlier, John Quincy Adams had made the same trip, but after he had left the presidency. On February 14, 1845, James K. Polk became the first president-elect to travel by train to his inauguration when, after traveling by coach from Cumberland to Relay, he boarded the train for the ride to Washington. President-elect Abraham Lincoln passed through Relay en route to his inauguration in January 1861. In early October 1862, he changed trains at Relay on his way to Harper's Ferry; along the way he stopped and visited the Antietam battlefield. A year later, in November 1863, he traveled through Relay on his way to Gettysburg, Pennsylvania, where he delivered his famous Gettysburg Address at the dedication of the national military cemetery.

Of all the historical events connected with Relay, none had more impact than the application of the electric telegraph. In 1843, Samuel F. B. Morse, inventor of the telegraph, secured permission for his Magnetic Telegraph Company to build an experimental line along the B&O right-of-way between Baltimore and Washington. The line would pass through Relay, run along the Thomas Viaduct, and then proceed to Washington. It was Morse's original intention to lay underground wires along the sleepers of the B&O's Washington branch. In November 1843, a lead pipe carrying four insulated copper wires was buried ten to twelve inches from a signal station at Mount Clare Station to the Relay House. Testing done at this time showed that none of the wires was sufficiently insulated to conduct electricity. Plans for underground construction were immediately abandoned, at a cost of $15,000, half of the budget allotted by Congress.

John H. B. Latrobe, who recommended construction of the telegraph line to B&O officials, wrote an interesting description of the event in his memorandum of the period:

> In these days, incredulity as to Morse's success was very general, and the majority hooted at the idea of an electrical telegraph.
>
> It is my impression that Mr. Morse's description to me contemplated a double wire, one for each direction. I have no recollection of his referring to the earth as completing the circuit. I know, however, that the idea of the present poles was not what he began with. His wires were crossed with threadlike women's bonnet wires, and were enclosed in a three-inch pipe which coiled on a spool in the rear of a plow and laid in the furrow which it made, being carried by a couple of rollers that pressed the earth, removed by the share, upon the tube.
>
> This plan was pursued as far as the Relay House seven miles from Baltimore. There was double difficulty met here. The furrow could not be made across the bridge [Thomas Viaduct], and the water condensed in the tube and destroyed the insulation. This led to the adoption of the poles, which I have every reason to believe that Mr. Morse regarded at first as but a temporary contrivance.
>
> My country residence being hard by the Relay House, I saw the work going on from day to day. (Latrobe 1868)

Morse solved his problem by stringing the telegraph wire along poles. In April 1844, after developing an effective but primitive telegraph pole, Morse resumed construction from the Washington end of the line. The line was completed without further delay, and on May 24, 1844, Morse sent the first electric telegraph message, "What hath God wrought," between the Supreme Court chamber in Washington and the B&O's Pratt Street Station in Baltimore.

WOODSTOCK

Woodstock remains, as it has for years, a collection of frame houses scattered on the rolling hillside above the Patapsco's south bank, approximately six miles above Ellicott City. At one time a post office, a tavern, and a railroad station stood by the tracks, designating the village. A number of handsome summer houses lined the hillside, making the village a retreat for the wealthy seeking to escape city life. The station was torn down in 1951 after passenger service along the line was discontinued. The post office is now west above the ridge, while a tavern is still near the tracks.

The origins of the village remain obscure. It is believed that the name is taken from the English town of Woodstock, on the River Glyme. The name dates back to Anglo-Saxon times, when the English town was called Wudestoc, meaning a clearing in the woods. The records of the B&O show the main line extending west to the Forks of the Patapsco, while passing Davis' Tavern at the site of the village. The first settler in the Woodstock area was Thomas Brown, who was appointed ranger of the Patuxent region in 1692. Brown surveyed two tracts of land along the Patuxent and established a plantation called Ranter's Ridge, running roughly southwest from what is now called Woodstock. Brown's son Joshua inherited Ranter's Ridge and disposed of it in three parcels. The name Woodstock first appeared in 1836, when the US Post Office was opened at "Woodstock, Anne Arundel County [later Howard County], Maryland." By 1838, the northern part of Anne Arundel County had been given its own organization as the Howard District, and in 1851 it became a separate county.

During the early 1830s, when the B&O began to stretch west from Ellicott's Mills, the settlement started to take shape. The work of building the roadbed for nearby sections of track was contracted to two local builders, Peter Gorman and Caleb Davis. In 1848, the B&O acquired land for a station at Woodstock and for many years it shipped granite from local quarries to Baltimore and other major Eastern cities. With the passing of the railroad and the closing of the major quarries, the economy returned to farm commodities, mainly wheat and corn, for its economic base.

Henry Gassaway Davis, US senator from West Virginia, was born in Woodstock, and Arthur Pue Gorman, US senator from Maryland, grew up in Woodstock and received his education in the county's free schools. In the post-Civil War years, the town's leading citizen was Brigadier General James Rawlings Herbert. A lieutenant colonel commanding Maryland units in the Confederate Army, Herbert was a veteran of the valley campaigns and a wounded hero of Gettysburg. When Herbert's Maryland regiment was in the Patapsco River Valley and bogged down for lack of transportation, Woodstock farmers rallied to his assistance and supplied enough wagons to enable Herbert and his men to rejoin the main body of the Confederate Army. Federal authorities took a dim view of outwardly aiding the enemy. Beale Cavey, who had recruited the rolling stock to transport Herbert's forces, was forced to temporarily hide out in the wilderness known as Soldier's Delight.

During the course of its existence, the tiny village on the south bank of the Patapsco has been praised and condemned by visitors and tourists.

In 1871, an English visitor sent home this description:

The river is like the Hodder at Stonyhurst, and it flows through the hollows of high wooded hills, wild and picturesque. The Baltimore and Ohio railroad runs along its winding course; and, at a distance of twenty-three miles from Baltimore, but only sixteen miles in a straight line, the little village of Woodstock nestles in a crevice between two hills. Indeed, a poorer apology for a village, or a feebler aspirant for municipal dignities could scarcely be imagined: for its sum total of constituents is a railway station, a post office, a few shanties and a county bridge over the Patapsco. (Jones 1873)

A Canadian visitor in 1873 was somewhat more kindly disposed:

The hills on either side of the river are abrupt and in many places precipitous, crowned with cedar groves, or woods of oak, maple, hickory, the tulip poplar, the gum, the fragrant sassafras and the more humble dogwood whose profuse white flowers in the full blossom of spring are in striking contrast with the crimson blossoms of the Judas tree, and whose blood red berries in the glow of an Indian summer show even brighter than the brilliant hues of our American forests in autumn. (Jones 1873)

As for the sluggish Patapsco, it has probably never been more lyrically described than by the same writer:

The serpentine course of the Patapsco, so far down beneath us that the noise of its waters as they dash over the rocks at the ford is toned down to a gentle murmur, the vista between the hills whose rough contour is softened by the woodlands on their slopes, the strip of fertile meadow at the margin of the stream, the island with its rank growth of reeds and willows, the stream, itself silvered by the distance and the play of light, the pearly mist hanging veil-like midway down the valley, and the haze at the horizon which, with more than artist's skill heightens the atmospheric perspective, the stark piers of the broken bridge, suggestive of scenes of violence amidst one of peace and beauty, such is the rough outline of a charming picture.

The unpretending hamlet of Woodstock, consisting of scarcely half a dozen houses, nestles snugly in a fold of the hills halfway up the southern slope, seemingly unconscious that it lies within a score of miles of one of the great centers of American civilization. (Jones 1873)

Woodstock College

The sleepy village of Woodstock was revived in 1866 when the Society of Jesus, commonly known as the Jesuits, purchased 243 acres of land on the north side of the Patapsco. On September 26, 1869, Woodstock College, or the College of the Sacred Heart as it was formally dedicated, opened its doors as the first permanent scholasticate, or house of studies, for the Society of Jesus in North America. Although located in the township of Granite, the institution derived its name from the village across the river, which served as its post office. The location, on the southwest tract originally surveyed in the late 1600s as Ranter's Ridge, was ideal. The site offered almost complete isolation, yet was only twenty-six miles from Baltimore. The only interruption in the rural tranquility was the occasional passing of a B&O train on the tracks below.

During the first phase of construction, nine acres of woodland were cleared. The main building, in the shape of an I, was made of gray-brown granite, cut and hauled from nearby Fox Quarry and then placed by hand. The 1.25 million bricks for the partition walls were burned on the premises. The main building, three stories with a dormer type roof, housed classrooms, 298 student rooms, an auditorium, an infirmary, 43 small chapels to accommodate 80 priests for daily Mass, dining rooms, offices, and guest parlors. As the college grew, the main building was expanded. The east wing and the chapel were added in 1924 and the two towers and the west wing in 1925. The science building was erected in 1927, and the O'Rourke Library, which contained 130,000 volumes, including a priceless collection of rare books and manuscripts from the fourteenth, fifteenth, and sixteenth centuries, was built in 1929. The college property expanded to 687 acres and eventually became a self- contained community. Artesian wells were drilled for water and a working farm supplied many of the daily food items. The college included a laundry, a radio station, a barbershop, a print shop, and a twenty-man volunteer fire department, which later became part of the Baltimore County system. The manicured grounds offered walking paths through gardens, and outdoor recreational facilities, which included a pool and athletic fields. At the village of Woodstock, a brick passenger station was built due to the political influence of the wife of General William Tecumseh Sherman, commander of federal armies in the West during the Civil War. General Sherman gained notoriety as the "plague inflicted on the South," when in the spring of 1864 he marched his armies through the heart of the Confederacy. Mrs. Sherman stayed in the Woodstock area for the scholastic year 1889-1890 to be on hand for the ordination of her Jesuit son, who was studying at the college. Additional complaints about the lack of communication with the outside world resulted in the B&O extending the rail telegraph line to the college.

In 1870, the college conducted its first ordination ceremonies. From that time to its closing, the college ordained and graduated more than 2,600 men to serve as administrators and professors in more than fifty prestigious Jesuit secondary schools and colleges in the United States and abroad. Many graduates engaged in pastoral and missionary duties throughout the world. The college, at one time the largest Jesuit college of theology in the world, was devoted exclusively to the final academic preparation of Jesuit seminarians for the priesthood. The four-year course of study provided a rigorous curriculum of arts and sciences, with an emphasis on church philosophy and theology. Ordination to the priesthood occurred at the end of the third year. A final or fifth year of study, called a tertianship, was offered as an option to graduates and was devoted to a renewed concentration on the spiritual before they entered the active ministry. The college granted the professional degrees of bachelor, licentiate, and doctor of sacred theology. Although physically isolated on the grounds of the college, the Jesuits did not isolate themselves from the community. The staff and seminarians were active in the local neighborhoods and performed social work in Baltimore and the nearby areas. Good relations between the Jesuits on the hill and the people of the valley continued throughout the life of the college. One instance of the warm welcome given the Jesuits occurred three months after the opening of the college, when seventy-five farmers gathered to raise the roof of the first barn on the grounds.

Woodstock College's greatest contribution to the local area was the part the faculty and seminarians played in the development of Catholic life. Before 1869, the nearest Catholic church was the chapel at Charles Carroll's Doughoregan Manor, located five miles west of Ellicott City. Within ten years, the Jesuits opened churches at Harrisonville, Elysville, and Poplar Springs. Catechism missions were established at Woodstock, Granite, Marriottsville, Elysville, Dorsey's Run, and Sykesville. In further response to the needs of the local communities, the college chapel was opened to the laity and served as a parish church until the Church of the Holy Ghost was opened in 1887. This church, later renamed St. Alphonsus, was a graceful granite structure located on the slope leading to the river, south of the college. In 1968, a fire gutted the structure, leaving only a picturesque ruin. In earlier years, before the fire, the Jesuit pastor of St. Alphonsus served as chaplain for the sanitorium at Henryton.

On August 1, 1970, in response to the need for a more challenging academic environment and greater opportunities for involvement, the Jesuit college moved to New York City. After being purchased by the State of Maryland, the college became a job training center. On February 23, 1972, after extensive renovation, Woodstock College officially reopened as a federal Job Corps Center. Its goal was to provide vocational and academic training for economically disadvantaged young adults.

GRANITE

The tranquil rural village of Granite, lying at the western end of Baltimore County where the Patapsco serves as a county border through the river valley, offers few hints of its illustrious past. Large frame houses are spread over the rolling countryside, and only the local churches with "Granite" in their names signal to the casual visitor that he or she has arrived in Granite. The granite industry, which has preserved the history of Granite in many of the nation's landmarks, still remains visible in the surrounding countryside. The abandoned quarries are now filled with water and concealed by dense woodland and thick underbrush. Narrow roadbeds constructed with a base of granite chips still wander through the woods to many of the quarries. For almost a century, the finest granite in North America was quarried from the natural crystalline rock formations. Dr. David Owen, on an inspection tour of building material sources for the Smithsonian Institution, made the following report on the Fox Rock and Waltersville quarries: "For about a mile square at this locality is an outburst of quartzose, granite of magnificent quality, both as regards beauty of appearance, compactness of structure and uniformity of color, texture and composition. I have never seen anything superior in this country. Indeed, I doubt whether it can be excelled in any country. It cannot be surpassed for strength and durability by any building material in the world." (Morgan 1967)

Bright speckled gray and composed mainly of quartz, mica, and feldspar, much of the rock at Granite was remarkable for its sharp joints, horizontal or vertical, which gave the appearance of having been built up layer by layer in huge blocks. This "jointing" was brought out by weathering as the great slabs slowly decomposed at the edges and corners over many years and became rounded, with sand in between.

These joints sometimes caused trouble in quarrying blocks and slabs. But at other times, they made quarrying fairly easy. The rocks broke cleanly when wedges driven in about three or four inches and a few inches apart in a series were tapped lightly and evenly. Rock ledges were so extensive that pillars forty to fifty feet high could be cut from the granite without a seam.

In the 1830s, the first customer of importance for the Granite quarries was the B&O, which bought stringers for tracks—slabs four to five feet long and eight to ten inches wide, dressed to correspond to the flange and tread of the car wheels.

In 1835, Putney and Riddle obtained a twenty-year lease for the Waltersville quarry, the largest in the area, from the owner, Captain Alexander Walters, a descendant of the original owner. A second quarry, Fox Rock, was operated by a Mr. Eaton and at one time was part of the Worthington estate. The last owner-operator of the quarry located in the backwoods of Woodstock College was the Peach family, who used the trade name Woodstock Granite Company.

About one mile east of Woodstock was Putney and Riddle's granite bridge. Lessees of the Waltersville quarry built a railroad two miles long from the bridge to the quarry so that slabs could be transported over the B&O. Waltersville was the only quarry served by rail facilities. The quarry company owned its own locomotive and flatcars.

The smaller quarries used horse-drawn teams and threshing machine engines to haul granite to the B&O station at Woodstock and later even to the Pennsylvania Railroad station at Ruxton. Ox teams frequently moved the slabs of granite around in the quarries. Water seepage was controlled by hand pumps.

Manual labor, mainly provided by slaves, was used during the first few decades of quarrying, beginning in the 1820s. In the most flourishing era of the Granite quarries, the 1870s through the 1890s, Fox Rock quarry employed about fifty men; Waltersville employed many more. The first steam drills were installed about 1900. Portable derricks lifted slabs weighing 50 to 100 tons each.

As many as 130 stonecutters and artisans from Scotland, Wales, England, France, and Italy were hired to work in long sheds cutting and polishing the granite rock for its many uses and custom orders. Granite dust cut up the lungs of many workers and almost solidified their bronchial tubes. As a result, a number of stonecutters died at an early age.

Using surfacing and polishing machines operated by compressed air, the workers effected a glaze and a polish so unusual that the stone was said to be unequaled by any other granite in the world. During the early 1900s, stonecutters were paid four dollars per day. Laborers received seventeen cents per hour. The working day was from 7:00 a.m. to 5:00 p.m., with one hour for lunch.

From the Waltersville and Fox Rock quarries at Granite came blocks used in the construction of numerous Washington, DC, buildings, including the Smithsonian Institution, the Library of Congress, the old US Treasury Department, the Patent Office extension, the main Post Office, and parts of the inner walls of the Washington Monument. In Baltimore, granite from Granite was used in building the Custom House, the old Post Office Building, the Court House, a monument to the Sons and Daughters of the American Revolution on Mount Royal Avenue, the Polytechnic Institute, St. Ambrose Catholic Church, the Fidelity Building, and many other churches, cemetery monuments, and commercial buildings.

The railroad viaduct at Relay was built of Granite's stone, as was one of the main buildings at Hood College in Frederick, Maryland. Locally, the main building at Woodstock College and St. Alphonsus Catholic Church in Woodstock were built with granite from the Fox Rock quarry. Major construction projects, in which material from Granite's quarries was used, were the Pressor Building in Philadelphia, a public building in Cuba, and the US Naval Hospital in Washington, DC. Up until 1900, all of the stone used in the National Cemetery at Arlington, Virginia, came from Granite. The nine bridges along the Mount Vernon Highway from 14th Street in Washington, DC, to Mount Vernon, Virginia, were built of granite from Granite. Stone for the Studebaker Monument, in South Bend, Indiana, came from Granite quarries. A by-product of Granite quarries was crushed stone used for roadbeds.

In the 1920s and 1930s, when the construction industry turned to building materials easier to handle and obtain, the quarry industry at Granite faded. As the demand for cheaper housing increased, the demand for granite lessened. Belgian blocks, cobblestones, and granite curbs for streets and roadways were replaced by asphalt and concrete. The hard, heavy stone blocks from Granite were supplanted by softer North Carolina granite and Indiana limestone. Cement and concrete blocks and the introduction of prefabricated building supplies dealt the fatal blow to the industry. Drills and hammers were silenced forever when the quarries at Granite were squeezed out by competing industries and new trends in construction.

In 1956, modern technology found a brief home at Granite. The US Army and the Department of the Defense utilized the upper plateau on the north side of the Patapsco for the installation of a Nike-Hercules antiaircraft missile base. The missiles were removed in the late 1960s when advancements in rocket weaponry made them obsolete.

SYKESVILLE

The arrival of the B&O in 1831 saw a rural farm village along the banks of the Patapsco develop into a prosperous town with a colorful and romantic history. The town was named after James Sykes, the son of John Sykes, a famous Baltimore merchant. In 1825, James Sykes bought 1,000 acres from the Springfield estate of the Patterson family. One of the land tracts included the site of the town, which at the time consisted of a sawmill and a gristmill. Recognizing the potential of the property with the coming of the railroad, Sykes in 1831 replaced the old mill and constructed a five-story hotel next to the tracks. The town quickly developed as a summer vacation spot for tourists from Baltimore, and the hotel gained a reputation as one of the finest in Maryland.

In 1845, Sykes enlarged his stone mill and converted it into the Howard Cotton Factory. Company houses for mill workers were constructed, and businesses were established, creating a company town. Prior to the recession of 1857, the mill employed over 200 workers. For a short period during the Civil War, the mill was run by James A. Gary. In 1847, the Elba Furnace was erected by James W. Tyson, on the north bank of the Patapsco about 150 feet east of the railroad station. It was a steam and water charcoal furnace 30 feet high and 8.5 feet wide. The stack was built of granite lined with brick. During thirty-three weeks in 1855, 956 tons of car-wheel were produced. The bulk of the ore for the furnace was obtained from the Springfield mine north of the town. In addition to the local businesses involved in lumber, lime, coal, and fertilizers, iron and copper mines were opened on the Springfield estate of George Patterson, the son of William Patterson.

The Flood of 1868 swept away much of the town of Sykesville and its industry. The mill, hotel, and business district disappeared under the floodwaters. When the river receded, only stone foundations were left. Wary merchants and citizens rebuilt the town along the higher ground on the river's north side. In 1972, Tropical Storm Agnes caused severe water damage, but it did not succeed in destroying the town.

At the foot of the business district, the railroad station stands along the side of the river, a constant reminder of the town's link to the railroad. The history of Sykesville has always been tied to the developments of the railroad. The town became the scene of one of the most dramatic confrontations between labor and management during the building of the B&O. Sporadic labor problems, arising from the work force, plagued the B&O in the early years and reached a climax when serious riots broke out at Sykes Mills in the spring of 1831. No sooner had the bad reports about Truxton Lyon, the highly recommended contractor, filtered into Baltimore, when word came that Lyon's workmen had walked off the job. Superintendent Stabler was immediately dispatched to the scene and within minutes after arriving reached a temporary truce by promising the workers that the directors of the railroad would see to their needs. Despite this hasty agreement, the situation remained tense. Lyon had somehow gone in debt to the workers for a considerable amount in back wages. Unless the money was paid immediately, the workers threatened to tear up the track.

As promised, John H. B. Latrobe made the trip to Sykes Mills and entered into an agreement with the workers. Latrobe distributed some $2,000, due Lyon as payment for his contract, to the workers who were stranded without money or credit. The tension eased, and Latrobe returned to Baltimore, thinking the matter settled. When the workers realized that only $2,000 had been paid to them, they once again called on Stabler and protested bitterly that they had been duped by the railroad and Lyon. It appeared that the actual sum due the workers was closer to $9,000, and Latrobe's payment was construed as a bribe to keep them working for little or no wages. The workers demanded a cash payment, in full, on the barrel head. When Lyon tried to explain that he would have to return to Baltimore and consult with the directors to get the money, the workers marched over to the track and began pulling up the rails.

Stabler, realizing the desperate situation, quickly returned to Baltimore and, on the advice of Latrobe, obtained a riot warrant, which was turned over to the sheriff. The sheriff, Stabler, and the posse, consisting of only William Patterson, proceeded to Sykes Mills to quell the uprising. The inevitable showdown between labor and management was not long in coming. Some 135 workers walked down the line behind a makeshift flag, armed with stone hammers and construction tools. Both parties stopped within a few feet of each other along the tracks east of Sykes Mills. The silent seconds of uneasy stares, which seemed like hours, were disrupted when Hugh Reily, one of the leaders for the workmen, came forward and seized Stabler's horse by the bridle. Hard words were exchanged, and the verbal confrontation served to incite and anger the workers. To ease the difficult situation and effect their own escape, the three men capitulated to the workers' demands and returned to Baltimore.

At a meeting of the directors, it was decided to end the uprising as quickly as possible by whatever means necessary. The warrant was turned over to Brigadier General Steuart, who embarked immediately on a special train with over 100 militiamen. Arriving at dawn in a surprise move, the soldiers arrested fifty of the rebellious workers, including Hugh Reily. A new contractor was hired, and the work on Lyon's original contract was completed without further incident. Whether the workers were ever fully paid was not mentioned in any official records pertaining to the incident.

Through the Springfield estate of the Patterson family, part of which became Sykesville and another part of which became Sykesville State Hospital, the Patapsco claims a connection to one of the most intriguing love affairs in American history. The international romance, played out against a background of a rising monarch and his new nobility, captured a worldwide audience. Betsy Patterson, the daughter of William Patterson, a wealthy and influential Baltimore merchant, achieved universal fame when she became the bride of Prince Jerome Bonaparte, the youngest brother of Napoleon I.

Born into the aristocracy of colonial America, Betsy received the proper education required for one of Baltimore's Southern belles. Lessons in the social graces, well learned in the finest schools and academies, would allow Betsy to easily circulate among the elite of high society. Her gracefulness and beauty were captured by the noted colonial portrait painter Gilbert Stuart, on her eighteenth birthday in 1803. The essence of her beauty — hazel eyes, dark curly hair, soft clear skin, delicate facial features, and graceful sloping shoulders — was impeccably mirrored and interpreted by the artist's skillful brush. Betsy claimed that Stuart had been the only painter to bring her beauty to life on canvas. In her later years, when time had stolen the innocent beauty of her youth, it was said that Betsy would often stand admiringly before this portrait.

During the early 1800s, Europe was in upheaval. Napoleon Bonaparte, riding the wave of success for his military campaign in Italy, became first consul and the most powerful man in France. Jerome, fifteen years younger than his famous brother, was swept into a seat of political power, as were his sisters and his other brothers. A supporting role in the new nobility was well suited to the handsome youth, who delighted in wearing colorful military uniforms. After a brief adventure in Haiti as part of a military expedition, Jerome concocted an excuse for making a trip to the United States. After wending his way to Washington, the social hub of the States, Jerome befriended Commodore Joshua Barney. Barney became his social tour guide and invited Jerome on a number of occasions to see the sights and sounds in the bustling seaport of Baltimore. While on one of these social excursions to Baltimore, the young Bonaparte was first introduced to Betsy Patterson.

Every Baltimore socialite claimed to have hosted the party where the eyes of these lovers first met. One of the more romantic stories tells of a prophetic incident at a ball where a gold chain worn by Betsy became entangled in Jerome's uniform. Betsy herself claimed that their first meeting was at a fashionable dinner party given by Louis Pascault, the Marquis de Poleon, in honor of his daughter. Infatuation quickly blossomed into love, and the couple became the toast of Washington's social circle. The concern of French officials in the United States and the disapproval of William Patterson failed to cool the romance, as did a forced period of separation.

Eventually, and reluctantly, William Patterson consented to the marriage. Bishop John Carroll, a personal friend of Patterson, graciously consented to perform the ceremony at the Patterson home. To give the marriage the appearance of official sanction, the social event of the year 1803 was attended by the mayor of Baltimore and the French consul of state.

When Napoleon learned of the marriage, he was outraged. Jerome had not only violated French law by contracting a marriage without his family's consent but also interfered with Napoleon's plans for strengthening his political position through nepotism prior to declaring himself emperor of France. Napoleon appealed to Pope Pius VII to annul the marriage; the pontiff refused. Napoleon then ordered Jerome to return to France, but Jerome ignored the mandate. In 1805, Jerome and Betsy sailed to Lisbon in an attempt to persuade Napoleon to allow them into France. Napoleon, embarrassed and angered by the actions of his brother, remained adamant in not allowing Madame Jerome Bonaparte to set foot on French soil. When the French council of state, at the direction of Napoleon, declared the marriage illegal, Jerome deserted Betsy and returned to France. In spite of promises to rejoin her shortly, Jerome never again saw Betsy, except for an accidental glimpse of her many years later on a chance meeting in the streets of London. For his obedience, Jerome was elevated to the throne of the newly created kingdom of Westphalia, and given a royal wife, Catherine, the daughter of the king of Wurtemberg.

Denied entry into France after Jerome left her, Betsy took refuge in London, where she gave birth to a son, Jerome Napoleon. Despite an occasional letter from Jerome declaring his eternal devotion, Betsy had given up all hope of ever being reunited with her husband.

In 1815, through the influence of William Patterson, the Maryland Legislature granted Betsy a divorce. In 1840, at the age of fifty-six, Betsy returned from Europe to reside permanently in Baltimore, a city she openly scorned. Her attitude was most peculiar in light of the fact she was treated like royalty in her hometown. At the time of Napoleon's death, Betsy made a point of praising his genius even though she had said "he hurled me back on what I hated most on earth, my Baltimore obscurity." (Beirne 1957)

Betsy was last remembered on the streets of Baltimore as a withered, miserly old lady who carried a dilapidated umbrella and lived in a one-room apartment in a boardinghouse on Cathedral Street. As a result of the trouble and expense incurred by her father during the romance with Jerome, she was left only a few city lots and houses in his will. William Patterson had at one time been the second wealthiest man in the state (the wealthiest was Charles Carroll, who was reputed to be one of the wealthiest men in the country). Betsy lived off the income from her rental properties and remained a noted figure until her death in 1879 at the age of 94.

The family line of the American Bonapartes was short-lived. Betsy's son, Jerome, nicknamed "Bo," had only two sons, Jerome and Charles Joseph. Jerome left the country to serve in the French navy, and little was ever known in the United States about his descendants. Charles Joseph remained in Baltimore and became one of its most distinguished citizens. He served in Theodore Roosevelt's cabinet as attorney general and later as secretary of the navy. He died leaving no heirs to the Bonaparte name. His passing marked the end of one of the most colorful and glamorous international episodes in American history.

MOUNT AIRY

Situated on the crest of Parr's Ridge in the southwestern corner of Carroll County, Mount Airy remains an important but unnoticed link in the history of the Patapsco because just south of the neighboring community of Ridgeville, the Patapsco has its beginning at a small farm pond known as Parr's Spring.

Mount Airy, conveniently located in the rich farm and dairy lands of four counties, has achieved a position of importance as a business center. Servicing farm operations, local industries, and residential communities, the town enjoys a healthy business environment unequaled by rural towns of similar size. The residential sections, populated by an ever-increasing number of commuters forsaking city life, are spread out over several hills completely surrounding the business and shopping district. From the heights of Parr's Ridge, a panorama of landscaped farmland, framed by lines of woodland, unfolds against the distant background of sky and the foothills of the Blue Ridge Mountains.

Mount Airy had its beginning in the early 1830s, when the main line of the B&O extended its rails from Ellicott's Mills to Frederick. At the time, it was reported that six families settled the area, headed by the Bussard family, who owned much of the original town. An Irish railroad worker is given credit for giving Mount Airy its name. The story claims the worker remarked the weather was rather "airish." It was then agreed that the country would be called Mount Airy.

With the cultivation of the surrounding farmlands and the development of the railroad, which built a spur leading into the town, Mount Airy began a slow but steady growth. Schools, churches, and businesses were built to meet the needs of the people. In 1846, the Ridge Presbyterian Church, financed by Henry Bussard, became the first permanent church in the small settlement. During the Civil War, the church, located on Mount Airy's highest hill, served as the headquarters for Company K of the New Jersey militia, who were guarding the railroad station. An unknown Confederate soldier was the first soldier to be buried in the Pine Grove Cemetery.

In 1888, Mount Airy numbered about 30 homes and 100 residents. The tranquility of the quiet, rather religious community was shattered in 1890, when the B&O decided to build a half-mile tunnel outside Ridgeville. The village became an overnight boom town, home for an estimated 300 rough, brawling, hard-drinking railroad construction workers. In the early 1890s, it was reportedly unsafe for unescorted women to venture out on any of the town's streets. While the railroad and its workers pumped large sums of money into the local economy, they remained unpopular guests. Saloons became social centers for the workers and provided them with much-needed entertainment. In response to the new construction and population boom, a jail was built to temporarily house the more boisterous and unruly.

Prior to the construction of the tunnel, trains had been forced to make the long and slow ascent to the summit of Parr's Ridge, at an elevation of 828 feet above sea level. Before the use of a practical steam engine, one powerful enough to make the climb unassisted, both horse-drawn and steam-powered trains made use of inclined planes. Designed to ease steep ascents and descents, these sloped and graded dirt fills caused considerable delay and inconvenience. The use of inclined planes was short-lived; in 1839, the line was rerouted farther west, at an elevation of 760 feet.

With the completion of the tunnel, the boom era of Mount Airy ended. The town, which for a short period had resembled the frontier of the Wild West, returned to its quiet ways. In 1894, the town was chartered and became officially known as Mount Airy. Byron Dorsey, a local merchant, was elected the first mayor.

The growth of the Mount Airy business community was continually hampered by devastating fires. On February 24, 1903, at 2:00 a.m., the northern section of the business district was destroyed by fire—within a few hours, a dozen business establishments were reduced to ashes, with an estimated loss of $50,000. On March 25, 1914, at noon, a fire started in the milling company and spread to the business section north of the railroad station. The same business district that had been destroyed in 1903 again went up in smoke. Mount Airy had no fire department, and the call for assistance went out to Frederick, some twenty miles west of the town. The lack of water was a problem until three B&O engines were pressed into service. The engines took turns running to a pumping station eight miles away. Fire engines were coupled directly to the tender, and water from the tender was pumped to the fire. In spite of heroic efforts to contain the fire, five buildings burned to the ground and a half-dozen others were damaged. The loss was placed at $75,000. On the evening of June 4, 1925, the business district north of the railroad was again hit by fire. Hood's Dry Goods Store was the only business to survive the flames. More than a dozen stores were destroyed, and damage was estimated at $200,000. Once again, B&O engines were used to transport water.

This third disastrous fire in twenty-two years proved the need for a permanent, well-equipped, and well-trained fire protection unit. In 1921, Charles Parker Glover had founded the first fire protection unit in Mount Airy. When he died a short time later, however, the unit was disbanded. Finally, in 1926, a volunteer fire department was organized. On May 22, 1969, the business district was once more threatened. This time the outstanding fire-fighting unit of Mount Airy was able to contain the spectacular blaze, although the Mount Airy Milling Company burned to the ground.

In spite of the destructive fires, Mount Airy continued to rebuild and prosper. By 1938, the town had one of the largest canning houses in the country and one of the largest flour mills in the state. During this time, it was also the chicken-hatching center of the United States. More than a million baby chicks were hatched each season and mailed or trucked to all parts of the country.

In 1949, Mount Airy and the B&O again made news. On December 31 of that year, the B&O made the last passenger run on the old Main Branch. The termination of service from Baltimore to Mount Airy marked the end of

America's oldest operating commercial passenger railway run. The service had begun in 1868 when the connection from Washington to Point of Rocks, known as the Metropolitan Branch, was completed. West-bound trains from Baltimore, Philadelphia, and New York were routed on this circumvention of the Main Branch. Travelers going west from Washington could save time and mileage on the new branch. Before this, trains had to double back to Relay from Washington before heading west on the original line. By 1941, passenger service on the old Main Branch from Baltimore to Point of Rocks was limited to two commuter runs via Mount Airy. Faced with a continuing loss of operating revenue, the B&O made an inevitable decision.

CHAPTER EIGHT

First Threads in the Magic Carpet of Steel: The B&O Railroad

The tracks along the first thirteen miles of commercial railroad in the United States still shine from the passing of an occasional coal train. However, the glitter and glamour once associated with some of the most memorable events in railroad history have long ago faded. The horn of the diesel locomotive still echoes lonesomely through the wooded river valley, a sad refrain to the song of the iron horse. The birth of the railroad not only revolutionized transportation but also ushered in an unprecedented era of technological development and economic prosperity. The B&O, born out of necessity and baptized by inventive minds, solved the problem of how to connect the great farming areas of the Ohio Valley with the population and industrial centers of the Eastern Seaboard.

Twelve years after the close of the War of 1812, America's major East Coast cities—Baltimore, Philadelphia, and New York—were competing vigorously for the recently opened commodity markets in the fertile Ohio Valley. In 1827, the Erie Canal, which had established an unbroken waterway from the shores of Lake Superior to New York City, was reaping the benefits of cheaper water rates to the Midwest. Attracting a large share of trade that had previously been shipped south, New York leaped ahead of Baltimore and Philadelphia as a trade center. Baltimore, despite its rapid growth as a city and commercial seaport, stood in the shadow of economic disaster. The city's dependence on the National Road as its link to the West seriously threatened its continued progress. The National Road, heading westward from Baltimore and passing through Ellicott's Mills, could not compete with the Erie Canal. If Baltimore were to remain a key center of transportation, then a way had to be found to link Maryland with the Ohio Valley. This would enable the city to recapture the trade lost to the Erie Canal. A barrel of flour that cost one dollar in Wheeling, West Virginia, sold on the Baltimore market for five dollars. The difference was absorbed by freight charges and passed on to consumers. To prevent a collapse of the local economy, it was imperative for business leaders to quickly find a solution to the transportation problem.

One possible solution to the problem was the building of a Baltimore leg to the Chesapeake and Ohio Canal. The C&O canal was to run parallel to the Potomac River and would consist of a series of locks to be traversed by barges pulled by teams of horses or mules. The idea, which now gained new popularity, had first been proposed by George Washington in the late 1700s. When the C&O Canal was chartered on March 3, 1825, Baltimore merchants hoped to benefit in some way from this project. A meeting of Maryland state delegates decided that "the practicability of a canal from Baltimore to intersect and unite with the Chesapeake and Ohio Canal, then to Pittsburgh, and thence to Lake Erie, no longer admitted of a doubt and should be carried out" (Hungerford 1928), and induced the Maryland Legislature to subscribe $500,000 to the stock of the canal company. Philip E. Thomas of Baltimore was made a commissioner representing the state's interest in the canal project. Subsequent surveys revealed that a canal extending from Washington and connecting with the Patapsco at Elkridge was not feasible. The rolling hills between the Patapsco and Potomac valleys would make the digging of a canal almost impossible. In addition to being cost-prohibitive, there was an insufficient supply of water at the higher levels. Baltimore was desperate. Businessmen searched frantically for another solution to their problem.

In the fall of 1826, at the Baltimore home of Colonel John Eager Howard, the Revolutionary War officer later immortalized in the Maryland state song, a group of influential bankers and merchants first gave serious consideration to the idea of a railroad. Evan Thomas, the brother of Philip E. Thomas, had just returned from England, where he had inspected the Stockton and Darlington Railway, upon which coal trains were being drawn by cumbersome engines from the mines to the coal docks. The dinner guests listened with great interest but remained relatively passive and undecided. Philip E. Thomas, the president of the Merchants Bank—noted for his self-possession, energy, clearness of perception, and rare judgment—believed the railroad was the answer to their problems. Thomas, who had resigned as commissioner to the C&O Canal in July, persisted in his belief and eventually convinced the others of the project's practicability. After a series of meetings, a charter was drawn up, approved, and submitted to the Maryland Legislature. On February 28, 1827, the act that formally sanctioned the incorporation of the Baltimore and Ohio Railroad was passed by the State of Maryland.

The excitement that the railroad project aroused throughout the state was translated into action when stock in the company became available to the public. The remarkable demand for the first stock of a new railroad was mentioned in newspapers all over the country. The subscription books for the shares of the B&O were opened on March 20 at the Mechanics Bank in Baltimore, the Farmers Branch Bank in Frederick, and the Hagerstown Bank. Although the subscription books remained open in Baltimore only twelve days, 36,788 shares, representing more than 22,000 individuals, were subscribed. This was exclusive of the 5,000 shares taken by Baltimore City. Large subscriptions also came from Frederick and Hagerstown.

The B&O was formally incorporated on April 24, 1827, when, in accordance with its charter, directors and first officers were elected. Philip E. Thomas was elected the first president and George Brown, a banker and the son of the early merchant Alexander Brown, was chosen treasurer. The first directors were Charles Carroll of Carrollton, George Hoffman, Philip E. Thomas, William Patterson, Robert Oliver, Alexander Brown, Isaac McKim, William Lorman, Thomas Ellicott, John B. Morris, Talbot Jones, and William Steuart. The State of Virginia confirmed the charter of the B&O on March 27, 1827, and the State of Pennsylvania did the same on February 22, 1828. The era of railroad mania, which opened in Baltimore, had officially begun.

THE FIRST RAILS

Baltimore City now had its railroad, but it existed only on paper. If America's first railroad was to become a reality, it would be necessary to call on the nation's human resources for help. The success of the B&O would be a result of the untiring effort, dedication, ingenuity, and inventiveness of America's great minds and strong backs. Their achievements were remarkable when one considers that there was no model or predecessor to copy. Much of the technical information about railroads was gained firsthand through trial and error.

The first step was to find the most suitable route for construction. For this project, the B&O chose Colonel Stephen H. Long of the US Army, and Jonathan Knight of the National Road. Knight brought along his superintendent of construction, Casper W. Wever, who built much of the road in Ohio. Since there was no established school of engineering in the United States except the US Military Academy at West Point, it was not unusual for private companies and state governments to call on West Point graduates for their technical skills.

Knight and Long sent promising reports from the preliminary surveys. The route from Baltimore to Point of Rocks, Maryland, would be difficult but by no means impossible. In light of grade limitations, the railroad would have to follow a waterway to ensure a level route. The best location would be a compromise between terrain features and current and predicted technology. After studying alternative sites, such as the Potomac River valley and the Monocacy River basin, the decision was made to follow the Patapsco River from Baltimore to Mount Airy, Maryland, and then west.

No sooner had the final report of survey been completed than the first of many problems arose. The Baltimore City Council refused to pay any of the $500,000 that had been subscribed to the B&O unless the railroad's Baltimore terminus was located exactly sixty-six feet above tidewater. Politicians feared that the city's downtown commerce center would shift if the railroad made the decision to follow the Main Branch of the Patapsco and build a terminal near the southern edge of the city where the river emptied into the harbor. The squabble was ended when B&O officials agreed to the council's demands. The terminal would be located sixty-six feet above tidewater at Pratt and Amity Streets, the present site of the Mount Clare Station. The "66 feet agreement" had immediate impact on the engineering of the railroad. Laying the first tracks from Mount Clare Station to Relay would be a time-consuming and financially draining construction project, involving cuts, fills, and bridges on a scale never before attempted. Although the agreement was questioned by officials on both sides, it quickly proved to be in the best interests of the B&O, which at the time was financially strapped for construction funds. The city's money proved to be crucial when the B&O was turned down for federal funding in December 1828.

The Fourth of July, 1828, was an unforgettable day of pageantry and ceremony to celebrate the past and future of the country. At Little Falls, near Washington, President John Adams lifted a spade of dirt, which marked the commencement of the C&O Canal. In Baltimore, a similar scene was repeated on a farm owned by James Carroll, in a remote spot between Gwynns Falls and Gwynns Runs where the proposed route crossed the city line. Charles Carroll, the last surviving signer of the Declaration of Independence, lifted a spade of dirt, marking the commencement of the B&O Railroad. At this ceremony, Carroll, who also assisted in the laying of the first stone, remarked to a friend who stood beside him: "I consider this among the most important acts of my life, second only to the signing of the Declaration of Independence, if second even to that." (Hungerford 1928) The day of parades and festivities in Baltimore and Washington sounded the beginning of the great westward race between the canal and the railroad.

On July 7, 1828, Captain William G. McNeil and a group of army engineers began the definitive locating of the railroad. Seven days later, Knight and Long published advertisements announcing the opening of proposals for the construction of the railroad's first thirteen miles. The route would extend northwest from the city to the Patapsco, where it would then parallel the river to Ellicott's Mills. The construction of the line was divided into twenty-six separate sections and contracts.

By October 1, 1828, the laying of the permanent track had begun. But due to a nationwide labor shortage caused by other large public-works projects, the work proceeded painfully slowly.

The "Deep Cut" west of Gwynns Run, through a hill 78 feet high and 1,300 yards long, proved to be the chief obstacle to early progress on the line. The contracts for this work amounted to one-third of the total cost allocated for preparing the line of rails from Baltimore to Ellicott's Mills. The problem was solved by filling in some of the excavation work and making a grade of seventeen feet to the mile. This grade, which saved thousands of dollars in excavation costs, was steep enough to promote runoff of rainwater but would not significantly reduce the pulling power of the horses.

Two different methods of construction were used on the first thirteen miles. The first rails were laid by carpenters who put down wood rails (called stringers) along wood or stone ties (called sleepers) and then attached metal strips to the top of the wood rails. The section of seven and a half miles from Baltimore to the Patapsco was done with wood sleepers and stringers. Due to the plentiful supply of stone at Ellicott's Mills, the remaining five and a half miles were laid with stone blocks as ties and wood rails as stringers. Prior to the permanent track, temporary track was installed. In Ellicott's Mills, a short portion of track was laid to facilitate transportation of materials to the Patterson Viaduct, whereas in Baltimore about one-and-a-half miles were used to move materials and to conduct experiments with horse-drawn passenger cars. At the time the track was laid, the

Army Board of Engineers adopted a roadbed of twenty-six feet for a double-track railroad with track centers of twelve feet in a gauge of four feet, eight-and-a-half inches. The final decision for the gauge (track width) was made with uncertainty. This measure was one of the two most frequently used on railroads in England. Different gauges were being used in the United States, and it was not until the 1880s that the gauge used by the B&O was made the standard for the nation.

A major decision was reached by B&O directors after they debated whether to use wood or stone bridges. In spite of the impressive wood bridge built by Colonel Long, the project engineer, to carry the Washington and Baltimore Turnpike over the tracks of the new railroad, the company opted for stone bridges, which were endorsed by Wever. The first bridge built by the B&O, the Carrollton Viaduct, had the distinction of being the first railroad bridge built in the United States. Named after Charles Carroll of Carrollton, the bridge measured 312 feet in length. The height of the structure, which traversed Gwynns Falls, was fifty-one feet, nine inches. The structure, whose stone was quarried in the vicinity of Ellicott's Mills, was divided into two arches. The larger arch, some eighty feet in length, passed over the water of the falls, and the smaller arch on the south bank was used for wagon traffic. The engineering concepts and construction techniques that were developed and used in building the Carrollton Viaduct were employed in later bridges on the B&O line. In December 1829, Charles Carroll again participated in a special ceremony. This time it was the laying of the last stone in the bridge bearing his name. The bridge remains in use today.

December 1829 also marked the completion of the bridge spanning the Patapsco about halfway between Relay and Ellicott's Mills. The stone arch structure — four spans totaling 375 feet in length — consisted of graceful curving arches in the style of the Carrollton Viaduct. It was named after B&O director William Patterson. On December 4, 1829, Patterson had the honor of being the first person to cross the Patterson Viaduct on horseback.

In 1868, the flood swept away the center sections of the majestic bridge. The Patterson Viaduct was never rebuilt and was temporarily replaced by a steel span called a Bollman Truss. When the track in that section of steep valley was straightened in the early 1900s and carried through a tunnel, the steel bridge was abandoned.

On January 7, 1830, the B&O transported its first revenue passengers. In response to public demand, the railroad opened its line from Pratt Street at Mount Clare to the Carrollton Viaduct. One-way tickets for the excursion ride were nine cents each, or three for twenty-five cents. Four cars, with a combined capacity of 120 passengers, were put into operation. This marked the first time in the United States that a railroad was operated for public use.

The horse-drawn excursion train (one horse pulled all four cars) proved the superiority of flanged wheels on rails over wagon wheels on an ordinary road. The fact that such loads were pulled with relative ease was a tribute to the work of Ross Winans. Winans, a horse trader from New Jersey who came to Baltimore to sell horses to the railroad, quickly addressed himself to the problems that horses were having in pulling coaches. Studying the mechanics involved, he came up with the friction wheel, a design that made the wheels and their axles revolve as a unit, with the entire rolling portions set in bearings outside the wheels. The friction wheel is still in use today, with modifications, on every railroad in the world. Working to perfect rail travel, Winans built the first coned wheels, which have a slanted tread allowing railroad cars to negotiate curves. He also devised flanges or ridges on the inside of the railroad wheels to keep them mounted on the track. Winans's brilliant work for the B&O resulted in major accomplishments in the invention and development of railroad equipment. He assisted in the development of Peter Cooper's Tom Thumb and Phineas Davis's York and later designed his own engines. He revolutionized the railroads by designing a locomotive named the Crab, the first engine to use horizontally placed pistons. Next came the Mud-Digger, an engine whose drive was so close to the ground that it threw mud and stones as it moved. This was followed by the Camel, whose superior hauling power played a large part in the B&O conquest of the Alleghenies.

In 1844, Winans left the B&O to open his own shop, where he continued to build railroad locomotives and work on other inventions. Years later during the Civil War, the controversial Winans would surface again and play a role in another historic event along the Patapsco.

After the first year of the B&O's construction, the building pace quickened, and by 1830 the thirteen miles to Ellicott's Mills were finished. The double track was completed at an average cost for gradation and masonry of $46,496 per mile. In addition to engineering obstacles encountered in conquering the diverse, rugged terrain, early problems included inclement weather and an unstable work force. Casper Wever, superintendent of construction, became so concerned with the use of "ardent spirits" that, at the beginning of July 1829, he mandated that all contracts for either gradation or masonry construction contain a clause prohibiting the use of alcohol. Liquor was freely sold at the workmen's camps, which comprised mostly immigrant workers, and brawls were frequent. The heat and the hard work during the summer months brought increased reports of violence—violence that eventually erupted into a riot. On August 14, 1829, the fighting culminated in the killing of one man and the wounding of several others. Quarrels were not confined to the workers. Arguments between contractors and laborers increased the atmosphere of tension and hostility. A few days after this ugly incident, the home of Thomas Ellicott, one of the contractors, was ransacked, and Ellicott was severely wounded.

On May 24, 1830, the first thirteen miles of line on the B&O were opened for public traffic. The American and other newspapers printed this simple but significant advertisement: "Office of the Baltimore and Ohio Railroad, 20 May 1830. Notice is hereby given, That the Railroad between Baltimore and Ellicott's Mills will be open for transportation of passengers on Monday, the 24th inst." A one-way trip took only one-and-a-half hours to complete. The new railroad was an immediate success, with more business than it could handle. Within the first four months of operation, revenues amounted to $20,012.36, far exceeding operating expenditures.

The termination of the first thirteen miles of track at Ellicott's Mills was not a coincidence. The mill town was a thriving industrial center and the most convenient point where travelers could take the stage to proceed westward on the Frederick Turnpike. The quarries at Ellicott's Mills and nearby Granite provided an abundant supply of stone for bridges, viaducts, and sleepers. A stone depot, constructed in 1831 and still used today as a railroad museum, became the center for passenger and freight movement and provided repair and storage facilities.

THE IRON HORSE ARRIVES

When the B&O was formed in 1828, a practical steam engine had not been developed to operate on American railroads. Although the B&O directors believed that the future of the railroad was in the steam engine, the horse remained the moving force. In the fall of 1828, the B&O dispatched Jonathan Knight, Captain William G. McNeill, and Lieutenant George W. Whistler (father of the American painter James A. McNeill Whistler) to England to study the first railways being built there. Special attention was to be given to the progress of the steam locomotive. The reports the men sent to B&O President Philip E. Thomas focused on the unlimited potential of the steam engine and its adaptability to the B&O line. Although interested in the developments of the steam engine, Thomas could not give the matter his undivided attention. He was totally absorbed in seeing the first order of business for the railroad completed: the construction of the first thirteen miles. Until the time came that the practicability of the steam locomotive was proven, the horse would remain the mode of transportation for the line. Because of the sharp curves of the B&O (as compared to the usually straight tracks and easy curves on the English railroads), and the light construction of lines in the United States, there was considerable doubt that an English- built locomotive could operate successfully. The failure of the English-built *Stourbridge Lion* on the Delaware and Hudson Canal tramway confirmed this suspicion.

While construction of the railroad progressed in 1828 and 1829, efforts were underway to increase the efficiency of the horse-powered train. Experiments were limited only to the imagination of the inventor. A railway car operating on the treadmill principle was innovative but unsuccessful. The *Cyclopede* was a railcar powered by a horse that walked up a slanted treadmill built on top of the car. The experiment came to an abrupt end when, on a test run, the cart hit a stray cow, thereby dumping the horse, the B&O directors, and members of the press into the brush by the side of the tracks. Evan Thomas, Philip's brother, designed a sail-powered car. Named *Aeolus* after the Greek god of wind, it carried a square sail on a single mast in a boat-like railway car. Catching the right wind, the car was able to move at a good speed, but speed proved incompatible with direction. The project was abandoned when experiments to sail the rail-locked car against the wind failed.

The replacement of the horse came with an invention of Peter Cooper, a New York real estate investor, inventor, philanthropist, and millionaire, who had made his fortune in the glue business. In the fall of 1829, he persuaded Philip E. Thomas to allow him to build an experiment steam locomotive for the B&O line. Cooper, who had invested heavily in real estate on the south side of Baltimore's harbor, believed the future of Baltimore and his own Canton company rested with the B&O. He was troubled that the railroad company, which had built such an elaborate and sturdy line, was having difficulty in making definite plans for the motive power by which the railroad was to be operated.

In June 1830, Cooper began to piece together his engine. The boiler was a round, fire-tube type, twenty inches in diameter and sixty-six inches tall. It stood upright on a car frame about the size of handcars later used by track crews. The wheels on the car were thirty inches in diameter. The lower part of the boiler served as the firebox; the upper part was filled with pipes. Cooper improvised and used musket barrels to connect the engine to the boiler. To force air into the boiler, he invented a blower to furnish a draft for the coal-burning firebox. A one-cylinder rotary engine, which he invented, was used (as opposed to reciprocating engines, which were being employed at the time).

In spite of repeated industrial sabotage, which included the theft of copper pipes and brass fittings and damage to the principal drive wheel, Cooper was able to complete the diminutive locomotive, dubbed *Tom Thumb*. The engine, which weighed about one ton, proved its ability to negotiate curves and demonstrated principles in locomotive engineering still in existence today. One of the test runs in the summer of 1830, at the time a seemingly insignificant event, was to become a railroad legend. John H. B. Latrobe, the chief counsel for the B&O and an early railroad historian, described the events of that day:

Mr. Cooper's success was such as to induce him to try a trip to Ellicott's Mills; and an open car, the first used upon the road, already mentioned, having been attached to his engine, and filled with the directors and some friends, the speaker among the rest, the first journey by steam in America was commenced. The trip was most interesting. The curves were passed without difficulty at a speed of fifteen miles an hour; the grades were ascended with comparative ease; the day was fine, the company in the highest spirits, and some excited gentlemen of the party pulled out memorandum books, and when at the highest speed, which was eighteen miles an hour, wrote their names and some connected sentences, to prove that even at that great velocity it was possible to do so. The return trip from the Mills—a distance of thirteen miles—was made in fifty-seven minutes. This was the summary of 1830.

But the triumph of this Tom Thumb engine was not altogether without a drawback. The great stage proprietors of the day were Stockton & Stokes; and on this occasion a gallant gray of great beauty and power was driven by them from town, attached to another car on the second track—for the Company had begun by making two tracks to the Mills—and met the engine at the Relay House on its way back. From this point it was determined to have a race home; and, the start being even, away went the horse and engine, the snort of the one and the puff of the other keeping time and tune. At first the gray had the best of it, for his steam would be applied to the greatest advantage on the instant, while the engine had to wait until the rotation of the wheels set the blower to work. The horse was perhaps a quarter of a mile ahead when the safety valve of the engine lifted and the thin blue vapor issuing from it showed an excess of steam. The blower whistled, the steam blew off in vapory clouds, the pace increased, the passengers shouted, the engine gained on the horse, soon it lapped him—the silk was plied—the race was neck and neck, nose and nose—then the engine passed the horse, and a great hurrah hailed the victory.

But it was not repeated; for just at this time, when the gray's master was about giving up, the band which drove the pulley, which drove the blower, slipped from the drum, the safety valve ceased to scream, and the engine for want of breath began to wheeze and pant. In vain Mr. Cooper, who was his own engineman and fireman, lacerated his hands in attempting to replace the band upon the wheel: in vain he tried to urge the fire with light wood; the horse gained on the machine and passed it; and although the band was presently replaced, the steam again did its best, the horse was too far ahead to be overtaken, and came in the winner of the race. But the real victory was with Mr. Cooper, notwithstanding. He had held fast to the faith that was in him, and had demonstrated its truth beyond peradventure. All honor to his name. (Latrobe 1868)

The victory was to be short-lived. That summer day along the Patapsco marked the beginning of a new era for the iron horse. On August 25, 1830, the *Tom Thumb* made its first successful trip between Baltimore and Ellicott's Mills, covering the distance of thirteen miles in about two hours.

Encouraged by the success of the *Tom Thumb* and that of the Rainhill Trails in England, the B&O directors decided to have their own contest to find a steam locomotive. On January 4, 1831, advertisements stating the contest's conditions and specifications were published in various newspapers. Five locomotives were entered in the contest, which was held in June of that year. Phineas Davis, a watchmaker from Pennsylvania, won the contest with his locomotive, the York. The engine, weighing three-and-one-half tons and capable of speeds up to thirty miles per hour, was the first locomotive whose wheels were coupled to form a pair of drivers. After some modifications, the engine was put into service between Baltimore and Ellicott's Mills. The moderately successful engine was retired in the summer of 1832 and replaced by the Atlantic. Built by Davis, with the assistance of Ross Winans and Peter Cooper, it proved more efficient than its predecessor in fuel consumption and in pulling the steeper grades encountered in expanding the line west.

In 1836, while taking a special excursion to Washington following the opening of the Washington branch, Davis was killed in a tragic railroad accident. On the return trip, a new engine that he had constructed for the line struck a loose rail and derailed. Davis was killed instantly, as he was thrown from the engine and then crushed as the engine's wheels passed over his body. All others aboard escaped serious injury. The untimely death of Davis was a blow to the technological efforts of the B&O. Davis had not only been improving on his practical line of steam engines but also had been working on methods to improve overall operation of the railroad. Although the contributions of Davis to the B&O were monumental, many railroad experts believe he had only begun to realize his potential.

The building of the B&O did not end in Ellicott's Mills. In August 1830, with the completion of the Oliver Viaduct over the Frederick Turnpike at Ellicott's Mills, the B&O continued its march westward. On April 1, 1832, the C&O Canal and the B&O met at Point of Rocks, Maryland. The state's geography forced both companies onto a narrow strip of land between the Potomac River and a steep Appalachian mountain slope. A bitter legal battle over right-of-way claims ensued, which resulted in a year's delay in construction and the B&O subscribing $266,000 to canal company stock. By 1842, the railroad had entered Cumberland, Maryland, a point that marked the canal's western terminus eight years later. At Roseby's Rock, near Wheeling, West Virginia, on Christmas Eve of 1852, the final rail connection was made that linked the victorious railway between Baltimore and the Ohio Valley. The dream of Baltimore's businessmen and the B&O became a reality, and the future of the city as a trade center was ensured.

THE THOMAS VIADUCT:
THE IMPOSSIBLE SPAN OF STONE

With the completion of the B&O to Point of Rocks in 1832, plans for the construction of a branch line to Washington began to be formulated. From the beginning of the railroad in 1828, arguments had been put forth proposing that a railroad between Baltimore and Washington would be more practical and profitable than one extending westward. President Philip E. Thomas, in his fifth annual report of October 1, 1831, gave favorable consideration to the proposal of such a line. The major problem facing construction of the line was politics.

Early days on the B&O: steam power versus horsepower.
Courtesy Maryland Historical Society.

"The Marvelous Span of Stone." Looking upriver at the Thomas Viaduct.
Courtesy Maryland Historical Society.

The State of Maryland was in no great hurry to purchase a stock subscription to the Washington branch. Its reluctance was in no small part due to the delay in receiving its substantial returns from the original investment in shares of the B&O. The first act empowering the state to subscribe to stock in the Washington branch was dated February 22, 1831. This act and subsequent others, similar in purpose with modifying clauses, were passed by the Maryland Legislature but left to die without further legislative action being taken. However, in the spring of 1833, a measure that was acceptable to both proponents and opponents of the bill was finally passed authorizing the purchase of stock.

After lengthy deliberation on the exact location of the new branch, it was decided the line would extend south from Relay near the Patapsco through Bladensburg and then to Washington. The concentration of mills and manufacturing concerns along the Patapsco River Valley, combined with the fact that a quarter of the entire route from Baltimore to the Patapsco was already built, weighed heavily in the final choice of location.

On this new line came one of the major advancements in track construction. Jonathan Knight, the chief engineer, suggested the track be laid with wood sleepers three feet apart (as opposed to four feet), and that stringers be placed below and above the crossties. He proposed that on the upper stringers a continuous flat iron rail be installed; each rail would be fifteen feet long, with a base three and a half inches wide and two inches high. The weight would be about thirty-two pounds per running yard, and about fifty tons for each mile of single track. The rail was the first form of the T rail used on the B&O and most likely anywhere in the United States.

Work on the line continued uneventfully and the branch into Washington was completed on August 25, 1835. However, tragedy struck the line in March 1835, four miles outside Washington, when what local newspapers termed a "riot" occurred. In the disturbance, five or six Germans were wounded by muskets and other weapons, and eleven Germans and one Frenchman were taken into custody and held over for trial. The riot was the result of a demand for higher wages. The assault by disgruntled workers was made upon those coworkers who were content with their wages.

The highlight of the Washington branch construction was meeting the monumental challenge of building a bridge across the Patapsco. "Ridiculous!" and "Impossible!" cried the critics and nonbelievers when the initial plans were revealed for accomplishing this prodigious task. On July 4, 1832, construction began on a multiple-arch stone viaduct across the gorge of the Patapsco between Relay and Elkridge. Philip E. Thomas secured the talents of the famous Baltimore architect, Benjamin H. Latrobe. Benjamin, the brother of John H. B. Latrobe, proposed an interlocked span of granite blocks set in a series of eight elliptical arches. Some engineers were critical, insisting that the span would not even support its own weight, much less that of a moving train. The distance across the Patapsco exceeded 600 feet, and the world had not yet seen a railroad viaduct of these dimensions. Undaunted by the critics, Latrobe proceeded with his plans, firm in his conviction that the bridge could be built. He contracted John McCartney, an engineer from Ohio, to undertake the actual construction.

Stone for the viaduct was quarried at Granite and transported by rail to the construction site. More than 26,000 cubic yards of stone were carefully cut, fitted into place, and grouted before the span was complete. Eight elliptical arches, each measuring from fifty-seven feet, ten and a half inches to fifty-eight feet, four and a half inches, were constructed to support the sixty-foot-high structure. The arches allowed small ships to pass freely under the bridge and permitted flood waters to pass unobstructed without causing any damage to the bridge.

On July 4, 1835, after two years of construction (at a cost of $142,236) the new span of stone, playfully nicknamed "Latrobe's Folly," was officially opened. The event attracted considerable media and public attention. Hundreds of spectators came from Baltimore, Washington, and the surrounding communities to watch the bridge dramatically collapse in a cloud of dust and debris. Anxious anticipation grew into suspense as the excited crowd, holding its breath, watched the six-and-one-half-ton steam engine, the Atlantic, pull onto and across the bridge. The crowd lining both sides of the river erupted into a deafening roar when a second train crossed the span.

The viaduct was named in honor of Philip E. Thomas. However, contractor John McCartney, aiming to ensure his place in posterity, erected a granite monument at the east end of the span. The obelisk, which still stands today, honored McCartney, Thomas, Latrobe, and other B&O principals. Legend has it that McCartney became so jubilant with the successful crossings that he served generous portions of whiskey to his stonemasons to commemorate the event. As they knelt before him, McCartney baptized each worker with a pint of whiskey.

The Thomas Viaduct still stands as the world's oldest multiple-arch stone bridge. Now halfway through its second century of existence, it has continued to carry the weight and ship the freight. Modern 300-ton diesel locomotives, which have replaced the first tiny six-ton steamers, have had no impact on the bridge's function or engineering. Repairs have consisted principally of replacing mortar in the stonework. Designated as a National Historic Landmark by the Department of the Interior, the viaduct stands as originally built: 612 feet long, 26 feet wide, and curving four degrees in a graceful arc across the Patapsco.

CHAPTER NINE

Blue and Gray Clouds over the Water:
The Civil War

Prior to and at the outset of the Civil War, the State of Maryland and its loyalties became one of the key factors in determining the fate of the Union. The border state, lying south of the Mason-Dixon Line yet north of the Potomac River, was sharply divided on the issues of slavery, states' rights, and secession. The balloting in the state for the 1860 presidential election reflected the differences in political opinion. Southern Democrat John C. Breckinridge, a staunch defender of slavery and the secessionist movement of the South, received 42,497 votes, only 720 more than Constitutional Unionist John Bell, who campaigned to preserve the Union. Democrat Stephen A. Douglas received 5,873 votes, while Republican Abraham Lincoln, a strong supporter of the antislavery movement, received only 2,294 votes. After the election, many citizens petitioned Governor Thomas Holliday Hicks to call for a special session of the Maryland General Assembly to determine and clarify the state's position. Fearing that the many Southern sympathizers in the assembly would influence the passing of an act of secession, Governor Hicks wisely resisted the pressure and refused to call a special session. As the Civil War drew near, most Marylanders took a compromise position toward both sides and hoped the seceded states might be brought back into the Union. They saw the darkness of war descending upon them and feared Maryland would become the main battlefield for the great armies of the North and the South, bringing only destruction and leaving behind only the ruins of its cities and the blood of its citizens.

Into this excited atmosphere, filled with tension and uncertainty, finally came the opening shots of the Civil War on April 12, 1861, at Fort Sumter in Charleston, South Carolina. Reflecting the political division of the state, Baltimore became a concentrated hotbed of political rhetoric and activity, most of it pro-South. Tension surfaced so quickly that on April 17 Baltimore Mayor George William Brown publicly asked all citizens to refrain from acts that might lead to violence, and to assist authorities in keeping peace and order in the city.

THE SIXTH REGIMENT OF MASSACHUSETTS TROOPS FIRING INTO THE MOB AT THE CAMDEN DEPOT, BALTIMORE, WHILE TAKING THE CARS FOR WASHINGTON, APRIL 19, 1861.

The first blood of the Civil War was shed on April 19, 1861, when the 6th Massachusetts Regiment fired into the mob at Camden Depot. *Courtesy Maryland Historical Society.*

The desperate plea produced a peace lasting only two days. On April 19, the 6th Massachusetts Regiment, which was en route to Washington, arrived by rail at the President Street Station of the Philadelphia, Wilmington, and Baltimore Railroad. Since the station was located at the northern edge of the harbor basin near Jones Falls, soldiers were forced to depart the train and board horse-drawn carriages for their final departure point at the Camden Station of the B&O line, which was located across the basin about a mile to the south.

While the soldiers were boarding at the station, a mob of several thousand citizens gathered along the water's edge at Pratt Street to taunt and harass the troops. Cobblestones were ripped from the street and hurled at the passing carriages. The fuse to ignite the crowd was slowly burning and it was only a matter of minutes until the emotions of the crowd would explode in violence. After a number of carriages safely passed through the streets, the mob placed obstructions and makeshift barricades on the tracks, thus forcing the soldiers to leave the carriages and make their way to the Camden Station on foot. As the soldiers crossed the bridge over Jones Falls in a double-quick march, a shot rang from the crowd. Untrained officers panicked and ordered their troops to turn and fire a volley. Several in the crowd were instantly felled by the gunfire. The soldiers quickly regrouped and resumed their march, but were now being chased and attacked by the enraged mob. More shots rang out, and a soldier lay dead in the streets. The chaos and bloodshed were briefly interrupted by Mayor Brown when he led a group of soldiers through the city's street. Despite the mayor's courage and heroic gesture, the fighting continued. By the day's end, twelve citizens and four soldiers were dead and numerous other citizens and soldiers wounded.

While the South rejoiced over this ugly incident, convinced now that Maryland would join the Confederacy, Brown hurried to Washington and begged President Lincoln not to send any more troops through Baltimore. In haste to avoid another conflict between soldiers and citizens, authorities in Baltimore ordered the destruction of railroad bridges and telegraph lines to the North. A force of approximately 3,000 Union soldiers, camped at Cockeysville awaiting orders to enter the city, returned to Harrisburg. Meanwhile, the makeshift army of civilians, who answered the call to arms by enlisting in the Maryland Guard, dispersed from the streets of Baltimore. Lincoln temporarily acquiesced to the pleas of Mayor Brown, but only until troops could be moved into the city. The events in Baltimore had shown how quickly and easily the transportation and communication routes between northern cities and the federal capital could be interrupted. Northern states demanded access to Washington and urged the use of force, if necessary, to keep Maryland in the Union. If Baltimore fell, the battleground would shift from south of the Potomac to south of the Susquehanna River. Lincoln's reply was quick and decisive.

On April 21, 1861, US Army Brigadier General Benjamin F. Butler landed at the Naval School (US Naval Academy) grounds with the 8th Massachusetts Regiment. Butler, who had been in Philadelphia, sailed from Perryville, at the head of the Chesapeake Bay, in order to bypass Baltimore and avoid another bloody confrontation. Butler's first priority was to repair the damaged tracks of the Annapolis and Elkridge Railroad, which connected with the B&O's Washington branch at Annapolis Junction, and thus to reestablish the vital railway link with the North. After reaching the Washington branch, Butler and his forces, which now included additional regiments from the Northern states, undertook the task of repairing damaged tracks and bridges as they advanced toward Washington and Baltimore. On April 25, the 7th New York Regiment marched by the White House and saluted the president. Union forces now controlled an unbroken route for transporting reinforcements and supplies from Washington to Annapolis Junction. Baltimore remained the only obstacle to unifying the North.

On May 5, General Butler, under orders from Lieutenant General Winfield Scott, commander-in-chief of the armies of the United States, occupied Relay with the 6th Massachusetts and 8th New York regiments (numbering 2,080 men) and Major Cook's battery of Boston Light Artillery. Cannons were immediately placed on the hills overlooking the Thomas Viaduct and the railroad junction, earthworks were constructed, and camps formed. Butler's mission was to stop the supply line from Baltimore sympathizers to the Confederates at Harper's Ferry and to provide a first line of defense against attempts to attack Baltimore or Washington from the Patapsco valley. Relay, approximately six miles southwest of Baltimore, was the key to any military strategy along the railroad corridor. It provided the only direct rail connection to the North and a main link to Harper's Ferry and points west, and served as the gateway to the Patapsco valley, which contained a large number of mills and manufacturers vital to the war effort.

The days that followed the occupation of Relay were filled with constant military preparation. Camp Relay, also called Camp Relay House, was composed of a number of camps and fortifications on both sides of the river. Union soldiers made their first camp, Camp Essex, on George Dobbins's property near the south end of the viaduct. Tight security was placed around the camp, and no one was allowed to pass the picket lines without proper identification. The camp became the main artillery position for the protection of the railroad and the viaduct. Cannons were placed on the high bluffs behind earthen breastworks, and a magazine was dug out and covered with a high mound of dirt. Guards stopped all trains and searched them for arms and contraband. They turned back or arrested all armed passengers and seized all shipments to the South. Within a few days, they were authorized to search personal baggage and effects. At the viaduct's north end, a second fortification was constructed on the bluffs overlooking Relay. Fort Dix, named in honor of General John A. Dix, was another artillery emplacement of sandbags and earth. Several wood buildings were erected as sleeping quarters and one was used as a hospital. The village of St. Denis, just east of the fort, was used as the parade grounds for the garrisoned troops. Several days each week, soldiers headed by a brass band would march from the fort to the village for several hours of close order drill.

On May 7, the first casualty was recorded when Private Charles Leonard was accidentally killed by the discharge of a musket from which he was drawing a charge. The *Baltimore American and Commercial Advertiser* of May 9, 1861, reported on the funeral of Leonard and the military activity at the camp:

> The funeral of Charles Leonard, a Private of the New York regiment, whose accidental death was noticed yesterday, was conducted with due solemnity. In the absence of the chaplain, the funeral services were conducted by Dr. Smith of the Surgical Corps. When the line was formed, the funeral cortege extended nearly half a mile and proceeded by the beautiful winding road to the cemetery of the Methodist Episcopal Church, where the interment took place. The usual volley of musketry was fired. There was no music except the deep rolling of muffled drums, and as the column marched down the declivity of the road which divides the two camps, the Massachusetts Regiment appeared on the roadside and saluted the cortege with uncovered heads. Many of the villagers attended the funeral and a deep solemnity prevailed . . .
>
> . . . When the troops occupied positions on Sunday, the work of erecting batteries was commenced on the hill commanding the approaches to the place, both by rail and turnpike. The work, although arduous and required to be done during a heavy storm of wind, and rain, has been accomplished, and their effectiveness was fully demonstrated yesterday afternoon. For the purpose, with the approval of Colonel Jones, an old frame shanty situated on the south side of the valley nearly a mile distant was selected as a target, and the accuracy of the firing was excellent. Notwithstanding the pieces were depressed at an angle of nearly 10 degrees almost every ball hit its mark, and about 30 were fired. In addition to these batteries, there is now stationed on the main branch of the road, just above the bridge, two brass six pounders with caissons.

On May 9, John W. Garrett, president of the B&O, and William P. Smith, master of transportation, visited Relay House to observe the inspection procedures for stopping and searching trains. An agreement was reached with Butler to avert the annoyance to which shippers of freight were being subjected in the seizure of "contraband" goods.

The second week in May was a whirlwind of military activity, beginning with the capture of the Winans's steam gun during the Raid of Ellicott's Mills, the most exciting wartime event to occur along the Main Branch of the Patapsco. On May 11, 1861, the noon train from Baltimore to Ellicott's Mills was halted at Relay House and pressed into service to transport a Union artillery company with two cannons and several hundred infantry troops. Their urgent mission was to capture the infamous centrifugal steam gun, which was reportedly being drawn by six mules over the Frederick Road from Baltimore to Harper's Ferry. There the gun was to be sold to the Confederates.

The troop train and the gun wagon arrived at Ellicott's Mills almost simultaneously. The gun was captured and returned to Relay along with its reported inventor, Charles S. Dickinson, and the three men who were transporting it. The exhibition of the gun's powers, scheduled for the next day, was canceled when it was discovered that some parts were missing. *The Baltimore Sun* of May 13, 1861, reported that "some very material and indispensable parts of the machinery were found wanting, and the steam gun, that all came to look upon as a death dealing engine, stood harmless as an old barn fan. It now turns out that the inventor, who was not taken with the gun, had with him in a buggy, a short distance off, all the important parts of the machinery used in the working of the gun and escaped with them by driving rapidly away."

Designed by Ross Winans and constructed by Charles S. Dickinson (who in 1859 took out a patent on the invention), the steam gun was an engineering marvel in the mechanical application of steam power for military purposes. It was a steam-powered cannon mounted on a four-wheel steam-propelled carriage. Iron balls, ranging from an ounce to twenty-four-pound shot, were shoveled into a large hamper, which tapered down to a groove. The groove allowed the projectiles to slip down into cup-like attachments, which revolved at an enormous rate. These attachments threw the iron balls forward with great force and velocity (the effect was similar to that of a modern-day pitching machine). The machinery was carefully protected by iron plates so that the gun could be run up close to enemy artillery without losing its steam power to opposing fire power. An armor shield was also provided to protect the operator. Designed for maximum efficiency, space inside the gun allowed the same man who shoveled the iron balls into the hamper to shovel coal into the firebox.

Tests of the gun showed its potential as a weapon of unbelievable destruction. William H. Weaver, a Civil War artist for *Harper's Weekly* and other publications, witnessed a test of the gun at Winans's factory in the western suburbs of the city. Weaver described the test in the *Baltimore News* of April 12, 1861:

> Against a brick wall about a foot thick, heavy timbers, each a foot thick, were piled up. When finally placed ready for the test, there was about three feet of wood and one foot of brick ready to receive the discharge of the gun. The gun was some 30 or 40 feet away from the target. At a given signal an awful uproar was begun. In less than a minute the gun had been stopped. In that short time the heavy timbers had either been smashed or thrown into the air. Every one of us was convinced that the discharge would have mowed down a whole regiment.

Union battery overlooking the Thomas Viaduct
and the Patapsco.
Courtesy Maryland Historical Society.

Union troops inspecting the captured Winans steam gun.
Courtesy Maryland Historical Society.

After its capture, the steam gun was ignored. Despite the interest displayed by members of the press and some military men, such as Butler, the gun remained at Relay House without ever receiving a thorough test. Some Union soldiers who saw the gun said afterward that "the contraption" never actually worked. They claimed loudly that most of the balls discharged from the gun merely trickled from the barrel and fell to the ground. The gun's critics clamored about unimpressive test results despite the fact that the trigger mechanism had been deliberately removed and, most likely, destroyed before the gun's capture. Others who examined the gun were quick to express faith in its capabilities.

Just two days after the capture of the steam gun, Union soldiers again swung into action when they boarded trains and headed northeast for the military occupation of Baltimore. From President Lincoln via General Scott, Butler received orders to use prompt and efficient means to put down any uprising of Maryland against the United States. If necessary, Butler was to suspend the writ of habeas corpus—the official court order established in American and British law which stated that any person accused of a crime could demand to be brought into court, where the charges against him were to be openly stated. Butler, a Massachusetts man, hadn't forgotten the riot in Baltimore and promptly reported several Baltimoreans suspected of actively aiding the Confederacy. When Scott replied that "it is probable that you will find them . . . proper subjects for seizure and examination," Butler translated the response into permission to move against Baltimore.

On May 13, as sunset settled over Baltimore, two trains, containing General Butler and about 1,000 troops, pulled into Camden Station from Relay House. Included in the assault force were 500 troops from the 6th Massachusetts Regiment, which had been stoned and fired upon less than a month earlier. By midnight, the troops had occupied the high ground at Federal Hill, which overlooked the harbor and most of the city from the south side of the harbor basin. Butler sent a note to Major Morris, commander at Fort McHenry, stating that he had "taken possession of Baltimore," and requesting the major to fire upon Monument Square in the city if an attack came during the night. The next day Butler issued a proclamation in an effort to quell continuing Confederate sympathies. All city, state, and federal laws would be strictly enforced, and all munitions to aid the South would be seized. The display of any flags, banners, or other items representing the Confederacy would be prohibited. Almost 3,000 muskets and 3,500 pikes (long wooden shafts with pointed steel heads used as foot soldiers' weapons) were confiscated and stored at Fort McHenry. Many of the pikes were manufactured by Ross Winans and had been stored under the floors of John Colley's residence near Strieker and Hollins Streets, where they were found by Butler's troops.

Under orders from Butler, soldiers rounded up and took into custody Southern sympathizers who were aiding and abetting the enemy. At Relay, the train carrying Governor Hicks and other members of the Maryland Legislature en route to Baltimore from Frederick (where the Maryland General Assembly held session), was stopped and boarded. Delegate Ross Winans was immediately arrested, charged with high treason, and transported to Annapolis, and then to Fort McHenry for safekeeping. He was released without a trial after he took a prescribed loyalty oath. Outraged at his arrest, his friends nominated him for Congress; however, the military law in effect in the city prevented any attempt to politically canonize Winans. Winans was again arrested as a traitor after loading a schooner with arms for the South. The ship was seized before it left port, and Winans was released from custody.

May 14 also marked the end of Butler's command in Baltimore. He was relieved of his duties and recalled to Washington for his "hazardous occupation of Baltimore" without the "knowledge" of General Scott. Lincoln did not agree with the recall of Butler and appointed him to the command of the department of Fort Monroe. Butler kept his rank of major general, which he had received during the occupation of Baltimore.

Within a few days, replacement troops were moved to Federal Hill, and the occupying force returned to Relay. Under martial law, the city became an armed fortress. Construction began immediately on a number of forts to ring the city. Their twofold purpose was to prevent a civil uprising by a show of force, or to level the city with artillery fire if an uprising could not be controlled in the streets.

Fort Federal Hill and Fort Marshall, both utilizing the high ground next to the Patapsco and looking down on the city, were established to serve as sentinels on both sides of the harbor. At Federal Hill, earthworks were constructed to cover the entire crown of the hill. Angled bastions were erected at the corners of the fort to allow artillery to cover all avenues of approach. Magazines were constructed totally underground. The inner layout of the fort consisted of three large wooden barracks, a command post and headquarters, a guardhouse, and an observation tower. A dry moat encircled the exterior of the fort. It was protected by more than fifty heavy guns and garrisoned by approximately 1,000 soldiers. Fort Marshall, located across the harbor on Murray's Hill (now the site of the Sacred Heart Church in east Baltimore), was almost identical in design and construction to Fort Federal Hill. From the northeast bank of the river, a garrison of 400 soldiers protected the rails and roads heading north to Philadelphia.

Following the dramatic events of April 1861, military life at Relay returned to normal. Soldiers' duties centered around the protection of the railroad, including bridges, culverts, switches, tracks, and cars. Infantry units were frequently trained at Relay and then rotated to various campaigns. By the end of May 1861, the 1st Maryland Regiment, numbering six companies, had been recruited and moved to Relay. This was the first organized Maryland regiment accredited to Maryland's quota in the Civil War. In June, the regiment relocated to Camp Carroll near Baltimore, where Colonel John R. Kenly assumed command. On September 25, 1861, the Patapsco Guard, also known as McGowan's Independent Infantry Company, was formed at Ellicott's Mills and initially assigned to General Dix's command at Baltimore. The unit performed guard and police duties in Maryland and Pennsylvania, usually at the site of railroad bridges. During the Gettysburg campaign, the unit skirmished with Confederate forces at Wrightsville, Pennsylvania. On July 30, 1864, the unit again skirmished at Chambersburg, Pennsylvania, during McCausland's Raid.

As more artillery units were assigned to duty protecting the vital railroad link at Relay, the camps became heavily defended fortifications, commanding a large arsenal of weapons. A report from the Army Requisition and Supply

Division, Ordnance Office, listed the following pieces at the Washington Junction in Relay (US National Archives):

Class I Ordnance on hand January 1, 1865
Field Guns and Howitzers

NUMBER	DESCRIPTION
2	12-pounders, Mountain Howitzer, Bronze, Smooth Bore, 4", 62 Bore
1	24-pounder, Field Howitzer, Bronze, Smooth Bore, 5", 82 Bore
3	10-pounders, "Parrott," Model 1863, Iron, Rifled guns, 3" Bore
20	12-pounders, "James," Bronze, Rifled guns, 4", 62 Bore

Siege, Garrison and Sea Coast Guns

NUMBER	DESCRIPTION
2	8" Siege Howitzer, Model 1841, Cast-Iron Howitzer, Smooth Bore

Although duties at Relay became routine as the war progressed and shifted fronts, a constant state of readiness was required. Rumors of impending attacks from sympathizers or dissident citizens, also called Baltimore's "roughs" by General Butler, kept the forces alert and on guard. The rumored attacks never materialized, but a number of fatalities were recorded. Policing the area proved as dangerous as combat, and resulted in a number of railroad-related deaths and numerous injuries. The unfortunate experiences of the 60th Regiment New York State volunteers showed the hazards and dangers of life near the railroad. William McDonald, Company E, New York State Volunteers, became a statistic while on night guard duty. Feeling ill, McDonald sat down on the track to regain his composure. He then fainted, falling backward to the outside of the track, with one leg remaining over the track. When the *New York Express* passed through the area, it severed his leg below the knee. Luckily, McDonald did not lose his life in the accident.

The explosion of a railroad locomotive proved to be one of the most spectacular and almost unbelievable accidents at the camp. Chaplain Richard Eddy of the same New York regiment vividly described the incident in the history of the regiment.

On the night of the 11th, between 11 and 12 o'clock, our camp was alarmed by a terrible explosion, evidently quite near, followed by a whistling noise in the air, much resembling that caused by the passage of a bomb, which Col. Hayward felt quite confident it was. A corporal in charge of a relief guard was going the rounds with his squad, when the strange noise-maker fell on their path, and only about three feet in their rear. They also thinking it was a bomb, got out of the way in a "double quick." No explosion following, the corporal reported that something had fallen near him, and was sent by the colonel to ascertain what it was. He returned bringing a piece of locomotive boiler-flue about three feet long, and weighing ten or fifteen pounds. As it was still very hot, we of course concluded that the explosion took place not far from us, and at once as many as were up went down to the track, about a hundred yards from camp. While going down the side of the deep cut through which the road here passes, I came upon the body of a man, horrible mutilated, his countenance so disfigured as to have but little of a human appearance remaining. He had evidently been blown into the air, and to such an elevation that coming down feet first, both legs were driven into the mud to some distance above his knees. The man had a soldier's uniform, but we never learned what regiment or State he belonged to. The locomotive, one of the kind called "camel back," lay upon the side of the track, a wreck. Fragments of it were strewn in every direction, some to the distance of four hundred feet. The engineer was found two hundred and sixty-four feet from the track, having been thrown, before striking the ground, through the top of a large tree, breaking off in his passage limbs of the tree three inches in diameter. The dome of the engine, weighing at least eight hundred pounds, was found twenty-five feet beyond the engineer. The fireman remained at the tender, but was so badly scalded that he survived but a few hours. Capt. Ransom was standing with one foot on the steep of the engine, having got on only a few moments before for the purpose of riding down a mile or more to visit his guard. He was thrown on the side of the track, but received no injury. A most surprising escape! (Toomey 1975)

The camps at Relay were utilized by both civilians and soldiers. During December 1864, several civilians were arrested in the Baltimore area and sent to Fort Dix for confinement. Records list a Robert Thompson having served a sentence of thirty days of hard labor for the charge of disloyal language. The fortifications on both sides of the river remained in operation until the end of the war. With the surrender of the Confederate Army in April 1865, Fort Dix and Camp Essex were dismantled, and the troops sent home.

Military activity along the Patapsco River Valley was not limited to Relay. Towns located on the B&O line witnessed daily the passing of long trains loaded with troops, horses, cannons, wagons, and other military supplies. The main roads crossing the Patapsco were frequently clogged with infantry and cavalry moving to and from the battlefronts. In an attempt to harass the rear guard and disrupt supply lines, marauding bands of Confederate cavalry and irregulars, many of them Marylanders, conducted sabotage missions along the valley. Farmers sympathetic to the cause of the South made upper sections of the river valley friendly territory for these raiding parties.

In June 1863, while en route to Gettysburg, a detachment of General J. E. B. Stuart's troops under General Fitzhugh Lee cut the telegraph lines and tore up the railroad track at Marriottsville, Sykesville, and Hood's Mill. Stuart's excursion through Hood's Mill proved untimely and costly. The one-day delay resulted in Stuart's cavalry being unavailable for deployment in the initial stages of the Battle of Gettysburg.

On the evening of July 9, 1864, the streets of Ellicott's Mills bristled with excitement and anticipation. Earlier that day General Lewis Wallace and his Union forces were routed at the Battle of Monocacy. Union soldiers, retreating in confusion, poured into the mill town. Train loads of wounded were brought into Ellicott's Mills and then sent to Baltimore. For days, the Frederick Turnpike, which led into Ellicott's Mills, was filled with ambulances and stragglers. At daybreak on July 10, word of the Union defeat reached Baltimore, sounding the general alarm throughout the city. Evacuation of the city proved needless, as the Confederates under General Early moved against the Union forces guarding the nation's capital.

The final footnote to the war along the Patapsco occurred in April 1865, following the assassination of President Lincoln. On April 21, the funeral train carrying Lincoln's body passed through Relay on its way from Washington to Baltimore. From the Camden Street Station, a funeral procession of politicians and soldiers escorted the hearse to the Latrobe Exchange and Custom House building at Lombard and Gay Streets. Under the great rotunda, an estimated 10,000 mourning Baltimoreans viewed the body of the Great Emancipator. Later that day, the body was returned to the funeral train for the trip north to Harrisburg, Pennsylvania, the next stop on Lincoln's funeral journey to his final resting place in Springfield, Illinois. Lincoln's final appearance took place a block away from the Pratt Street waterfront where on April 19, 1861, the first blood of the Civil War had been shed in the streets of Baltimore.

CHAPTER TEN

Hell and High Water: The Floods of 1868 and 1972

THE GREAT FLOOD

A dreadful calamity befell the Valley of the Patapsco on Friday, the 24th day of July. A flood of unprecedented dimensions and incalculable powers swept nearly the whole valley, from Mount Airey down to the Ridge carrying along with it destruction to annihilation, and misery to a maddening extent. What handicraft and human genius had wrought, what nature herself had beautifully built up, what human industry and self-denial had accumulated — all, all went, swept away as if it never had been, or leaving only the saddest of ruins, the most mournful reminiscence of things that were . . . over these vacant places, over these ghastly ruins hover the spirits of nearly half a hundred of human beings; men, women and children whose mad despair was only ended by the dreadful certainty of death, death in the raging element, a grave in the irresistible billows, that dashed down seaward and lashed the flanks of the granite-built hillsides with ruin-breathing madness, while a thousand eyes, tearless but burning with feverish excitement, bore to the trembling heart hope and despair upon despair, watching incessantly, or returning stubbornly, if turned away by the maddened mind, as if fascinated by the fatal magic of a hopeless sympathy and a helpless will. Helpless, yea, helpless as babes were all the many friends, crowding at the waters edge; for the wild billows and what they carried in their dreadful embrace rendered every attempt of approach to the isolated sufferers impossible, and with such unknown swiftness had the flood grown beyond any known mark, that a few seconds of time had severed the thread of aid, had cut off the sympathetic chord of hope, had clipped the last fibre of the Patapsco's artful web, and family after family sank down into the endless night of death. But I must come to particulars. (*Common Sense*, July 29,1868)

Life along the Main Branch of the Patapsco in the 1800s could best be described as the peaceful yet precarious coexistence of man and nature. The river provided the power for a thriving mill industry, and the valley provided a scenic rural setting for the workers and their families. Interruptions of the lives of the river people were few but extremely violent. Fire and rain, which wreaked havoc on the valley like a predestined plague, seemed nature's way to test the will and spirit of the people in overcoming adversity. Although fire devastated many of the mills, it was the floodwaters that almost succeeded in sweeping away any evidence of man's existence. Residents and businessmen, resigned to living with the unpredictable and uncontrollable flooding, could never have imagined such horror as was to be inflicted by rising, swirling waters. On July 24, 1868, the most destructive flood in the history of Maryland, commonly referred to in printed material as a "freshet," occurred along the Patapsco. The death and destruction would range from Ellicott City to Baltimore City. "Black Friday," as the day would be known, claimed some fifty lives and cost millions of dollars in damages. Along the Patapsco River Valley, thirty-nine persons drowned or were fatally injured. Twenty-eight houses were washed away, and the mills and the railroad were extensively damaged. The event drew national attention, as leading newspapers and magazines sent artists and reporters to cover the story. The *New York Times* reported the "Maryland Flood" on the front page of the July 25 and July 26, 1868, editions.

The light rain that began to fall early Friday morning on Ellicott City gave little indication of the impending disaster. But already along the western reaches of the Patapsco, eighteen inches of rain had fallen within half an hour. Between 8:00 and 10:30 a.m., the water fell in such vast torrents throughout the valley that, in one ten-minute period, the rise in the river was estimated at five feet. At 9:30 a.m., the surging waters tore apart the residential communities and industrial centers of Ellicott City.

The destruction began at the appropriately named community of Watersville, later known as Mt. Airy. The old main line of the B&O was washed out in numerous places. Railroad track was left hanging limply over the gouged-out riverbank, and the railroad bed was twisted into grotesque shapes. This would be a common sight where the railroad paralleled the river through the steep rocky canyons. Woodbine saw its gristmills and sawmills go underwater, and, at Hood's Mills, the lime mills and sawmills were swept away. At Sykesville, a store, a hotel, and twelve houses were engulfed. The watchman at the railroad tunnel between Sykesville and Marriottsville lost his life while remaining at his duty station. The Elba Furnace in Sykesville, which had been recently blown out, was severely damaged and never rebuilt. At Marriottsville, the Reeves Mill was destroyed. The angry waters rushed into Woodstock, sweeping away two houses and several bridges.

At Alberton Mills, between Woodstock and Ellicott City, owner James Gary and his daughter, Pamelia, narrowly escaped with their lives. Deciding to remain in their mansion to weather the storm, Gary and his daughter were forced to the second floor after floodwaters destroyed a brick building behind their home. As the water rose and the walls of the house began to crack, Pamelia jumped from a bedroom window and landed on the first-story roof. By clinging to some passing debris, she was able to drift to a nearby sturdy oak tree. She was quickly followed by her father. The pair remained marooned in the tree until the floodwaters subsided. Structural damage and equipment loss at the Alberton Mill was estimated at $150,000.

Downriver at Hollofields (the site of Ellicott's Upper Mills), a mother and her son were listed among the first casualties when their house crumbled like cardboard in the wake of the raging river. The Union Mill at Oella, situated on the high ground next to the river, suffered only the loss of its cotton inventory and water damage to the machinery. As the rampaging water approached Ellicott City, it became an uncontrollable fury, its rage intensified by reinforcements from many swollen tributaries. By the time the first wave of floodwater reached Ellicott City, it had uprooted and carried away trees, houses, and bridges. At Ellicott City, the tremendous force of the river was funneled into the steep canyon that lined the river above and below the business district at its edge. The devastating results were unpredictable and unbelievable.

In the bustling mill town of Ellicott City, July 24, 1868, was a day that began much like any other day. It started with the usual gathering of people on the B&O station platform awaiting the arrival of the 9:00 a.m. train from Frederick to carry them to their places of employment in Baltimore. Among those waiting were the honorable John Lee Carroll, Judge Richard Merrick, former governor Thomas Watkins Ligon, James McCubbin, and J. R. Clarke. The village children were already in their classrooms, and housewives were well into their rigorous routine of daily chores. Groaning and whirling sounds from the colossal flour and cotton mills that clung to the river's banks filled the air and signaled the start of another working day.

At approximately 9:15 a.m., Charles W. Harvey, the B&O station agent, announced the arrival of the westbound mail train from Baltimore. As the train departed the station, it disappeared into an eerie darkness that had slowly covered the river canyon. About a mile west of the station, an avalanche of water engulfed the locomotive and its cars. The train's engineer, fireman, conductor, and passengers frantically scrambled up the steep canyon walls to safety.

By 9:30 a.m., an uneasy calm had settled on the village. The darkness had intensified and now shrouded the mills and houses. Accompanied by deafening claps of thunder, brilliant flashes of lightning pierced the darkness, illuminating the ill-fated structures lining the river. The sights and sounds of the approaching storm overwhelmed every living creature in the valley. Birds ceased to sing, and people in the streets paused to search the sky with a tense look of uncertainty. Workers inside the mills stopped their activities, unable to see in the darkness. The Patapsco had risen nearly ten feet to the bed of the turnpike bridge connecting the Howard County (south side) and Baltimore County (north side) portions of the village. During the next thirty minutes, the water rose more than twenty-five feet and quickly overflowed the banks of the river. Communication between opposite banks became impossible. Attempting to cross the river was suicidal.

A short distance west of the railroad station was the Granite Mill. It was situated on a sharp turn in the canyon along the river. The mill, along with the mountainous rocks on the opposite side of the canyon, had acted as a breakwater and held the Patapsco in check. By midmorning the river had risen sixteen feet higher than ever before witnessed. A frothy mass of spray shot upward an additional twenty feet above its surface. Within minutes, the mill's stone walls, some of which were said to be twenty feet thick, began to sway. The tremendous pressure and weight created by the forty-foot-high crest began to buckle and dismantle the enormous stone structure. Horrified workers streamed from the massive building and scrambled up the canyon walls to safety. All escaped except one man who could not swim. Vain efforts were made to rescue the terrified man as he sought refuge in the mill's swaying granite tower. Seconds later, the tower rocked violently and the entire building collapsed with a thunderous roar. The man and $250,000 worth of equipment were swept out of existence.

The raging waters then turned their full fury on a row of thirteen houses standing between the B&O bridge and the Patapsco Flouring Mills on an island created by the millrace and the river. Houses of wood, brick, and stone crumbled like eggshells and disappeared into the boiling forty-five-foot-deep torrent. As each succeeding house in the row was destroyed, the occupants fled to the roof of the next building. Finally thirty-six persons had gathered on the roof of the last house. Friends, relatives and those children who were unable to return home after early dismissal from school stood helplessly on the riverbank and watched in terror as the raging waters began to rip the house from its foundation. The location of the house away from the riverbank made rescue attempts impossible. Frantic efforts to throw a line to the survivors failed. The hopes and whispered prayers of the villagers went unanswered as the last roof disappeared beneath the swirling waters. Only two families escaped from the thirteen homes.

Dr. T. B. Owings, returning from a house call, was a horrified witness to the loss of his own family. It was reported in local newspapers that Owings

> saw all the dear ones of his household in imminent peril, unable to render them the slightest assistance and watched them, as they fled across the roofs, almost frantic with grief. When he saw them go down with the building on which they had finally obtained a foothold and engulfed in the raging waters, it was more than human nature could bear, and the sympathizing friends who surround him carried him to the hotel almost insensible. He is in a constitution of deep melancholy and exhibits indications of insanity. At a late hour this evening he was said to be hopelessly insane and fears were entertained . . . that he would attempt to take his own life.
> (*American and Commercial Daily Advertiser*, July 27, 1868)

In 1936, the *Ellicott City Times* interviewed Charles Cramblitt, the only survivor. Cramblitt recalled the heroic operation made to rescue the Owings family.

> One of the most pitiful and yet brave things which I saw while I was stranded in the mill was the drowning of Dr. Owings' youngest baby and William, one of the colored men who worked for him. After the other members of the family had been drowned, this colored man took the baby in his arms and went to the roof.
> Of course the water was coming down harder all the time and the force of all this dislodged Dr. Owings' house which was built and sent it into the river. This colored man was still on the roof with the baby in his arms and just as the house floated to a point about opposite where I was in the mill, it must have struck a rock. . . as it turned over and over and the colored man and the baby were drowned before my eyes.

Following the destruction of the last house, the Chesapeake and Patapsco mills, belonging to the estate of Charles Carroll of Carrollton, came face to face with the raging waters. The Chesapeake Mill, built of large granite blocks, quickly succumbed to the overwhelming torrent. Its elaborate machinery and vast stores went bounding down the river with two employees. One of the employees succeeded in taking hold of a piece of timber and rode the crest for two miles to Ilchester, where he gained a foothold on a rooftop. Almost instantly, the roof was dashed against a protruding rock and the man disappeared beneath the surface.

Although greatly damaged, the Patapsco Mill, constructed of wood, survived the onslaught. From a small bridge at the rear of the mill, five young men carried out a valiant rescue operation. After rescuing several persons being carried downstream by the waters, they suddenly found themselves trapped by the rising water. Carrying flour barrels as life preservers, they climbed to the gallery on the mill's roof. For seven hours, they stood helplessly on the slanting and crumbling building before they could be rescued.

John Pendleton Kennedy described the destruction at Gray's Cotton Mills, about a mile downstream from the Patapsco Mill:

> Every tree and street, the conservatory, the fences, the out buildings are all swept away. A great part of the dwelling house is in ruins, a deposit of three or four feet of white sand spread over the grass plots; quantities of stone brought down the river from the mills destroyed above, strewed over this deposit, the porches carried away, my entire library taken off, leaving no vestige of books, prints, busts and other articles with which it was furnished, the factory shockingly injured, requiring $50,000 worth of repairs. Mr. Bowen's house is lifted up from its foundations and borne bodily away upon the flood. The devastation has so completely altered the aspect of the place that I should not know it. (Davidson 1967)

In a letter to E. L. Stanley, Kennedy further described the disaster:

> In the summer of 1868 a terrible freshet, unequalled in its sudden eruption and devastating course, burst over the valley, swept away massive stone walls, bridges and dwellings and changed the whole aspect of the scene. As many as forty-two persons lost their lives at this time. In consequence of a bend in the river Mr. Gray's mill escaped destruction, as far as the edifice was concerned, but its machinery and surroundings were submerged and ruined and more than half of the dwelling houses and all the choice trees were carried off, leaving a debris of stones and slime where once the garden bloomed. A more striking and painful contrast cannot be imagined than that presented by photographs of the scenery before and after the flood. (Davidson 1967)

From Ellicott City, the raging waters roared down the valley unobstructed. Damage to Gray's Mills was similar to that sustained by other mills downriver. At Ilchester, the Thistle Cotton Mill, situated on a narrow, soft curve in the steep valley, suffered major damage. The majestic Patterson Viaduct of the B&O received structural damage to each of its four arches and was rendered nonfunctional. Railroad tracks running next to the river were twisted and torn for miles. Downstream at Orange Grove, the flour mill was severely damaged and much of its machinery and stock carried away. Gun Road, which passed through the mill's lower floor, was washed away from the river's east bank.

Two miles below Orange Grove, the industrial center of Avalon was almost completely swept away. Only ruins remained as evidence of the town's existence. The wave of water slammed into the Avalon Iron Works, destroying buildings and machinery. Gone were the four smokestacks between the long brick buildings, where nails, iron plates, and bars were manufactured. The small town, located east of the industrial center, absorbed much of the damage from the initial wave of water, thus protecting portions of the ironworks. The houses, stores, churches, and school, some twenty buildings in all, disappeared under the swirling currents. The flood also destroyed the wharves and the channel used by scows and small tugs to ferry pig and scrap iron to Avalon and manufac- tured iron to Baltimore. The small wharves, located just below the Avalon Iron Works, were built by Ross Winans and the owners of the ironworks. On the morning of the flood, a small steamer, the *Great Western*, was moored to a large willow tree at one of Winans's wharves. When the water began to rise higher and higher, James Biden, the manager of Winans's operation, and his brother and two other men tried to safely secure the boat. As the water continued to rise, the men climbed higher in a tree in order to secure the fastenings. The water rose so rapidly that within minutes they became stranded. A large mass of debris floating downriver uprooted the tree, carrying both it and the boat into the floodwaters. Biden remained on the tree until he was rescued near the Light Street Bridge in Baltimore. Although exhausted by the ordeal, Biden survived. The three other men drowned.

Below Avalon at the Rockburn Branch on the river's south bank, Mrs. John Humphries, forced from her home by the river's backwater, witnessed the carnage wrought by the flood from a nearby hilltop. Mrs. Humphries saw, in addition to recognizable debris from homes and businesses, a cradle go by, but she was unable to determine whether there was a baby inside. A doghouse floated past with the animal still chained to it. The dog tried vainly to swim away from the house but tired in the effort and returned to the house. Clinging desperately, it disappeared when the doghouse rolled over and under the water.

The Thomas Viaduct stood strong against the gigantic wave of water. Homes and businesses on the south side of the structure suffered extensive damage. Damage to the Hockley Mill, known at that time as Robert's Flour Mill, was reported by the *American* on July 25, 1868: "Robert's Flour Mill located at the western end of the viaduct over the Patapsco near the Relay House was inundated on the first and second floors, the machinery greatly damaged, and the large stock of barreled flour and grain washed away causing a loss of many thousand dollars." At the fall line near Elkridge, the floodwaters spread out into the lower terrain and decreased in intensity. Nevertheless, the flood ripped through Elkridge Landing, destroying any traces of the original colonial settlement. The early ironworks at the Elkridge Furnace were damaged but not totally destroyed.

As the floodwaters receded, the gruesome task of searching for the victims began. The following days were filled with memorial services, the clearing of wreckage, and the rebuilding of homes and businesses. The bodies of a young man and his wife and child were found caught in a treetop. Three days after the disaster, the flats below the Thomas Viaduct yielded six more victims. The search among piles of debris, driftwood, and mounds of silt and mud continued for months. Bodies were found wedged in debris near the river's mouth at the edge of Baltimore, some fifteen miles downriver from Ellicott City.

The *Baltimore American* on July 24, 1868, provided an accurate summary of the preceding day's events: "On Saturday afternoon we visited the scene of destruction at Ellicott City . . . Indeed, there has probably never been any instance in this country where the fearfully irresistible power of water has been so fully demonstrated, where the strongest and most scientific works of men have proved but as straws in its way."

Baltimore and the Flood

The great flood along the Patapsco River Valley was also the worst flood in the history of Baltimore. It struck at a time when the city was experiencing the pangs of a growing boomtown. After the Civil War, new homes and industries began springing up overnight. The population stood at over half a million. Cotton mills and gristmills lining Jones Falls, as well as sugar refineries and ironworks near the harbor, were prospering.

By the time people going to work in the eastern section of the city were passing Jones Falls (the stream that carried the runoff from outlying hillsides into the harbor), the stream was spilling over its walled embankments into the cobblestone streets. At the time, the flooding was considered a side effect of the passing storm, and no evacuation plans were put into operation.

By noon, the storm was at its peak. The wind-blown curtain of water was now receiving the serious attention of all citizens. The south wind blew in a high tide that joined with the rain-swollen falls to produce a sudden and dramatic flood crest. Reports indicate that the falls rose as much as five feet in ten minutes, and that it eventually reached a height of twenty feet. Wooden bridges spanning the falls and its feeder streams were the first to feel the force of the flood. Stone from the uprooted Eager Street Bridge was swept away by the rushing waters into a collision course with other downstream bridges. Bridges collapsed so suddenly that many people on them could not escape. Debris-filled waters tore away at outbuildings, trees, fences, and oil tanks. Telegraph lines were torn down. Horsecars were either swept away or stranded in the flooded streets. Water and gas service was disrupted.

Ellicott City after the Great Flood of 1868.
Courtesy Maryland Historical Society.

Harrison Street, close to the falls, was one of the first streets flooded. Squealing rats were seen scampering to higher ground as if fleeing a sinking ship. When the floodwaters crested later in the day, only one lamppost at Baltimore and Harrison Streets was visible. The Centre Market near the falls was hard hit and became a hell of high water. A theatrical company was rehearsing in a hall above the market when cries came from below. A hole was broken in the floor, and the actors viewed a tragedy unfolding. The doors were completely blocked, and terrified people were clinging to the framework above the market stalls as the water quickly rose. A rope was lowered and more than thirty people were hauled to safety. At about 1:00 p.m., a horsecar was lifted from its tracks and carried down Harrison Street. When it reached Fayette Street and lodged against a restaurant, the driver managed to free himself and the horses.

As the day wore on, more flooding occurred in streets near Jones Falls close by the harbor. The police commandeered all the boats they could find and turned the front of the flooded Holiday Street Theater into a dock area and headquarters for rescue operations. Police Commissioner James E. Carr was proclaimed a hero for his leadership and actions. A newspaper account related that "he led the men in his boat in places of great peril, and rescued women and children from death. Two parties he rescued from Davis Street were in the upper story of the house, holding each a child above their head, with water to their necks." The aftermath of the disaster was not without its lighter moments. On some streets, men and women "revelled in semi-nudity, catching waifs and strays borne down by the tide. Barrels of flour and whiskey, articles of household furniture and all other imaginable floating stuff was captured."

The tragic statistics compiled for the Flood of 1868 were grim. The final count for Ellicott City and Baltimore was some 50 dead, 4,000 unemployed, 2,000 homes and businesses flooded, and millions of dollars in property damage. By nightfall on that fateful Friday, the flood-waters began to recede, making the streets passable and cleanup operations possible.

THE FLOOD OF 1972

After the Flood of 1868, communities and industries along the river learned to live with the uncertainties of the weather and its effect on the river's composure. Likewise, they learned to cope with the aftermath of floodwaters, and to regroup, repair, and rebuild as quickly as possible. In most cases, the inconvenience was temporary. Although the river continued to cripple occasionally, it was never the killer it had proved to be on July 24, 1868. However, the false sense of security that grew for over a century was shattered on June 21, 1972. Like a wild animal, trained but never really tamed, the river turned into a killer once again. Death and devastation rode the crest of floodwaters down the Patapsco River Valley. The flood was immediately compared to the disaster of a hundred years earlier. Destruction of property was enormous, but death did not reign supreme.

That day proved anything but promising for the first day of summer. The sporadic rain showers of the past several days had made it difficult for anyone to envision sunny vacation days at beach or mountain resorts. Most people, staying indoors to avoid the tedious raindrops, were thankful that the rain would

A view of receding 1972 floodwaters from Main Street in Ellicott City. At upper right is the George Ellicott house. *Courtesy Library, Howard County Historical Society, Ellicott City, Maryland, #637.*

probably not ruin the first official summer weekend. As another uneventful Wednesday ended and evening settled over the valley, Tropical Storm Agnes rolled into the area unnoticed. For days, the storm had moved deceptively up the East Coast from the Florida Panhandle. Weather alerts and flood watches were announced on local radio and television broadcasts, but few people paid any attention to a summer storm that did not carry fierce hurricane winds.

As evening progressed along the valley, the downpour steadily increased. The region's watersheds, already saturated with heavy spring rains, could not absorb the excess. The runoff was quickly funneled into nearby streams and creeks. The Patapsco rose slowly at first, giving no cause for great concern. By 11:00 p.m., the river had crept over its banks in Ellicott City. Within the next hour, it rose dramatically, drowning the banks under ten feet of water. The river's rage had just begun. Main Street appeared to be a lake. Residents living near the river were forced to evacuate as water reached the second story of apartment buildings. Many were rescued by boat, whereas others were plucked from rooftops by helicopters.

Authorities quickly mobilized emergency and rescue forces. The night of terrifying danger was not allowed to escalate into a night of panic and chaos. As the water rose higher and higher, police and fire personnel, assisted by local volunteers, warned people in imminent danger to seek safety on higher ground. National Guard helicopters rescued two men from the roof of the plant at Daniels. Two railroad engineers near Marriottsville were ordered to abandon their 137-car coal train. Marooned by high water in the process of trying to save the diesel locomotive, the pair had to be rescued by helicopter. In Elkridge, a family of six was forced by rising water from their home into a small boat. While they were trying to reach high ground, the boat capsized and all six held onto the boat for several hours until it drifted into shallow water.

A disaster relief center was established in Ellicott City to aid the hundreds of homeless residents. The 121st Engineer Battalion of the National Guard was called up to evacuate and aid flood victims and to assist in emergency repairs. The flooding continued through the night, uprooting trees, knocking out electric and phone service, and sweeping away cars and trucks. Roads and bridges were washed out, leaving many communities and citizens stranded.

Thursday morning's light lifted the curtain of darkness and revealed an unbelievable spectacle. Even though the river had crested to record heights during the early morning hours, the floodwaters still raged. Spectators lined the riverbanks to witness the destructive power of the river. Grotesque scenes of twisted and ensnarled debris protruding from the receding river, which was now light brown in color, provided sights that hadn't been seen in over a century.

In Ellicott City, more than fifty businesses suffered major damage, exceeding $1.2 million. The former home of Jonathan Ellicott, the son of one of the city's founders, was ripped in half. The granite structure, which had survived nearly two hundred years, was finally defeated by the river. Two gas stations, a used-car lot, and an auto-parts agency, located on the north bank, were reduced to rubble and junk. At Elkridge, two gas stations, a restaurant/laundromat, and a new-car dealership received extensive water damage.

Established industries that had survived the Great Flood of 1868 were once again hit hard. The Wilkins-Rogers flour mill, constructed on the original site of Ellicott's Lower Mills, suffered damage to its building and supplies, for an estimated loss of $50,000. The C. R. Daniels Company, located above Ellicott City at the former town of Alberton, was destroyed. The river rose so fast that five workers caught inside the main mill building had to be evacuated by helicopter. The water's force washed the town store downriver. Cars, trucks, trees, bridge girders, and other debris lodged among the mill buildings. The C. R. Daniels Company incurred an uninsured loss of $2.7 million. The mill complex, coated inside and out with slimy river mud, would never be restored. The property was eventually sold for $25,000 and was used as a warehouse and still later as a light manufacturing concern. At Elkridge, the I&R Equipment Company and the Adley Express Company suffered damages estimated at $2 million, but were able to resume limited operations by August.

The lower portion of the Patapsco Valley State Park extending from Ilchester to Elkridge was devastated. Land bordering the river was leveled. In that area, large portions of roadbed were washed away, and sections of the railroad line were left dangling in midair. Bloede's Dam and the Avalon Dam suffered major damage. The superstructure at Bloede's was destroyed, and at Avalon the river washed away the dam's north end and then changed course, circumventing the remaining section. Hundreds of trees were ripped from the riverbanks and carried downriver to inflict more damage. The Orange Grove and Avalon recreational areas were hit the hardest. Picnic shelters, park equipment, buildings (including the park headquarters at Orange Grove), and water and electrical systems were uprooted and swept away. Two of the park's unique attractions were destroyed. The Swinging Bridge, spanning the river at Orange Grove, and the Lost Lake at Avalon disappeared with the floodwaters. The Avalon pumping station, built on the site of the Avalon Iron Works and used as a park maintenance facility, was flooded to the top of its twelve-foot doors. The sanitary sewer interceptor line running next to the river was uncovered and ruptured in four places, spilling raw sewage into the river. One of the few bright spots was the uncovering of the original railroad line with granite sleepers laid in 1830. Damage to the park was close to $2 million.

The grimmest statistic was the seven deaths attributed directly to the flood. Several stranded motorists became victims when they fled their vehicles to try to reach safety. One victim was a thrill seeker who drowned when his canoe became snagged in the top wires of a utility pole. A heroic but tragic rescue operation occurred at Daniels, when Harry Shiflett, the innkeeper at the Hollofield Inn, and Carroll L. Greniger, attempted to rescue two women stranded in separate vehicles. In the rescue attempt, all four became trapped by the rising water. For three hours, they clung to a tree awaiting help before Greniger and one woman tried to float downstream on a log. The other woman and Shiflett remained hand in hand clinging to the tree until floating debris broke their grasp and separated them. Shiflett was rescued hours later still clinging to the tree. The bodies of the others were recovered downriver. In an ironic twist of fate, one of the women was reported to be Greniger's fiancée.

On the second day after the flood, recovery operations were well under way. The backbreaking job of shoveling out mud and debris and restoring ruined businesses and homes became a spirited community effort. People helping people, working hand in hand, became a common sight along the valley. Discouraged but not defeated, the river people bounced back with a remarkable resiliency. Morale remained high as the tedious task of cleaning up continued for months. A big boost came from the Army Corps of Engineers, who played a major role in large-scale recovery operations. The corps cleaned debris from the river, restored bridges, and repaired damaged sewer lines. Working with disaster relief funds, the corps awarded engineering and building contracts once damage surveys were conducted to determine priorities in repair and replacement work.

On the Friday following the flood, President Richard Nixon declared Maryland a federal disaster area, allowing needed federal money to be funneled into the hardest-hit areas. The following Wednesday, Vice President Spiro T. Agnew stopped at Ellicott City on his inspection tour of flood areas along the East Coast.

While surveying the damage from a helicopter, the former governor of the state remarked that he "couldn't remember anything as bad." Tropical Storm Agnes did benefit the river by flushing away debris and sediment that had built up over decades. However, the cleansing of the river's bottom and banks was not without drawbacks. Ravaging floodwaters had broken the sewer interceptor line running parallel to the river along its southern bank and dumped millions of gallons of untreated sewage into the water.

Scientists compared Tropical Storm Agnes to the Flood of 1868 and labeled it a "hundred-year storm." Although they stated that a flood of such magnitude is a very infrequent event, they quickly pointed out that such a flood could happen at any time. While the rebuilding was taking place, county and state officials were revamping and updating information on flood prevention and evacuation plans. Designated flood areas were established, and a number of construction projects were designed to reduce local flooding. (The flooding in 1972 had been compounded by the runoff from large areas of residential development. Water collected by rainspouts, gutters, and paved areas channeled into storm drains and culverts. The result was a tremendous volume of water being quickly fed into the already swollen river.) Monitoring devices were also installed at strategic points along the river to record flow changes. Despite these preventive measures, flood experts agreed that only so much could be done and that the valley's fate rested with the uncertainties of the weather and the temperament of the river.

Over the years, floods of a lesser nature have plagued the valley. Scattered between the two major floods were numerous natural disasters that were smaller but still deadly and destructive. The Flood of 1923 inundated Main Street in Ellicott City, causing considerable water damage to homes and businesses. In 1934, a storm, whipped up by winds exceeding sixty miles an hour, thrashed the valley for nearly twenty-four hours. The resulting floods were responsible for at least three deaths and the destruction of numerous homes, businesses, and bridges. In 1952 and 1956, the river flooded its banks and caused considerable property damage. In the 1960s, Hurricane Camille lashed the valley with heavy rains. Later, in 1975, Tropical Storm Eloise roared through the region, resulting in $1.2 million in flood damages and losses.

The epitaph for the Patapsco River Valley floods was unknowingly written after the Flood of 1868 as an address on a letter to a resident of Ellicott City:

To Jesse R. Reynolds, of Ellicott Mills
In the land of old Maryland, among the huge hills,
Where torrents from Heaven down the steep mountain rolled, Destroying men,
women and children, as at Sodom of old;
A warning from Heaven, a chastening rod.
Repent and be saved is the command of your God.

Washington, DC
(Kreh 1920)

CHAPTER ELEVEN

Harnessing the Force and Fury: River Dams

The Patapsco, frequently called the "River of History," can also be appropriately entitled the "River of Historic Dams." From Hockley Mill above Elkridge to Hood's Mill below Marriottsville, dams of earth, stone, wood, and concrete were built across its swift waters in order to harness waterpower for the various mill operations. Every commercial mill and almost every private mill had a dam for its source of power. Ranging in height from eight to fifteen feet and spanning the river's width, the dams were built to pool a supply of water with enough force to power the machinery. Often the dams were constructed with a millrace. These narrow and deep canals, running parallel with the river away from the dam, diverted water directly to the waterwheel, which was the main power source. The canals supplied mill operators with a way of controlling the river's force and flow. The dams were monuments to their builders, who did not always have access to the latest engineering techniques or large powerful machines needed to move tons of raw material. Many dams have disappeared, but a number still remain in a nonfunctioning capacity. Abandoned and gradually deteriorating with time and wear by the elements of nature, they serve as reminders of man's early attempts to tame the river. Over the years, the dams have fired iron furnaces and forges, ground wheat into flour that made the name Patapsco famous, driven looms for cotton and silk sold in worldwide markets, threaded and stitched sails for the fleet of Baltimore clippers and tents for the armies of the United States, generated electricity for nearby communities, and supplied drinking water to the city of Baltimore. The greatest number of dams in the state and perhaps the country occurs along the nine-mile stretch of river from the railroad community of Relay, just above Elkridge, to the mill complex at Daniels, situated between Ellicott City and Sykesville.

The first dam on the river was located at Relay, under the shadow of the Thomas Viaduct. Designed to furnish waterpower to the Hockley Forge, and later Hockley Mill, the dam was later replaced by another and used by the

Viaduct Electric Company to power electric generators. The last dam at this site was destroyed by floodwaters in 1933.

The next upriver dam was an earth and stone structure used by the Dorsey Forge. Located about 500 feet below the Gun Road Bridge in the present-day Patapsco Valley State Park, it was replaced by a stone structure for the Avalon Nail and Iron Works. The new dam, constructed about 300 yards upriver, was partially destroyed when the Flood of 1868 swept away the village and the ironworks. The dam was rebuilt in 1901, when the Baltimore County Water and Electric Company built a plant for water purification. In 1972 the floodwaters of Hurricane Agnes washed away a substantial portion, but a stone section of the dam extending from the north bank still stands today. The storm of 1972 cut a path around this section, leaving the ruins standing among dry rocks.

There was another dam about a mile upriver at the site of the Orange Grove Flour Mill complex. The wooden overshot dam, curved in a half-moon, was anchored on the river's north bank by a heavy timbered cage filled with large boulders, and on the south bank by an abutment of stone masonry. Its spillwater fell on the backwater pooled by the Avalon Dam and furnished power to the large mill on the river's north bank. Today the only remaining portion of the dam is the stone and masonry abutment.

At Ilchester, approximately two miles above Orange Grove, a dam was erected to power the Dismal Mill and later the Thistle Cotton Mill. The location for a dam was well chosen. Even though its narrow gorge makes it subject to severe flood damage, a dam still stands at the site of a paper and cardboard manufacturing operation.

Two miles upriver stood the stone dam at the Patapsco Cotton Mill, which later became Gray's Cotton Mill. Evidence of the mill, which was twice destroyed by floods, can be seen on the north bank. The last visible traces of the dam vanished with the Flood of 1972.

Above Gray's Cotton Mill stood the most diminutive of all the dams. In Ellicott City, at the site of the two flour mills that the Ellicott brothers built in the early 1770s, stood a small dam five feet in height. This structure survived the Flood of 1868 but later fell victim to floodwaters and construction projects. Just above Ellicott's Mills also stood the massive stone dam of the Granite Cotton Company. At the time of the Flood of 1868, it was the highest dam in the valley, measuring nearly thirty feet in height. The dam and the mill were swept away by the flood and never rebuilt.

In 1810, the Union Manufacturing Company constructed a dam for its mill operation at Oella, just above Ellicott's Mills on the north bank. The millrace connecting the dam with the mill was believed to be the longest race serving a single mill in the United States—1.75 miles. Although the rumor was never authenticated, it was said that the millrace had been dug by slave labor. The Union Dam, also known as the Oella Dam, was severely damaged by a flood in 1817. The original stone structure was rebuilt with concrete, a commercial building material that gained widespread usage in 1812. Damage to the structure during the Flood of 1972 revealed portions of the original dam within the present structure. The abandoned dam still remains today, although large sections have been washed away.

Further upriver at the Daniels mills, formerly Alberton, stands a concrete dam used to power the mills at the site. Although the mill complex has been ravaged by fire and flood and is no longer used, the dam remains intact. The most easily accessible of all the Patapsco mill dams, it stands as a fine example of the design and construction that created a power source which used only water pressure, well before the introduction of electricity and liquid fuels.

The newest dam on the river is the Liberty Dam, located on the North Branch, approximately two-and-a-half miles north from where the Main Branch of the Patapsco forks into the North Branch and South Branch. Built in 1954 to contain a water supply for Baltimore, the dam cut off a large potion of the water flow to the Main Branch of the river. The dam and reservoir were built as a result of the demand for water following the period of increased industrial activity after World War II. Water from the Liberty Reservoir flows through a concrete-lined tunnel ten feet in diameter to the Ashburton Filtration Plan in Baltimore, a distance of over twelve miles, through solid rock. When it was finished, the water behind the concrete gravity dam inundated approximately 3,400 acres and eight-and-a-half miles of old streambed. The dam measures 160 feet in height above the streambed and 704 feet in total length, with a spillway of 480 feet. The reservoir has a capacity of 43 billion gallons.

BLOEDE'S DAM

Of all the dams on the Patapsco, the most historic and significant is Bloede's Dam. Located between the Orange Grove Flour Mill and the Thistle Cotton Mill, the dam was built in 1906 by the Patapsco Electric and Manufacturing Company of Ellicott City (eventually to become part of the Baltimore Gas and Electric Company) and named for the company's president, Victor Gustav Bloede. At the time of its completion, the dam represented a milestone in construction technology. Not only was it among the earliest reinforced concrete dams built in the United States, it was also the first to use the technique of housing electricity-generating machinery in its hollow interior. Bloede's Dam was recognized as the world's first underwater hydroelectric plant. The dam was described in many scientific and engineering journals, both in the United States and Europe, and was visited by noted hydraulic engineers from all parts of the world.

In 1901, the newly formed Patapsco Electric and Manufacturing Company answered the demand for electricity by deciding to build a new dam and power station. Their power plant at Gray's Mills was replaced in 1902 but it failed to produce enough electricity. The new dam was designed and built by the Amberson Hydraulic Construction Company of Boston. H. von Schon, of Detroit, was the consulting hydraulic engineer; Newton and Painter, of Baltimore, were the electrical engineers. The reasons for the unusual construction of the dam were the result of cost and location. At the time, the Patapsco Electric and Manufacturing Company was a small concern and did not have the capital to finance the building of an expensive dam. Due to the very low riverbanks further downriver, a high dam would have caused the backwater to overflow into residential communities. The submerged powerhouse secured the highest obtainable hydraulic efficiency of available flow and fall and represented the greatest economy in powerhouse construction. The underwater plant was used year-round because the water did not freeze as far down as the inlet, which was six feet below the surface of the water. The water was taken through trash racks into short penstocks and discharged vertically downward below the floor of the power plant into the tailrace.

Bloede's Dam was a flat-slab reinforced-concrete buttress dam of the half-apron type. The frontal view showed the dam to be a small, tight, curving slope or slide with the bottom section cut off to form a short vertical drop. It had a total length of 220 feet and was forty feet wide at the base. The height from normal tailwater was twenty-six-and-a-half feet. At each end, the buttresses and deck rose ten feet above the spillway, which was 168 feet long. The backwater originally extended about one mile, with an average width of about 500 feet. The dam was built of reinforced concrete, and the deck was supported by nineteen buttresses, which tapered from a thickness of twenty-four inches at the base to sixteen inches at the top. The dam's shell was eighteen inches thick at the base and ten inches thick at the top. With the apron or curve extending halfway down from the crown or top, the remaining portion was open and portholes provided light, though with a heavy flow of water, they proved of little use. Water going over the crest of the dam was carried to within sixteen feet of the tailwater. The end of the apron allowed water to fall uninterrupted into the river's downstream side. Originally, a fish ladder was placed at one side of the dam, as required by law. The ladder was about 200 feet long and had the proper slope and fins so that fish could easily ascend the dam.

The power equipment inside and underneath the dam originally consisted of two 34-inch horizontal Leffel waterwheels fitted with Woodward governors. Each turbine ran at 240 rpm and was directly connected to an Allis Chalmers 300-kilowatt, 1,100-volt, 3-phase 60-cycle alternator. Water was fed to the turbine through steel pipes passing through the upstream spillway shell and discharged by draft tubes into the base of the dam, dropping into a well some three feet below the riverbed. Intake was about six feet below the crest of the spillway.

In 1913, the dam and other electric systems were purchased by the Consolidated Gas and Electric and Power Company of Baltimore. The new owners found the dam to be greatly in need of repairs, and renovations were begun immediately. Sediment in the pond above the dam, which reduced the flow to the waterwheels and decreased output, was cleared. The operating parts of the dam were refurbished, and a new head gate and sluice gates were installed. (The gates were operated from motor-driven pedestals mounted in concrete houses above the dam's crest.)

In 1924, operation of the plant ceased. Larger and more capable powerplants were now operating, and the power equipment, which had never been replaced, was becoming worn and outdated. The considerable amount of trash and debris from upstream industrial operations hampered the efficient operation of the plant.

Bloede's Dam, at one time a monument to a remarkable engineering feat, is now a scarred and deteriorating concrete shell. Equipment that had not been removed when the dam was closed was washed downriver by floodwaters. In 1972 Tropical Storm Agnes did considerable damage to the dam, washing away much of the riverbank and sweeping away the gatehouses and columns on top of the spillway. The pond above the dam has filled with so much sediment that the intake pipes are no longer visible. Large cracks and leaks inside and outside the dam mark its state of general deterioration. In 1980, a feasibility study was conducted by the Maryland Department of Natural Resources to determine if the dam could be renovated as a historic attraction for visitors and possibly be restored as a functioning powerplant. The results of the survey were discouraging. The dam had reached a point of decrepitude where any type of repair was now financially unfeasible. Even the cost to renovate the structure for visitor use was prohibitive, for it involved extensive repairs to make the dam structurally sound once again. With the passing of time, it has become another monument to a past era and its people. The dam's only visitor today is an occasional hiker stopping near the top of the structure for a sweeping view of the river valley.

The history of Bloede's Dam is also the story of Victor Gustav Bloede, the man responsible for its construction. He made his initial fortune by manufacturing an obscure but essential product used in conducting everyday business: gum on postage stamps. At one time, Bloede had the monopoly on the market, making nearly 7 million pounds of gum a year. The gum was a result of his own work in pioneering the development of dextrins and carbohydrates derived from vegetable starches.

Born in Dresden, Germany, in 1849, Bloede immigrated to the United States in 1850 with his family after his father was forced to leave Germany because of his involvement in the 1848 Revolution. The family settled in Brooklyn, New York. As a young man, he aspired to be a chemist. He enrolled at Cooper Union, where he caught the eye of Peter Cooper, who encouraged and helped him. At seventeen, Bloede filed his first dextrin-process patent. In 1877, Bloede moved to Catonsville, Maryland, where he set up a plant manufacturing inks, dyes, and adhesives. During this time, he became widely recognized for his experiments in starches and dextrins. In 1908, he endowed the first of many philanthropies when he built the Marie Bloede Memorial Hospital at the Eudowood Sanitarium.

In addition to being the president of the ink-manufacturing company bearing his name, Bloede also had an interest in organizing the National Bank of Catonsville and was the moving force behind the formation of the Patapsco Electric and Manufacturing Company. The utility business, although small, made him better known than his chemical business. For years, his company supplied power to the western edge of Baltimore at cheap rates, but in 1910 he was turned down when he applied for a bigger, permanent license to operate. This unsuccessful attempt to expand his utility business set off a court battle that raged for months.

Frustrated at losing his expansion bid to the Consolidated Company, his competitor, he sold his utility business in 1913. In 1929, Bloede sold his manufacturing company, but stayed close to his laboratory until his death in 1937 at the age of eighty-eight. In 1980, Bloede's descendants donated funds to the Patapsco Valley State Park for the construction of a historical display commemorating his accomplishments.

CHAPTER TWELVE

A New Deal for the Nation's Human
and Natural Resources: The CCC and the COs

THE CIVILIAN CONSERVATION CORPS

I pledge you, I pledge myself, to a new deal for the American people.
— Franklin Delano Roosevelt
Democratic National Convention Chicago
June 1932

Within three weeks of taking office on March 4, 1933, President Roosevelt sent a special and urgent message to Congress proposing "to create a Civilian Conservation Corps, to be used in simple work, not interfering with normal employment, but confining itself to forestry, the prevention of soil erosion, flood control, and similar projects." The reply was quick: two weeks after the request, Congress approved legislation setting up the Civilian Conservation Corps, more commonly referred to as the CCC. The CCC was one of the first New Deal programs, and it paved the way for other agencies concerned with general social relief. It succeeded not only in putting the unemployed youth of the nation to work but also instilled a sense of new hope for a country burdened by the Great Depression.

A restoration of confidence in the federal government was long overdue. By the time Roosevelt was inaugurated, following the overwhelming defeat of Hoover, the economic situation was desperate. An estimated 15 million Americans were unemployed. Of this total, approximately 2 million were roaming the country looking for any type of work. Makeshift cities of ragged tents, cardboard boxes, and wood structures appeared on the fringes of the larger cities. The run on the banks by panic-stricken people caused the majority of banks to close; many of them never reopened. The troubled nation looked to its new leader to show the way to a new prosperity.

The success of the CCC was a result of the program's simplicity and its back-to-basics philosophy. Its primary function was to ease unemployment by taking young men off street corners and teaching them basic job skills in the nation's forests and parks. Although much of the work involved manual skills—such as clearing and cleaning of woodlands, planting trees, and constructing roads, buildings, and bridges— the program instilled the old-fashioned American work ethic in the CCC recruits.

In order to keep down government expenditures, the CCC was administered by existing government agencies. President Roosevelt placed the Department of Labor in charge of recruitment and gave the army the authority and responsibility to run the camps. The Department of Agriculture and the Department of the Interior were assigned the task of developing needed and useful work projects. The success of the program was immediate and the response was overwhelming. Roosevelt's goal of placing 250,000 young men in the CCC within three months of legislative authorization was quickly exceeded. By July 1, 1933, over 300,000 recruits were living and working in 1,300 camps scattered throughout the country. Armed with picks, shovels, saws, and other pioneer tools, and quartered in tents and rough wooden barracks, the young men of the CCC were soon turned into a productive work force.

To be eligible for the program, a young man had to come from a family on the social relief rolls. In many cases, unemployment alone was accepted as qualification. Eligibility was limited to men between the ages of eighteen and twenty-five. In addition to receiving free room and board, clothing, transportation, medical treatment, and educational training, a recruit received a cash allowance of $30 a month, $25 of which was sent home to his family. Enrollment was for a period of six months, with a maximum total service time of two years. Camp quotas were placed at 200 men.

The 356th Company, CCC, Camp SP-2-MD, which was established in the Patapsco Forest Reserve (later to become the Patapsco Valley State Park), was typical of CCC camps throughout the state and the country. Formed on June 6, 1933, at Camp Holabird, Maryland, the company was moved two days later to a field along the south bank of the Main Branch of the Patapsco, near the junction of Gun and River Roads. This first campsite, comprising tents and hastily constructed wooden buildings, was inundated and swept away by surging floodwaters on August 23, 1933. The sudden storm destroyed everything in the camp, except for a few personal articles saved by the retreating recruits. As a result of this unfortunate occurrence, the company was moved temporarily to Fort George G. Meade, Maryland. On September 15, the company was back at the Patapsco River forest. This time the camp was situated on higher ground along the river's north side. The new location required extensive work to make it suitable for CCC administrators. Load after load of sand and topsoil was needed to put the area into shape. Six hundred tons of dirt were hauled and leveled so that the company area could be landscaped. With the completion of wood barracks and other support facilities, Camp Tydings became formally established as the home of the 356th Company, CCC.

Although Camp Tydings was located in a state park at the edge of Baltimore City rather than in a large secluded forest reserve, the work done was similar to that in CCC camps set up in more isolated areas throughout the country. Each camp had designated priorities in work assignments. One of the first projects at Patapsco was the construction of firebreaks. The clearing of dead trees and brush from a strip about eight feet wide contributed to a significant drop in the number of forest fires and consequent damage to timber stands. The firebreaks were also used to mark boundaries and provide a convenient series of trails. Secondary roads and hiking trails were built through remote areas to allow easier access for hikers and campers. Considerable attention was also given to the construction of bridle paths. With new and improved trails, horseback riders were provided with an easy ride up and down the steep slopes and across the many streams. Improvements and additions were later made to the camping and picnic facilities. The hard work performed by the 356th Company did not go unnoticed. For sixteen months, Camp Tydings was designated and honored as the "gold star" company of the Third District, a feat unequaled by any other CCC camp.

A typical day in the life of a CCC member began at 6:00 a.m. with reveille, breakfast, and the traditional army policing of the grounds. There were daily inspections by the army officers who ran the camps. The CCC, though not organized on military lines, also had members whose duties corresponded to those of sergeants and corporals. Before 8:00 a.m., the recruits went off to the woods and fields to clean up the areas and to build everything from firebreaks to picnic grounds. Once away from camp, they were supervised by Agriculture Department and Interior Department employees, many of whom were recruited in the area of the camp because of their special knowledge of local conditions and needs.

The forestry work at Camp Tydings was directed by H. F. Meyer, who was assisted by two young graduates of Penn State's forestry school. During the day, recruits were turned over to foresters who arranged and planned their work program in cooperation with the state forestry department. All camp improvements were carried out on a recruit's own time, but each recruit was required to put in seven hours a day, five days a week, in forestry work.

By late afternoon, the young men were back in camp and under army supervision once again. Floors were scrubbed, gardens tended, and maintenance and painting carried out. Before dinner there was always a short military drill, but the CCC recruits were never issued arms. Evenings were generally free for Ping-Pong, pool, checkers, reading, or even a trip into town. As the CCC developed, classes were instituted for illiterates and for youths who wanted to learn a trade. For the young men at Camp Tydings, a night out usually meant a trip to nearby Arbutus for a date, a movie, or just to take in the sights outside the camp. Proud to wear their regulation army olive drab dress uniform, CCC members of Camp Tydings were easy to recognize among the civilian population.

Despite the emphasis on work production, progress was also measured in personal development and growth. Army Captain Samuel Glazier, commander at Camp Tydings, often pointed with special pride to the record of his group for its average weight gain — eighteen pounds — instead of the twelve-pound average gained by the entire CCC. The men were fed army rations, but they often ate almost twice as much as the average soldier. The allowance for food was thirty-six cents per man per day, and the commander of each camp supervised all the buying, giving the business to local dealers.

The layout of the buildings along the Patapsco was typical of the winter quarters set up throughout the country. It included five barracks, each with a capacity of forty men, a mess hall, a headquarters building and dispensary, a bathhouse with showers and hot and cold running water, a garage, and a recreation hall. The recreational hall was used for lectures, dances, and movies. There was a good-sized athletic field near the old Avalon pumping station. Boxing was one of the popular winter pastimes. An officer confided that about the only fighting in camp took place in the ring.

The camp had a radio, subscribed to newspapers and magazines, owned a few books, and each month received an allotment of 100 books as part of a circulating library.

The proximity of Baltimore created a special problem for this camp, because most of the men preferred to go to the city whenever possible. The opportunity to leave the camp was used by the more ambitious recruits to attend night schools in Baltimore. Two men attended night classes at the Johns Hopkins University, and others enrolled at City College and Polytechnic or took courses at various vocational schools. Classes in automobile and airplane mechanics and similar vocational work were more popular than so-called cultural subjects. Although the camp had one or two college graduates and a number of high-school graduates, the schooling of the average man stopped at about the fifth grade. The US Office of Education and the Department of the Interior provided each camp with an educational director and programs developed in accordance with the needs of each camp.

A system of rating was instituted within the camp. Competition among barracks was keen. Residents of one barracks went to work at 9:00 p.m. to scrub out their quarters, but another group, not to be outdone, arose at 5:00 a.m. the next day and made their own building more presentable.

Between March 1933 and the outbreak of World War II in December 1941, the CCC provided jobs and a new life for almost 2.5 million young men around the country, including thousands who served in the more than twenty-five camps scattered throughout Maryland. Much to the dismay of many labor critics who feared the program would be a military training camp similar to Hitler's youth movement in Germany, the CCC compiled a record in saving and developing the nation's natural resources unparalleled to the present day. The work done by CCC members is often evident today in many parks and forests. Although much of the work goes unnoticed or has disappeared with the passing of time, the sense of pride and responsibility instilled through army discipline and hard work forever remains a part of those men who breathed life into the Civilian Conservation Corps.

CONSCIENTIOUS OBJECTORS:
PACIFISM HOMESTEADS ALONG THE PATAPSCO

The call to arms that sounded with American participation in world war drained the surplus of manpower in the nation and brought the CCC to an end. During the war years, the National Youth Administration continued the work started by the CCC. However, Camp Tydings would merit special consideration and attention by becoming the first camp for conscientious objectors — commonly called COs — in American history. On May 15, 1941, a group of twenty-six pacifists withdrew to the woods of the Patapsco Valley State Park to form a service community as an alternative to military service. Under the provisions of the Selective Service Act of 1940, COs who were recognized by local draft boards were assigned to "work of national importance under civilian direction." In World War I, universal conscription forced everyone into the armed service, including COs. COs were to be placed in noncombat roles; however, in reality their assignments often depended on the feelings of the commanding officers. This system led to numerous abuses, which often went uncorrected. During World War II, the system of alternative service for COs changed greatly. They could again choose noncombat roles in the armed services, but those who, on religious or moral principles, refused assignment to the armed forces were placed in civilian public service. An estimated 25,000 men served in noncombat roles and approximately 12,000 men chose civilian public service.

The Civilian Public Service, which was the administrative body handling the COs, was a compromise resulting from negotiations between the Selective Service System and the pacifist groups led by the historic peace churches: the Friends, Mennonites, and Brethren. It resulted in a peculiar marriage between the government and the pacifists. Peace groups administered COs in camps, but authority to assign men and select work projects rested with the director of Selective Service. The Patapsco camp was run by the American Friends Service Committee, while the Maryland Department of Forests and Parks supervised the men in their work projects.

Using the facilities at Camp Tydings that had been built by the CCC in the 1930s, the community of COs found themselves in a most inappropriate location. The camp was located on Gun Road, which took its name from the Revolutionary War activity in the area. Munitions trains rumbled day and night within a few feet of the camp. Across the river on the grassy fields that were the first campsites of the CCC, new army conscripts from Fort Meade performed training maneuvers. Sometimes when participating in war games, soldiers came into the dining hall of the COs (often called "conchies" by army personnel) for a cup of coffee and a few taunting comments.

The work assigned to the men at the Patapsco camp was a continuation of the projects previously started by the CCC: development of recreational facilities (including the building of picnic tables, shelters, latrines, and fireplaces), conservation, reforestation, and fire prevention.

The men who came to the Patapsco camp were a reasonably homogeneous group in terms of their background. Rosters from the camp in December 1941, when its total reached seventy, and in June 1942, when it reached ninety-nine, indicate that the camp members were predominantly Friends and mainstream Protestants. Each of these two groups constituted one-third of the total camp population. The remaining third was generally split between members of smaller Protestant sects, such as Christadelphians and Jehovah's Witnesses. In June 1941, the camp had only one Brethren, one Catholic, and two Jews. Most of the community's members were from Pennsylvania and New Jersey. Only a small number were from Maryland. The occupational and educational backgrounds of camp members were more diverse than their religious affiliations. Professional men, such as teachers, doctors, and lawyers, composed the largest group. The second largest group was made up of those in business, clerical, and sales professions. The remainder included those in skilled technical fields and unskilled jobs. Generally well-educated, articulate, and earnest, the men would often have late-night talk sessions in which they discussed and argued pacifist principles.

In spite of personal ideological differences, the camp thrived. However, its continued growth from the initial twenty-six members in May 1941 to seventy in December 1941 and ninety-nine in June 1942 seriously eroded group cohesiveness. The system of self-government in which decisions were made on the basis of consensus, or "sense of meeting" as in the Quaker custom, was challenged. The added input to the process of self-government resulted in splitting the various groups into numerous factions. In the end, the camp managed to maintain a system of self-government, but the decreased role of the individual in directing his own actions suggested the decline of the community ideal. By the end of the first year, men were beginning to talk about "the end of the honeymoon."

Although the men generally performed well in their work assignments, they became increasingly frustrated with them. They complained that building picnic tables and shelters was make-work and not of particular national importance. The frustration increased with the attack on Pearl Harbor and America's entrance into World War II. Many men entered the Civilian Public Service with the hope that they would be trained in the much-needed skills for relief and reconstruction and be eventually assigned to such work in this country or overseas. In this way, they could publicly demonstrate their silent opposition to the war and their willingness to help bind up the wounds of the war. When the Selective Service backed away from sending COs overseas, many camp members volunteered to leave the camp and work on special detached service assignments. Many men opted for this type of work and were assigned to state mental hospitals, which were pitifully understaffed at the time. Job frustration was one of the major causes leading to the camp's decline and downfall. It sapped morale and enthusiasm and had a demoralizing effect on the men and their purpose.

A side issue on which the highly idealistic camp members focused their attention was the policy of segregation in the park. In the course of their work, the men became aware that the facilities they were developing were "white only." Several camp meetings addressed what was referred to as the "Negro in the park question," and the COs decided that the issue should be taken up with project officials. They received the answer that facilities were planned for blacks on a hundred acres of undeveloped land set aside for this purpose. The social concern of camp members was ahead of Maryland's border-state sensibilities. Little came of their advocacy of this cause, representing another blow to their attempt to infuse their work with idealism. The COs were able to resist building an air-raid tower, but their efforts to resist local racial policies proved fruitless.

Although the men assigned to this involuntary community were committed to their beliefs of public service, problems arose that eventually eroded the prevailing spirit of brotherhood and the manifestos of cooperation and service. Situated between Baltimore and Washington, the COs were well aware of their existence in a fishbowl. Their actions were scrutinized daily by the local community. The contempt and disgust shown toward them was never reflected in their own attitudes toward the public. Although their political stand was never understood or supported, they never made any serious attempts to convert the public to their way of thinking.

In August 1942, a little more than a year after it had opened, the Patapsco camp completed its work and closed. Most of its members were transferred to Powellville on Maryland's Eastern Shore to work on the Pocomoke River drainage project. In late 1945, with the end of the war, the American Friends Service Committee and other peace groups withdrew from their role in administering Civilian Public Service camps, partly in protest of peacetime conscription and partly because of second thoughts about the wisdom of close cooperation between pacifists and the government. The Civilian Public Service was quietly phased out and with it the idea of the community camp experiment for COs. The decision of these men to act in accordance with their religious beliefs and moral convictions, while face-to-face with the overwhelming cynicism and criticism of a country unified by war, was a display of immense silent courage. For these men, the victory was not to be found on the battlefield but within their own hearts and souls.

CHAPTER THIRTEEN

Preserving the Legacy: Prescription for the Future

The ongoing chapter in the history of the Patapsco River belongs to the State of Maryland and the city of Baltimore. The governing bodies of these two entities will formulate and administer the regulations that determine the future of the river. As the river is divided into two major components, so is its future. The history of the Northwest Harbor and the Middle Branch is constantly being revised and updated, while the history of the Main Branch has remained unchanged for decades.

In the closing years of the twentieth century, the port of Baltimore remains, much as it did in the 1700s and 1800s, a hardworking seaport. Despite face-lifts to the shoreline, the waterfront has retained its nautical charm and salty personality. Looking downriver, the eastern horizon still serves as a backdrop for a maritime collage of ships and seagulls. Although the port is economically healthy and from all outward appearances thriving, it is undergoing a change never before witnessed. This change, which began in the early 1970s, marked not only a transition but also a transformation. Starting at the harbor basin, industrial emphasis has been replaced by commercial, residential, and recreational interests. The port, or place where the maritime industry conducts business, is slowly receding down the Patapsco toward the Chesapeake Bay. The large ships now load and unload their cargoes on the lower Patapsco, away from the eyes of the city.

From atop the manicured slopes of Federal Hill on the southern rim of the harbor basin, the changes in character of the working waterfront are most evident. While shipyard cranes downriver stand as silent sentinels over empty drydocks and abandoned warehouses, directly across the river a new hustle and bustle fills the air and echoes across the water. Tourism is the new industry that has taken hold on the river's banks. The birth of the industry occurred in 1979 when Harborplace was completed. These European style twin marketplace pavilions, designed by the James Rouse Corporation, became the magnets to attract people to the Inner Harbor district. The commercial success of the marketplace resulted in the construction of the Baltimore World

Patapsco Valley State Park today, looking downriver from Route 40.
Photo by the author.

The Inner Harbor in the 1990s, a landscape of geometric designs and shapes.
Photo by the author.

Trade Center, the National Aquarium, and the Maryland Science Center. The addition of these buildings, each unique in design and appearance, fostered the renovation boom along the water's edge. Rotting piers and terminals have been replaced by shops, restaurants, and hotels, while the freighters, schooners, and steamboats have been replaced by a fleet of sailboats, yachts, and historic vessels. The transformation in the last decade, which has earned Baltimore the title of "Renaissance City," has not been confined to the harbor basin. Downriver, the massive brick warehouses at Fell's Point and Canton have been renovated as waterfront condominiums, complete with backyard marinas.

Under the leadership of Mayor William Donald Schaefer, the dreams of a modern and prosperous waterfront district have become a reality. Although Mayor Schaefer justly earned accolades for the success of the Inner Harbor, the original planning for the harbor renovation project is credited to Mayor Theodore R. McKeldin, who developed and coordinated planning efforts in the early 1960s. However, the ideas of harbor development can be traced back even further to the Great Baltimore Fire in 1904. According to an article in *The Baltimore Sun* on February 20, 1946, Paul E. Burkhard presented his ideas for inner harbor development in a small brochure a few months after the fire. Burkhard envisioned a public waterfront area with parks and promenades encircling the harbor basin. Piers were to be removed and wreckage from the fire was to be used for landfill. A terraced skyline was to be created by carefully orchestrating building construction. A front row of ornate public-use buildings, four to six stories high, would stand in the foreground, against which the city's skyscrapers would rise from the ashes. A diagonal park would connect the waterfront parks to the heart of the downtown area. Burkhard imagined the harbor area as an aesthetic center, comparable in beauty to the Alster Basin at Hamburg, the graceful lakeshore landscapes of Zurich, Luzerne, and Geneva, and the panorama of Naples and its bay. In his brochure, Burkhard wrote:

> For Baltimore will thenceforth engage the attention of travelers of all nations—as a spot where the beauty of nature and the beauty of architectural art and—last, but not least the famed beauty of Baltimore's women all unite to form an aesthetic and recreation center of extraordinary charm. Can Baltimore afford to shoulder the responsibility of not taking advantage of the pronounced natural advantages that God has given her?

The plans to make Baltimore one of the world's most beautiful cities were immediately rejected by business leaders who sought to rebuild as quickly as possible. While the essence of Burkhard's vision would become a reality in the 1980s, he remains a mystery person. Except for the 1946 article, there is no record that Burkhard existed. Although he is listed as an architect in the article, there is no record of him in membership lists of professional and scientific societies. Likewise, a search of libraries, archives, and historical societies proved negative. There is no known copy of his waterfront development brochure.

Despite the praise and profits currently being enjoyed along the banks of the inner harbor, the future of the waterfront is clouded. Critics claim that the city and state are covering up their inability to attract and maintain new industries by substituting a gaudy and glittering tourist attraction catering to well-to-do residents and out-of-state visitors. The accusations do have a degree of validity. Statistics reveal that for years the port of Baltimore has been gradually losing business to other ports on the Eastern Seaboard. The inability to effectively compete with other regions had been linked to restrictive labor practices dockside and higher terminal fees. Perhaps the most overlooked reason for the continuing decline of business is the location of the port. Baltimore's major advantage over its competitors has always been its inland location. Until recently it has always been more profitable to move freight on water than over land. With the deregulation of shipping rates, it is now cheaper to move freight over land routes to ports with closer access to ocean waterways. The extra hours required to steam up the Chesapeake Bay or through the C&D Canal have proved too costly to many shippers. It is ironic that the port that gave birth to the commercial railroad in the United States is now being threatened by railways whose own existence was in danger just a few years ago.

Although concern is voiced over the future of the port, Baltimore's history will always be connected to the waters of the Patapsco. The port has survived through the centuries by being able to adapt. Technology and trends have continually been accommodated to ensure the survival of the maritime industry. Trade, not tourism, argue critics, is the economic base for the city and state. While the historical record of the port supports the claims of industrialists, the success of the recreational seaport cannot be viewed as a superficial and transient business investment. While the distant future of the port is impossible to predict, it is not impossible to foresee the cycle of change making a complete circle. In the next hundred years, condominiums and marinas might give way to warehouses and shipyards. The billowing sails of a new generation of tall ships could once again grace the skyline.

While the history of the harbor continues to be written, the history of the Main Branch has been static. In the twentieth century, the river valley plays host to a new audience as a state park under the auspices of the Maryland Department of Natural Resources. The Patapsco Valley State Park, located on the southern outskirts of Baltimore, presently comprises 11,000 acres, beginning seven miles upstream from the mouth of the Main Branch and extending to Liberty Dam on the North Branch, and Sykesville on the South Branch. The park, stretching nearly thirty miles in length and averaging one-half mile in width, contains a variety of outdoor opportunities, including picnicking, camping, and hiking. Throughout the park, history abounds. The curious and adventurous visitor can discover the sites and ruins of the Thomas Viaduct, Relay Hotel, Avalon Iron Works, Hockley Mills, CCC camp, Avalon Dam, Orange Grove Flour Mill, Bloede's Dam, Patterson Viaduct, Ilchester, and Gray's Mill. Many other historic towns and landmarks are adjacent to, or within reach of, the park's boundaries. In the late 1960s, the park began a "River of History" bus tour. The weekend tours lasted until the Flood of 1972.

Land bordering the Patapsco was private property until 1912, when a number of citizens decided to preserve the beauties of the Patapsco River Valley for the public. With the help of the Maryland Legislature and a few public-spirited people, such as John M. Glenn and Richard Norris, the Patapsco Forest Reserve was created. Soon after this initial gift, the Maryland Legislature appropriated funds to purchase about 1,500 acres along both banks of the river from Relay to Hollofield. Agreements were made with some of the large riverfront companies, such as the Thistle Company, J. W. Dickey and Sons, the Baltimore County Water Company, and the Consolidated Gas and Electric Light Company, whereby the State of Maryland could use part of their land for recreational purposes. These areas were known as Auxiliary State Forests. Edward Prince was the first forest warden (predecessor of today's park ranger). A rugged individual who patrolled the forest on horseback, dressed in a military-type uniform with campaign hat, Sam Browne belt, and sidearm, Prince epitomized the spirited outdoor man who ranged the hills and valleys protecting natural resources.

During the first two decades of the park's existence, little work was done to improve its recreational facilities. Despite increasing use by the population of an expanding metropolitan area, the park was plagued by a lack of adequate funding. When Franklin D. Roosevelt inaugurated the Civilian Conservation Corps in 1933, the Patapsco Forest Reserve became one of its first camps. Under the CCC, the park finally received some much-needed attention and development. Conservation and recreational projects included the building of roads, trails, picnic areas, and campsites. During the time of the CCC, the name of the forest reserve was changed to Patapsco State Park. Later, when the administrative department for parks and forests in Maryland was reorganized as the Department of State Forests and Parks, the name was again changed — to Patapsco Valley State Park. In the early 1940s, the void left by the CCC was filled by the National Youth Administration and the COs. The work started by the CCC was continued until the end of World War II. From then until the 1950s, the park again saw very little construction or maintenance work; this resulted in the deterioration of the existing facilities.

In 1957, Maryland Governor Theodore R. McKeldin had the honor of dedicating the Theodore R. McKeldin Recreational Area near Marriottsville, at the fork of the North and South Branches of the Patapsco. Since his days as mayor of Baltimore, McKeldin had been a leading advocate of expanding the park from the mouth of the Main Branch at the harbor basin to Liberty Dam on the North Branch and Sykesville on the South Branch. In 1946, Mayor McKeldin had appointed the Patapsco River Valley Commission to formulate ideas for the park's expansion. The commission drew up a comprehensive plan calling for an expansion of the park to 15,000 acres and for a riverside parkway to connect the major areas. It called for a linear park that would extend thirty-seven miles, with an average width of half a mile, from the Hanover Street Bridge to Sykesville. Although many of the proposals failed to materialize, a number of Mayor McKeldin's ideas were later incorporated in follow-up planning projects.

In 1972, the lower section of the park from Ilchester to Elkridge was devastated by Tropical Storm Agnes. Restrooms, picnic shelters, the swinging bridge at Orange Grove, and the park headquarters were swept away by the raging floodwaters. In the river gorges where floodwater funneled through the valley, erosion was severe. Large chunks of the riverbank were completely washed away. When the floodwaters finally receded, the lower section where the river valley widens became the resting place for mountains of junk and natural debris. Restoration of the park was a slow process, which caused displeasure to many visitors and local residents. In the early 1980s, however, construction projects to fully restore the park were at last completed.

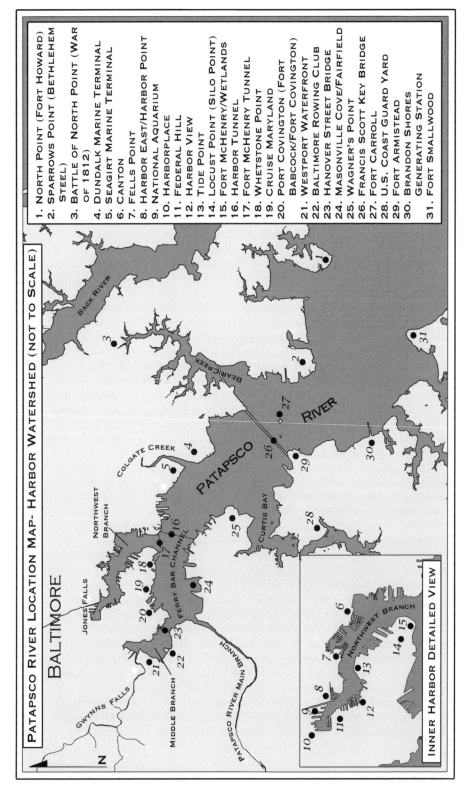

BALTIMORE

1. North Point (Fort Howard)
2. Sparrows Point (Bethlehem Steel)
3. Battle of North Point (War of 1812)
4. Dundalk Marine Terminal
5. Seagirt Marine Terminal
6. Canton
7. Fells Point
8. Harbor East/Harbor Point
9. National Aquarium
10. Harborplace
11. Federal Hill
12. Harbor View
13. Tide Point
14. Locust Point (Silo Point)
15. Fort McHenry/Wetlands
16. Harbor Tunnel
17. Fort McHenry Tunnel
18. Whetstone Point
19. Cruise Maryland
20. Port Covington (Fort Babcock/Fort Covington)
21. Westport Waterfront
22. Baltimore Rowing Club
23. Hanover Street Bridge
24. Masonville Cove/Fairfield
25. Wagner's Point
26. Francis Scott Key Bridge
27. Fort Carroll
28. U.S. Coast Guard Yard
29. Fort Armistead
30. Brandon Shores Generating Station
31. Fort Smallwood

Inner Harbor Detailed View

Patapsco River – Harbor Basin. *Illustration by Jedediah Kahl.*

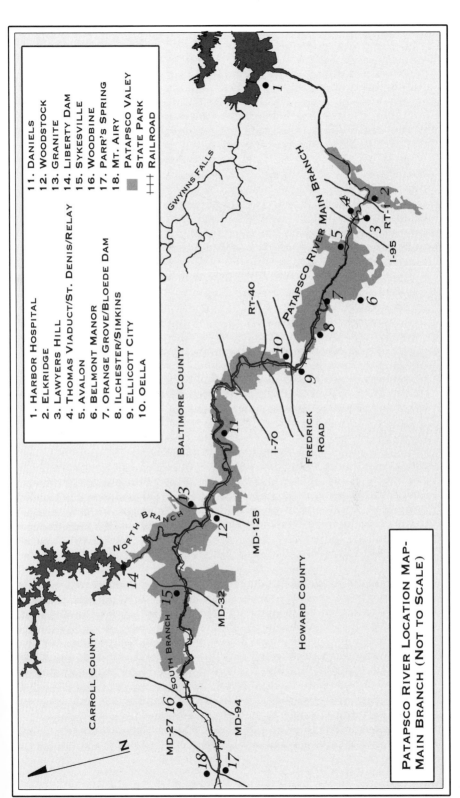

PATAPSCO RIVER LOCATION MAP-
MAIN BRANCH (NOT TO SCALE)

1. HARBOR HOSPITAL
2. ELKRIDGE
3. LAWYERS HILL
4. THOMAS VIADUCT/ST. DENIS/RELAY
5. AVALON
6. BELMONT MANOR
7. ORANGE GROVE/BLOEDE DAM
8. ILCHESTER/SIMKINS
9. ELLICOTT CITY
10. OELLA
11. DANIELS
12. WOODSTOCK
13. GRANITE
14. LIBERTY DAM
15. SYKESVILLE
16. WOODBINE
17. PARR'S SPRING
18. MT. AIRY

▨ PATAPSCO VALEY
STATE PARK
╫╫╫ RAILROAD

Patapsco River—Main Branch. *Illustration by Jedediah Kahl.*

CHAPTER FOURTEEN

A Tired and Troubled Tributary

POLLUTION PROBLEMS

On any day in any season, given the right weather and right atmospheric conditions, the views of the Patapsco River are postcard visions of natural beauty, inscribed with platitudes from the pen of Mother Nature herself. Blue sky and blue water slightly stirred by a sweet and briny breeze overwhelm the senses as people play and work on the water. Vessels of all shapes and sizes crisscross the water in a floating collage against a background of new and old Baltimore that gently hypnotizes. When spectators reluctantly awaken from their daydream, they walk away with the impression that local advertisers brainstormed in 1975 to promote the city's pending harbor renaissance. Baltimore truly is a "Charm City," a seaport town with hidden charms begging to be explored. Since that time, part of that prophecy has been fulfilled. Tourist attractions around the harbor's perimeter, such as Harborplace and the National Aquarium, have refreshed themselves, waiting to be rediscovered by legions of new and old visitors. High-rise buildings, beckoning new generations of residents and workers, have risen from the rubble of vacant lots to create glistening canyons of steel and glass along the riverbank. On any given day, it can be an idyllic scene waiting to be captured by the artist's brush and palette.

But dreamers beware! On any day in any season, given the wrong weather and the wrong atmospheric conditions, the harbor is a horror story, a toxic tale of deceit and death with bizarre plot twists that could have easily been penned from the "Master of the Macabre," former Baltimore resident Edgar Allan Poe. On these days when church bells toll from the old ethnic neighborhoods, they mourn the slow death of the river. Instead of slow-moving watercraft adrift in the harbor, the water is fouled with sewage and trash as small schools of dead fish bob on the surface, suffocated by the water they breathe. A nauseating

Stormwater runoff creates a new species of "plastic"
tree along the Patapsco's feeder streams.
Courtesy Blue Water Baltimore.

Islands of plastic debris from the harbor after heavy
rainstorms. Baltimore's version of the Great Pacific
Garbage Patch. *Courtesy Blue Water Baltimore.*

stench hangs heavy in the air over a body of florescent green water that appears to glow in the tidal shadows. The river is dead on arrival. That is also part of the river prophecy that has become part of its current legacy.

Despite the on-going economic progress of the river reflected by the growth of tourism and commercial/residential development, the on-going environmental problems related to the Patapsco River have not changed. Stormwater runoff, raw sewage, and organic (industrial) contaminants remain the chief sources of pollution. They have not faded with age, but have become more complex due to population growth and changing ecosystems. As usual, they have been compounded by political indifference and public apathy, or vice-versa, to produce a stalemate on cleanup efforts that has plagued seaport cities in the United States for centuries.

Within the last twenty years, scientists have identified stormwater runoff from construction, industrial, and municipal sites as the biggest threat to the watershed, especially the harbor system as it extends to the Chesapeake Bay. The untreated water that drains from the city of Baltimore contains a "witch's brew" of sediment, oil, road salt, fertilizers, toxic chemicals, pesticides/insecticides, and animal waste. With heavy industry slowly migrating downriver to the lower reaches of the Patapsco, continued population growth in the metropolitan area has resulted in a flurry of building projects that break open the land and bleed the earth into the rivers. While sediment spills from construction sites are often viewed as a temporary pollution source, the remaining permanent structures increase the amount of impervious surfaces, such as parking lots, sidewalks, and roofs, which increase the volume of stormwater entering an overloaded river system.

In recent years, industrial runoff has abated due to the declining presence of heavy industry along the river; however, toxic contaminants remain a constant health threat to the river and its inhabitants. Tainted stormwater from over 3,000 companies located in the Patapsco watershed causes two main problems. It sweeps surface contaminants into the river and its tributaries, and then permeates the ground to release buried toxins, which slowly seep into the water. Downriver at the Curtis Bay industrial zone (home to chemical processors, shipyards, and power plants) and across the river at Sparrows Point (former home of the world's largest steel mill) legacy contamination is a never-ending environmental battle.

When talking about municipal runoff, environmentalists always "talk trash." Heavy rains, which are usually accompanied by high winds, sweep tons of trash into the harbor. Gwynns Falls and Jones Falls, two of the city's largest freshwater tributaries, become conduits for a tidal wave of stormwater filled with glass bottles, cans, sports balls, fast-food cartons, styrofoam containers, cigarette butts, tree branches, lawn furniture, and a variety of plastic bags and bottles. Wherever the river pools, especially around the piers and inlets, the surface of the water solidifies as an undulating junkyard of filth. Visitors find it disgusting; residents find it embarrassing; politicians find it irritating; and environmentalists find it enraging.

Even more appalling than the images of trash are the sight and smell of raw sewage emptying into the harbor. In the city, environmentalists debate whether stormwater or sewage is proprietary, but for city residents, it depends on the type of broken pipe in their yard. What most people don't realize is that stormwater and sewage issues in the Patapsco watershed are physically and historically intertwined. While the stormwater and sewage systems use different pipelines, the routes often run parallel in a gravity-fed system that utilizes the terrain of the region. Stormwater flows into storm drains that empty into low-lying feeder streams, and raw sewage flows through a spider web of pipes that empty into large concrete pipes, known as interceptors. These interceptors, which often run alongside moving bodies of water, carry the sewage to a pumping station, which then pumps it to a sewage treatment plant. In theory, it sounds like a feasible plan. In reality, it's a disaster that's explained with simple arithmetic.

In addition to cracks from shifting earth, boring tree roots, and internal obstructions, thousands of miles of old pipes have millions of leaky joints. With increased volumes of rainwater from a storm, both pipe systems leak into each other and create volumes of liquid beyond the pipe's capacity. Leaks allow raw sewage to seep into storm drain pipes while rain-filled sewage pipes overwhelm pumping stations causing overflows. In both instances, diluted mixtures of stormwater and raw sewage flow into the Patapsco River. Clogs and backups inside the pipes add to the problem by increasing the chance of ruptures and collapses. Even without a rainstorm as a catalyst, wastewater routinely leeches through fissures in the decaying pipe. In others cases, raw sewage has been piped directly into storm drains through illegal connections that occurred during construction.

In 1997, the city was sued by the Environmental Protection Agency and the Maryland Department of the Environment for repeated overflows of raw sewage. Between 2010 and 2012, over 7 million gallons of raw sewage entered the river. To avoid fines that ranged up to $15,000, sanitary sewer overflows, or SSOs as they are called, were often underreported or conveniently not reported. On August 12, 2014, the problem was highlighted when a storm dumped more than six inches of rain over the Baltimore region. Rainwater overwhelmed storm drains and flooded the city's sewer lines, resulting in a diluted raw sewage overflow of 3.2 million gallons into the Patapsco River. Over the ensuing days, the estimate from city officials increased to 9 million gallons and finally to over 12 million gallons, nearly four times the original estimate. According to state records, it was the largest, single-day sewage spill since 2006. City officials acknowledged that state regulators would be reviewing the tardy report since state regulations require prompt public reporting of sewage spills. No one mentioned that fines for sewage spills are based on the amount of spilled sewage. Since 2002, the City of Baltimore has been under a federal consent decree to fix the antiquated, overflow-prone sewer system by 2016 at a projected cost of $1 billion.

In December 2015, an investigative report by the Environmental Integrity Project exposed the city's failed efforts to meet the consent decree deadline on January 1, 2016. The environmental nonprofit organization, which focuses on enforcement of environmental laws, environmental justice, and pollution of the Chesapeake Bay, reported that only half of the repairs and upgrades to stop the chronic sewage overflows had been completed. While this was no surprise to activists and environmentalists, who were monitoring the city's dismal progress rate, the report was an environmental bombshell that shocked everyone. It was discovered that over the past five years, the city had deliberately pumped more than 330 million gallons of raw sewage into Jones Falls, which empties into the harbor. The figure was fifteen times more than what was previously reported by the city. Blaming the problem on in-take pipes at the Back River treatment plant, city officials admitted that two of the sixty-two relief valves, which were supposed to be closed, had not been plugged. The valves, located along the pipe system, were designed to dump overflow sewage into the nearest stream and prevent sewage backups into homes and businesses. Much to the dismay of citizens and environmentalists, the city planned to file a new timetable for the consent decree in federal court. Transparency in city government, the latest buzzword among politicians and bureaucrats, once again proved as lucid as stormwater runoff in the harbor basin.

Most of the sewage and stormwater flows through pipes that were installed between fifty and a hundred years ago. The sewage system alone uses 3,000 miles of sewer lines and 110 pumping stations, which funnel raw sewage to city-owned wastewater treatments on each side of the river: the Back River Wastewater Treatment Plant in Essex and the Patapsco Wastewater Treatment Plant in Curtis Bay. The larger facility at Back River, which treats 180 million gallons per day from Baltimore City and Baltimore County, diffuses most of that water into Back River. Until the steel mill at Sparrows Point closed in 2012, approximately forty percent of the final effluent was diverted through two six-mile long pipelines for industrial purposes. On the other side of the river, the history of the Patapsco plant highlights many of the waste disposal problems facing large East Coast cities. When the state-of-the art plant opened in 1940, it could only remove approximately one-third of the pollutants from the wastewater that was discharged into the Patapsco River. Technology at the time could not meet the environmental demands. With major upgrades in the 1970s, the plant was finally able to meet the more stringent water quality requirements.

The city's sewage operation made headline news in September 1989 when a sixty-one car freight train, carrying 5,000 tons of sludge from Back River headed for a landfill in Louisiana. Upon arrival, residents complained so vehemently about the odoriferous cargo that it was moved to Moss Point, Mississippi. People there didn't want the train either. Now dubbed the "Poo Poo Choo Choo" by the national media, the train's contractor was threatened with daily fines of up to $2 million for not having the required state permit. The rail saga ended nine weeks later when the train returned to Baltimore with its cargo intact. The infamous cargo found a final resting place at a local landfill.

Despite the persistent pollution problems, there is hope for the river. River communities in other parts of the country, most notably in Boston and New York, have resurrected their dead rivers. The ultimate solution is money, but with a price tag in the billions, the likelihood of a financial quick fix is unrealistic. More "green" politicians to champion the cause of the Patapsco would help, but they are a rare species in Maryland politics where the cleanup of the Chesapeake Bay, the state's greatest natural resource, has languished for decades due to political self-interests. Such common sense legislation as banning plastic trash bags and limiting phosphorous wastes from chicken farms inherently falls victim to corporate lobbying and special interest groups.

To combat pollution problems, a plethora of city, state, and federal agencies monitor the watershed and collect scientific data. Together they are a unified voice for a call to action, but too often their cries are unheeded. While they can identify the problems, they have no power to implement the solutions because they do not control the public coffers. While progress is being made by local governments, it is too often subjected to political whims. As the Patapsco entered the twenty-first century, a power shift occurred. Calls for cleanup action from grass-roots movements became a unified choir that turned heads in the courtroom and boardroom. These wader and watchdog groups became the eyes, ears, and voices of the river. They proved the mantra "power to the people" from the late 1960s actually worked.

POLLUTION SOLUTIONS

The Patapsco River began its heralded "green" march into the new century with a tune from a small band of environmentalists and activists. Only this time, the song of the river was a clarion call that echoed a mystical refrain to the time when the first Indians appeared along the riverbanks to harvest the natural bounty. Modern verses of this ancient song of the Patapsco reaffirmed the sacred bond between the river and its people and provided a spiritual compass to guide the river into the future. Although the ancient chants were performed in different tongues with different rituals, the subtle message was uninterrupted: the waters in this holy garden are sacred; treat them with reverence. Beginning in the 1900s, that folk spiritual was muted by the apocalyptic din of man and machine that accompanied the dawn of the Industrial Revolution. The ensuing decades of progress saw the sacred waters blasphemed, polluted by its caretakers until all life forms were gasping for their last breaths or ceased to exist. Now, a hundred years later, the turbulent cacophony of industry had been largely silenced. In its place, a new song of hope emerged, one that praised the ideals of environmental stewardship.

In the 1770s, the fertile farmland in the Patapsco River region provided the Ellicott Brothers with an abundance of wheat to successfully launch their milling operations. Over 200 years later, the region surrounding the river valley provided a fertile spawning ground for local activists and concerned citizens to successfully launch the Patapsco Heritage Greenway and the Patapsco Riverkeeper, two grassroots organizations for the preservation and protection of the Patapsco. Experiencing various degrees of success and failure, these nascent groups became embroiled in a bitter custody battle for a section of the river. In the end, both groups created blueprints for success that would be copied by other grass-roots movements. Eventually, these groups would provide a network of environmental watchdogs along the entire length of the Patapsco River.

The battle of the Main Branch originated in 1990 when Governor William Donald Schaefer called for a Maryland Greenways program to create a system of connecting natural corridors that would protect natural resources and offer recreational opportunities. To administer the program that eventually focused on the novel concept of heritage tourism, the Maryland Heritage Areas Program was created under the domain of the Maryland Historical Trust.

In 1997, the Patapsco Heritage Greenway Committee, a private group organized by Oella developer Charles Wagandt, was formed with the stated purpose of protecting the river valley. The committee hired a consulting team to develop a proposal for the greenway along a twenty-four mile section of the Patapsco River from Elkridge to Daniels. This arbitrary boundary also annexed the lower section of the Patapsco Valley State Park. The proposal, which would be the cornerstone for their "greenway" application, included nature trails, paved bicycle trails, bridges, train stations, visitors' centers, parking lots, concessions, upscale accommodations and an aggressive marketing campaign to attract tourists. Designation as a heritage area would qualify the greenway and the group for grants, tax credits and low-interest loans for tourism-related activities.

The response from environmentalists, such as the local chapters of the Audubon Society and the Sierra Club, was fast and furious. Claiming the greenway proposal had been prepared without any environmental impact studies or public participation, they argued that section of the state park was already suffering from overuse and overcrowding. A plan to attract more people to the park seemed contrary to the original intent and purpose of the greenway. Their pleas raised a number of red flags that attracted the attention of local residents. Wagandt attempted to ease everyone's worries by stating the greenway would build a bigger constituency for environmentalists and aid them in protecting the natural resources of the valley. His comments fell on deaf ears, not mute tongues. Environmentalists asserted the tourist-based plan was simply a ploy to expand residential and commercial development in the area, most notably in the state park, and pointed the finger at Wagandt as the villain.

For many environmentalists, community groups, and local residents, Charles Wagandt, the savior of Oella, was an enigma. At heart, was he a dyed-in-the wool real-estate developer or a born-again historical preservationist? The great-grandson of former mill owner William J. Dickey, Wagandt purchased the dilapidated seventy-acre mill town of Oella in 1973 and single-handedly transported it into the twentieth century. Under his master redevelopment plan, he salvaged every historic building to include the log cabins and lobbied for the installation of water and sewer systems to eliminate the dumping of raw sewage into the Patapsco. He arranged for mill workers to remain in their homes, conducted oral histories of former mill workers, and donated mill artifacts to the Smithsonian. He was a founding member of the Friends of Patapsco that helped relocate the George Ellicott House and locate Benjamin Banneker's home site. Over the years, he had received prestigious awards for his work in historical and architectural preservation. Yet, despite the accolades, he was not trusted by his current adversaries. They pointed to his tenure with the Maryland Historic Trust as board member, treasurer, and chairman and opined the greenway project reeked of political cronyism since the Maryland Historical Trust was the funding source for the Maryland Heritage Areas Program.

The Maryland Conservation Council, a collation of environmental groups in the Chesapeake Bay watershed, joined the fray with a letter to Governor Parris Glendening, voicing opposition to the greenway and alerting him to the growing controversy over using publicly owned land for private commercial interests. To greenway foes, this was the fundamental issue of the controversy. Was the mission of the state park to provide an outdoor recreational experience in a wilderness setting or a tourist-based excursion against a background of trees and streams? If the latter was true, did a public, non-profit group have the authority to dictate policy in state-owned lands?

At the first public meeting in October 1999, about 100 residents voiced their concerns about crowds, pollution, and the destruction of wildlife habitat. To appease the opposition, Wagandt subsequently stepped down as chairman amid rumors that he stood to gain financially from the project. His replacement John Slater, president of Slater Associates, a Columbia-based landscape architect firm, pledged to work more closely with environmental and community groups in the future. That promise did little to quell the opposition. With opposition increasing and local towns backing out of the project, Baltimore and Howard Ccounties withdrew their financial support for the greenway. Sensing the momentum had shifted against them, the committee abruptly and quietly ended their certification process in spring of 2000.

In fall of 2000, the Greenway Committee changed its name and revised its strategy. Now called the Friends of the Patapsco Valley and Heritage Greenway (FPVHG), the group released new details about its vision for the heritage area that still included the state park. Proposed enhancements with a projected cost in the millions included a parking garage and visitors' center in Ellicott City, an interpretive site at the Thomas Viaduct, a visitors kiosk inside the park, hike and bike trails leading into the valley from the south, and a salaried, four-person staff with a payroll of $160,000.

With a new name, the group hoped to acquire non-profit status and renew its agreement for an additional $20,000 in grants from the local counties. The changes in name and tactics did not quell the simmering discontent from opponents who staunchly equated "heritage area" with "tourist destination." They immediately questioned the group's fiscal management, noting the group had received approximately $70,000 in public funds to provide a management plan that was agreeable to all parties. With neither side willing to compromise, there would be no peace in the valley. This latest proposal only rekindled the heated rhetoric.

The flashpoint occurred at a public hearing in June 2001 when the Maryland Department of Natural Resources proposed a 1.25 mile paved extension of the Grist Mill Trail inside the state park. State officials claimed the multiple-use trail would allow the casual visitor, including the handicapped and disabled, more access to the rugged terrain inside the park. Strongly supported by the FPVHG, which had proposed the trail in 1999, the project drew sharp criticism from environmentalists. They saw it as a marketing ploy by real-estate developers to expand residential development around the park's borders. To mount a legal challenge to the project, the Sierra Club of Howard County claimed the paved surface would increase runoff into the Patapsco River in violation of non-tidal wetlands and waterways permits.

In March 2002, the Sierra Club appealed the state's permit to cross 100 feet of wetlands as part of the trail extension. After lengthy discussions, state officials negotiated an agreement. The Sierra Club agreed to stop all legal challenges to the project and the Department of Natural Resources agreed not to build any additional paved trails in the park for ten years. In November 2002, the ten-foot wide trail that extended north to the old Patterson Viaduct was opened. Outdoor enthusiasts now had a smooth, paved surface to trek through the steep terrain of the river valley that accessed Ellicott City and Oella. The FPVHG had access to the greenway and the opportunity to demonstrate the benefits of a heritage area. As for the greenway opponents, all they had was a long wait to determine the intentions of the FPVHG.

Following the dedication of the trail, an uneasy truce settled over the valley. For the next ten years, the FPVHG, later renamed the Patapsco Heritage Greenway (PHG), developed an admirable record in environmental stewardship. True to their word, protection of the valley's natural resources and preservation of its cultural history became their primary goals. To connect with the communities, they sponsored river-cleanups, tree plantings, invasive species round-ups, history walks, and kayak trips. Hundreds of volunteers donated thousands of hours to cleanup the river and beautify the valley.

Outreach programs included historical presentations, environmental education, and a stream watch program where volunteers adopted a section of a stream flowing into the Patapsco. One of the more popular events through the years was the Garlic Mustard Challenge. Every spring, groups of volunteers gathered in the state park and pulled hundreds of pounds of the invasive plant, which was believed to have been transplanted from Europe in the 1800s as an herb for cooking. The harvest celebration featured an amateur chef contest with free sampling of the recipes, old-fashioned games, and old-time music along the banks of the Patapsco.

In 2013, following the expiration of the construction ban in the park, the PHG resurfaced in their pursuit for certification as a heritage area. At public forums, the group's presentation "Envision the Valley" unveiled their repackaged vision for the river valley that included redefined boundaries and a full-time, paid executive director. Expanding the valley's borders would incorporate more residential areas to form a coalition of supporters who would have more political clout with county and state officials. There was no denying that more political clout translated to more legislative funding. The group pointed out the visitors' center at Avalon and the Thomas Viaduct as projects that could benefit from greenway certification. Later that year, the group was awarded a $75,000 grant from Howard County to pursue certification. Part of the money would be used to hire a consultant to undertake the application process.

Environmentalists had a chance to make a final plea in December 2014 at the last public hearing before the final certification vote. Once again, members of the Sierra Club contended that including the state park in the greenway master plan would pave the way for construction projects within the park boundaries at the will of PHG without any oversight from outside groups. Once again, they were rebuffed when a greenway spokesperson politely reminded them that any projects in the state park require approval of the Maryland Department of Natural Resources. Some skeptical residents, worried about protecting the ambiance of their historic communities, still feared that cultural preservation translated to commercial development.

In January 2015, after two years of fostering support from residents and appeasing county governments and state park officials, the PHG proudly announced that Patapsco Valley had become the thirteenth certified heritage area in the state. The group now managed 24.6 square miles of land that included Patapsco Valley State Park and the bordering communities of Catonsville, Arbutus and Relay. Certification meant that qualified local jurisdictions, nonprofits, businesses and individuals could be eligible for state grants.

Talk about money underscored the announcement. Money for promotion, a museum, and historic markers filled the air like soft, sweet raindrops after a prolonged drought that began in 1998 when the Patapsco Valley became a designated heritage area not eligible for funding. However, the celebration turned bittersweet when a week later it was announced there would be a $300,000 retroactive cut to funding for the state's heritage areas.

Even though the PHG emerged as the clear winner in the end, opponents could eventually claim an indirect victory. The fallout over the Main Branch of the Patapsco migrated downriver to Baltimore's harbor which was in dire need of a guardian. While the battle over the heritage area languished in the court of popular opinion, a handful of concerned citizens, who had opposed the idea of transforming the Patapsco Valley into a tourist hub, sensed the need for a new voice in protecting the Patapsco River. With little fanfare in the late 1990s, a small group of activists and outdoorsmen from Elkridge and Ellicott City formed the Patapsco Riverkeeper.

The idea of a grassroots movement without political and financial ambition to save a river had been successfully demonstrated and was waiting to be copied. In 1966, the Hudson River Fisherman's Association (HRFA), the nation's first Riverkeeper, was created by a group of blue-collar commercial and recreational fishermen to save the dying Hudson River. Robert Boyle, avid fly fisherman, noted outdoor writer with *Sports Illustrated* and one of HRFA's founders, stumbled across two overlooked laws that provided the legal sword to battle polluters around the country. The Rivers and Harbors Act of 1888 and the Refuse in Harbors Act of 1889 forbade pollution of American waters and provided a bounty for reported violations. In essence, these laws allowed private citizens to sue corporate polluters to cleanup the nation's waterways.

With a powerful legal tool at their disposal, HRFA began tracking down and prosecuting polluters one at a time until none remained. In 1968, they collected their first bounty of $2,000 and began a succession of lawsuits that toppled corporate polluters like dominoes. In 1983, they hired their first full-time river keeper and launched a patrol boat. In 1986, they changed their name to Riverkeeper, based on the 1980 book *Death of a Riverkeeper* by famed fly fisherman Ernie Schwiebert. Years later, Riverkeeper became part of the renowned Waterkeeper Alliance, founded by environmental attorney and activist Robert F. Kennedy Jr., that would eventually patrol and protect waterways around the world. Starting in 1966 with the birth of the HRFA, a new militancy emerged in American environmentalism that later saw the creation of the global environmentalist group Greenpeace. A handful of concerned citizens who lived along the Patapsco saw no reason why they shouldn't be part of these success stories.

In 2002, under the leadership of Lee Oxenham, the Patapsco Riverkeeper was created. Oxenham, who had served as ad hoc spokesperson for the Howard County Sierra Club in their fight against the greenway, became the first executive. Steve Stover, outdoorsman and naturalist, served as the first riverkeeper. Residing near the state park, Stover, who spent ample hours hiking, fishing, canoeing, and studying the river, was highly knowledgeable about the environmental challenges it faced. The group immediately aligned itself with riverfront communities to aggressively fight pollution. The weapon of choice was the citizen's lawsuit. Armed with the motto "Your Right, Your River,

Your Riverkeeper," Oxenham quickly mounted an ambitious legal campaign to protect, promote, and advocate on behalf of the river with pro bono legal aid from law school extensions and non-profit environmental law groups. The hardball tactics caused a philosophical rift that resulted in the departure of some original members.

The first battle to save the Patapsco occurred in 2002 when the Riverkeeper teamed with neighborhood community groups in the Curtis Bay area to sue Erachem Comilog over the issue of pollution permits. Erachem, the world leader in processing raw manganese for electronics (batteries) and agrochemicals (fertilizers) had been routinely discharging toxic amounts of manganese wastewater into the tributaries of Curtis Creek under a five-year, renewable permit from the Maryland Department of the Environment (MDE).

After thirty years of dumping, residents made the permit a rallying cry and demanded a hearing after studies found that chronic exposure to manganese could lead to manganism (manganese poisoning), a condition of psychiatric disorders and motor disturbances with symptoms similar to Lou Gehrig's disease and multiple sclerosis. In response to the public outcry, company officials pointed out the improvements in waste disposal over the years while state regulators reaffirmed the permits were legal. Residents became outraged when they discovered the Environmental Protection Agency (EPA) did not have a standard for acceptable levels of manganese in discharge water. Instead, individual states were allowed to determine appropriate discharge levels for permits under the Clean Water Act. Maryland had not established a standard. Residents demanded an explanation and promptly received one from the chief of MDE's Industrial Discharge Permits Division who called for further study due to concerns about toxic levels and stated that manganese posed no threat to humans, but could harm aquatic life. The statement noted that Erachem had become more ecologically conscious over the years. Since 1990, their water-recycling program reduced the amount of wastewater from 1 million gallons a day to 60,000 gallons a day.

The comments were of little consolation to the local residents who worried about their health. To exacerbate the issue, Erachem had been listed by the EPA as the largest discharger of EPA-listed chemicals into surface water according to EPA's own toxics-release index. In 2000, Erachem discharged 1.8 million pounds of nitrate compounds into Curtis Creek, more than any of the other eighteen companies and government agencies on the EPA database's list.

While the lawsuit was eventually dismissed, the legal action highlighted the serious problems between corporate polluters and state regulators. Toxic wastes were legally allowed to accumulate in the Patapsco watershed under the eye of state regulators who routinely rubber stamped renewal permits. Due to bureaucratic oversight, regulators were ignoring the mandates of the Clean Water Act of 1972 to reduce the amounts of discharged pollutants. This blatant violation of the law raised the foreboding question: How much toxic waste can a watershed sustain without imposing a health hazard to its inhabitants? To answer that question, a new phrase, Total Maximum Daily Load, became part of the vernacular in referencing toxic wastewater discharges and other pollutants. While the Riverkeeper claimed a small victory, the debate over discharge permits became a hotly contested issue that would surface in subsequent battles to save the Patapsco. The pollution problem with Erachem Comilog resurfaced in February 2016 when the Environmental Integrity Project and Blue Water Baltimore announced plans to sue the company for failure to comply with its nitrogen discharge permit. Public records, collected by the Baltimore Harbor Waterkeeper, disclosed that in 2014 and 2015 the company discharged more 350,000 pounds of nitrogen into a tributary of the Patapsco. That amount exceeded their permit by more than twelve times, placing the watershed at a high risk for algae blooms that create oxygen depleted "dead zones." In 2013, the company had entered into a consent decree with the MDE that limited the amount of nitrogen discharge to 13,800 pounds annually. It simultaneously reached an agreement with MDE that temporarily doubled that limit under the threat of fines while the company upgraded its wastewater treatment operations. One of those upgrades was the installation of a denitrification plant, which was to be operational by September 4, 2015, to filter effluent. Environmental groups claim the plant was never installed; Erachem officials claim it was installed but not working properly at start-up. In its defense, MDE stated that it had fined the company $10,200 in 2013 and was assessing penalties for 2014 and 2015. In spite of repeated promises to clean up its act, data from 2014 showed that Erachem Comilog retained its title as the single largest polluter of Maryland's waterways.

In 2005, the Riverkeeper finally claimed a major victory with a lawsuit against Constellation Energy Group and its power plant, the Brandon Shores Facility, located just south of the entrance to Curtis Bay. With the aid of the Mid-Atlantic Environmental Law Center, a not-for-profit law firm providing legal assistance to individuals and public interest groups on environmental matters, the Riverkeeper cited a pattern of on-going violations of opacity limitations (particle pollution) under the Federal Clean Air Act. Over 9,000 violations were recorded over a three-year period. According to EPA statistics, the plant was the nation's leader in the emission of hazardous air pollutants. Smoke billowing from the twin smokestacks around the clock filled the air with a toxic blend of sulfur dioxide (acid rain), nitrogen oxide, and mercury. Once again, the residents of Curtis Bay and surrounding region were suffering the consequences of unregulated pollution. Nearby neighborhoods were reporting the highest levels of mercury pollution in the country. Even in small doses, mercury poisoning (mecurialism) causes damage to the brain, heart, lungs, kidneys, and nervous system.

Protracted legal proceedings concluded in April 2007 when Constellation Energy agreed to upgrade the plant and provide a $50,000 water improvement grant for non-profit use. To meet state requirements for the reduction of air-borne toxics, the plant built a new 400-foot desulphurization stack and installed "scrubbers" (apparatus to clean gases passing through the smokestack of a coal burning power plant) at a cost of $875 million.

When the updates to the power plant were finally completed in February 2010, area residents breathed easier. Yet, despite this victory, they worried. Quality of life in an industrial zone required industrial-strength diligence and vigilance. Partnering with other regional and national grassroots environmental groups, such as the Energy Justice Network, community groups in the Curtis Bay area gained the expertise to successfully battle corporate giants in their war for a healthy habitat. In the process, they learned the language of the environmental warrior. The lexicon of the Patapsco now included the term "environmental justice," a concept rooted in the 1960s that flourished in the 1990s under President Clinton's Executive Order 12898. Signed in February 1994, the law mandated that no population base, regardless of race, color, national origin, or income, had to disproportionately bear any negative environmental effects from commercial, industrial, and government operations and policies. A few years later, the clamor for environmental justice would be echoed by the residents across the river at Sparrow's Point and upriver at Westport.

Despite success in confronting polluters, the Patapsco Riverkeeper failed to generate a viable membership base and garner media attention, both crucial components in attracting funding sources to expand programs and meet the funding requirements of the Waterkeeper Alliance. Due to persistent money problems, which plagued the organization from its inception and may have been related to its aggressive litigation tactics, the organization folded in early 2006. Polluters along the watershed breathed a sigh of relief. To their disappointment, the respite was brief. While the Patapsco Riverkeeper was gone, it was not quickly forgotten. One person remembered and resurrected the vanquished riverkeeper with a new name and a new image to fulfill a lifelong dream in her beloved hometown.

Later that year, Baltimore native Eliza Steinmeier returned home after spending the last eight years on the West Coast attending law school, working on clean water issues, teaching ecology classes, and conducting marine research. Her resume was custom-tailored for the job. After graduating from Bucknell University with a degree in environmental studies, she attended law school at UCLA where she clerked for the Santa Monica Baykeeper and their attorneys for Lawyers for Clean Water. In 2004, as an attorney for Lawyers for Clean Water, she settled a landmark case against the City of Los Angeles for sewage spills into the Santa Monica Bay. The suit forced the city to repair and upgrade their infrastructure of antiquated sewage plants and pipes at a cost of 2 billion dollars. In that year, she also founded the Magdalena Baykeeper in Baja California Sur in Mexico.

With her expertise in the courtroom and experience on the water, she overcame many of the obstacles that faced her predecessor and established the Baltimore Harbor Waterkeeper as the official watchdog on the Patapsco River. At the helm of her sixteen-foot C-Dory, she became a familiar and friendly face on the water, conducting shoreline inspections and water samplings at the numerous monitoring sights along the river. On land, she parlayed her hometown roots and love of the river into a blue-collar persona that captured media attention with numerous articles and interviews and paved the way into the public arena for education and outreach programs.

Focusing primarily on the harbor from the edge of downtown Baltimore to the mouth of the Chesapeake Bay, Steinmeier quickly realized that stormwater runoff had replaced industrial toxins and raw sewage as the river's environmental priority. City streets, alleys, and parking lots had become collection points and launching pads for a laundry list of pollutants and trash. While sewage pollution could be directly traced to the city's crumbling infrastructure, the trash issue was far more perplexing because it represented a behavioral problem, not an institutional one, on the part of city residents. So much trash was flowing down the storm drains after rainstorms that on September 4, 2008, the Environmental Protection Agency Region III approved the listing of Baltimore Harbor (the Middle Branch extending from the mouth of the Main Branch northeast to lower Canton) as an impaired waterway. As a result of this advocacy by the Baltimore Harbor Waterkeeper, the MDE was required to establish a TMDL (total maximum daily load) for trash reduction. In January 2015, the EPA finally approved a plan for preventing trash from entering the shoreline along the Patapsco.

But the volume of trash was only half the problem. Mixed with the trash was an invisible killer that had life threatening consequences for humans and marine life. Fertilizers, raw sewage, and animal wastes were overloading the river with nutrients, such as phosphorous and nitrogen, which triggered excessive amounts of algae growth. Algae blooms, commonly known as red tides, blocked sunlight to aquatic plants and eventually died and dissolved in the water, depleting the dissolved oxygen for fish and replacing them with dead zones. Even more alarming was the health hazard caused by the amount of *e-coli* bacteria from human waste that was five times the limit for human contact. Sampling the harbor for bacteria levels became a mandatory task to ensure . Baltimore City was complying with its 2002 consent decree.

Before stepping down from her position, Steinmeier spearheaded the move to consolidate five watershed groups in the region. On January 27, 2011, environmental leaders gathered to proudly announce the creation of Blue Water Baltimore, a non-profit that merged the Baltimore Harbor Waterkeeper with the watershed associations from Baltimore Harbor, Gwynns Falls, Herring Run, and Jones Falls. With a common goal to restore and protect the Patapsco River and Back River watersheds, the group could now pool their talents to secure more funding for a variety of green projects and wield more political clout in halls of government.

The transition proved the adage that likely allies did not always make a likely alliance. The merging of five disparate groups began in 2008 as lawyers wrangled over the budget, staff, funding, legacy debts, and a headquarters building. While the administrative issues would eventually be mediated with some bruised feelings, the major stumbling block was a philosophical one over the issue of litigation. The four associations were primarily focused on watershed maintenance that included tree plantings, stream cleanups, water monitoring, and outreach programs. Advocacy, awareness, and education were their core components. Although their programs overlapped in some instances, each group had achieved success in establishing solid membership bases and receiving funding from local governments. Would the tree planters, as they were affectionately called, alienate their members and donors by aligning with the more aggressive Waterkeeper who wielded the civilian lawsuit? The debate, however peaceful and polite, had the potential to scuttle the merger. However, in the end, the common goal became the common good when all parties agreed that a loud unified voice for the watershed was more important than a lone cry in the wilderness. A measure of immediate success was apparent when the list of new donors dramatically expanded following the merger.

While the new group was a compromise of projects and policies, the mission of the Waterkeeper remained intact. At the inaugural luncheon for the organization, Steinmeier clarified the new-forged relationship between activism and awareness. "They realized having a hammer in their toolbox gave them a very powerful tool," she replied in response to questions from reporters. "They didn't want to shut the Waterkeeper out and be a happy-go-lucky, kumbaya organization."

Steinmeier also had a chance to comment on the vexing problem of public apathy that she constantly addressed during her time on the water. "Nobody cares about urban rivers anymore. They just assume that they're dead. People are told not to go near them, and they have no experience otherwise," she proclaimed passionately. "We're fighting to get our rivers back, so people look at it as a resource for us, not just a dumping ground."

To Steinmeier, "out of sight was and out of mind" was simply a convenient excuse for not restoring the river. Her comments echoed the sentiments of environmentalists all along the river. Watershed residents needed to realize they were geographically and spiritually connected to a diverse natural resource that impacted all aspects of their lives. The Patapsco River was a living entity that needed their attention and intervention. It was too easy to classify the river as part of the Chesapeake Bay and hope that restoration of the bay would be the remedy for the river. Each individual watershed faced unique problems. In the case of Patapsco, the problems facing the river were the same problems facing the citizens of Baltimore as an urban society. The health of the city was reflected in the health of its river. Her comments not only outlined the upcoming agenda for Blue Water Baltimore, but provided a template for future environmental groups on the river.

In October 2005, the elusive connection between the river and its people was dramatically forged when a group of Baltimore businessmen formed the Waterfront Partnership of Baltimore. The private, non-profit organization brought together businesses, other non-profits (such as the National Aquarium and the Maryland Science Center), and city agencies to manage, promote, and advocate the inner harbor basin as it extended in a semi-circle from the Bond Street Wharf in Fells Point to the Rusty Scupper restaurant across the river. Unlike the battle over tourism development along the Main Branch, there was no philosophical conflict with the mission of the Partnership. Entertainment and the environment were the core values to be promoted in an effort to return the luster that once made Harborplace a world-class tourist destination. However, the focus would now be on reconnecting the local population to their river by hosting tourist-themed events, creating waterfront parks with green spaces, staffing safety and security teams, and providing landscaping and maintenance services. With a staff of only six, the Partnership adroitly developed its skills as a talent broker in recruiting people and money with astounding results.

Beyond the glitz and glamour of media-hyped events that drew large crowds to the harbor's edge, the management team knew intuitively that their success hinged on the Patapsco. The river was the prized centerpiece for once again making the harbor Baltimore's playground. If Baltimore wanted to grow its reputation as a place to call home for businesses and residents, it would have to cleanup the river. This simple proposition was a daunting challenge. With the harbor being one of the most polluted waterways in the nation, the idea of a clean river, which had languished for decades, seemed impossible.

To counter the critics, the Partnership and its supporters pointed north. By 1990, the Charles River, which flowed eighty miles from Hopkinton to the Boston Harbor, was a cesspool. The river's environmental profile reflected the same problems that were affecting the Patapsco, namely sewage, stormwater runoff, industrial pollution, and trash. In 1995, the Charles River Watershed Association began a data-driven restoration project, incorporating monitoring sites and a team of scientists and engineers, to make the river fishable and swimmable by 2005. The cleanup effort galvanized universities, non-profits, and community groups who partnered with the association and demanded immediate action. As a result, the City of Boston updated its infrastructure and the federal government began strictly enforcing disposal/dumping permits. Success was measured in small increments. By 1999, the Charles River met boating standards. In the early 2000s, the river began hosting swim meets. Finally, in July 2013, the river was opened for public swimming. If Bostonians could rally to save their river, why couldn't Baltimoreans?

Michael Hankin, CEO of Brown Advisory and co-founder and Board Chair of Waterfront Partnership, saw the problem firsthand in 2002 when he moved his investment company to offices in Fells Point. From his window, he had breathtaking views of maritime Baltimore looking across the river. Looking down at the river, his heart sank in despair. If he was disgusted with islands of floating trash, he could only imagine what visitors thought as they first approached the river.

Although the Partnership quickly achieved its goal of improving the aesthetics around the harbor, something was missing. Hankin's office panorama provided the answer. There was no quality of life around the river if there was no quality of life in the river. The organization's vision for the future of the Patapsco was lacking in commitment. In April 2010, the Partnership triumphantly announced the creation of the Healthy Harbor Initiative. With the goal to make the harbor swimmable and fishable by 2020, the connection between the river and its people was publicly reaffirmed. Residents applauded; environmentalists rejoiced; and critics snickered. With all of the trash in the harbor, there was a better chance of walking across the river than swimming across it. Despite the guffaws, the bold prophecy signaled a new era for the river restoration. For decades, people had been brought to the river. Now was the time to get them in the river for an ecological baptism. Ecology for the masses was the gospel to be preached around the harbor.

The Partnership went right to work to fulfill their prediction. With generous grants from the Abell Foundation, the Partnership developed a data-based water quality program and a floating wetlands project to demonstrate options for improving water quality. Collaborating with Blue Water Baltimore, which already had an extensive water sampling program to include bacteria monitoring, water quality data was collected, analyzed, and evaluated to measure cleanup progress. In conjunction with EcoCheck, a partnership between the National Oceanic and Atmospheric Administration and the University of Maryland Center for Environmental Science, an annual State of the Harbor Report Card was unveiled. Modeled after the annual Chesapeake Bay report from the Chesapeake Bay Foundation, the graded pollution indicators painted a grim picture of the harbor's current health. Despite the troubling findings, the report established a benchmark to measure future progress.

Again with funding from the Abell Foundation, the Partnership recruited volunteers and students from the Living Classrooms Foundation to install 2,000 square feet of floating wetlands near the World Trade Center. Designed by

Biohabitats, a Baltimore-based consulting firm that specializes in conservation planning and ecological restoration, the construction project utilized empty soda bottles retrieved from the harbor and other recycled materials. An evaluation of the wetlands by the National Aquarium concluded the floating wetlands were capable of supporting robust and diverse communities of native plants and aquatic organisms that may be more efficient than natural wetlands per square foot.

On October 13, 2013, building on the success of the floating wetlands, the Partnership in conjunction with the Chesapeake Bay Foundation and support from business leaders and local schools announced the Healthy Harbor Oyster Partnership. Oysters had once been a food and filtering staple for the bay. Their return to the Patapsco as a viable ecosystem would demonstrate the unlimited potential when man and nature work in harmony. Five oyster gardens, wire mesh baskets hanging from a pier with baby oysters (spat) were installed around the inner harbor. Local businesses adapted each garden and provided employee volunteers to maintain the cages with assistance from student oyster gardeners. The following spring, 22,000 oysters were pulled from the gardens and transported to an oyster sanctuary near Fort Carroll at the mouth of the Patapsco. While survival rates for wild oysters were extremely low due to predators and low oxygen levels in the water, the Patapsco oysters achieved a seventy-percent survival rate. With a success rate that far exceeded expectations, the number of spat was increased to 165,000 the following year.

To combat the harbor's trash problem, an $800,000 waterwheel, funded by the Maryland Port Administration and Constellation Energy, was unveiled in May 2014 where the Jones Falls empties into the harbor. The odd looking contraption, weighing nearly fifty tons, was best described by its inventor John Kellet as "cross between a spaceship and a covered wagon and an old mill." Measuring fifty feet in length, thirty feet in width with a fourteen-foot wheel attached to the side, the design employed new and old technologies to remove up to 50,000 pounds of trash daily. Floating booms funneled debris onto a conveyor belt that deposited the debris into a dumpster. The conveyor belt was powered by the waterwheel as it slowly turned with the current. When the current was too slack, solar panels on the canopy provided electricity from rechargeable batteries to turn the wheel. The premise was simple; the results staggering. In less than a year, the waterwheel collected 80,030 plastic bottles, 96,649 polystyrene containers, over 4 million cigarette butts, 1,953 glass bottles, 36,160 grocery bags, 66,409 chip bags, and 249 sports balls.

History buffs quickly noted that waterwheels, which once powered the Industrial Revolution along the Patapsco, were now being used to solve a modern-day problem on the same river. Despite its success, everyone hoped the waterwheel, though well-loved, was short-lived. The ultimate goal was to put the wheel out of business as soon as possible and then take the next step forward. The "greening" of the Patapsco through a marriage of tourism and environmentalism was generating a bounty of good publicity that had people taking notice. Perhaps, a fishable and swimmable harbor was not a pipe dream by 2020, or shortly thereafter. Seeing was believing, and believing was finding a host of green converts along the harbor basin, one project at time.

One simple solution to the trash problem is the inner harbor water wheel that removes tons of junk from the harbor. *Courtesy Adam Lindquist/ Waterfront Partnership of Baltimore.*

Floating wetlands become living laboratories in restoring ecosystems that create a healthy river. *Photo by the author.*

CHAPTER FIFTEEN

All That Glitters—The Patapsco Gold Rush

THE EASTERN HORIZON

While environmentalists were battling over control of the Main Branch, developers along the inner harbor were building. Taking advantage of low-interest financing deals from global investment firms and generous tax breaks from the city that outraged taxpayers, developers began buying property in the 1980s along both sides of the harbor. Building on recycled industrial sites that required environmental remediation was always a risky proposition, but once the first building started leasing space, the race was on. Despite the political consensus to transform the harbor district into a national showplace, the task was difficult. Funding, tax incentives, the recession, and environmental regulations routinely sabotaged the projects. Ironically, an apocalyptic financial disaster in 1985, followed by a broken promise, spurred a long-term construction project that created a new riverfront landscape appropriately dubbed "The Gold Coast" by the local media.

The local real-estate stampede started in 1982 when President Ronald Reagan signed legislation deregulating the thrift banking industry. Jeffrey Levitt and his partners jumped on the financial juggernaut with the purchase of Old Court Savings and Loan Association in Baltimore. Thrift banks, most notably savings and loan associations, were community-based institutions that made their money from individual deposits and long-term, low-interest mortgage loans. They were trusted institutions throughout the ethnic neighborhoods where blue-collar families invested their nest eggs for a modest, but safe, return. Nobody ever dreamed their savings would finance a high-stakes game of speculative real-estate that would ultimately ruin them. After two years of financing risky commercial developments around the county and funding lavish lifestyles for its owners, Old Court collapsed. Ignoring regulations in commercial and construction loans, the free-wheeling bank had been loaning money, literally giving it away, without a sufficient interest rate to guarantee a margin of profit to maintain fiscal health.

On May 9, 1985, the run on the bank began after a private insurance fund audit announced "management difficulties" at Old Court and the removal of Levitt. Depositors raced to nervously line up outside the bank, hoping to withdraw their accounts or what was left of them. Hot on their heels were federal and state regulators who immediately limited withdrawals and placed the bank in conservatorship. Customers, who wanted their money, had to wait until the bank's assets were liquidated. The owners, who later served prison sentences for embezzlement and misappropriation convictions, had to wait for federal banking officials to complete their criminal investigation.

One of Old Court's high-profile casualties was Michael Silver, former aide to Governor Marvin Mandel turned real estate speculator, who financed his business deals through the bank. Within a few years, he had amassed an expansive, jaw-dropping portfolio of expensive waterfront property. Now bankrupt, Silver was battling creditors who were threatening foreclosure on his properties. One of those properties on the radar of city hall was a twenty-acre plot of vacant lots, warehouses, and lumberyards in southeast Baltimore. Fearing a bankruptcy auction of the property could result in ownership that did not share his vision of the inner harbor renaissance, Mayor William Donald Schaefer called on John Paterakis, one of Baltimore's wealthiest businessmen, for a favor. If Paterakis bought the property for the $11 million asking price, the city would buy it back a year later for $13 million. Paterakis, a behind-the-scenes power broker and no stranger to risky business deals, was interested. In 1953, he inherited the H&S Bakery upon the death of his father, and turned it into the largest, privately owned bakery in the US. In 1965, the avid poker player, always willing to take a gamble, invested in high-speed bakery equipment to become the largest supplier of hamburger buns to McDonald's in the US.

At Schaefer's urging, Paterakis bought the property. A year later, Schaefer reneged on his promise, telling him the city didn't have the money and the appearance of sweetheart deal for a heavy-weight party fundraiser would have political repercussions. Paterakis didn't panic. Instead of immediately auctioning the property to recoup his investment, he formed a development company, H&S Properties, with Michael Beatty to explore options for the site. The team included architect Stanton Eckstut, the man who planned Battery Park City, the renaissance waterfront development at the foot of Manhattan in New York City. Eckstut strongly believed the concept of a "green" commercial and residential complex within a traditional neighborhood setting could be successfully transplanted in Baltimore.

After traveling to New York with Eckstut, Paterakis was sold on the idea of a mixed-use complex where residents walked to work, shopped around the corner, and lived upstairs. There he witnessed a vibrant neighborhood community that had been built atop a ninety-acre landfill and dredge site. It was East Baltimore along the Hudson. Despite the similar scenarios, not everyone in Baltimore shared the dream. Developers, who were behind the Inner Harbor renaissance, told Paterakis to stick with building homes in the suburbs. In the late '80s, Baltimore, like many other East Coast cities, was feeling the effects of crime, drugs, and unemployment that had city residents fleeing to the tree-lined cul-de-sacs in the country. The green was in the green, his critics admonished, but Paterakis was undeterred. He liked what he saw in New York, rolled up his sleeves, and opened his wallet.

Initial construction began in 1995 with Paterakis writing start-up checks before he had any financing or tenants for his buildings. Two years later, he had his first building and his first tenant as the staff from Sylvan Learning Systems unpacked their boxes. When construction finally ended in 2011 with the opening of the Four Seasons Hotel, a soaring glass tower offering luxury accommodations, Harbor East was complete. With the help from generous tax incentives, Paterakis had bankrolled the largest development in the city's history. The dream of a new downtown with offices, hotels, condominiums, stores, restaurants, and a movie theater had been realized. Harbor East, valued at an estimated $1.1 billion, encompassed 1.4 million square feet of office space, 300,000 square feet of retail, 2,100 hotel rooms, 650 apartments and condos, and 4,500 parking spaces. To business analysts, Harbor East marked another dramatic shift in Baltimore's downtown district. From the 1850s to the 1950s, the intersection of Howard and Lexington Streets had been the center of downtown before shoppers fled to the urban malls. Thirty years later, it migrated a few blocks south with the opening of Harborplace as tourists flocked to the water's edge. Now another thirty years later, it was relocated a few blocks to the east, Harbor East to be exact.

To the casual observer, the view from Harbor East to Canton appeared congested. A continuous corridor of high-rise buildings and townhouses snaked along the waterfront and stopped at the eastern edge of Canton where the mammoth brick rectangles that once housed the National Brewing Company and the original Gunther Brewery had been converted to luxury apartments. But there was one plot of prime real estate next to Harbor East that was bypassed. The twenty-seven acre parcel was the former home of Allied Chemical, later Allied Signal, where chromium was processed and manufactured to make chrome for over 145 years. In the early 1880s, Isaac Tyson Jr., a Quaker businessman from Baltimore who studied geology, mineralogy, and chemistry in France, began mining chromite around the local countryside. In 1845, he established the Baltimore Chrome Works, a chromium ore refinery, along the banks of the Patapsco River to refine the mineral into pigments. The works, which became part of the Mutual Chemical Company in 1908, merged into Allied Chemical in 1954.

In 1985, the plant closed after company officials announced the market for chromium compounds used for paint and leather-tanning had been replaced with less hazardous chemicals. At the same time, environmental officials discovered that approximately sixty-two pounds of chromium per day, eight percent of it an inhaled carcinogen known as *hexavalent chromium*, was seeping into the harbor and groundwater. Although never declared a Superfund site, the plant produced seventy percent of Maryland's annual chromium waste. While much of the waste was simply dumped outside the buildings, some of it was used as landfill for the expansion of Dundalk Marine Terminal, at the time an accepted practice for this type of industrial by-product. On September 29, 1989, the Maryland Department of the Environment (MDE) and the Environmental Protection Agency (EPA) signed a consent decree that required the company to fully investigate the environmental impact of the site and implement remedial measures approved by state and federal agencies. Looking to the future, the decree stated that any redevelopment plans had to be approved by the MDE and EPA to ensure they did not compromise cleanup efforts.

Allied Chromium Plant in the early 1900s along a congested industrial waterfront. Proximity of the river to similar industries made it a convenient dumping site before the clean water regulations.
Courtesy Honeywell International.

Artist's sketch of the completed Harbor Point proves that brownfields can be successfully reclaimed with an eye to the future environment.
Courtesy Beatty Development.

In 1990, Allied began dismantling the plant. To minimize additional releases of contaminants, a number of reconstruction projects were completed. To support failing bulkheads, a stone embankment was constructed around the water's edge. Dredge material was then transported to Hart-Miller Island for disposal. A hydraulic barrier, or slurry wall, was constructed around the perimeter to intercept groundwater at a depth of seventy feet, the depth of the soil and water contamination. After completion of the barrier, a three-tiered cap (consecutive layers of synthetic clay, a plastic membrane, and a layer of clean soil that measured a thickness of five feet) was installed to seal the property. The final project was the head maintenance system designed to extract contaminated groundwater from sixteen wells and lower the groundwater level below that of the river. The groundwater was pumped to on-site storage tanks for transport to a hazardous waste facility. Ten years and $110 million later, the project was finished with total containment. Honeywell International, who acquired Allied Signal in a 1999 merger, would be responsible for monitoring and maintaining the property in perpetuity.

In May 2003, EPA and MDE signed the nation's first Prospective Lessee Agreement with Harbor Point Development, a joint venture between Struever Bros., Eccles and Rouse, and H&S Properties Development. The agreement, which offered relief from future environmental liabilities, allowed the developer to sign a long-term ground lease with Honeywell. These redevelopment plans became a benchmark for the restoration of former contaminated industrial sites, known as brownfields. EPA later cited the plan as a model for their Land Revitalization Program. But despite the cleanup progress, Harbor Point languished for nearly a decade, beset with environmental hurdles and financing issues caused by the recession. When Struever Bros., Eccles, and Rouse pulled out in 2009 due to mounting debts, the project appeared to be teetering on the brink of a financial chasm.

In January 2013, Michael Beatty split from the H&S Properties to lead Beatty Development Group (BDG) as the sole developer. Through patience and perseverance, the new management team battled the same issues that faced its predecessor and prevailed. In September 2013, over the protests of activists who cried political cronyism, the Baltimore City Council approved $107 million in Tax Increment Financing for public infrastructure improvements that included roads, curbs, gutters, sidewalks, and public open space. In March 2014, Beatty received permission from the EPA and MDE to begin construction after his air-monitoring plan for the site was finally approved. Health concerns by local residents were more than justified. Penetrating the surface caps during the initial construction phases could release airborne carcinogens into a densely populated area. Only five months earlier, Beatty's air-monitoring plan had been rejected for flaws in equipment and data collection methodology. By promptly and openly responding to the concerns of environmentalist and residents, BDG was able to assuage any fears about the project and establish a bond of trust between the company and the surrounding communities that was crucial for success.

In June, workers began hammering 1,100 steel piles into the ground for the foundation of the twenty-one-story Exelon Building, the cornerstone of the multi-building complex and regional headquarter for the Exelon Corporation. When full build-out is completed in 2022, the $1.5 billion mixed-use district, similar in concept to Harbor East, will offer over 3 million square feet of hotel, office, residential, and retail space with nine-and-a-half acres of open green space. At that time, the Baltimore Waterfront Promenade, the nearly seven-mile, paved walkway that hugs the shoreline from the Canton Waterfront Park to Fort McHenry, will be completed and uninterrupted.

POINTING TO LOCUST POINT

While Harborplace has been lauded as the cornerstone of the city's economic revival, the foundation had been laid years earlier with the city's rowhouse rehabilitation effort called the Dollar House Program. In 1973, urban pioneers could buy a house, most of the time just four walls with or without roofs and floors, for a dollar or more and rehab the structure with various government loans. Starting in distressed neighborhoods on the west side, the program quickly expanded to include Fells Point and other waterfront enclaves. As the yuppies (young urban professionals) flocked to these trendy, bohemian communities, the number of houses dried up. By the 1990s, the only remaining structures were old warehouses, factories, and industrial sites. The riverbank extending east from Federal Hill to Fort McHenry, traditionally known as Locust Point, was one of first harbor sections to be rehabbed and renovated.

In 1986, Richard Swirnow and a partner bought the former Bethlehem Shipyard on Key Highway at auction for $24.4 million. By 1992, the forty-two-acre plot with drydocks and berthing piers had been transformed into Baltimore's first luxury, high-rise waterfront development. Harborview Tower, built over one of those former drydocks and rising twenty-seven stories with 252 units was later expanded to include a marina, yacht club, and clusters of townhouses. Despite some difficulty in leasing space and finding tenants due to the recession, other developers were taking a closer look at the waterfront.

In 2009, the Turner Development Group opened Silo Point, a $200 million conversion project on a fifteen-acre plot just west of Fort McHenry. The five-year construction project converted the old Baltimore and Ohio Locust Point Grain Elevator into high-rise condominiums with twenty-four floors and 228 units with adjacent office and retail space. The grain elevator, which was completed in 1924 and soared to nearly 300 feet, was at one time the largest and fastest in the world. Ten miles of conveyor belts moved almost 4 million bushels of grain annually from rail cars to silo to ocean-bound freighters. Throughout the middle of the decade, grain exports marked the heyday of the seaport when it was ranked the fourth largest in the country. With the demise of the grain silos in Locust Point, grain was replaced by coal as the chief export in the late 1990s.

Even the National Park Service joined the newsmakers along Locust Point on two notable occasions, one with a twist of green. In September 2014, Fort McHenry National Monument and Historic Shrine hosted one of the biggest celebrations in the city's history with the Star-Spangled Spectacular, the bicentennial celebration of the national anthem. The week-long celebration featured tall ships, reenactments, a living flag where over 6,600 school children donned red, white, and blues ponchos to create a fifteen-star and thirteen-stripe flag, music concerts highlighted by a PBS Great Performance, visits from the president and vice president, and air shows by the Blue Angels. When the city officials tallied up the figures, they calculated that 1.43 million visitors spent $164 million on area hotel rooms, meals, and entertainment, which resulted in tax revenue of $6.4 million to the state and $1.5 million to the city.

While the events garnered national media attention, the real headline news for environmentalists and tourists occurred on March 3, 2011. Eighty years to the date after President Hoover signed a congressional act making the "Star Spangled Banner" the official national anthem of the United States, the park dedicated its new Visitor and Education Center. The old center, built in 1963 under the Park Service's Mission 66 program, featured "park service modern" architecture. Within a few years, the "modern" facility was obsolete, unable to accommodate the increasing number of visitors. With its new building, the Park Service would not make the same mistakes.

Designed by Baltimore-based GWWO, the structure was inspired by the Star Spangled Banner. Two curved exterior walls, contrasting in volume and height, represented the fort and the dynamics of the unfurled flag. The juxtaposition of these walls expressed the meaning of the flag's stripes: red brick symbolizing the valor of the red stripes, and the zinc façade symbolizing the innocence of the white stripes. The sloping walls were created to establish a visual dialogue and directed the visitor's attention to the flag flying over the fort.

To environmentalists, the 17,655-square-foot facility, three times larger than the old building, was another major step in promoting the green agenda along the Patapsco. Using recycled brick, native plants in landscaping, a geothermal system to heat and cool the building, and low-flush sinks and toilets, the building received the LEED (Leadership in Energy and Design) Gold certification from the US Green Building Council in 2012.

For visitors, the three interconnected galleries provided the much-needed space for more exhibits from the fort's unseen collection. Touch screens allowed visitors to vote on the War of 1812, explore the life of Francis Scott Key, and connect with the Battle of Baltimore. Interactive screens played various interpretations of the "The Star-Spangled Banner" that included the US Marine Corps Band and Jimi Hendrix at Woodstock. The new movie, likened to an IMAX presentation, featured computer-generated imaging and special effects that brought the battle sequences to life. As with the old movie in the old building, the grand finale was the inspirational and emotionally charged vision of the actual fort appearing beyond the screen as the US Naval Academy Choir sang the national anthem. Through teary eyes, visitors unanimously agreed that there were some things that technology could never improve.

In 1994, Procter & Gamble Co., a stalwart of Baltimore's industrial waterfront for six decades, closed its Locust Point manufacturing plant and eliminated 215 jobs. For over sixty decades, the sprawling red-brick complex, located next to the Domino Sugars plant, produced a line of soap, laundry, and dishwashing products that were found on the shelves of every American household. The site for the once state-of-the-art facility was originally selected for its ship, rail, and truck facilities. Despite its age and prior use, its location on the river made it an ideal candidate for renovation as office space.

Struever Brothers bought the property in 1998 for $6 million and began a $67 million renovation that transformed the factory complex into Tide Point, a fifteen-acre corporate campus with 400,000 square feet of office space. The project was the brainchild of C. William Struever, a locally based developer who gained a reputation for converting obsolete and antiquated industrial structures into fashionable commercial office buildings, such as the American Can Company in Canton and the Power Plant at the inner harbor.

In 2003, Under Armour, the global high performance sportswear company, left its cramped offices in Pigtown to become the largest tenant at Tide Point. The company had been founded in 1996 by Kevin Plank who started his apparel empire in the basement of his grandmother's house. With a handful of synthetic athletic shirts and a handful of employees, the former football player at the University of Maryland began his quest to replace the cotton t-shirt on the playing fields around the world. Within a decade, the company found itself competing in the global market with iconic athletic brands, such as Nike and Adidas, and needed space for its ever-expanding workforce and product line.

In January 2011, the company announced plans to buy the Tide Point complex and invested $14.2 million to expand the campus with showrooms, a top secret "innovation" lab, meeting spaces, and a basketball court. To "green" the campus, buildings featured recycled carpet, energy-efficient lights, previously used workstations, skylights, and white roofs to reflect the sun. Two years later, the deal was completed for $58 million. Along the gritty, hard-edged, blue-collar Patapsco River, Kevin Plank finally found a permanent home that reflected the company's gritty, hard-edged, blue-collar attitude.

Despite the ever-changing landscape, visages of old Baltimore's glorious manufacturing and maritime history still exist at the inner harbor. One of the most famous landmarks is the Domino Sugars refinery just upriver from Tide Point. Opened in 1922, the facility still takes advantage of the shipping, rail, and truck vehicle transportation options that first attracted industry to the harbor basin. Large tanker ships regularly dock next to the plant and unload hundreds of millions of pounds of raw sugar, which is eventually processed into over forty sugar products. An estimated 6.5 million pounds of raw sugar are processed daily throughout the plant's eight stories.

While sugar is king to consumers, it's the neon sign atop the "sugar house" that attracts tourists. The massive 120 by 70 foot neon sign, erected in April 1951, has become the most visible Baltimore icon from its perch 160 feet above the harbor. Using 650 elongated glass tubes that spell out "Domino Sugars," the sign casts a warm and welcoming blood-orange glow over the nighttime harbor. In 2014, the company installed solar panels on one of the rooftops to light the sign. Solar energy was one of the many "green" initiatives to make the plant environmentally friendly.

Like every other industry along the river, the refinery has environmental issues, which are readily being addressed. In 2010 and 2011, the Maryland Department of the Environment fined the company $150,000 for discharges of sugar into the harbor. In 2012, the Environmental Protection Agency levied a fine of $200,000 and entered into a consent decree to reduce emissions of nitrogen oxides, which contribute to the smog problem and eventually find their way into the river and the bay. To remedy the situation, the plant has cut its air emissions by more than half and installed a detection system to prevent accidental discharges of sugar water.

Standing upriver from the sugar refinery is the last of the many shipyards that once lined the inner harbor underneath the shadow of Federal Hill. General Ship Repair, which has been owned by the Lynch family since its founding in 1924, opened as a marine machine shop on Light Street. In the late 1920s, the company moved to its present location where it tenaciously survived the Great Depression. Sold at auction after going bankrupt, the company was quickly bought back by its founder Charles "Buck" Lynch.

After WWII, the company's success extended into the '50s and '60s with the renovation of Victory and Liberty ships for the Korean and Vietnam wars. In its heyday, the shipyard employed over 600 workers. By continually upgrading its repair capabilities to include a state-of-the-art dry dock, the company methodically became a major ship repair facility along the mid-Atlantic seaboard. With a finely tuned ear to the needs of the industry, the shipyard found its niche in handling small to mid-size vessels, such as dinner cruise ships, tugboats, fireboats, and barges.

Resiliency, as proudly noted by the Lynch family, has been the trademark of the company, which will hopefully keep them in business. The looming question along the gentrified harbor is: Where will that business be located as residential developments steadily encroach on the boundaries of the shipyard? In 2008, the company partnered with Baltimore City to develop a master plan that would rezone the company's two-acre site for mixed-use development and allow the extension of the harbor promenade. The sale of the waterfront property would offset the high costs of building new facilities capable of supporting the ponderous dry dock repair equipment. A move to Canton, which had been mentioned as a possible site, would bring the company closer to the ships that it services at the port's major terminals and hopefully create an industrial buffer that would prevent future residential development at any new site. To date, the company remains at its present location. No activity has been reported in selling the property or relocating the company.

THE MYSTIFYING MIDDLE BRANCH

What if? That was the question that defined the history of the Middle Branch of the Patapsco at the turn of the twenty-first century. It was also the question that intrigued Baltimore residents and developers after the city's bid to host the 2012 Olympics was rejected. In the blink of an eye, billions of dollars and thousands of jobs vanished when New York was announced as the winner during the preliminary round. The Washington-Baltimore 2012 Regional Coalition had invested three years and $9.5 million in their 600-page proposal. The bid had predicted an influx of more than 5 million visitors and the creation of 70,000 jobs. A financial forecast had projected a total operating budget of $2 billion with a return of over $5 billion in total economic impact.

Olympic events for the two-week extravaganza would have been staged in a fifty-mile "Olympic corridor" extending from Baltimore to northern Virginia. Four hundred and sixty miles of rail would have transported athletes and spectators around the region against a background of history and architecture that showcased the nation's capital and the City of Baltimore. Baltimore would have hosted soccer, gymnastics, triathlon, cycling, and field hockey. Olympic sailors would tack on the Chesapeake Bay near the Naval Academy, and mountain bikers would climb the steep hills in Patapsco Valley State Park. The University of Maryland at College Park would be home to the Olympic Village.

Although Olympic fever quickly dissipated after the announcement from the US Olympic Committee, the idea of Baltimore, not Baltimore and Washington, hosting the Olympics was an irresistible daydream. One person dared to theoretically prove the Olympics were not only for athletes but for scholars. In his 2013 thesis for a master's degree in city and regional planning, Patrick Terranova described Baltimore's Olympic dream in vivid detail. His paper titled "Gold Standard: Applying Best Practices in Olympic Development to a Baltimore Bid," convincingly presented an analytical study for the development of an Olympic infrastructure to rival any other bidders for the imaginary games.

The Olympic Ring, three downtown waterfront districts within a one-and-a-half-mile radius, would utilize current sports venues, accommodations, and convention facilities to stage games and media events. The two districts along the Middle Branch of the Patapsco were envisioned as showcase centerpieces for the bid. The River District that ran from Whetstone Point to Point Covington would host games in newly constructed facilities as the official Olympic Park; the Village District along the Westport waterfront would house athletes in the official Olympic Village. After the games, both sites would be converted to mixed-use communities for commercial and residential endeavors. In compliance with the Middle Branch Master Plan adopted in 2007 by the Baltimore City Planning Commission, the renovated Olympic waterfront would have also provided a restored ecosystem that offered outdoor recreational opportunities. Although Terranova's thesis was a hypothetical scenario that came ten years too late for serious consideration by Olympic bidders, it demonstrated the unbounded potential of the Middle Branch.

The idea of fun and games along the Middle Branch was not a new concept. In the 1880s, the river basin was the home to yacht clubs, beer gardens, bathing beaches, summer resorts, and boathouses. The sport of rowing, or sculling, started there in 1864 with the founding of the Baltimore Rowing Club, later renamed the Ariel Club. As more local clubs were formed, they collectively called themselves the Patapsco Navy and held an annual championship known as the Navy Day Regatta.

In 1905, the Ariel Club and the Arundel Boat Club, the only remaining clubs, which had become premier powers in regional and national competition, revived the annual championship and developed a fierce rivalry that matched the intensity of any other sport from that era. The race course, dubbed the Spring Garden course, began at Ferry Bar Point and ran west underneath the Hanover Street Bridge before turning northward along the cove. The coveted prize was a maroon and blue triangular pennant with a white inset at the base containing the initials "P.N." and the year of the regatta. Races were held for nine straight years until bitter disputes over crew eligibility ended the association.

Two of the sport's biggest names had Baltimore connections. Jim Wray, the Harvard coach who led the 1914 Crimson crew to the first American eight-man victory in the Royal Henley Regatta (the sport's most prestigious race), started his career with the Arundel Boat Club. Harry "Dad" Vail, famous crew coach at Harvard and Wisconsin, trained national championship boats for the Baltimore Athletic Club and Ariel Rowing Club from the early 1890s to 1911. Today the largest collegiate regatta in the US bears his name.

Through the 1920s, Baltimore clubs hosted several regional and national championships that attracted crowds of up to 10,000 people along the shoreline. Local newspapers covered the races as major sporting events. Beginning in the 1930s, the sport started fading as Americans discovered the automobile and other pastimes. Suffering from declining membership, the Great Depression, and a renovated boathouse that led to bankruptcy, the venerated Ariel Rowing Club was the first club to disband. At one time, it had been the fourth oldest rowing club in the United States. Industrialization of the waterfront during WWII effectively ended the era of the sport. Boathouses disappeared and the yacht clubs relocated downriver. In 1979, rowing in Baltimore was revived when a group of former college oarsmen began gathering on the river. In 1987, the city of Baltimore built the Baltimore Rowing and Water Resource Center, a multi-use facility that provided offices and storage space for rowing shells. Within a decade, the sport had attracted a number of college, high school, and club teams that were eager to experience the metropolitan waterfront. The center became the headquarters for the Baltimore Rowing Club, which offered training programs for amateurs and inner-city youths.

Apart from its storied history as a recreational area, the Middle Branch had been targeted by real-estate developers for decades. However, unlike projects around the inner harbor that flourished with an infusion of corporate financing and tax incentives from the city and state, development around the Middle Branch would languish after initial interest in the property faded in the 1980s. Twenty years later, there was once again hope as developers turned their sights away from the inner harbor in a search for other waterfront areas.

In 2004, Patrick Turner, envisioning the success that he experienced at Silo Point, bought just over forty-three acres of waterfront property between Waterview Avenue and Interstate 95 for $13 million. Residents of the adjacent Westport community, tucked away in the far west corner and cut-off by railroad tracks and interstate overpasses, were elated. The blue-collar enclave had fallen on hard times with the shuttering of local manufacturers that had employed many local residents. By 2000, twenty-two percent of the homes were abandoned and the community became noted for its high crime and unemployment rates. In July 2009, Westport made the news for another wrong reason when state officials found toxic vapors seeping into homes from nearby abandoned industrial sites. These sites had been cleaned up and cleared in 1981 under the federal Superfund law. To remedy the problem, ventilation systems were installed in the dwellings. At the same time, state and federal officials also reported cancer-causing cleaning solvents in the groundwater beneath the site that were believed to be the source of the vapors. Westport was desperate for a savior to revitalize the local economy and restore the community. They hoped that Turner's dream could make their dreams come true.

With a half-mile of waterfront on a body of water five times larger than the inner harbor, the project, known as Westport Waterfront, was being hailed as the next Harbor East. The $1.2 billion complex of shops, hotels, restaurants, offices, townhouses, and condominiums also advertised amenities such as water-related recreation and a wildlife refuge. Plans were discussed to renovate the nearby abandoned railroad "swing" bridge and create a loop around the Middle Branch for walkers and bicyclists. With $160 million in tax incentives from the city of Baltimore, the project appeared to start on solid financial footing.

Improvements on the property began in 2008 with the demolition of two familiar landmarks, the old Baltimore Gas and Electric's Westport Power Station and the Carr-Lowery Glass Company. The coal-burning power plant, constructed in 1906 and operated until 1993, was at one time the largest, reinforced-concrete building in the world. At the time it was razed, it still housed its suspended system of coal cars and tracks for storing and moving coal throughout the building, even though the plant changed to oil in 1971.

The glass company, founded in 1889 by local businessmen William W. Lowrey and Samuel J. Carr, became famous for its line of intricate perfume/cosmetic bottles and other decorative specialty bottles, many using the cobalt-colored glass known as "Baltimore Blue." Despite the move to automation in 1927 and the mass production of the popular Avon bottles in the '40s, the company struggled for decades to sustain a profit in the labor-intensive industry of glass making. By the time the company closed in 2003, it had expanded its product line to include tableware, candle holders, and food and beverage containers, but it was too late to fend off foreign competition and the popularity of plastic.

In 2010, after refinancing delays caused by the recession, the first phase of construction to transform twenty-five acres of barren waterfront into a living shoreline commenced. With a $620,500 grant from the MDE, an environmental soil cap, a wetland sill of boulders to control erosion, and a floating boom to reduce trash in the wetland were installed. This was to be followed by new roads, bicycle paths, and landscaping before breaking ground in 2011 for a luxury high-rise apartment.

Unfortunately for Turner and local residents, the first phase of construction was also the first and last step in overhauling the green infrastructure along the shoreline. In December 2012, a Baltimore judge ordered a default judgment for about $100,000 against one of Turner's companies for non-payment of wetland work at the property. This cash-flow problem was only the latest in a chronology of financial maneuvers that included defaulted loans, refinancing deals, foreclosures, a bankruptcy, and two auction proceedings. In January 2015, Turner's dream collapsed on the steps of a Baltimore downtown courthouse when the property was sold at auction for $6 million to Westport Property Investments. While the name of the new owner was not revealed, the small group of savvy spectators noted the winning bid was represented by a lawyer from Ballard Spahr, a national law firm who had represented Under Armour interests in the past.

Another waterfront dream that became tangled in the financial web across the Middle Branch belonged to the National Aquarium. Their more modest pursuit was the Center for Aquatic Life and Conservation, a 50,000 square-foot facility dedicated to conservation programs, environmental education, and animal care. Like Turners' project, the Aquarium started out on solid financial footing with a state grant for $5 million in December 2004. In 2006, they acquired a twenty-acre plot and began remediation of the brownfield with a $200,000 award from the EPA. Aquarium officials were elated at their good fortune. Earlier the EPA had previously denied a similar request stating that since the property had been polluted by the city, the city was responsible for restoring the site. Tons of debris were removed from the property and the ground was capped with a layer of clean dirt. Aquarium officials stated that cleanup expenses would be funded with proceeds from the sale of an eight-acre section of the site to Patrick Turner for $8.3 million.

Despite an optimistic attitude, the financial future for the center was bleak. Development along the Middle Branch did not generate the same excitement as the inner harbor. Money was scarce; investors even scarcer. Citing recession-related financing issues and fundraising challenges, the Aquarium was forced to scale back its original concept. In May 2010, aquarium officials unveiled plans for the Center for Aquatic Life and Conservation's Environmental Demonstration Area, a $5.4 million "conservation demonstration park" on a twelve-acre site that featured habitats for migratory birds and native insect populations, a recreational pier, and a network of trails.

One footnote to the aquarium's troubled business venture revealed the extent that property along the Middle Branch and rest of the river was changing hands for financial survival. City court records disclosed that in June 2012 the Center for Aquatic Life and Conservation Inc., a division of the National Aquarium, filed suit against Patrick Turner for repayment of an $115,000 loan that had defaulted. The loan was to a Turner subsidiary for the purchase of a seven-acre site that housed the city's maintenance garage near the Middle Branch. To satisfy the debt, Turner was negotiating to transfer ownership of another Westport property. In this latest chapter, money and mortgages repeatedly changed hands, but nothing changed in the community of Westport. Residents and city officials would have to wait for a new savior to come to the rescue.

Dreams lived easy and died hard on the Patapsco. Just as one was sinking under the rippling surface, another one was splashing from murky depths. In 2008, Under Armour's Kevin Plank had discussed expanding his inner harbor campus to the Middle Branch, but any preliminary plans were quickly scuttled when the city planned to take control of the land under eminent domain. He had hoped to build a company campus to rival that of his chief competitor Nike, headquartered in Beaverton, Oregon. With its futuristic architecture of white, glass-walled buildings and sports facilities set amid a breathtaking 270-acre landscape of trees, fields, and water, the complex was the envy of every sports company, if not every company, around the world. The campus captured the contemporary business ethic and lifestyle that mirrored the vision of the company. It reflected success and superiority. It reflected precisely what Kevin Plank wanted for his company.

Seven years later, with the eminent domain threat defeated, the public learned that Plank's dream had been discreetly revived. Real estate records disclosed that his private development company, Sagamore Development, had acquired 120 acres for $90 million along the north side of the Main Middle, a stretch of land extending from Fort Whetstone to beyond Port Covington. Following the practice that had become standard business procedure for developers, purchases had been completed through private holding and investment companies to effectively shield the parent company from any unwanted media attention.

Speculation about the future of the property ended in March 2015. While making his first public comments about his waterfront acquisitions, Plank stated that he wanted to create a "new neighborhood" in Port Covington with shopping and restaurants, anchored by a relocated Under Armour headquarters. In addition, there would be a distillery and horse stables for possible use by the Baltimore City Police Department. None of his comments raised any eyebrows. Horses and distilled spirits had been Plank's long-time pet projects.

In the past, Plank had commented to the press about building a distillery to produce rye whiskey under the brand name of Triple Rye. Maryland, once synonymous with straight rye whiskey, led the nation in 1936 with fifteen distilleries that produced over 14 million gallons of rye grain. America's unquenchable thirst for rye whiskey following the end of Prohibition in 1933 lasted only a decade. With Americans drinking more scotch, gin, vodka, and other distilled spirits after WWII, the rye industry slowly faded until the last barrel of Pikesville Maryland straight rye whiskey was sealed in 1972. The distilling of rye whiskey in Maryland dated to the 1700s when tobacco farmers planted rye and wheat as cover crops to replenish the soil. With the resurgence of the cocktail culture, Plank quite possibly found the business opportunity to create a new brand with a historical connection to the city and state that he proudly promoted at Under Armour.

In January 2016, Sagamore Development Company, Plank's real estate firm, unveiled plans for developing 266 acres in Port Covington. The presentations, which included a master plan to the city's Urban Design and Review Panel, finally provided details about Plank's vision to transform a ramshackle industrial waterfront district into a global riverfront destination. The plan included up to thirteen million square feet of office and residential space, restaurants, entertainment venues, and forty acres of public parks and green zones. The cornerstone of the project was the new Under Armour headquarters, which will include a fifty-acre complex for 5,000 employees near the site of the defunct Sam's Club. The sprawling waterfront campus will feature three skyscrapers, a 5,000-seat stadium, a field house, product development spaces, and an expanded Ferry Bar Park. As part of the company's "green" commitment to environmental sustainability, a man-made lake will filter water runoff and water from the Patapsco to cool buildings before being released back into the river. No specific timelines or price tags were disclosed, but the mixed-use development was expected to cost billions over the next twenty years. Developers expected that it would take at least a year for the master plan to work its way through the city's planning and review process before phased construction projects begin.

In March, Sagamore Development announced they were requesting $535 million in tax-increment financing (TIF) from Baltimore City to pay for infrastructure improvements (new roads, bridges, sewers, utilities and parks) at Port Covington. The money from city-sold bonds would be repaid by new property taxes generated by the project. While the practice has financed other developments along the harbor, this would be the largest in the city's history and one of the largest in the nation. In addition to the bonds and their own money, the company would also seek $574 million in state and federal funds. The infrastructure package totals $1.1 billion of the estimated $5.5 billion for the entire project.

Learning a lesson from past TIF developments that raised the ire of watchdog groups, politicians and city residents, Sagamore launched a political-styled media campaign to win the hearts and mind of the public and loosen the purse strings at City Hall. Print and TV ads with the mantra of "We will build it together" featured "everyday" citizens and entrepreneurs extolling the economic virtues of the project in terms of new businesses and more jobs. An artist's rendering of the completed project showcased a sparking and sprawling city by the river with modernistic high-rise buildings, marinas, parks, and playing fields.

Seemingly overlooked in the media blitz and political controversy was the fate of the iconic Hanover Street Bridge, officially renamed the Vietnam Veterans Memorial Bridge in 1993, which served as the backdrop for the TV ads. Constructed in 1916 and designed by world-renowned Baltimore engineer John E. Greiner, the Beau Arts-style bascule bridge is literally crumbling into the river below. With its graceful arches and four towers framing the center drawbridge, the 2,290-foot bridge is a main thoroughfare for heavy industry in South Baltimore and a gateway to Anne Arundel County.

In January 2016, Baltimore's Board of Estimates approved a nearly $1.2 million study to determine if the aging bridge, riddled with potholes and exposed rebar, should be repaired or replaced. The study is expected to be completed by 2018.

CHAPTER SIXTEEN

A "Green" Port Report

A PORT OF OPPORTUNITY

Although the harbor basin has been transformed into a bustling metropolis, the lower half of the Patapsco remains a muscling seaport that fuels the economic engine of the state. Over the past twenty-five years, the landscape of the maritime industry has changed in proportion but not purpose. As the Port of Baltimore entered the twenty-first century, it weathered fluctuating economic climates and adapted to ever-changing maritime demands to retain its ranking as a top-tiered port. Among US ports, Baltimore has been first in handling autos, light trucks, farm and construction machinery, forest products, gypsum, aluminum, and sugar; and second in coal exports. The success of the port in the 2000s was a dramatic turnaround from the 1980s and 1990s when the port's viability was threatened by rail deregulation, conflicts with maritime labor unions, loss of shipping lines, and the building of super ships.

With expanded terminal capacity and channel improvements, the port experienced dramatic increases in yearly cargo tonnage since 2000. With shipping containers still the main staple, the port expanded its share in niche cargo, basically anything too large to fit in a container, such as autos, light trucks, forest and pulp products, farm implements, and construction equipment. For this type of cargo, the port's inland location within an overnight drive of one-third of the nation's population proved more cost effective to shippers than transporting these goods by railroad from ports closer to the ocean. The inland advantage, which once propelled the port into prominence and prosperity before the cost-cutting ascendency of ocean ports, had returned.

The Maryland Port Administration (MPA), owner and operator of the five largest terminals in the port, led the way in upgrading facilities to accommodate current and future clients. In 2010, Maryland officials signed a fifty-year agreement with Ports America, the largest terminal operation and stevedore in the United States, to operate the Seagirt Marine Terminal, the state-of-the-art, computerized facility that opened in 1990. In return, Ports America agreed to construct a fifty-foot deep berth and install new cranes. In May 2013, the port dedicated four new 400-foot cranes that would triple the unloading capacity. The cranes arrived from China aboard the *Zhen Hua 13* after a two-month ocean voyage that captured media attention from its first day at sea. Each crane weighed 1,706 tons with booms that cleared a fourteen-story building and extended 206 feet from the edge of the wharf to the opposite side of a docked ship for a reach of twenty-two containers.

During the passage, each crane had its boom locked skyward to increase stability. As the ship approached the Chesapeake Bay Bridge with a vertical navigational clearance of 186 feet and then the Francis Scott Key Bridge with a clearance of 185 feet, the crane booms were lowered to fit under the bridges. The Coast Guard closed the shipping channel to all traffic, and traffic on the bridges was stopped to prevent distracted drivers from causing or being involved in an accident. With tugboats clinging to its hull, the ship moved forward at a speed of two knots. Expected to clear the Chesapeake Bay Bridge by four feet at low tide, the ship passed under the bridge with approximately ten feet of clearance. Concerns about the clearance margin had prompted transportation engineers to calculate the amount of bridge sag as the result of the hot weather.

With the new berth, the terminal became only the second East Coast port with a fifty-foot berth and a fifty-foot shipping channel that was part of the 50-Foot Channel, the north-south route running 150 nautical miles from the harbor to Cape Henry, Virginia. The port was now equipped to handle the larger ships that would be passing through the widened Panama Canal in 2016.

In 2006, cruises officially joined cars and containers as a major cargo with the opening of a new cruise terminal at the South Locust Point Marine Terminal. Cruise ships had been making port-of-calls at the Dundalk Marine Terminal since the early '90s, but the port wasn't able to cash in on the lucrative, recession-proof cruise industry without a dedicated facility that could be a home port. Following 9/11, travelers and travel agents clamored for a secure mid-Atlantic terminal that offered easy access to the interstate and an airport. In addition to satisfying those transportation requirements, Baltimore offered a home port getaway with hotels, restaurants, and entertainment at the Inner Harbor just two miles away. For the cruise lines, the demographics proved irresistible. Maryland had the highest median income in the nation, and the Baltimore-DC-Northern Virginia corridor topped the list as the most affluent region. The new terminal, the closest East Coast port as far west as Chicago and Indianapolis, was also within a four-hour drive of the eight wealthiest counties in the country and a six-hour drive for forty million people.

The major cruise lines, such as Carnival and Royal Caribbean, responded to the demand with their biggest ships and year-round cruises. Baltimore quickly became the home port for cruises south to Bermuda, the Bahamas, and the Caribbean; and north to New England and Canada. In December 2012, Cruise Maryland announced that it had sailed its one millionth passenger from the South Locust Point. The old paper warehouse, converted at a cost of $13 million, was a financial gold mine, providing nearly 500 jobs and pumping $90 million into the state's economy. In 2012, the port became the fifth busiest cruise port on the East Coast.

The cruise boom almost went bust in June 2013 when Carnival announced it was leaving Baltimore due to new federal emission regulations that required cruise ships to burn cleaner fuels within 200 nautical miles of US and Canadian coastlines. Carnival stated the higher fuel costs of low-sulfur fuels would make it unprofitable to sail from Baltimore. The Carnival Pride, a 2,124 passenger ship that sailed weekly from Baltimore to the Bahamas and the Caribbean would reduce its sailing schedule before relocating to Tampa, Florida. The move would leave the port with only one large cruise ship, the Royal Caribbean's Grandeur of the Seas, and postpone any expansion plans for the terminal.

In response, state officials and the governor vigorously lobbied the Environmental Protection Agency on Carnival's behalf while searching for another cruise line to fill the void. As a compromise, Carnival offered to spend $200 million over the next three years for air "scrubbers" on its ships as they went into drydock for overhaul, but federal regulators procrastinated in making a decision. Finally, in September 2013, Carnival and the EPA announced they had reached an agreement where Carnival would install pollution control equipment on one-third of its ships. The good news for Carnival was bad news for the port. The deal came too late to amend Carnival's deployment schedule for 2014. Port officials were stunned at the turn of events that excluded them from the bargaining table. While they had just lost half of their lucrative cruise business, they were optimistic. Carnival officials left the door open for returning to Baltimore, stating they would evaluate all viable options in complying with air-quality regulations and itinerary changes. For delighted port officials, the door opened as quickly as it closed. In late 2014, Carnival announced they would be returning to Baltimore in March 2015 with the Carnival Pride.

In October 2014, port officials officially opened a new auto berth at the Masonville/Fairfield Terminal. At 1,175 feet in length and 130 feet in width, the new berth was not only longer and wider than the old one, but also had rail capabilities that were capable of supporting 1,000 pounds-per-square-inch as compared to 100 pounds for the old one. Demand necessitated action, and the port responded to meet the demands of automakers and shippers. In 2005, Mercedes Benz signed a twenty-year lease, and in 2012, BMW signed a five-year lease. In 2012, the port had surpassed New York as the nation's leading car handler, and in 2014, it handled over 800,000 vehicles to maintain its grip on the top spot. With two operational berths, an ever-increasing number of vehicles could be quickly unloaded, processed, and prepped for delivery.

Transportation managers for car manufacturers and dealers praised the terminal complex, noting experienced stevedore crews in unloading vehicles from RoRo (roll on/roll off) vessels, access to on-site vehicle processors, and truck and rail options. The biggest benefit for shippers was the expanded space. A guaranteed berth allowed ocean-going car carriers, usually loaded with four to six thousand vehicles, to steam across the oceans at slower speeds. At reduced speeds, ships burned less fuel and released less hazardous emissions. As with niche cargo, the port's proximity to population centers and transportation routes worked to its advantage in the car import/export business. The extra eight to ten hours to steam up the Chesapeake Bay were offset by the port's inland location, which reduced trucking expenses. With the globalization of the auto industry, the port began to import Ford vans from Turkey and General Motors compacts from Mexico, and export high-end American sedans, sports car, and SUVs to the Middle East.

As the Port of Baltimore entered the twenty-first century, it faced challenges similar to what was experienced over the past three centuries. Economic turmoil, emerging technology, competition from ports home and abroad, labor unrest, and political whims were conquered by a coalition of dedicated maritime leaders whose vision and leadership continuously reinvented the port. No one was more instrumental in the port's success in the last fifty years than Helen Delich Bentley.

The "champion of the port" started her career as a maritime reporter and editor for *The Baltimore Sun*. Beginning in 1950, she also produced and hosted a local TV program *The Port That Built a City* that presented maritime and transportation news. The show, later renamed *The Port That Built a City – and State* ran until 1965 and included live remotes aboard ships in Baltimore harbor. Her coverage of the supply problems during the Vietnam War led to the widespread use of containers as the preferred method of cargo transport.

From 1969 through 1975, Bentley served as chairman of the United States Federal Maritime Commission. From 1985 through 1995, she served in the US House of Representatives where she sat on the Committee on Merchant Marine and Fisheries. Following her political career, Bentley served as a consultant to the Maryland Port Administration. In 1995, she founded Helen Bentley & Associates, Inc., a consulting firm specializing in government relations and business development. To honor her tireless efforts in promoting the Baltimore maritime industry, the port was officially renamed the Helen Delich Bentley Port of Baltimore to celebrate the port's 300th anniversary in 2006.

A NEW SHADE OF GREEN

In 2006, the economic engine of the state became the big green machine when the MPA developed an Environmental Management System (EMS) in response to more stringent federal environmental regulations. The EMS was a fluid set of processes and procedure to blend environmental stewardship with daily port operations. Many of the problems facing the port, such as air emissions, stormwater management, spill prevention and response, and trash reduction, were the same problems facing the city. However, the port's problems were occurring in highly concentrated industrial zones that were impacted by unique problems inherent to the shipping industry, such as monitoring dredged material and eliminating invasive species from arriving ships. To inform the workforce about the port's new priorities, the EMS also included employee training in environmental awareness and stewardship opportunities.

Realizing they were the last line of defense in the battle to save the river and embracing the mantra "green business is good business," port officials installed screens on storm drains, removed underground storage tanks, and converted to clean diesel technology in cargo-handling equipment, dray trucks, locomotives, and harbor craft. Tugboats ran at slower speeds to burn less fuel. Seagirt Marine Terminal recycled used oil, batteries, and scrap metal. Wallenius Wilhelmsen, the Scandinavian line that shipped automobiles and farm equipment at Dundalk Marine Terminal, drove electric and hybrid diesel-electric yard vehicles and recycled water from its car wash facility.

With over 1,100 acres of impervious surfaces, stormwater runoff at the terminals contained diesel fuels, oils, road salt, chemicals, exhaust tracings, and rubber residue. To combat this on-going problem, a massive stormwater vault was constructed at the Seagirt terminal to collect and treat the runoff. At the Dundalk terminal, an algae turf scrubber, which won a first place award from the Chesapeake Stormwater Network for Innovative Best Management Practice, was installed. Measuring 300 feet in length, the scrubber pumped water from the Patapsco into a shallow screened trough where the growth of natural algae fed on nutrients in the water and released dissolved oxygen for marine life.

While the EMS documented the port's commitment to green initiatives, the actual greening of the port began in the early 1980s with the Hart-Miller Island dredge project. As it has been since the 1700s, the viability of the port depended on accommodating the ever-increasing draft (distance between the waterline of a vessel and the bottom of the hull) of modern-day cargo ships. To maintain a navigable depth, the port was annually required to dredge million of tons of muck, consisting of gravel, clay, sand, and silt, from the entrances to the harbor. For decades, dredge material had been dumped in deep troughs on the floor of the bay. By the mid-1980s, that practice had been banned due to toxins in the dredge material. With 126 miles of waterway, the port had the greatest dredging requirement in the country. Each year, nearly 1.5 million cubic yards of material had to be scooped from the bottom of the harbor and deposited somewhere in the Chesapeake Bay watershed. Without alternatives, the port would die a slow death. Logistically and financially, the easy solution to the problem was to build containment dikes; however, they raised environmental issues that adversely impacted local communities and ultimately poisoned any public relations campaigns.

By the time the last scoop of dredge material was dumped at Hart-Miller Island in December 2009, over 100 million cubic yards had been dumped to create 1,100 acres for a wildlife refuge and recreational area. Everyone praised the island reclamation project once it had been completed, but success did not come easy. For twenty-five years, port officials battled residents and environmental groups over a string of broken promises for the broken islands that left bitter feelings. During the life of the project, state officials repeatedly reneged on their agreement and raised the dike's containment cells to continue dumping while searching for other disposal sites. The controversy ended in 1997 when a state law ordered the project to be closed by 2009 and legislation was passed to reclaim Poplar Island in the mid-Chesapeake Bay as a dredge disposal site. To their credit, port officials learned from their mistakes.

In the 1990s, Poplar Island, which consisted of 1,100 acres of forest, fields, and marsh in the 1800s, was broken into three pieces totaling less than ten acres. The former home to colonists, moonshiners, and a presidential retreat was eroding into the bay at a rate of thirteen feet a year. Using technology from the Hart-Miller Island project, port officials began dumping "clean" dredge material from the port's access channels. But the Poplar Island project solved only part of the problem. There was still plenty of dredge material that needed a dumping site. Due to the cost of transporting dredge material offsite, port officials looked to the western side of the Patapsco River at Cox Creek and Masonville for the solution.

In 2007, the MPA began one of the greatest environmental success stories in Maryland with the construction of the Masonville Dredged Material Containment Facility near the mouth of the Middle Branch at Fairfield. In 2010, the containment dike, which enclosed 127 acres of open water, began receiving dredged material that would be compacted into solid soil. With a capacity of 15 million cubic yards, the site would fill dredging needs for about thirty years and allow for expansion of the auto terminal at Fairfield.

While port officials were looking to the future, they were also looking to the past, hoping to avoid the public-relations pitfalls that marred the Hart-Miller Island project. While the project was still in the design phase, they began soliciting input from local residents and community groups to strike a deal that was amiable to both sides. To prove their good intentions, the Masonville Citizens Advisory Committee was created to provide citizen oversight that was routinely missing from these types of multi-faceted dredging projects. Port officials knew that public support was crucial in streamlining environmental impact statements and fast-tracking state and federal wetlands permits. Their concerted effort to embrace the community was quickly rewarded when the anticipated four-year wait for permits was reduced to twenty-eight months.

With the permit hurdle cleared, the local communities were as eager as port officials to begin construction. As part of the Baltimore Harbor Dredged Material Management Plan, state officials agreed to a package of community enhancements that included the restoration of Masonville Cove for public use. Prior to acquisition in 1978, the property had been the site of the Arundel Sand and Gravel Company, which stored mountains of sand and gravel along the river. In the summer, the "Cove" became the popular beach for residents of Masonville, Curtis Bay, and Brooklyn. Until pollution in the 1950s created health risks, it was the place where neighborhood kids first learned to swim or catch a fish. For former residents, it was the home of many fond memories before the B&O Railroad purchased the houses and bulldozed the history of their tiny, tight-knit community.

Since the isolated property had never been fully developed, it became a convenient dumping ground for inconvenient wastes from nearby industries. Due to its proximity to Fairfield, it suffered the devastating effects from the shipyards where large, ocean-going vessels were built, repaired, and most recently broken apart. In July 1993, the 979-foot long, aircraft carrier USS *Coral Sea* arrived at Fairfield for what was billed as the largest ship-breaking project in American naval history. Four years later, the dismantling project became a national environmental disaster that pulled back the curtain on the dark side of the ship-breaking business. In May 1997, Seawitch Salvage and its owner were convicted by a federal jury of violating environmental laws and making false statements to a government agency. It was the nation's first criminal case involving environmental violations and the ship-scrapping industry. Investigation disclosed the company had exposed workers to hazardous asbestos and haphazardly dumped oil and debris into the Patapsco River. This incident was only the latest in a long list of violations that extended back to WWI. By the time port officials were studying the site for dredge disposal in 2004, the fifty-two-acre refuge had become a toxic, underwater junkyard with some debris dating back to the Great Baltimore Fire of 1904 according to local lore.

Masonville Cove, an undeveloped waterfront in a heavy industrial area, suffered from decades of abuse as an illegal dump. *Courtesy Maryland Port Administration.*

A restored Masonville Cove becomes a model of environmental stewardship between industry, environmentalists, and local communities. The "greening" project also restored a spectacular view of the Baltimore skyline. *Courtesy Maryland Port Administration.*

Coinciding with the construction of the dike in 2007, the MPA began a massive and hurried $22 million cleanup effort at the cove. More than 61,000 tons of refuse were removed or recycled, to include unexploded ordnance, wooden barges, 27 abandoned vessels, 306,000 gallons of petroleum-tainted water, 17,400 tons of timber, 6,600 tons of concrete rubble, 5,300 feet of electrical wire and cable, and 4,000 pounds of electrical equipment containing PCBs, mercury, and asbestos.

Two years later on Earth Day, April 22, 2009, port officials and politicians dedicated the Masonville Cove Environmental Education Center, a "near-zero, net-energy" building with "green" features such as a ground-source air-conditioning system, solar energy, rain barrels to collect roof runoff for greenery and flowers, a reflective roof to decrease the amount of heat transferred into the building, and an energy recovery ventilator to efficiently heat or cool the air inside the building. Environmental programs were offered to the community on weekends, and a variety of ecological learning experiences were developed for school children by the Living Classrooms Foundation and the National Aquarium Baltimore.

With the opening of the center, work shifted to land restoration. Hot spots on the property were capped with clean soil, and invasive species of plants were removed and replaced with native trees, shrubs, and wetland plants. After the ground was remediated, public recreational enhancements quickly followed that included hiking/walking trails, a fishing/kayak pier, a boat ramp, and a bird sanctuary amid the restored wetlands. Nearly seventy acres of water and fifty-four acres of land were reclaimed by the project. An added bonus was the return of the stunning view of the Baltimore City skyline rising from the sparkling waters of the Patapsco River.

In 2004, the Port received the American Association of Port Authorities' Community and Public Involvement Award, a national award in recognition of the public outreach policy and program that led to the creation of the Masonville containment site. In 2010, the MPA's $153 million initiative to transform one of the harbor's most contaminated sites into a healthy habitat received an Environmental Excellence award by the National Association of Environmental Professionals. In September 2013, the urban wilderness at Masonville Cove was recognized as the nation's first Urban Wildlife Refuge Partnership by the US Fish and Wildlife Service. In the end, the MPA had polished a discarded emerald from the fouled waters of the Patapsco into a shining jewel. Environmental stewardship had found a home at an abandoned industrial outpost on the riverbank.

CHAPTER SEVENTEEN

Guardians of the Patapsco

They are known worldwide as Guardians of the Seas, but along the Patapsco River, the dedicated men and women of the US Coast Guard at the Curtis Bay Coast Guard Yard are the unsung "heroes of the harbor." Unheralded and unnoticed, they conduct search and rescue missions, maintain navigational aids, enforce maritime laws and regulations, and monitor port security and shipping operations. True to their motto *Semper Paratus*, this small band of specially trained and highly skilled professionals is "always ready" to answer the call. Their presence along the river since the 1790s has produced a seabag full of intrepid tales that exemplify their commitment to serve and protect. In the 1980s, one of those fabled stories had a green tint as the yard affirmed its environmental commitment to the region.

The Curtis Bay Coast Yard, tucked away on a 113-acre corner of land inside Curtis Bay, had its beginning in April 1899 when the Revenue Cutter Service purchased thirty-six acres of farmland surrounding Arundel Cove. The land had previously been part of a ninety-seven-acre farm owned by William Hall, a freed Civil War slave, who was reputed to be the largest African-American farmer in Maryland. In June 1899, an experimental shipyard was established, and a year later the crew from the training ship *Chase* set up permanent quarters at the cove to mark the beginning of a training academy that in 1910 relocated to New London, Connecticut, as the US Coast Guard Academy. In 1905, Congress authorized the purchase of additional land, and the "Revenue Cutter Station at Curtis Bay" was permanently established.

Throughout its first decade, the depot repaired lifesaving boats, constructed small boats, and overhauled revenue cutters. By the 1930s, many of the original buildings and much of the equipment were outdated. To modernize the depot, Congress funded construction for new trade shops and the installation of a forty-ton marine railway. When the Lighthouse Service was transferred to the Coast Guard in 1939, buoy construction became a major function. In the years leading up to WWII, the depot upgraded its facilities to include a 3,000-ton floating dry dock, two shipways, and a concrete pier with tower crane. At this time, the depot officially became the US Coast Guard Yard. During the war, the civilian workforce ballooned to 3,100 employees with an additional military complement of staff, trainees, and students from the numerous schools that were based at the yard.

In March 1942, the Coast Guard opened a Training Station (boot camp) across Arundel Cove, east of the yard. The new base, consisting of thirty-nine wooden buildings that included barracks, schoolrooms, an auditorium, a mess hall, a sick bay, a ship's service store, and a firehouse, was completed within sixty calendar days. Workers poured concrete and pounded nails during two shifts, much of the time under giant floodlights. Just days before the base was completed, the first complement of 400 recruits, or "boots," arrived to begin an intensive one-month training program that prior to the war lasted three months. In addition to recruit training, schools for gunners' and radio operators were also established.

To keep pace with the Army and Marine Corps and expand their wartime capabilities, the Coast Guard created the War Dog Training Base in November 1944. With the wartime Coast Guard tasked with guarding navy installations, the use of war dogs released "Coasties" for other duties. Basic training for 250 dogs lasted from two to four weeks and focused on physical fitness, basic obedience commands, and off-leash activities. If successful, the canine candidates, a select group of German Shepherds and Doberman Pinschers, graduated to advance training, which consisted of trailing, scouting, message carrying, and attacking. Following the surrender of Japan on August 15, 1945, most of the war dogs were "detrained" at the base to prepare them for their entry into the civilian world as household pets. The others remained in the service for sentry duty.

Following the war, the flurry of shipyard work continued for the next three decades with repairs, overhauls, conversions, and the construction of lighted buoys, patrol boats, buoy tenders, surfboats, motor life-boats, tugboats, and cutters. In the 1970s, operations at the yard expanded to meet the cutting edge of marine science and technology. The highlight of the decade was the construction of the Stable Semi-Submerged Platform, a twin-hull vessel with a removable center section for lowering research equipment into the water. In the 1980s, the yard constructed the Zero Relative Velocity Skimmer, a prototype oil skimmer used to clean up oil spills. As that decade closed, the yard started the construction of six river barges for Coast Guard use on the Mississippi and Missouri Rivers. Despite the steady work throughout the '80s, the yard faced its greatest challenge when Reagan administration budget cuts threatened its closure. As Maryland legislators lobbied to save the yard and its 654 jobs, the Coast Guard began sending its yard work to private companies. At the eleventh hour, the yard was saved when a Norfolk contractor could not meet the Coast Guard production schedule. The ships were sent back to Baltimore for the necessary repairs.

In the 1990s, the yard found its niche as a mid-sized shipyard focusing on ship repair, renovations, and conversions. In April 1999, the yard celebrated its centennial, and on July 10, a former Navy salvage tug was re-commissioned as the United States Coast Guard Cutter *Alex Haley*. Haley, who retired after twenty years as the chief journalist of the Coast Guard and the first African-American to reach the rank of Chief Petty Officer, achieved literary fame for his Pulitzer Prize winning novel *Roots: The Saga of an American Family*. The conversion highlighted the extraordinary work performed at the yard to maintain and modernize the Coast Guard's fleet. Work involved removing the stern towing machine, forward crane, and A-frame; installing a flight-deck, a retractable hangar, and air-search radar; and replacing the four diesel engines with modern sixteen-cylinder Caterpillar diesels.

In October 2014, the yard returned to its roots in working with wooden ships. On a cold and rainy day under the cover of a gray sky, the sloop-of-war *Constellation*, part of the fleet of historic ships operated by Historic Ships in Baltimore, was towed down the Patapsco River from its berth at the Inner Harbor and gently nudged into dry dock to begin a four-month renovation. The $2.1 million project replaced spars and rigging and up to 4,000 square of timber that was rotting from rainwater inside the hull. This was not the ship's first major or most costly overhaul. Beginning in the 1990s, the aging vessel, built along the banks of the Patapsco, was literally falling apart at the seams.

In 1994, the warship was condemned by the Navy as an unsafe vessel due to deterioration (rotting) of the frame and closed to the public. Two years later, the stripped-down, forlorn hulk with no rigging was meticulously pushed across the harbor to a shipyard near Fort McHenry to begin a $9 million overhaul that saved the historic vessel from the scrap yard. Talk about replacing the old ship with a traditional rebuild, which would destroy its historical integrity, ended when cost estimates soared to over $25 million. With most of the vessel below the gun deck being the original wood, the ship was suffering from the effects of age and weather. Over time, the hull had gradually lost its ability to support the ship, making it susceptible to any water pressure against its futtock frame, the curved timbers that form the ribs. Navy divers measured the hogging, or arching of a vessel amidships, and found the bow and stern had dropped thirty-six inches from the amidships. To keep the vessel from coming apart, nylon strapping was run under the hull at five points and a "hogging strap" ran lengthwise to support the sagging hull. In addition to replacing frame, planking and decking were replaced with laminates to prevent rainwater from seeping to the lower decks.

On July 2, 1999, the *Constellation*, the last all-sail ship built by the US Navy and now restored to its appearance as the last floating warship from the Civil War, returned triumphantly to the inner harbor after completion of the largest maritime restoration project by a non-government agency. Thousands lined the harbor promenades amid a gala celebration that included a Navy flyover, a cannon salute from Fort McHenry, water cannonade from fireboats, and a parade of ships. As spectators celebrated, maritime historians and enthusiasts quarreled. Research to ensure that any modifications to the ship were historically accurate resurrected the on-going debate about the provenance of the ship. Hoping to quell the controversy once and for all, *Constellation* officials reported that laser surveying of the hull produced a surface model that matched the original 1853 drawings by the ship's designer John Lenthall.

Was the war sloop *Constellation*, built in Norfolk and commissioned on July 28, 1855, a separate ship with the same name as the first, or was it the original frigate, built in 1797, with a succession of modifications from 1812 to 1853? That was the question to be definitively answered. While both sides of the argument claimed to have evidence supporting their position, naval historians concluded the *Constellation* was a newly designed ship that "possibly" could have used timber from the original. Newspapers accounts from the 1850s reported the frigate was broken up within a couple yards of Ship House B where the keel for the new *Constellation* was being laid as a sloop-of-war. Since the sloop was longer and wider than any other vessels in that class, she was manned and equipped under the table of allowance for a "raze frigate."

While conducting a reexamination of the historical documents that claimed major changes to the ship occurred before the 1850s, the Navy's David Taylor Ship Model Testing facility uncovered several suspicious pieces of paper at the National Archives. With assistance from the FBI, it was determined that a faked National Archives rubber stamp and a modern typewriter were used in creating archival files to support the "original ship" argument. Another issue that contributed to the confusion about the age of the ship was related to the paperwork at the Norfolk shipyard in the 1850s. Since there was no congressional authorization to build a new *Constellation*, funds were authorized for "repair" of the *Constellation*. The new vessel would be "administratively rebuilt" while retaining the name of its predecessor.

Wood or steel hulls mattered little to the workers at the Coast Guard yard. Over the years, they had accumulated the expertise and experience to handle any tall ship. One of the most welcomed tall ships to ever sail up the Patapsco River was the Coast Guard's *Barque Eagle*, America's Tall Ship. The three-masted, 295-foot steel-hull vessel was seized from Germany after WWII as a war prize. With more than 23,500 square feet of sail and six miles of rigging, the *Eagle* has served as a classroom at sea for academy candidates and officer candidates since 1946. A permanent crew of seven officers and fifty enlisted personnel staff the vessel as trainees sail her while learning the ways of the ancient mariners. In addition to damage control, engineering and deck seamanship, trainees must master the traditional skills of celestial navigation, knot tying, hauling and stowing the sails, and climbing the rigging.

After completing an extensive, four-year repair project at the yard in the 1980s, the ship returned to the yard for repair availability (period of time when a ship is assigned to undergo maintenance or repair activity) in 1995 and 1998. In 2001, she came to the yard for a repair availability and experienced her first lift on the land-based ship handling facility. In winter 2010, the yard completed a remarkable emergency availability. Despite back-to-back blizzards that dumped more than four feet of snow over the Baltimore area, the ship was repaired and returned to sea in a record eight days. In September 2014, the yard began one of the biggest overhauls in the history of the *Eagle*. The four-year, $28 million project was so encompassing that families of crew members were moved to the area as the yard became the temporary home port for the ship.

In 1967, the skills of yard workers were put to the ultimate test after a maritime accident almost sent the *Eagle* to the bottom of the Patapsco River. On January 27, after months of maintenance and repair, the ship started its journey home to New London in a heavy fog. Under power with a skeleton crew and a chief warrant officer at the command, the vessel strayed from the shipping lane in the harbor and was struck by an inbound Philippine freighter. The impact of the collision tore off the *Eagle's* bowsprit and peeled back the upper section of the bow, leaving a jagged sheet of twisted and crumbled steel hanging over the gunwales. Utility boats from Curtis Bay responded promptly to the ship's

America's Tall Ship, the *Barque Eagle*, undergoes renovations at the Coast Guard Yard in 2014/2015. During that time frame, highly-skilled, modern shipwrights also repaired the wooden ship USS *Constellation*. *Courtesy US Coast Guard.*

USS *Constellation*, flagship of Baltimore's historic fleet, berthed at the inner harbor after the latest restoration. *Photo by the author.*

distress call and towed the *Eagle* back to the yard for months of more repair. Damage to the bow was assessed at $200,000, but the *Eagle* was lucky. A few seconds earlier, she would have been cut in half by the freighter.

In 2002, the Environmental Protection Agency announced the yard had been added to its Superfund list. The listing, which would supply federal cleanup money, mandated a thorough environmental study to determine the scope of the contamination. A century of blasting paint off ships, welding and cutting steel, storing oil and batteries, burning waste, and dumping bilge had taken its toll on the ecosystem and workers' health. Environmental problems, dating back to WWII when the yard worked three shifts around the clock to meet war demands, included low levels of soil contaminants, such as metals, volatile organic compounds, polychlorinated biphenyls (PCBs), pesticides, and dioxins. Contamination extended deep into the sediments of Curtis Creek below the drydocks.

In the 1980s, the Coast Guard began studying the problem and worked with state and federal environmental officials to formulate a cleanup plan for nine contaminated parcels. At an unpaved salvage yard where drums of lubrication oil, lead acid batteries and transformers were stored, 2,900 tons of soil were excavated. At a burn pit near the salvage yard where oil, liquid and solid wastes, batteries, and asbestos material were incinerated, 6,700 cubic yards of soil were removed and an oxygen-release compound was injected into the ground to treat groundwater. At "Site 9," along the cove where bilge spoils from ships had been deposited, sediment was dredged and ground soil removed.

To allow for future use of the remediated sites, the Coast Guard applied the more stringent residential cleanup standards in place of industrial standards. Sustainable environmental practices were also incorporated in the solution. To control storm runoff, low impact stormwater options, such as porous pavers and green space plantings, were installed. Reducing the carbon footprint also included a crane electrification project and recycling. During the cleanup, over 2,600 tons of concrete and 20 tons of steel were recycled, and about 25,000 tons of contaminated soil were treated on site for shipment to a non-hazardous waste landfill. Environmental innovation even extended beyond the front gate. On Earth Day in April 2009, the yard opened the Coast Guard's first Landfill Gas Renewable Energy Center where methane gas from a nearby landfill owned by the city was converted to electricity and steam for use at the shipyard.

In May 2012, after eleven years and $16 million, the EPA and Coast Guard signed a Record of Decision formally acknowledging that toxic wastes at the nine sites had been removed. This agreement started the process to have the yard officially removed from the Superfund list. EPA officials praised the yard for the quick turnaround, noting that many Superfund projects extend for decades. Community leaders from nearby neighborhoods in Pasadena and Glen Burnie lauded the yard for keeping residents updated with meetings and newsletters during all phases of the cleanup. Through their dedicated partnership with federal and state agencies, the yard emerged as a leader in the field of environmental management.

CHAPTER EIGHTEEN

The Reign of King Steel

The environmental history of Sparrows Point as it entered the twenty-first century was a twisted tale of two questions: Who's in charge and who's responsible? Over the ensuing years, both questions would be answered by many different voices, as industrialists and environmentalists skirmished over the plot of land that dated back to Thomas Sparrow's land grant in 1652. These blended voices narrated an epic story of good and evil as industrialists conveniently concealed the truth while environmentalists vigorously exposed the lie. The fall of the steel mill closely paralleled the rise of environmental activism. In certain aspects, the final chapter in the history of Sparrows Point mirrored the frenzied events that had occurred between environmentalists and industrialists along the Patapsco River. Only this time, the stakes were even higher.

Environmental stewardship was an elusive concept for the Bethlehem Steel Corporation throughout its history. Following the ascent of Sparrows Point as an industrial giant after WWII, the steel mill's owners acted with impunity. For them, pollution was merely a discarded variable in the company's equation that production plus profit equaled progress. For steel workers, pollution was merely a discarded by-product in the union's equation that production plus corporate profits equaled higher wages. Steel was the cash commodity in the 1900s, much like tobacco was the cash crop in the 1700s. Sparrows Point executives were the modern-day plantation owners who built a large company town, a larger shipyard, and the largest steel mill in the country that routinely accounted for ten percent of the state's economy.

King Steel built America's war machines, its bridges and skyscrapers, and its cars and refrigerators. The King ruled arbitrarily and capriciously and answered to no one while openly flaunting the federal clean air and water acts of the 1970s. State regulators routinely turned their heads and politicians cast a blind eye as the high tide of "steel" money inundated the state. It was common knowledge that contributed to the common good. Who could argue? Upgrading the mill for environmental purposes would be an out-of-pocket expense that reduced the company's profit margin. While pollution was ignored year after year, the environmental bill was accumulating day by day. After a hundred years, it would become an incalculable debt that would eventually devastate the land and its people.

In 1973, the Council on Economic Priorities (CEP), a public service research group that analyzed the social and environmental records of corporations, ranked the Sparrows Point plant in the top five of the worst water and air polluters in the country. At the time, the plant was dumping hundreds of pounds of arsenic and thousands of pounds of cyanide daily into the Patapsco River. Bethlehem Steel executives, worried about their image in the enlightened environmental age and more worried about losing money in fines and penalties, were quick to react. In December 1973, *The Baltimore Sun* reported that they clandestinely met with federal officials and state representatives in Philadelphia to address the indiscriminate violations of environmental laws. Their solution was not to fix the problem but to alter the permit. The new permit increased the daily discharges for chromium by 347 percent, soluble zinc by 86 percent, and soluble iron by 55 percent. Although King Steel emerged victorious on the water, it was forced to compromise in the air. To address the issue of air pollution, the plant installed abatement equipment at a cost of $65 million to reduce sulfur dioxide in the air.

Environmentalists and residents viewed this expenditure with guarded optimism, fearing the steel mill would continue its longstanding practice of paying the fines instead of installing environmental upgrades on aging blast furnaces and coke ovens. That practice had been proven to be cheaper in the long run. Five years later, the guarded optimism soured to full-blown pessimism to no one's surprise. In 1977, the CEP termed the mill's efforts to reduce water pollution as "abysmal." In 1978, the Maryland Occupational and Safety Health fined the mill $11,000 for twenty-six counts of endangering workers' health from exposure to toxic gas leaking from the coke ovens.

The tragic wake-up call for cleaning up the mill was sounded in 1981 when Baltimore attorneys Peter Angelos and Howard Schulman filed the first lawsuit against Bethlehem Steel for asbestos exposure. Older workers were dying from lung disease and other cancers at an alarming rate. Many new retirees saw only a handful of retirement checks before they painfully gasped their last breath, usually accompanied with an oxygen bottle. Asbestos was a natural fireproof mineral that was ubiquitous in steel mills to protect equipment and workers from the extreme heat. Pipes, wires, and panel boxes were covered with it; coats, aprons, and gloves were manufactured with it. When inhaled, the colorless and odorless asbestos fibers imbedded themselves in the soft tissue of the lungs. The resulting scar tissue reduced lung capacity and created a condition known as asbestosis. Years later, the debilitating disease often led to mesothelioma, a fatal cancer directly related to asbestos exposure.

In 1991, with asbestos cases snowballing, Angelos filed a federal class action lawsuit in Baltimore against asbestos manufacturers on behalf of thousands of workers. Before the trial, many of the defendants agreed to out-of-court settlements, which quickly became the norm in asbestos lawsuits. For the remaining seven, a jury ruled that asbestos manufacturers had knowingly sold hazardous products to companies since the 1930s and awarded the plaintiffs compensatory damages. Thousands of dollars went to steel workers while millions went to the lawyers. But few steel workers begrudged Angelos for his one-third fee. Instead, they praised him as the hometown hero, another rags-to-riches story from the streets of east Baltimore, who came to their rescue when no one else would listen to their complaints, much less champion their cause.

Born on the Fourth of July in 1929, just months before the Great Depression, Angelos was the son of Greek immigrants who grew up in Highlandtown, a collection of ethnic neighborhoods that was home to many steel workers. While attending law school at night and working at the family's restaurant and tavern during the day, he befriended many steelworkers who stopped off after their shifts for a shot and a beer. Later, these friends would become his clients. In 1993, the hometown hero came to the rescue again when he led a local group of noted investors to buy the Baltimore Orioles for $173 million at a bankruptcy auction. The new owners had paid $70 million more than the previous record for a baseball team.

In June 1989, Bethlehem Steel Corporation agreed to spend $92 million to end the pollution from its Sparrows Point plant. For decades, the mill had choked the area with thick, black clouds of toxic smoke that contributed to acid rain and smog. Among Maryland companies, the steel maker was the third-largest producer of cancer-causing chemicals. The legally binding agreement with the Maryland Department of the Environment (MDE) required the company to install new equipment to reduce air pollution by 1994 without jeopardizing the 8,000 jobs at the mill. The coke ovens alone would receive a $24 million upgrade. If the company failed to meet compliance dates, state officials could levy fines up to $100,000 for violations. To back-up their threat, MDE fined the mill $150,000 for violating pollution laws during the year-long negotiations.

Improvements were made in reducing air pollutants, but ground pollution continued. As a result, the Environmental Protection Agency (EPA) and the MDE sued Bethlehem Steel for numerous hazardous waste violations. The case was settled in 1997 when both parties signed a Consent Decree that required Bethlehem Steel and any subsequent owners to correct violations and perform studies to fully evaluate contamination at the plant. One of the studies that would later prompt litigation was a comprehensive assessment of migrating contaminants that could present a health risk to humans and marine life. For environmentalists, the decree was a major victory that would establish accountability for the indiscriminate pollution, or so they hoped. For prescient federal and state officials, the decree was an omen that Bethlehem Steel's reign along the Patapsco, which began in 1916, was in peril.

To stop the financial hemorrhaging that year, Beth Ship, the once highly profitable and productive shipyard that dated to 1889, was sold to Veritas Capital. The 250-acre shipyard, renamed Baltimore Marine Industries (BMI), continued repairing ocean-going vessel, building tank and container barges, and breaking ships for the US government's naval reserve. Six years later, with the ship repair industry suffering the effects of a sluggish economy, BMI filed for Chapter 11 Bankruptcy. In November 2003, the shipyard was sold by court order to Barletta-Willis, which continued the ship repair and breaking business. North America Ship Recycling, a subsidiary and the first tenant on the site, was awarded contracts for nearly $3 million to scrap ships from the "ghost fleet" in Virginia's James River.

On October 15, 2001, the nightmare for steel workers began when Bethlehem Steel filed for bankruptcy protection under Chapter 11. Citing $400 million in losses for the year, the nation's third-largest steel manufacturer said it would cut jobs, renegotiate labor contracts, and take "all possible steps" to reduce expenses. Those steps included eliminating health benefits and realigning retirement pensions. Complaining that foreign steel was being dumped in the country at unfair discounts, the company pleaded for trade restrictions from the federal government. While the federal government could be partially blamed, they were merely a convenient scapegoat. Foreign imports were only part of the problem. Cracks in the king's armor started appearing in the mid-1970s with increased lay-offs and decreased production. Unfunded pension portfolios, union labor contracts, and an outdated physical plant were the culprits that sabotaged the company's financial health. The company's woes ended in 2003 when International Steel Group (ISG) announced the purchase of the company for $1.5 billion. As part of the deal, the 1997 consent decree would remain intact.

In August 2005, ISG acknowledged to state regulators that runoff containing benzene, a human carcinogen, was seeping into the Patapsco River from the coke oven area. Company officials contended the rate of discharge was low in comparison to the substantial mixing of groundwater and surface water that was simultaneously occurring at other areas. As a result of this logic, no steps were taken to reduce or stop the runoff because the harbor could assimilate the trace metals without harm. Despite elevated levels of various metals in sediment at the southern end of the shipyard, the company asserted that toxic wastes, such as benzene, did not pose a hazard to humans.

A few years later, the extent of the pollution was fully exposed by the AES Energy Corporation, which had commissioned sediment testing for its proposed liquefied natural gas terminal at Sparrows Point. Tests found sediments in the Patapsco River laced with chromium, copper, lead, mercury, zinc, and other toxic metals. Concentrations of many chemicals around the steel mill and harbor were higher than reported in 1996. Environmentalists were shocked and outraged at the lack of federal and state oversight. With no enforcement, the consent decree proved to be worthless as many had feared.

While the plant had downsized over the years, it still remained the largest steel mill in the Northeast and the only mill on the East Coast that made steel from scratch. Despite the consent decree, many hazardous substances produced during the steelmaking process, such a semi-molten slag that was dumped in landfills near the waterfront, were still being released into the river. High levels of metal contaminates in the upper water layer were recorded near the shipbuilding docks. On land, elevated concentrations of carcinogenic metals were found in surface sediments, including chromium from steel plating and lead and zinc from blast furnace slag. Other carcinogenic chemicals detected at the sites were anthracene, benzopyrene, and fluorine.

Environmental groups publicly chastised the EPA and MDE for their failure to enforce the consent decree. Attempting to deflect blame, MDE officials stated the decree was outdated and called for a new pact with the current owner Severstal to establish an expedited timetable for cleaning up landfills and smokestack emissions. Severstal responded by stating it had fully complied with the agreement, which it inherited from the prior owners

ArcelorMittal, and would vigorously defend itself against the threatened lawsuit. In 2008, the Russian-based Severstal had purchased the mill for $810 million after ArcelorMittal was ordered to sell it. After merging with ISG in 2005, Mittal took over Arcelor a year later to form ArcelorMittal, the largest steel maker in the world. In response, the Department of Justice filed an anti-trust lawsuit to ensure fair competition in the tin-plate market. In 2007, a federal judge ordered the sale of Sparrows Point to break up the monopoly in the steel industry.

Unlike Severstal, ArcelorMittal acted to comply with the consent decree. Upon purchasing the steel mill, it paid a fine of $98,500 that had been levied against ISG for air-pollution violations. In the two years of ownership, it built two $85 million state-of-the-art wastewater treatment plants and spent millions in upgrading pipe and duct work. In contrast, Severstal's main contribution to clean up the air was a $2 million roof repair at the sinter operations plant.

In May 2009, the Chesapeake Bay Foundation (CBF) and the Baltimore Harbor Waterkeeper (BHW) filed a Notice of Intent to sue the EPA, the MDE, and the current and prior owners of the mill for failing to uphold the consent decree. To avoid any follow-up litigation and more bad publicity, the EPA and MDE pressured Severstal to take action. As a result, Severstal announced plans for a preliminary cleanup as it challenged its legal obligation to investigate contamination beyond the plant's borders. The stalling tactic infuriated environmentalists who saw this action as another attempt to outmaneuver the consent decree.

A year later, with no tangible cleanup progress, CBF and BHW had reached the breaking point. On July 9, 2010, they filed a lawsuit against Severstal and ArcelorMittal for failure to abide by the 1997 consent decree. The suit alleged that both companies generated, stored, and disposed of hazardous waste without a permit in violation of the Resource Conservation and Recovery Act, the principal federal law in disposing of solid and hazardous wastes. The petition claimed that wastes found in Bear Creek and the Patapsco River were an imminent and substantial endangerment to human health and the environment. At one location, benzene had been found in groundwater at levels 100,000 times greater than the federal government's maximum contaminant level. At another location, near the coke ovens, an underground hydrocarbon plume was leaking light crude oil into Bear Creek.

The lawsuit once again raised the controversial issue of pollution permits. In 2009, the steel mill was discharging pollutants into the Patapsco under a state permit that had been expired for forty-five months and not been updated since 2001. In 2006 and 2007, the mill released 60,101 pounds of toxic chemicals into the nearby waters, a thirty-seven percent increase from two previous years. The release of chromium, copper, lead, manganese, and nickel was coming from the seven outfalls, man-made channels about twenty feet wide and two or three feet deep that discharged millions of gallons of wastewater used for making steel. Between January 2007 and June 2009, the mill violated their permit seventeen times. Despite being out of compliance for six of the last twelve fiscal quarters, MDE had not imposed any penalties on the facility. An MDE spokesperson acknowledged the discharge permit had expired in February 2008, but added they were working with Severstal for a renewal that would include total maximum daily loads for Baltimore Harbor and the Chesapeake Bay.

On July 12, 2011, US District Court Judge J. Frederick Motz ruled that ISG, who had purchased the mill from Bethlehem Steel, was not responsible for cleaning up the polluted site under the terms of the bankruptcy sale. In effect, the consent decree had been legally redefined but not voided. In March 2011, Severstal had petitioned the federal court to dismiss the suit as the plant was being sold for $1.2 billion to RG Steel, a subsidiary of the Renco Group. Attorneys for Severstal argued that Motz didn't have jurisdiction because of the ongoing consent decree with the state and federal government. Somehow their argument swayed the court. In response, CBF and BHW stated the plant had continued to pollute the bay and was seeking emergency action to stop it.

Any hope that RG Steel, the nation's fourth largest flat-rolled steel manufacturer, would be the savior who returned the workforce and restarted the furnaces was dashed only a year later. In August 2012, a federal bankruptcy judge approved the sale of the mill for $72 million to Hilco Industrial, a company that specialized in industrial liquidation. Once again, the cleanup of the mill was on the bidding block as the sale included an agreement to establish a $500,000 escrow fund to pay for investigating offshore water contamination. Hilco and its partner Environmental Liability Transfer, which owned the land at Sparrows Point, also agreed with environmental regulators to assume RG Steel's obligations for a water-quality monitoring program. After a lengthy dispute over the scope of the program, RG Steel agreed to sample sediments no more than fifty feet offshore. Environmentalists immediately challenged the federal judge's approval of the agreement. They contended that because contaminants were being found farther offshore, the scope of the monitoring agreement in the 1997 consent decree should be expanded.

A day after the bankruptcy sale to Hilco, Sparrows Point residents filed their own lawsuit in Baltimore County against RG Steel and LaFarge North America, an on-site cement plant that used slag from blast furnaces in making cement. The suit claimed these companies were exposing residents to noxious odors and carcinogenic air pollutants. One of those pollutants was the red, gritty dust, called "kish" by locals, which had covered the local communities like a light dusting of snow since WWII. Though only two residents were listed as plaintiffs, the complaint sought to be treated as a class action suit on behalf of about 200 residents from Dundalk, Turners Station, and Edgemere, many who lived in modest waterfront homes near the steel mill. With all litigation stayed during the RG Steel bankruptcy proceedings, the legal firm representing the residents decided to proceed with the lawsuit after the bankruptcy judge allowed a lawsuit by the CBF to proceed.

While the legal wrangling continued over the consent decree, the fate of the mill continued its downward spiral. Any hope of reviving the comatose mill ended in December 2012 when Nucor Corporation announced it had purchased the cold mill from Hilco Trading for parts to be used at the company's four other mills. Built for $300 million in 1999, the cold mill allowed for the precision-rolling production of stainless steel and was the most modern and profitable part of the plant. No surprise to steel workers, Hilco also announced the next step would be to liquidate the remaining assets and dismantle the plant.

In January 2013, hundreds of spectators, hoping to snare a piece of steel history at a bargain price, and serious bidders that included scrap dealers and steel companies from around the country gathered at the mill for a public auction on everything from forklifts to snow blowers. Hilco auctioned about 1,600 lots of equipment over a two-day period to coincide with an online auction for tools. With over 100 years of accumulated equipment and tools at the one-time largest steel plant, Hilco officials were justified in claiming this event to be the largest steel auction ever conducted.

Baltimore City also felt the effects of the impending collapse of the steel mill when it became involved in a legal battle over treated wastewater from the Back River Waste Water Treatment Plant. In July 2013, Sparrows Point LLC, owned by Environmental Liability Transfer, informed the city that it planned to stop piping up to 40 million gallons of treated wastewater from the sewage plant. The company claimed the city breached its agreement by failing to make all of its $80,000 payments on time and by failing to monitor the toxic nature of the discharged water through the Sparrows Point pipeline. In response, the city sued the company, arguing that it would violate its federal pollution-discharge permit by discharging all of its wastewater into Back River.

When the mill was operating, water from the Back River treatment plant was used in the steelmaking process and then discharged into Bear Creek. With the mill shuttered, Sparrows Point LLC stated there was no need for treated wastewater and they wanted out of the water business. Following a series of temporary restraining orders that allowed up to 40 million gallons of wastewater to be accepted by Sparrows Point LLC, the lawsuit was dismissed in January 2015 when both sides reached a new, long-term agreement that paid the company $120,000 monthly for operating expenses.

Back on the environmental front, there was finally good news for environmentalists. In January 2014, Judge Motz vacated his previous decision limiting the scope of environmental testing in waterways around the steel mill. In March 2012, Motz had approved an agreement between RG Steel and government regulators that required testing for contaminants within fifty feet of the shoreline. The latest ruling, following an appeal by the CBF and BWB, allowed for extensive testing farther offshore.

In September 2014, the mill, which had remained idle since its closing in 2012, was sold to Sparrows Point Terminal LLC for $110 million. Encompassing 3,100 acres on a 5.3-mile peninsula, the property was the largest vacant industrial site with deepwater access in the country. The company was funded by Redwood Capital, a private equity firm owned by Jim Davis. Davis and his cousin, NFL Ravens owner Steve Bisciotti, had made their fortunes with the founding of Allegis, a staffing company worth $6 billion. Although the sale marked the sixth time in eleven years the property had changed hands, state officials were optimistic that local ownership with ties to the steel community would bring stability in strategic planning. However, any plans to redevelop the site into a transportation, light manufacturing, or supply center were secondary to the remediation of the property.

After tough negotiations, the new owners entered into an agreement with the MDE and Maryland's Office of the Attorney General to pay for the cleanup with $48 million in financial assurances. An independent third party was hired

Charges at the base of the "L" blast furnace are detonated. Seconds later, the massive structure crumpled to the ground, signaling the end to the reign of King Steel. *Courtesy Patrick Taylor/*East County Times.

to review the work every six months. If the cash reserve faltered, the company would automatically replenish the working money pool. Failure to comply with the agreement could result in fines up to $5,000 per day. Total cleanup costs could reach $75 million to include offshore environmental investigation and EPA oversight. While state officials, politicians, and the new owners parroted their commitment to the environment and the local communities, many residents remained skeptical. This was an "oldie but a goodie," a tired refrain that was sung every time the mill changed hands.

The final exclamation point to the reign of King Steel occurred on January 28, 2015, when the "L" Blast Furnace was imploded. Ironically, what had been the largest blast furnace in the Western Hemisphere opened in 1978 just as steel imports hit a record high. In seconds, the history of steelmaking at Sparrows Point disappeared in clouds of thick, black smoke as the intimidating thirty-two-story structure, weighing 8 million pounds, toppled to the ground in a crumpled heap of twisted and broken steel. All that remained was another pile of rubble in a jagged and gouged landscape that resembled the bombed out, post-WWII cities in Europe and Japan.

One historic icon was saved from the destruction. A month prior to the implosion, the large, lighted, steel-framed star, which stood atop the furnace and was known as the Star of Bethlehem, was removed and refurbished. For nearly forty years, the star hung brightly over the steel mill during the Christmas holidays as a sign of peace, prosperity, and goodwill. The site's new owner hoped to find a permanent spot for the star to symbolize a new era of prosperity. For the emotionally drained residents and former steel workers, they hoped it was the light at the end of a long, dark tunnel. From boom to bust and from rust to dust, the life of an American industrial icon had come full cycle, and they had been there to witness the spectacle.

Hoping to endear themselves to the nearby communities as promised, the mill's new ownership erected the restored "Star of Bethlehem" for the Christmas season. Placed atop the water treatment, one of the tallest remaining structures, the star continued the longstanding tradition of honoring the birthplace of Jesus and the history of steelmaking at Sparrows Point.

On January 12, 2016, Sparrows Point was unceremoniously consigned to the pages of history at a press conference. In breaking with tradition, CEO Michael Moore announced the mill property had been renamed Tradepoint Atlantic. The name change also introduced a new logo. Featuring the intertwined letters "T" and "A" to form the top three points of a star, the logo represented the property's land, rail, and water access while echoing the Star of Bethlehem. Much to the disappointment of many residents and former steelworkers who had already witnessed enough history in the making, the rebranding was deemed necessary to attract foreign business to a global transportation and logistics center that could create up to 10,000 jobs.

CHAPTER NINETEEN

Patapsco 21

RUN, RIVER, RUN

At the turn of the twentieth century, low-head, concrete reinforced dams along the Patapsco reflected the science of their era. A hundred years later, they symbolized arrogant attempts to overpower nature. But despite being battered and abandoned, the dams stood as strong as ever. As obsolete icons, these industrial nuisances blocked fish migrations and endangered citizens. If the river was to run to sea and rejuvenate itself through its natural cycles, the dams had to be removed. Among the fish species to benefit from a free-flowing river, such as shad, alewife, and river herring, the most notable was the American eel. While migrating to spawn throughout the tributary, the eel distributed freshwater mussels, which in the larval stage attached themselves to a host species, such as the American eel. Once transplanted, the mussels filtered enormous quantities of water, much like the oyster in the Chesapeake Bay.

While still maintaining their picturesque charm during the turning of seasons, the dams hid a dark side. Serious talk about dam removal usually occurred after a drowning. But when the price tag for the undertaking was discussed, the conversation faded to a whisper. As the river entered the twenty-first century, talk hovered over the river valley like a fierce and foreboding storm cloud. Between June 2005 and July 2014, there were six deaths at Bloede Dam alone. In the enlightened environmental era since the 1970s, human tragedies and the extinction of fish species had no price tags. It was time to take action whatever the cost. In 2005, the Friends of Patapsco Valley State Park, a not-for-profit foundation that provided charitable gifts for park enhancements, contacted American Rivers to make those dams disappear.

In June 2009, American Rivers, a national, non-profit river advocacy organization that specialized in dam removal and flood plain restoration, received $4 million from the National Oceanic and Atmospheric Administration (NOAA) for removing Union Dam and the Simkins Dam. The Patapsco River Restoration Project was among fifty chosen by NOAA from a list of 814 coastal

Before removal. Simkins Dam, typical of the reinforced concrete dams that powered the mills and destroyed fish migrations along the Main Branch. *Courtesy American Rivers.*

After removal. Looking upstream from the site of the former dam, a small section of the Patapsco returns to its natural and scenic state. *Courtesy American Rivers.*

restoration proposals under the American Recovery and Reinvestment Act of 2009, a federal economic stimulus program. Since the Union Dam was "shovel ready" with all the work and environmental permits secured, it was the first dam selected.

In September, workers started bringing in the heavy equipment to begin the long-awaited demolition of Union Dam. The 209-foot structure would become the largest dam removal project in Maryland's history. Breached near the Howard County shoreline in 1972 by Tropical Storm Agnes, the obsolete industrial relic posed a hazard for swimmers and paddlers, an obstacle for migrating fish, and a health threat. From a human health perspective, it was feared the turbulent water would erode the supports for the forty-two-inch sewer interceptor pipe that ran under the western embankment, causing a rupture that would dump millions of gallons of raw sewage into the river. Since the dam was broken with no sediment impoundment, heavy equipment was used to divert the stream, chisel apart the dam, and restore a river channel. A year later, the riverbank was replanted with native plants, shrubs, and trees, and the $1.5 million project was successfully completed. Engineers and environmentalists now set their sights on the next dam downriver.

In September 2010, the Simkins Dam fell to the hydraulic jackhammers in an $872,000 demolition project. Unlike Union Dam, Simkins employed a passive sediment management approach since the 10-foot high, 200-foot wide structure was intact. This procedure allowed impounded sediment to gradually flow downriver as the height of the dam was reduced. It was the first time that sediment studies were employed to determine physical and biological changes from a large-scale river restoration effort. While downriver, Bloede Dam prevented studies of migratory fish, geological surveys reported the former dam site had reverted to its former natural rock and cobble bed as the clean sand and gravel sediment moved downstream. From a biological prospective, there was a noted increase in the numbers of mayfly, stonefly, and caddisfly larvae.

Downstream where sand pooled, there was also an increase in burrowing aquatic bugs. For the first time, the restoration partnership included Inter-Fluve, an environmental engineering firm that specialized in investigations, design, and restoration of waterways. Since its founding in 1983, the company had completed more than 1,600 successful restoration projects around the world. The stage was set and the team now assembled to tackle the biggest obstacle on the river: Bloede Dam.

In August 2013, NOAA awarded American Rivers a $3.57 million grant for the removal of Bloede Dam. Since the underwater hydroelectric plant was abandoned in 1932, the dam had impeded migratory fish and imperiled public health. Fish ladders installed in 1992 were costly to maintain due to frequent clogging and did not effectively transport an abundance of the desired spawning species. In the 1960s, the dam became a popular hangout and illegal swimming hole with deadly results. Drownings occurred in 2013, 2014, and 2015 when daredevils sliding down the face of the dam or jumping from the curved lip became entrapped in the backwash of cascading water that created a spinning effect known as a drowning machine.

The procedures to remove the dam would be similar to those used at Simkins, except that Bloede would be on a much larger scale with a length of 220 feet and a drop of 26.5 feet. The proposed time line would relocate the forty-two-inch sewer line in winter 2015, remove the dam in winter of 2017, and restore the landscape by the following spring. The passive sediment approach would release downstream up to 312,000 cubic yards of sediment as compared with 88,000 cubic yards at Simkins. Following a controlled demolition to breach the dam, excavators with pile hammers would break the dam into pieces.

Dredging behind the dam was not a viable option since it would have added $20 million to the budget, required around-the-clock construction operations, and closed that section of the park for another year and a half. While sediment studies reported the river channel would recover within seven months, the long-term impacts of sediment release below the dam could result in deposits up to seven feet high and take from six to ten years to fully recover depending on flow events. Over time, deepwater habitats of sand and gravel would be replaced with swift water habits of cobble and stone. During the recovery period, the river would be stocked with shad and herring to rebuild the population. To preserve the cultural history of the site, a portion of the dam would be preserved on the Howard County side for historical interpretation, and viewing platforms would be constructed on both sides of the river.

With ongoing plans to complete the design phase, newly elected Governor Larry Hogan Jr. announced in January 2015 a proposed budget cut that would eliminate the state's $1 million contribution to remove the dam. Environment stewardship was once again a political orphan. The cut would have jeopardized $7.7 million in federal grants committed to the project. NOAA informed the Hogan administration that if the state rescinded its contribution, federal grants would expire with no future guarantees for funding. Opponents to the budget cut argued that if the dam stands, it would waste the millions already spent on removing the other dams and likely cost taxpayers at least $1 million in upgrades to comply with the state's dam safety laws. In early March 2015, the regional director for American Rivers and concerned citizens that included a former park ranger who witnessed a drowning at Bloede Dam testified before the Maryland Budget and Taxation Committee to restore the money. Later that month, the budget for fiscal year 2016 was passed with full funding for the dam's removal.

MORE THAN A FISH BOWL

Tucked away in the corner between Fort McHenry and Whetstone Point, the Fort McHenry Wetland survives as a monument to nature's resiliency and man's potential to restore an endangered ecosystem. The nearly eight-acre wetland was constructed by the US Army Corps of Engineers in the early 1980s as a mitigation project after shallow-water habitat was destroyed during the construction of the Fort McHenry Tunnel. For twenty-two years, the tunnel, which opened in 1985 and runs 107 feet below the surface of the Patapsco just downriver from the fort, was the most expensive underwater tunnel project in the United States. In 2007, that distinction was officially bestowed upon Boston's gargantuan tunnel and bridge project, unofficially known as the Big Dig.

Over the next decade, the three culverts that accessed the wetland slowly filled with silt and transformed the thriving wetland into an urban pond. The removal of the regular tidal flushing prevented fish migration, but did not hinder the flow of trash that became trapped and dispersed inside the riprap perimeter. Compounding the degradation was the invasion of *Phragmites australis*. The deep-rooted invasive reed with broad grass leaves and tall stems produced a toxin that wiped out native wetland plants. In February and March 2004, the wetland was reconstructed with mitigation credits when a nearby port slip was filled in. The new design promoted regular flooding, controlled debris collection, and enhanced plant and animal habitats. Invasive weeds and reeds were removed, and high tides were studied by National Aquarium biologists to determine where and when to plant various species of marsh vegetation.

Despite the reconstructive upgrades, the soft shoreline at the tip of a peninsula, which splits the river into two branches, remained a natural receptacle for thousands of pieces of plastic trash from stormwater runoff.

Before restoration. A neglected wetland becomes a tidal trash pond due to clogged inlets that have stopped the tides. *Courtesy National Aquarium.*

After restoration. The trash pond once again becomes a thriving ecosystem due to tidal flows that sustain wetland habitats. *Courtesy National Aquarium.*

Since assuming stewardship of the wetland in 1999, the Aquarium has sponsored Fort McHenry Field Days in partnership with the National Park Service. In spring and fall, a small army of volunteers descends upon the wetland to remove debris, plant vegetation, maintain trails, and tend the wetland's gardens. Today, the wetland, which is monitored and maintained by the Aquarium, functions as an outdoor classroom, a wetlands living laboratory, a bird sanctuary, and a community volunteer project aimed at promoting environmental awareness.

When it opened in 1981, the National Aquarium in Baltimore quickly became a premier tourist destination. With 1.5 million visitors a year and another 3 to 4 million tourists passing by its entrance, the Aquarium was a people magnet. Since its inception, the Aquarium proudly promoted its role in inspiring conservation of the world's aquatic treasures. Inside the building, the Chesapeake Bay was a featured ecosystem with "Maryland: Mountains to the Sea," an exhibit that created the illusion of traveling down a stream in the Allegheny Mountains until the journey ended in the Atlantic Ocean. Yet, despite the financial success and the rave reviews, there was an embarrassing disconnect. Right outside its doors, an aquatic resource was slowly dying, and nobody seemed to care. To remedy the situation and connect with the public at the river's edge, the Aquarium had to move outdoors.

In 2005, officials opened the Harry & Jeanette Weinberg Waterfront Park. The 90,000-square-foot interpretive plaza invited the casual visitor to explore Maryland's diverse ecosystems from the mountains to the ocean with interpretive signs and native plants against the backdrop of the harbor. By converting the old seal pool exhibit to a 40,000 gallon cistern, 281,000 gallons of recycled rainwater irrigated the park's gardens and provided a natural filtering system for the river. On September 9, 1981, the pool had been the site of Mayor Schaefer's famous "splash heard around the world." Wearing an orange- and yellow-striped Victorian swimsuit and straw boater, the mayor dipped into the pool while cradling a rubber ducky to fulfill a pledge if the aquarium failed to open by a promised date.

In 2012, the National Wildlife Federation declared the Weinberg Waterfront Park a Certified Wildlife Habitat, an area that provided wildlife with food, water, and shelter, and a place to raise their young. To reach a larger audience, the federation and the Aquarium launched a program in May 2013 to make Baltimore the largest community-certified wildlife habitat on the Chesapeake Bay by "greening" any space where plants could grow.

With the goal of improving local water quality and wildlife habitat, the Aquarium Conservation Team (ACT) expanded their efforts to engage the public with community-based restoration projects. The Fort McHenry Wetland, which marked a dramatic shift in the Aquarium's approach to local conservation in 1999, provided a successful blueprint for other river projects. At the Westport Waterfront, plantings to stabilize the shoreline and restore natural habitat were conducted until the project financially collapsed. Ironically, it was the environmental nemesis known as harbor dredging that ensured an abundance of ongoing restoration and reclamation opportunities. In addition to planting days at Masonville Cove and Poplar Island, the ACT held their first BioBlitz at the Cove in June 2014. For one day, scientists, naturalists, students, teachers, and volunteers gathered to identify and record as many living organism that could be found. Over 100 people identified 150 species that were included in the Maryland Biodiversity Project, a comprehensive photo collection of all Maryland species.

Also, in June 2014, the ACT installed eight "biohuts" along the bulkheads of the inner harbor. Similar in concept to the oyster baskets installed by the Waterfront Partnership, the biohuts were compartmented, rectangular cages with oysters on one side and an empty outer cage on the other to provide shelter for juvenile fish. Unlike the Partnership's cages that were used to harvest and replant oysters, these cages were designed to monitor species diversity and oyster (spat) growth. Eighteen different species were recorded at the cages, to include grass shrimp, blue crabs, American eels, sea nettles, and pink combo jellies. The program proved so successful that a year later additional "biohuts" were installed at the inner harbor and Masonville Cove.

In January 2016, Aquarium officials announced Phase One of a campus revitalization project. Plans called for the creation of a natural tidal and floating wetland between Piers 3 and 4. Expected to be completed by 2019 at a cost of $14 million, the green space will feature a diversity of floating wetlands, bay grasses, and a terraced ledge leading down to the water. In an effort to reconnect the people with its river, the 2.5-acre area will feature educational activities, interactive exhibits, picnic areas, and kayaking.

The Aquarium's commitment to transform their river campus into a model urban waterfront began in 2010 when the first floating wetland was assembled and launched in the harbor. The 200 square-foot, man-made island demonstrated the ability to provide the ecological benefits of a natural shoreline in place of a hardened environment. Using innovative technologies, the floating wetland improved water quality and clarity, removed excess nutrients, reduced low oxygen levels, and provided a natural habitat for plants and animals, to include estuarine organisms that filtered water and provided a food source for fish and crabs. The combination of "biohuts," oyster baskets, and wetlands demonstrated the potential to transform the old concrete docks into living seawalls and publicly display the unlimited potential to restore the Patapsco.

THE RISING TIDE

Since former Vice President Al Gore's book and documentary in 2006 titled *An Inconvenient Truth*, his effort to raise public awareness about climate change, global warming has been vehemently debated by scientists and politicians. Regardless of causes and effects, the air is warming and the seas are rising. Not only is it happening around the world, it's happening along the Patapsco River. While the Maryland Port Administration and the Corps of Engineers are busy creating new islands in the Chesapeake Bay from dredged material, Mother Nature is busy swallowing up the old ones in the lower bay. Businesses and governments in the Patapsco watershed have taken notice.

In September 2003, Tropical Storm Isabel delivered a frightening wake-up call that proved a glimpse into the future. Driving winds and torrential rains created a heavy storm surge that flooded low-lying areas along Patapsco. While residents in Fells Point accepted this latest nuisance flooding as a way of life, others faced costly consequences. At the National Aquarium, the generator failed and flooded the facility with more than two feet of water, placing the thousands of fish and animals at risk. Following the storm, the Aquarium created a comprehensive emergency plan to ensure that staff can be self-sufficient and exhibits self-sustaining during weather emergencies. Hydraulic floodgates, wind-resistant glass, and a new generator were installed to storm-proof the complex. Evacuation plans were developed and ample supplies of dry ice, oxygen, and batteries were stored. At the port's terminals, the eight-foot surge crested the bulkheads. The widespread flooding over acres of asphalt lots caused only minor electrical damage and left behind piles of flotsam and jetsam that washed ashore. The Baltimore Museum of Industry sustained $1 million in storm damage as sewage flooded exhibits and heating- and air-conditioning systems.

Flooding at the National Aquarium after Tropical Storm *Isabel*. With rising sea levels, cities are facing the reality of global warming.
Courtesy National Aquarium.

After the cleanup, everyone breathed a sigh of relief, imagining what would have happened if the full-blown hurricane had spiraled up the bay. That future possibility was now a stark reality with the emergence of the global warming phenomenon. In June 2012, the US Geological Survey reported that sea levels along the Atlantic coast from North Carolina to Massachusetts were increasing three to four times faster than the rest of the globe. The Chesapeake Bay was recognized as one of nation's "hot spots" with sea levels twice the national average. Over the last century, sea levels have risen four to eight inches, but more than a foot in the bay region.

Maryland's predicament is compounded by a combination of rising water and sinking land. The land in the Chesapeake region has been sinking over the past 1,000 to 2,000 years at a rate of 1.3 millimeters each year. While the bay has been sinking, the water has been rising due to the melting of the polar ice caps and thermal expansion as molecules in heated seawater expand. Sea levels in the Chesapeake Bay are estimated to rise 1.5 feet by 2050 and 3.7 feet by 2100. However, scientists urge state officials to allow a margin of safety and plan for a rise of two feet by 2050 and six feet by the end of the century to account for ocean currents, salinity, thermal layering, and the earth's rotation. The Union of Concerned Scientists reported that tidal floods in Baltimore could increase ten-fold over the next three decades to more than 225 inundations a year.

With 3,190 miles of shoreline and 265,000 acres of land situated less than five feet above the high-tide line, Maryland, along with Louisiana and Florida, is one of the most vulnerable states in the country. To combat the higher tides and greater storm surges, government agencies and private corporations are taking action. Options are limited. Adaptation, not prevention, is the mantra from government planners and climate scientists. The choices are categorized as defend, retreat, or accommodate. The euphemism "managed retreat," which incorporates a combination of options, has gained recent popularity.

While most local efforts are still mired in the early assessment stages, the city of Baltimore has moved to the forefront in disaster planning. In 2013, the city's Department of Planning created a new Disaster Preparedness and Planning Project (DP3) to address existing flood problems and expected higher sea levels. The city also identified vulnerable assets and critical facilities and established new building guidelines in the tidal flood plain to offset higher sea levels. Despite the progress in formulating policy, the debate continues on the best way to protect waterfront communities.

For the Port of Baltimore, life in the floodplain presents few options. When possible, certain operations can be moved to higher ground. To comply with state guidelines, new permanent structures can be built with a minimum of two feet of freeboard above the 100-year base flood elevation. Wet basins can be constructed with high dikes. And finally, upgrades can be made to storm proof structures and equipment. However, nothing can be done to raise the height of the Chesapeake Bay Bridge and the Francis Scott Key Bridge. One day, higher tides resulting in lower clearance margins could impede the super-ships of the future from accessing the port. Apocalyptic flooding by 2300 with sea levels rising from twelve to twenty-four feet would submerge current port terminals around the harbor and return Sparrows Point to a marshland.

For Baltimore, the only options are retreat or defend. The city could either buy homes in low-lying areas, such as Fells Point and the inner harbor, and relocate residents, or build a system of seawalls and floodgates to protect these areas, similar to New Orleans. Either option would destroy or drastically alter the historic waterfront communities that have become synonymous with Baltimore. The issue of rising sea levels also presents ethical questions related to environmental justice. Do city officials build protection for tourist attractions at the expense of other businesses? And do city officials build protection for the more affluent developments in the Inner Harbor at the expense of the poorer, blue-collar communities in the industrial zones downriver?

A BRIGHT "GREEN" CITY

In the late 1990s and early 2000s, consent decrees to clean up pollution in the Patapsco River were heralded as major milestones in environmental stewardship. Commitments were now in the form of legal and binding documents. The spotlight had been rightfully placed on improving water quality as a means to improving the quality of life along the watershed, but something was missing. For mostly political and social reasons, the city of Baltimore had always been considered part of the problem, but not part of the solution. That oversight was corrected in 1997 when the Baltimore Ecosystem Study (BES) was initiated by the National Science Foundation (NSF).

Designed to improve the quality of life for Baltimoreans into the future, the study engaged world-renown researchers from around the country to study the city as a human ecosystem. In 1980, the NSF created the Long Term Ecological Research (LTER) Network to conduct long-term and in-depth research on ecological issues in expanded geographical areas. Realizing that a large portion of the nation's population now lived in cities where knowledge about urban ecosystems was virtually nonexistent, the NSF selected Baltimore as one of its two research sites. In 1997, the LTER began to inspect and dissect the way Baltimore interfaced with its environment as teams of scientists and researchers trekked across the urban landscape in relative obscurity.

With its network of local universities, access to government agencies, proximity to the Chesapeake Bay, and abundant archival resources, Baltimore was the ideal research subject for exploring the ecosystems of an "old" city. Integrating biological, physical, and social sciences, the BES investigates ecological, cultural, and economic forces that interact to shape environmental quality in the metropolitan area. The ultimate goal of the BES is to develop Baltimore as a sustainable city in the twenty-first century. For scientists and researchers, sustainability translates to a habitat where citizens live, work, and play without damaging or destroying the natural environment and governing bodies make decisions that weigh social and biophysical consequences on the ecological balance.

Since the BES research region is contained within the Patapsco River watershed, water quality initiatives have added valuable information to the Patapsco database. In studying the urban stream syndrome, scientists discovered the crucial role that riparian zones, or streamside ecosystems, play in preventing nitrogen runoff from migrating downriver. From a social science perspective, researchers discovered that environmental concerns over air and water quality are equally shared by urban communities regardless of their ethnic composition and income levels. Delving further into the subject of social stratification, comparative studies of wealthy and poor neighborhoods raised the issue of environmental justice. By mapping the history of neighborhood change and zoning/permit requests for Baltimore City from 1920 to the present, researchers documented a history of racial bias in locating environmental liabilities, such as landfills and incinerators, closer to predominantly African-American communities than white communities. These findings highlighted the fact that environmental concerns may be equally shared across distinct and diverse urban communities, but access to environmental protection may not.

The diversity of research proved there were no research boundaries within the geographical borders. Everything that connected people to the environment was a research possibility, such the impact of vacant houses and lots, tree canopy, and mosquito and rodent populations. Over the years, the study has accumulated an ecological database to support education and community-based activities in the Baltimore area. To circulate their findings through educational programs, the BES researched how students and teachers learn about their city as an ecosystem. In response, they created the Baltimore Partnership for Environmental Science Literacy, a broad coalition of non-profits, schools, and businesses, to administer a variety of teaching and training programs in the environmental sciences.

To reach into the neighborhoods and connect with the public, BES partnered with the Parks and People Foundation. Founded in 1984 by Mayor William Donald Schaefer, the non-profit organization was formed to raise and manage funds, develop outreach programs (recreational and literary), and partner with public and private agencies to ease the city's administrative and financial burden in caring for its parks. Two of the more noted outreach programs were the Green Career Ladder and Revitalizing Baltimore. Green Career Ladder offered progressive environmental education for students from elementary school through post-secondary education to a full-time "green" job. Revitalizing Baltimore, a community reforestation project, provided tree canopy along city streets and urban streams. Using hundreds of volunteers and thousands of students who planted trees to foster environmental stewardship, the program became a national model in community reforestation and watershed restoration.

In 1989, the foundation partnered with Yale University and the Baltimore City Department of Recreation and Parks to create the Urban Resource Initiative. The program recruited talented college and graduate students to work with Baltimore neighborhoods to find innovative solutions for local environmental problems. Since its inception, the program, staffed and funded by Parks & People, has evolved into the "research and development arm" for recreation and parks issues in Baltimore. One of the most productive and publicized projects was the feasibility study for the Gwynns Falls Trail, a fifteen-mile winding greenway for hikers and bikers that connected 2,000 acres of publicly owned land just west of Baltimore.

With its proven track record of bridging with the public, Parks & People, a charter member of the BES, became a linchpin in connecting BES scientists to the communities where they worked. Every year Parks & People and BES hosted community "greeners" during the BES Open House and Community Greening Celebration, an event held in conjunction with the BES Annual

Science Meetings. In 2014, the annual BES symposium included a sustainability workshop that was open to the public.

PEERING INTO THE CRYSTAL BALL

As the Patapsco River flows into the twenty-first century, its path through the pages of Baltimore's history will be dictated by big business. While the reliance on heavy industry has receded, the river remains the workhorse for its people, a role it has played for 300 years. In July 2015, port officials and politicians gathered under the towering cargo cranes at Seagirt Marine Terminal to announce a new lease with Maersk that would bring three ships weekly and an additional 31,000 containers to the port. It was a welcomed homecoming for the world's largest shipping line, which had previously signed an historic ten-year lease with the port in 1991. The euphoria in the local maritime industry was short-lived. By 1996, the number of port calls had dwindled to forty due to the eight-and-a-half-hour trip up the Chesapeake Bay. In a decision that rescued the port, port officials deemphasized containers in favor of other cargoes. Two decades later, congestion at other container ports and supersized cargo ships, capable of utilizing the fifty-foot shipping channel, could signal the re-emergence of the container business at the port. Bigger ships also guarantee more dredging projects. With its established track record in environmental stewardship, port officials should be able to duplicate their success at Masonville Cove in fostering a "green" port.

Around mid-harbor, smokestacks have been replaced by high-rises as the Gold Coast expands downriver. The first business entrepreneurs, who built self-sufficient villages around their milling operations, have now been succeeded by real-estate partnerships that build self-contained, mixed-use communities. The concept of self-reliance among river people remains intact despite the advance of computer technology and the rise of the global community.

Along the upper reaches of the harbor, the Under Armour vision has begun to shape the landscape as a corporate campus. At Port Covington, the former Sam's Club building is being converted for the company's information technology and finance departments, the first small step in creating CEO Kevin Plank's vision of a company campus. Across the harbor from its current headquarters at Tide Point, work began in March 2015 to convert the old Recreation Pier into a 128-room boutique hotel.

In June 2014, Plank's development company purchased the venerable landmark from the city for $3.4 million. Built in 1914, the 500-foot pier had served as a cargo pier, municipal dancehall, harbormaster's office, Maritime Exchange headquarters, and homeport to Baltimore's tugboat fleets. When the children in Fells Point and South Baltimore needed space to play, the roof behind the "head house," the main building with the ornate brick façade, was converted into a playground. In the 1990s, the building served as production offices and the police headquarters for NBC's TV series *Homicide: Life on the Streets*. According to Plank, the $60 million project will expand the company's brand and provide guests with a unique Baltimore experience as they ferry across the Patapsco in Chesapeake Bay work boats. In July 2015, the development company officially announced the purchase of the Turner property in Westport.

Downriver at Sparrows Point, the massive demolition and cleanup project continues under the watchful eyes of environmentalists and residents. In April 2015, former owners HRE Sparrows Point LLC and Sparrows Point LLC along with their demolition contractor were fined by the Maryland Department of the Environment for violations involving stormwater runoff, sediment and erosion, illegal dumping and storing of trash and industrial waste, and improper handling of asbestos. Under the agreement, HRE Sparrows Point, which owned the buildings and equipment, was fined $375,000, and Sparrows Point LLC, which owned the land, and its contractor agreed to pay $3.375 million for environmental projects that could be completed outside the boundaries of the steel mill. Environmentalists were elated that money was being used for other "green" projects instead of being dumped into a general fund.

Just east of Sparrows Point, a battle between developers and local residents continues over a picturesque ninety-four-acre tract of land that juts into the Chesapeake Bay at the mouth of the Patapsco River. Steeped in military history, the property was the beachhead for British troops who began their ill-dated march to Baltimore in September 1814. From 1900 to 1940, it was an active army post until it was given to the Veterans Administration, which operated a five-story hospital with 377 beds from 1943 until September 2002.

In 2004, the Department of Veterans Affairs (VA) announced the campus would be redeveloped into the nation's largest continuing-care facility for veterans to be called Bayside at Fort Howard. Fort Howard Senior Housing Associates, a subsidiary of Federal Development LLC of Washington, signed a seventy-five-year lease to construct a state-of-the-art retirement community for 790 residents with discounted rental units being first offered to eligible veterans. The lease with a private vendor was the first in VA history and was touted by the VA as a national model for utilizing large tracts of government land for a profit while catering to the needs of veterans.

Developers envisioned a $100 million mixed-use community that would include 1,300 residential and assisted living units, a nursing care facility, a marina to moor over 100 boats, 30,000 square feet of retail space, a museum, a boardwalk, and a fishing pier. The historical integrity of the property would include preserving the sprawling parade ground and renovating a number of the remaining structures that include a theater and the nurse's home, which served as the III Corps headquarters for Major General Douglas MacArthur from 1925 to 1928. Ten acres would be set aside to build a veterans' home to be operated by the state.

In October 2007, developers, government officials, and politicians gathered at Fort Howard to proudly celebrate the grand opening of the Fort Howard Veterans Museum and the Bayside sales office. Two years later in August 2009, the lease agreement was terminated, and the search began for a new partner. To resolve a long-running feud between the developer and Baltimore County over building permits, zoning regulations, and property taxes, the VA sided with county officials. It was wryly noted that not one shovelful of earth had been turned since the grand opening. Nearly 1,500 veterans, many who had reserved spots at the new community with deposits from $500 to $5,000, began a protracted legal battle for refunds. Area residents, who were skeptical about the developer's intentions, were relieved. From the beginning, they had expressed serious concerns about increased traffic on inadequate roads and the lack of proper water and sewer lines. Most agreed that the property should be developed exclusively for veterans on a smaller scale. Both federal and county politicians supported the search for a new developer committed to creating a veterans community.

In November 2011, the VA signed an Enhanced Use Lease, later amended to another seventy-five-year lease, with Fort Howard Development LLC. Similar in concept to its predecessor, the $500 million project again highlighted veterans' preference options. The mixed-used community, to be called Landing at Fort Howard, proposed nearly 1,500 residential units, 130,000 square feet of office/retail space, a major supermarket, restaurants, and other commercial amenities not available to area residents. Once again, residents voiced their previous concerns, and, once again, their pleas fell on the deaf ears as VA officials and politicians voiced their overwhelming support. With its bucolic setting and stunning views of the bay and river, residents envisioned the secluded peninsula as a "healing place" for recovering veterans.

Since the signing of the lease, the project has stalled after apparently failing to receive approval from the Baltimore County Council for a planned-unit development (PUD) status that would allow flexibility in zoning rules to increase the number of homes if the project is deemed beneficial to the community. Newly elected in 2014, county councilman Todd Crandell, who represents the district, flatly stated the he would not support zoning regulations that called for a "megatropolis" on the peninsula. The site is currently zoned for 550 units. In June 2015, developer Tim Munshell failed to appear at a community meeting to update residents. This no-show, combined with a failure to meet permit and license deadlines, again fueled fears that "veterans' preference" was synonymous with large-scale commercial development.

True to his word, Crandell officially rejected the PUD application in September 2015, sending the building plans back to the drawing board with the developer and the VA. In his press release, the councilman promised to protect the peninsula from over-development. He also acknowledged the needs of veterans and stated: "Our veterans deserve better than to have their sacred land swallowed up by development. Any plan that seeks my support will have to have a veterans focus as well as be fit for the community."

Unlike the lower harbor basin, an uneasy truce has settled over the river valley on the Main Branch since the area was designated a heritage greenway. The future portrait of the river will be framed by the Patapsco Heritage Greenway and their interpretation of heritage tourism. Environmentalists on both sides, who battled passionately over this issue, will be closely watching as the master plan for the river valley unfolds. Will the organization continue to be a trusted environmental steward for the river or is "heritage tourism" another blandishment for commercial exploitation of a natural resource? That's the question only time will answer.

If properly implemented, heritage tourism could be the economic catalyst that finally brings peace to the valley. One example of heritage tourism at its finest is the Benjamin Banneker Historical Park and Museum in Oella. Dedicated on June 9, 1998, after nearly two decades of planning, the museum traces the life and times of Benjamin Banneker through exhibits that feature archaeological artifacts related to Banneker and the Ellicott family. In addition to an array of educational and environmental programs, the museum offers a calendar of special events that include the visual and performing arts. The 142-acre park, established on land that was purchased by Robert and Mary Banneker in 1734, also includes hiking trails through a wooded valley that highlight conservation of wildlife habitats and preservation of natural resources. In November 2009, Baltimore County officials formally opened a replica of the one-story cabin built by Banneker on his colonial farm. The 224 square-foot structure resulted from a $400,000 state bond for design and construction.

Environmentalists along the Main Branch will also be closely monitoring the transformation of the Patapsco to a wilderness river. When Bloede Dam is finally removed, Daniels Dam will be the last impediment to fish migration. Many observers fear that the dam will become the next battleground in the war over heritage tourism as historical preservationists have already expressed a desire to preserve the dam for its historical significance and aesthetic qualities.

Despite the plethora of construction and demolition projects that have transformed the landscape along the water's edge, the recent history of the Patapsco River is the story about a massive cleanup effort. While the restoration of the Patapsco River will involve time and money, the question remains: When will that last chapter be written? If left to its own devices, nature has shown the miraculous ability to undo the intrusions of man at little or no cost. However, that process takes considerable time measured in seasons and cycles, and modern man, who measures progress by clocks and calendars in his rush to progress, has little patience for the mechanisms of the natural world. By any standard of measurement, the recovery of the river will be a grueling marathon with progress manifested by slow and steady steps.

Who will ultimately save the Patapsco? It will be the responsibility of "we the people" when "we" finally raise our collective voice to demand that our birthright of clean water be prioritized without financial and temporal constraints. Until the voice of the people becomes the will of the politicians, the recovery of the river will be frustratingly slow. The encouraging news is that the environmental movement, which has rapidly expanded and accelerated within the last twenty-five years, will sustain the momentum, however slight it may be. Another seemingly contradictory force working in favor of the river is the proliferation of residential developments around the harbor. While new construction has placed additional stressors on the watershed, it has also raised the environmental consciousness about the river. The new river residents are young, highly educated, urban professionals who grew up with the "green" movement and are keenly attuned to the concept of environmental stewardship. They are new vibrant voices who have joined the environmental chorus in singing the praises of a clean river.

While the legion of supporters championing for a clean river has produced many unsung heroes, no one exemplifies the spirit of the Patapsco more than local activist and environmentalist Joe Stewart. A fixture at regional open-water swimming events since 1990 as a participant and organizer, Stewart eventually turned his energy to the plight of his beloved Patapsco River. On May, 19, 2002, Stewart made his first of five swims across the mouth of the Patapsco to raise funds for local watershed groups. Clad only in his Speedo (no goggles or wetsuit),

A glimpse into the future: a fishable Patapsco River.
Courtesy Waterfront Partnership of Baltimore.

Another glimpse into the future: a swimmable Patapsco River.
Courtesy Waterfront Partnership of Baltimore.

he braved chilly waters, strong currents, shipping lanes, recreational boaters, and floating debris to become the first person to swim across the mouth of the river. Escorted by kayakers and motorboats, he completed the 4.4 mile swim in three hours and fifteen minutes and raised over $5,000. A planned route from the Key Bridge to Fort McHenry was shelved due to health concerns with sewage, stormwater runoff, and chemical toxins that are prevalent in the upper harbor.

Since that first swim, Stewart has become a one-man crusade to save the river. To coincide with his swims and raise awareness of cleanup efforts, the avid photographer created "It's the Patapsco, Hon!: A Photo Essay." The traveling exhibit captured the ever-changing moods of the river on its journey from Parr's Spring to the Chesapeake Bay. At his annual "Save the Patapsco, Hon!" party in his Waverly home, Stewart gave away hundreds of his photo greeting cards in exchange for donations to conservation groups. In May 2004, the annual "Save the Patapsco" swim featured the river's first "wade-in" and "teach-in." Hosted by the Patapsco Riverkeeper and the Patapsco/Back River Tributary Strategy Team, the event drew a record crowd of concerned citizens and public officials who gathered at the water's edge to measure water clarity and clean up the beach. Meanwhile, out on the water, Stewart's escort flotilla measured water clarity along the route with a secchi disk.

Hopefully, one day in the not too distant future, Marylanders will once again line the riverbank and cheer wildly as swimmers splash ashore after swimming the length of the river from the inner harbor to the bay. That event along a "swimmable and fishable" river will be the last entry in the Patapsco's great comeback. Against all odds, the "River of History" will have completed another remarkable chapter.

The final words about the illustrious past of a river are, oddly enough, about its future. While there is little doubt that the river will continue to flow and ebb endlessly as time itself, there are serious concerns about its quality and character that will be bequeathed to future generations. Although legal ownership of the Patapsco resides with the city of Baltimore and the State of Maryland, the river belongs to the people of Maryland. We are the ones responsible for the river's future. To protect it, we must look to the past and preserve the legacy of the river's first caretakers. The Indians of the Patapsco left behind more than colorful names on a map echoing a forgotten era in American history. They left a respect and reverence for the elements of nature that today are being rediscovered and redefined as environmental awareness. To guarantee the river's future, we must instill the concepts of preservation and conservation in the minds of all the people. We must restore the philosophy of living in harmony with the land and the water. How do we accomplish these goals? Quite simply, we must educate ourselves. The river is a complex mechanism, but it is not beyond the comprehension of the average person; a degree in marine biology is not required to understand the needs of the river. Through educational programs about the environment and ecology, we can ensure that the Patapsco River will continue as one of Maryland's greatest natural treasures.

Bibliography

Ahen, E. Miller. *Lafayette's Second Expedition into Virginia, 1781.* Baltimore: Maryland Historical Society Fund Publication, 1891.

Alexanders, J. H. "Report on the Manufacturing of Iron — Addressed to the Governor of Maryland." Printed by the order of the Senate. William McNeir, Printer to the Senate, 1884.

Alpert-Levin, Helen. "A Negro Genius of His Day." *The Baltimore Sun,* July 28, 1929.

Alsop, George A. *A Character of the Province of Maryland.* Ed. William Gowans. Vol. 1. London, 1666. Reprint. Baltimore: Maryland Historical Society Fund Publication, 1869.

American. January 4, 1809; December 15, 1815; May 20, 1830; July 24, 1868.

American and Commercial Daily Advertiser. January 6, 1813; May 3, 1825; May 9, 1861; July 6, 1861; July 27, 1861; July 28, 1861; July 25, 1868.

Andrews, Matthew Page. *History of Maryland: Province and State.* Hatboro, PA: Tradition Press, 1965.

(2nd) Annual Report of the President and Directors to the Stockholders of the B&O Railroad Company. Baltimore, 1828.

(4th) Annual Report of the President and Directors to the Stockholders of the B&O Railroad Company. Baltimore, 1830.

(38th) Annual Report of the President and Directors to the Stockholders of the B&O Railroad Company. Baltimore, 1864.

(47th) Annual Report of the President and Directors to the Stockholders of the B&O Railroad Company. Baltimore, 1873.

"Armament of the Forts and Batteries of the U.S. from December 31, 1863, with Current Additions. Requisition and Supply Division, Ordnance Office." Entry 113 of Record Group 156. US National Archives, Washington.

Baltimore Sun. April 15,1842; May 11,1861; May 13, 1861; May 14, 1861; July 25, 1883; February 6, 1934; November 10, 1938; July 28, 1940.

Bedini, Silvio A. *The Life of Benjamin Banneker.* New York: Charles Scribner's Sons, 1972.

Beirne, Francis F. *The Amiable Baltimoreans.* New York: E. P. Dutton and Co., 1957. Reprint. Baltimore: Johns Hopkins University Press, 1984.

Bentley, Helen Delich, *The Great Port of Baltimore: It's First 300 Years, 1706–2006,* Baltimore: Port of Baltimore Tricentennial Committee by Media Two, 2006.

Bland, Joseph G. *Maryland Business Corporations, 1783–1852.* Baltimore: Johns Hopkins University Press, 1934.

Bloede, Victor Gustav. *Patapsco Electric and Manufacturing Company: A Short Story.* Baltimore, April 1912.

Bohner, Charles H. *John Pendleton Kennedy: Gentleman from Baltimore.* Baltimore: Johns Hopkins University Press, 1961.

Brand, Barbara. *The Story of Belmont.* Washington: Smithsonian Institution Press, 1974.

Breen, Robert G. "Progress versus Prosperity." *The Baltimore Sun,* March 25, 1953.

Brooks, Neal A. and Eric G. Rockel. *A History of Baltimore County.* Towson, MD: Friends of Towson Library, 1979.

Brown, Alexander C. *The Old Bay Line 1840–1940.* New York: Bonanza Books, 1940.

Buckler, Thomas H. *Baltimore: Its Interest — Past, Present and Future.* Baltimore: Cushings and Bailey, 1878.

Burgess, Robert H. *This Was Chesapeake Bay.* Cambridge, MD: Cornell Maritime Press, 1963.

Byrne, J. A. "Historic Relay." *Baltimore and Ohio Magazine,* November 1921.

Byron, Gilbert. *The War of 1812 in the Chesapeake Bay.* Baltimore: Maryland Historical Society, 1964.

Cadzow, Donald A. *Archaeological Studies of the Susquehannock Indians of Pennsylvania.* Vol. 3. Harrisburg: Pennsylvania Historical Commission, 1936.

Capital News Service of the University of Maryland, *Sea Level Rising in Maryland,* A Philip Merrill College of Journalism Investigative Project, July 2013.

Calendar of Maryland State Papers, No. 4, the Red Books. No. 8. Annapolis: Hall of Records Commission, 1953.

"Centenary of Famous Relay Bridge to Be Observed by B&O July 4." *Catonsville Herald,* May 3, 1935.

Chase, Arline. "Hell Loosed in the Streets of Baltimore." *Firehouse,* September 1981.

Civilian Conservation Corps Official Annual 1937. District No. 3, Third Corps Area. Washington: US Government Printing Office, 1938.

Colley, David. "Drive Slated to Restore Patapsco Institute." *The Baltimore Evening Sun,* May 24, 1967.

Daniel, Mann, Johnson, and Mendenhall. *Master Development Plan: Patapsco Valley State Park.* Annapolis: Maryland Department of Forests and Parks, 1971.

Davidson, Isobel. *Real Stories from Baltimore County History.* Hatboro, PA: Tradition Press, 1967.

Dilts, James D. "Can State Clean Up Polluted Patapsco?" *The Baltimore Sun,* August 20, 1967.

"Direct Descendants of Tom Thumb to Make Last Run December 31." *The Baltimore Sun,* November 30, 1949.

Dozer, Donald Marquand. *Portrait of the Free State: A History of Maryland.* Cambridge, MD: Tidewater Publishers, 1976.

Duffy, Edward P. "Only Memories and Ruins Remain Where John P. Kennedy Dwelt." *The Baltimore Sun,* July 22, 1928.

Dyer, Frederick. *A Compendium of the War of Rebellion.* New York and London: Thomas Yoseloff, 1938.

Elkridge Bicentennial Committee. *Elkridge: A Bicentennial Journal.* June 1976.

"Elkridge and Its Historical Background and Traditions." *Ellicott City Times,* July 22, 1948.

Ellicott, Andrew. *Journal of Andrew Ellicott, 1796–1800.* Philadelphia: Thomas Dobson Publishers, 1803.

Ellicott City Bicentennial Association. *Ellicott City Bicentennial Journal, 1772–1972.* 1972.

Ellicott City Times. April 22, 1916; March 27, 1967.

Evans, Oliver. *The Young Millwright and Miller's Guide.* Philadelphia, 1795. Reprint. New York: Arno Press, 1972.

Finlayson, Anne. *Colonial Histories (Maryland).* Nashville: Thomas Nelson, 1974.

Furguson, Alice L. *The Piscatazvay Indians of Southern Maryland*. Baltimore: Alice Furguson Foundation, 1959.

"Ghosts of Many Famous Men Haunt Old Gray Mansion on Banks of Patapsco." *Jeffersonian*, January 13, 1933.

"The Great Flood." *Common Sense*, Ellicott City, MD, July 29, 1868.

Griffin, Gerald. "A Maryland State Forest Has Its Face Lifted." *Baltimore Sun*, December 24, 1933.

Hall, C. C. *Narratives of Early Maryland, 1634–1684*. New York: Barnes and Noble, 1967.

Harper's Weekly. May 25, 1861.

Harwood, Herbert H. Jr. *Impossible Challenge: The Baltimore and Ohio Railroad in Maryland*. Baltimore: Barnard, Roberts, & Co., 1979.

Helewicz, Joseph. "Infectious Bacteria Thrive in Patapsco." *Ellicott City Times*, October 27, 1966.

Henry, Frank. "City Playground: Thirty-seven Miles Long." *The Baltimore Sun*, November 5, 1950.

Herald Argus. Catonsville, MD. March 8, 1967.

Herman, Benjamin. "The Great Baltimore Flood of 1868." *The Baltimore Sun*, July 21, 1957.

Hill, Michael. "Despite Its History, Sykesville Refuses to Die." *Baltimore Evening Sun*, September 21, 1973.

History and Roster of Maryland Volunteers, War of 1861–65. Vol. 1. Prepared under authority of the General Assembly of Maryland. Baltimore: Gugenheimer and Co., 1898.

Holland, Celia M. *Ellicott City, Maryland: Milltown, U.S.A*. Chicago: Adams Press, 1970.

Howard, George W. *The Monumental City*. Baltimore: M. Curlander Publishers, 1889.

Hungerford, Edward. *The Story of the Baltimore and Ohio Railroad, 1827–1927*. 2 vols. New York: G. P. Putnam, 1928.

Jones, Arthur E. "Woodstock: Its Surroundings and Associations." In *The Woodstock Letters*. Woodstock, MD: Woodstock College Press, 1873.

Kanarek, Harold K. *The Mid-Atlantic Engineers: A History of the Baltimore District, U.S. Army Corps of Engineers, 1779–1974*. Washington: US Government Printing Office, 1976.

Kay, Liz R., "Wary of Plans for Patapsco," *The Baltimore Sun*, November 12, 2002.

Keidel, George C. *Early Catonsville and the Caton Family.* Baltimore: J. H. Furst Co., 1944.

Keith, George C. *Baltimore Harbor: A Picture History.* Baltimore: J. H. Furst Co., 1982.

Kenny, Hamill. *The Origin and Meaning of Indian Place Names of Maryland.* Baltimore: Waverly Press, 1961.

Kobell, Rona, "Watershed Groups Unite to Form Blue Water Baltimore," *Bay Journal,* January 1, 2011.

Kreh, Charles F. "Saw Ellicott City Flood and Tells Grim Story of Awful Havoc There." *The Baltimore Sun,* February 15, 1920.

Latrobe, John H. *The Baltimore and Ohio Railroad: Personal Recollections.* Baltimore: F. Lucas Jr., 1868.

Lippson, Alice Jane. *The Chesapeake Bay: An Atlas of Natural Resources.* Baltimore: Johns Hopkins University Press, 1973.

Lord, Walter. *The Dawn's Early Light.* New York: W. W. Norton and Co., 1972.

McCord, Joel. "Fort Echoes with Sounds of Play." *The Baltimore Sun,* June 26, 1983.

McGrain, John W. *The Molinography of Maryland: A Tabulation of Mills, Furnaces, and Primitive Industries.* Towson, MD, 1968. Rev. and exp. 1976.

Oella: Its Thread of History. Oella Community Improvement Association, May 1976.

"The Development and Decline of Dorsey's Forge." *Maryland Historical Magazine* 72, No. 3, 1977.

Grist Mills in Baltimore County, Maryland. Towson, MD: Baltimore County Heritage Publication, 1980.

McKinsey, Folger. "Sykesville Boom Started in 1825." *The Baltimore Sun,* September 30, 1941.

McNamara, Joseph M. *The Archeological Resources of Patapsco Valley State Park.* Maryland Department of Natural Resources, Maryland Geological Survey, May 1977.

Manakee, Harold. *Maryland in the Civil War.* Baltimore: Maryland Historical Society, 1961.

Marye, William B. "The Baltimore County Garrison." *Maryland Historical Magazine* 16, 1921.

"The Maryland Flood." *New York Times,* July 26, 1868.

Maryland Gazette. June 14, 1764.

Morgan, Paul T. "The Granite Story: A Chronicle of the Most Unique Square Mile in Baltimore County." *Ellicott City Times,* March 27, 1967.

Mount Airy: Historical, Industrial, and Biographical Sketch. Mount Airy Chamber of Commerce, N.p., n.d.

National Park Service, NPS Form 10-900, USS *Constellation*, National Register of Historic Places Registration Form.

"Nature, Man Fast Filling Up Patapsco River Mud Flat." *The Baltimore Sun,* November 17, 1946.

Nawrozki, Joe. "VA Center to Undergo Transformation." *The Baltimore Sun,* February, 2004.

Niles' Weekly Register, November 12, 1813; November 12, 1814; February 21, 1829; May 15, 1830; May 20, 1830; May 29, 1830; December 24, 1830; March 19, 1831; March 26, 1831; July 16, 1831; March 31, 1832; April 26, 1834; March 14, 1835.

Offut, Scott, and Elmer R. Haile. *Baltimore: Its History, Progress, and Opportunities.* Towson, MD: Jeffersonian Publishing Co., 1916.

"Old Ellicott Millrace Is Victim of Modern Needs." *The Baltimore Sun,* July 28,1940.

Olson, Sherry H. *Baltimore.* Cambridge, MA: Ballinger Publishing Co., 1976.

Olsen, Sherry H. *Baltimore: The Building of an American City.* Baltimore: Johns Hopkins University Press, 1980.

Orser, Edward. "Involuntary Community: Conscientious Objectors at Patapsco State Park during World War II." *Maryland Historical Magazine* 72, No. 1, 1977.

Owens, Hamilton. *Baltimore on the Chesapeake.* New York: Doubleday, Duran and Co., 1941.

Papers of the Continental Congress, 17 January 1778. Folio 443. US National Archives, Washington.

"Patapsco Courses 50 Miles from Pond to Port." *The Baltimore Evening Sun,* November 2, 1976.

Patapsco Valley State Park: Draft Master Plan. Annapolis: Maryland Department of Natural Resources, 1977.

Patapsco Valley State Park: Environmental Statement Draft. Annapolis: Maryland Department of Natural Resources, 1978.

Phillips, Thomas L. *The Orange Grove Story.* Washington: N.p., 1972.

Piscataway Park: General Historic Background. Office of Archaeology and Historic Preservation, US Department of the Interior, National Park Service, September 1969.

"Power Plant inside a Dam on the Patapsco River." *Electric World* 1, No. 5, August 3, 1907.

"The Raid of Ellicott's Mills, Souvenir Program." Howard County Historical Society and Ellicott City Rotary Club, May 12, 1962.

"The River of Historic Dams." *Baltimore Municipal Journal* February 6, 1931.

Reutter, Mark. *Making Steel: Sparrows Point and the Rise and Ruin of American Industrial Might.* Urbana: University of Illinois, 2004.

Roberts, Robert B. *Encyclopedia of Historic Forts.* New York: MacMillan Publishing Co., 1988.

Rowland, Kate Mason. *The Life of Charles Carroll of Carrollton, 1737–1832.* 2 vols. New York: G. P. Putnam's Sons, 1898.

Ruckert, Norman G. *Fort McHenry: Home of the Brave.* Baltimore: Bodine and Associates, 1983.

Rudacille, Deborah. *Roots of Steel: The Boom and Bust in an American Mill Town.* New York: Pantheon Books, 2010.

Saunders, Keith. "Coast Guard Graduating Own War Dogs Shortly," *The Baltimore Evening Sun,* December 13, 1944.

Scarborough, Katherine. "The Evolution of Maryland's Highways." *The Baltimore Sun,* July 19, 1931.

Scharf, John Thomas. *History of Maryland from the Earliest Period to the Present.* 3 vols. 1879. Reprint. Hatboro, PA: Tradition Press, 1967.

Scharf, John Thomas. *History of Baltimore City and Baltimore County.* Philadelphia: Louis H. Everts, 1881.

Schmidt, John C. "World's Largest Jesuit School of Theology." *The Baltimore Sun,* December 27, 1959.

Semmes, John Edward. *John H. B. Latrobe and His Times, 1803–1891.* Baltimore: Norman Remington Co., 1917.

Semmes, Raphael. *Captains and Mariners of Early Maryland.* Baltimore: Johns Hopkins University Press, 1931.

Semmes, Raphael. *Baltimore as Seen by Visitors, 1783–1860.* Baltimore: Maryland Historical Society, 1953.

Shaner, J. Jean. "New Coast Guard School Completed in 60 Days," *The Baltimore Evening Sun,* March 6, 1942.

Sherman, Natalie. "Kevin Plank's Port Covington Land Rush." *The Baltimore Sun,* January 25, 2015.

Shoumatoff, Alexander. "A Town in Search of Itself." *Washington Post,* January 30, 1969.

Singewald, Joseph T. Jr. *Report on the Iron Ores of Maryland*. Baltimore: Johns Hopkins University Press, 1911.

Smith, John. *Travels and Works of Captain John Smith*. Eds. Edward Arber and A. G. Bradley. Edinburgh, 1910.

Spurrier, John E. "Relay Station Originally the Viaduct Hotel." *Baltimore and Ohio Magazine*, January 1920.

Stearns, Richard E. "Some Indian Village Sites of the Lower Patapsco." In *Proceedings of the Natural History Society of Maryland*. Baltimore: Natural History Society of Maryland, 1949.

Stein, Charles Francis Jr. *Origin and History of Howard County, Maryland*. Howard County Historical Society, 1972.

Stiehm, Jamie. "Swimming Against the Tide of Neglect." *The Baltimore Sun*, May 24, 2004.

Stidman, John Randolph. "July Fourths at Relay." *The Baltimore Sun* June 9, 1935.

Stone, Stephanie. "Baltimore Beat—A New Keeper in the Harbor," *SpinSheet*, March 2007.

The Story of Baltimore's Water Supply. City of Baltimore, Department of Public Works. Rev. ed. November 1981.

Stump, William. "The Man behind the Iron Horse." *The Baltimore Sun*, February 24, 1952.

Summers, Festus P. *The B&O in the Civil War*. New York: G. P. Putnam and Sons, 1939.

Terranova, Patrick. *Gold Standard: Applying Best Practices in Olympic Practices to a Baltimore Bid*. Applied Research Paper, Georgia Institute of Technology, School of City and Regional Planning, Spring 2013.

Titus, Charles. *The Old Line State: Her Heritage*. Cambridge, MD: Tidewater Publishers, 1971.

Toomey, Daniel C. *A History of Relay, Maryland, and the Thomas Viaduct*. Baltimore, 1972.

Tyson, Martha. *A Brief Account of the Settlement of Ellicott's Mills*. Baltimore: Maryland Historical Society, 1871.

Unger, Mike. "Shining Armour." *Baltimore Magazine*, August 2013.

US Army Corps of Engineers, Baltimore District. *Chesapeake Bay: Existing Conditions Report*. 7 vols. 1973.

Vogel, Steve. *Through the Perilous Fight: Six Weeks That Saved the Nation*. New York: Random House, 2013.

Warfield, J. D. *The Founders of Anne Arundel and Howard Counties*. Baltimore: Kohn and Pollock Publishers, 1905.

White, Andrew. *Relatio Itineris in Marylandiam*. Baltimore: Maryland Historical Society, 1874.

Wilstach, Paul. *Tidewater Maryland*. Indianapolis: Bobbs-Merrill Co., 1931.

"Winans Steam Gun Mystery Is Solved." *The Baltimore News American*, April 12,1911.

Wirth, Conrad L. *Civilian Conservation Corps Program — March 1933 to June 30, 1943: A Report to Harold L. Ickes, Secretary of the Interior*. Washington: US Government Printing Office, 1944.

Wood, Pamela, "Balto. Co. Councilman Says He'll Block Fort Howard Redevelopment," *The Baltimore Sun*, June 5, 2015.

Young, Edwin. "New Life for Lawyer's Hill." *The Baltimore Sun*, April 4, 1937.

Index

C

Choptican Indians, 16
Church of the Holy Ghost, 101
Civilian Conservation Corps, 150-154, 161
Civilian Conservation Corps, 365th Company
Civilian Public Service, 151, 15
Civil War, 3, 31, 36, 37, 46, 67, 91, 92, 115, 122-132
Claggett, Levi, 45
Clay, Henry, 68
Clayton, William A., 77
Clean Water Act, 174
Clemm, John, 45
Clermont, 30
Clinton's Executive Order 12898, 176
Cochrane, Alexander, 42, 44, 45
Cockburn, George, 41, 42
Cole, Thomas, 27
Colgate Creek, 26
Colonial Inn and Opera House, 68
Common Sense, 133
Conestoga, 25
Congress of Vienna, 30
Conowingo, 19
Conoy Indians, 16
Conrad, Joseph, 81
Consolidated Gas, Electric Light and Power Company, 81, 148, 149, 161
Congreve rockets, 45
Constellation, 29
Constellation Energy Group, 178, 180
Continental Army, 71
Continental Building, 33
Continental Navy, 28
Continental Treasury, 54
Cook's Battery, 124
Coolidge, Calvin, 47
Cooper, Peter, 29, 115, 116, 118
Cornwait, John, 79
Cornwallis, Charles, Earl, 55
Corpus Christi Catholic Church, 35
Council on Economic Priorities, 212
Council of Safety, 40
Craighill, William, 37, 38
Cramblitt, Charles, 136
Crandell, Todd, 233
Cruise Maryland, 198
Cully's Wharf, 30
Curtis Bay, 5, 26, 36, 166
Curtis Bay Coast Guard Yard, 205, 206
Curtis Creek, 5, 26
Cyclopede, 116

ཀ D ལྷ

Daniels, 6, 90, 91, 141-143, 145, 146
Daniels Company, 91, 142
Daniels Dam, 234
Davis, Caleb, 98
Davis, Henry Gassoway, 98
Davis, Jim, 217
Davis, Phineas, 115, 118
Deep Run, 51
Defence of Fort McHenry, 45
Delaware, 9, 21
Delaware Bay, 26
Delaware Indians, 19
Dick, James, 52
Dickenson, Charles S., 126 Dickey, William J., 86, 87
Dickeyville, 87
Dismal Mill, 79, 146
Dix, John A., 125, 129
Dobbin, George W., 96
Dodge, Samuel, 41
Dollar House Program, 187
Domino Sugars, 188, 189
Donaldson, Thomas N., 96 Dorsey, Caleb, 48, 51, 71
Dorsey, Edward, 48, 51, 71-73
Dorsey, John, 48, 51, 53
Dorsey, Robert, 71
Dorsey, Samuel, 51, 71
Dorsey, Samuel, Jr., 53
Dorsey, Thomas, 53, 54
Dorsey Forge, 55
Doughnut Corporation of America, 66
Doughoregan Manor, 48, 61, 62, 101
Dove, 27
Dredging, 36-68
Druid Hill Park, 94
Dundalk Marine Terminal, 5, 36

ཀ E ལྷ

Eckstut, Stanton, 183
Eddy, Richard, 130
Eighth (8th) Massachusetts Regiment, 124
Eighth (8th) New York Regiment, 124
Eisenberg, Benjamin, 40
Elba Furnace, 104, 136
Elkridge, 6, 7, 9, 10, 18, 22, 48-56, 138
Elkridge Battalion, 53
Elkridge Furnace, 51, 53, 138
Elkridge Hundred, 53

F

 G

Q

R

S

Seneca Indians, 22-24
Seneca Trail, 22
Seventh (7th) New York Regiment, 124
Severn River, 18
Severstal, 215
Sharpe, Thomas R., 94
Sherman, Mrs. William Tecumseh, 100
Shiflett, Harry, 143
Sierra Club, 170-172
Silo Point, 192
Silver, Michael, 183
Simkins Dam, 222, 223
Simkins, Leon, 79
Simkins Industries, 80
Sirnow, Richard, 187
Sixth (6th) Massachusetts Regiment, 123, 124
Sixtieth (60th) New York State Regiment, 130
Skinner, John S., 41
Slater, John, 171
Sledd's Point, 26
Smallwood, William, 39
Smith, Denis A., 95
Smith, John, 3, 4, 16, 20
Smith, Sam, 42, 43
Smith, Samuel, 68
Smith, William P., 125
Smith's Wharf, 77, 78
Society of Jesus, 99
Sollers Points Flats, 39, 40
South Branch, 10, 147, 160, 161
South Locust Point Marine Terminal, 198
Spanish-American War, 38, 40, 46, 95
Sparrows Point, 211-213, 228, 232
Sparrows Point LLC, 217, 231
Spesutia Island, 22
Springfield, 105
Stabler, Superintendent, 104, 105
Stamp Act, 52
Star of Bethlehem, 218, 219
""Star-Spangled Banner", 45
State Gazette, 56
Steinmeier, Eliza, 176-178
Stewart, Brigadier General, 105
Stevenson, John, 28
Stewart, Anthony, 52
Stewart, Joe, 235, 236
Stockton and Darlington Railway, 111
Stockton and Stokes, 117
Stony Creek, 4, 5
Stourbridge Lion, 116
Stover, Steve, 173
Stricker, John, 43, 44
Struever Brothers, 189
Struever Bros., Eccles, and Rouse, 186

Stuart, Gilbert, 105
Stuart, J. E. B., 131
Susquehanna Nation, 21
Susquehanna River, 19, 22, 23, 25, 124
Susquehannock Indians, 16, 18-25
Sutton, Samuel, 96
Swedish Council, 22
Sykes, James, 103
Sykes Mills, 104, 105
Sykesville, 6, 103-107, 134
Sykesville State Hospital, 105

≈≈≈ T ≈≈≈

Tangier Island, 42
Tarpeian Rock, 68
Taylor, Robert, 81
Taylor's Forest, 71
Terranova, Patrick, 191
Tide Point, 231
Thistle Cotton Mill, 138, 146, 147
Thistle Mill Company, 79
Thomas, Evan, 111, 116
Thomas, Philip E., 111, 112, 116, 119-121
Thomas Viaduct, 9, 56, 75, 93, 94, 97, 121, 124, 138, 145
Thornburg, Joseph, 67
Tiber River, 68
Tom Thumb, 115, 117, 118
Tongue Row, 68
Tonnant, 41
total maximum daily load, 177
Tottell, Richard, 53
Treaty of Ghent, 62
Treaty of Paris, 55 T
Treaty of 1652, 23
Treaty of 1663, 23
Triple Rye, 195
Tropical Storm Agnes, 76, 91, 104, 141, 143, 146, 149
Tropical Storm Eloise, 144
Tropical Storm Isabel, 226, 227
Trueman, Thomas, 23, 24
Turner Development Group, 187
Turner, Patrick, 192
Tyson, Isaac, 184
Tyson, James E., 69, 104
Tyson, John S., 69
Tyson, Martha, 64

U

Under Armour, 189, 194, 231
Union Bank of Maryland, 65
Union of Concerned Scientists, 228
Union Dam, 146, 222
Union Manufacturing Company of Maryland, 67, 84, 86, 87, 89, 146
Union Mill, 135
Union Shipbuilding Company, 36
US Army Corps of Engineers, 37-39, 143
US Army Hospital #2, 46
US Capitol, 10
US Coast Guard, 205-210
US Coast Guard Training Station, 206
US Geological Survey, 227
US Green Building Council, 188
US Military Academy, 40, 62
US Naval Academy, 124
US Naval Academy Choir, 188
US Olympic Committee, 191
US Patent Office, 63
USS *Coral Sea*, 202

V

Vail, Henry, 192
Veterans Administration, 39
Viaduct Hotel, 94, 95
Vietnam War, 39
Virginia, 28

W

Waddell, Matthew, 85
Wagandt, Charles, 169-171
Wallace, Lewis, 132
Walters, Alexander, 102
Waltersville Quarry, 102
Warfield, Charles Alexander, 52, 53
Warfield, Richard, 48
Warfield, Walter, 54
War of 1812, 30, 38, 41
Washington, DC, 9, 17, 23
Washington, George, 29, 41, 55, 62, 81
Washington, John, 24
Washington Monument, 10
Washington Turnpike, 56
Wastahanow, Chief, 23

Watchman, John, 30
Waterfront Partnership of Baltimore, 178, 226
Waterkeeper Alliance, 176
Waughn, Samuel, 68
Weaver, William H., 126
Weinberg Waterfront Park, 225
Welsh, Molly, 88
Westport, 176, 192, 194
Westport Waterfront Park, 193
Wever, Casper W., 112, 115
Whetcroft, William, 71-73
Whetstone Point, 27, 40, 45
Whig Club, 52
Whisman, James, 69
Whistler, George W., 116
White, Andrew, 17
White Rocks, 4
Wilkins-Rogers Company, 66, 142
Williams, William, 57
Winans, Ross, 46, 75, 114, 115, 118, 126, 128, 129, 138
Woodbine, 6, 134
Woodford, Helen, 68
Woodstock, 6, 98-101, 134
Woodstock College, 99-102
Woodstock Granite Company, 102
World Trade Center, 179
World War I, 32, 35, 39, 46, 66, 87, 95
World War II, 29, 35, 39, 66, 87, 91
Worthington, George, 75, 77

Y

Yaocomicoe Indians, 16
York, 115, 118
Yorktown, 55

Z

Zekiah Swamp Reservation, 19
Zhen Hua, 198